A HISTORY OF RUSSIA

BY GEORGE VERNADSKY

AND MICHAEL KARPOVICH

VOLUME 1

ANCIENT RUSSIA

ANCIENT RUSSIA

BY

GEORGE VERNADSKY

NEW HAVEN
YALE UNIVERSITY PRESS

Printed in the United States of America

First published, June, 1943
Second printing, March, 1944
Third printing, January, 1946
Fourth printing, August, 1952
Fifth printing, January, 1959

PREFACE

In the course of the last decades an impressive amount of new source material has been accumulated in the field of Russian history, and many new and significant viewpoints have been advanced in the monographic literature that has been produced both in Russia and in other countries. The scope of Russian history has been substantially expanded in time, with a further investigation of both its recent and its earliest periods, and many of its aspects that previously were not given adequate attention have received a much fuller although still a somewhat uneven treatment. The authors of the present series are convinced that by now the ground has been sufficiently prepared for a systematic presentation of the whole course of Russian history, on a large enough scale to permit an ample treatment that would utilize the accumulated documentary material as well as the results of special scholarly investigations.

It is planned to publish this history in ten volumes of which the first six, by Professor Vernadsky, will cover the period from the beginning of Russian history to the end of the eighteenth century, and the remaining four, by Professor Karpovich, from the opening of the nineteenth century to our own times.

While each of the authors will bear individually the responsibility for his part of the work, it is hoped that a certain unity of approach will be preserved, and some common features have been agreed upon for the series as a whole. Besides a presentation of the main trends of Russia's political, economic, and social history, an attempt will be made to integrate it with a treatment of the country's cultural development. Special attention will be paid to the history of the component parts of the Russian Empire, both before and after their unification under a single political authority. At each successive stage of Russian history the place of the Russian people in the world will be discussed, with reference not only to the foreign policies of the governments but also to the people's cultural contacts.

The authors, each of whom has been teaching Russian history in American universities for over fifteen years, feel greatly encouraged by the fact that of late Russian studies have struck firm roots in this country and have made considerable progress. Of particular significance is the formation, among the younger generation of American scholars, of solid cadres of specialists in the field of Russian history who already have to their credit an impressive number of valuable monographic studies. On the other hand there has been a steadily growing general interest in things Russian. Thus it may be hoped that the present attempt at a large-scale treatment of the whole course of Russia's historical development will answer a genuine need on the part of both the specialists and the general readers.

The publication of this work would not have been possible without the financial support of the Humanities Fund of New York City, and the authors want to express their gratitude to that organization.

George Vernadsky
Michael Karpovich

CONTENTS

MAPS

INTRODUCTION

THE volume which is now being presented to the reader covers the earliest period in Russian history down to the coming of the Varangians. The author's treatment of his subject matter in this volume calls for some explanation. Until recently it has been customary to start Russian history with the Varangians, while all that happened before their time was, if mentioned at all, considered "prehistory" from the point of view of the student of Russia's past. It was the archaeologists, starting from the base of "prehistory," who first attempted to examine the earliest trends in the history of Russia, and the publication twenty years ago of M. I. Rostovtzeff's *Iranians and Greeks in South Russia* may be considered an important turning point in Russian historiography.

The author's intention in writing the present volume has been to approach the early background not from the point of view of the archaeologist, nor of the classical historian, but from that of a historian of Russia; that is, to treat it as an organic part of Russian history. He therefore begins not with the ninth but with the second century; not with the Varangians but with the Antes and the early Rus tribes. While the validity of such a plan can hardly be denied, its execution meets with almost insurmountable obstacles because of the scarcity of adequate written sources, especially native sources, for the earliest period. One may liken the task to that of restoring a broken vase out of fragments of which only a few remain intact; as might be expected, because of the wide gaps it is hard to fit even what pieces we have to their proper place. It has been necessary on many occasions, therefore, to have recourse to the method of conjecture, but in each of these instances the author has tried to check and countercheck his surmise with all indirect evidence available. Because of the extensive migrations of early Slavic tribes, attention has had to be paid in this volume not only to events within the geographic area of Russia itself but likewise to developments in some neighboring countries, as for example the Balkan peninsula, and to the policies of contemporary empires, as the Byzantine Empire, the Turkish Kaganate, and the Caliphate. However, while the reader will find in this book much information on the history of the Byzantine Empire, the Bulgars, the Khazars, etc., the author wishes to make clear that this volume is in no sense a sketch of Byzantine or Balkan history. Only certain points in the history of the Byzantine world are brought out, which bear directly or indirectly upon the development of the Russian people and Russian civilization. As to Chapters I and II, dealing with prehistory and with the Scythian period, they are meant to serve merely as introduction.

This volume is the fruit of many years of labor, during which the author has received kind encouragement and help from several of his friends and colleagues. To Boris A. Bakhmeteff he is particularly indebted for his warm sympathy and interest in the work. Obligations to the published work of others are acknowledged in the notes, but M. I. Rostovtzeff's exhaustive studies of the Scytho-Sarmatian background call for special mention here, and the author certainly appreciates the privilege of having his personal advice on some of the important points. Many a moot problem of Byzantine background has been discussed with Henri Grégoire, and while sharing some of his opinions, as for example on the Magyar question, the author has not been able to accept his skepticism with regard to the early activities of the Rus in the Pontic area. But even when taking exception to Grégoire's views the author has always found them extremely stimulating. He also wishes to express his gratitude to Adolph B. Benson, Jacob Bromberg, V. F. Minorsky, Roman Jakobson, and A. A. Vasiliev for valuable suggestions, as well as to Nicholas Toll who read the first draft of Chapters I and II. Alfred R. Bellinger was kind enough to read the manuscript of Chapters I through VI and to criticize the text with regard to both style and content. The maps, except for No. 4, have been prepared and drawn by Nicholas Krijanovsky, of the American Geographical Society.

The author's thanks are also due to the staff of the Yale University Library for their unfailing coöperation, as well as to the staff of the Library of Congress and of the New York Public Library; to the Editorial Department of the Yale University Press and to Miss Annabel Learned for their assistance in preparing the manuscript for the printers.

G. V.

New Haven, Connecticut,
March, 1943.

ANCIENT RUSSIA

Chapter I

PREHISTORY

1. Approach to the Problem of the Origins of the Russian People.

The historical roots of the Russian people reach deep into the past. While early annals contain considerable information concerning the Russian tribes of the ninth and tenth centuries A.D., it is certain that their respective ancestral groups consolidated themselves long before, at least in the Sarmato-Gothic period, while the process of their consolidation must have started even much earlier, in the Scythian period. Generally speaking, the problem of ethnogenesis is, with any people, a very complicated one. We must not approach it in the light of such over-simplified traditional schemes as the theory of the genealogical tree of languages, which was for a long time considered a sort of universal panacea not only by philologists but by historians as well.

With regard to the prehistoric background of the Russian people we have specifically to avoid such generalizations as the "aboriginal Pan-Slav language" (*Ursprache, pra-yazyk*), supposed to exist prior to the ramification of the modern Slavic languages, or the "aboriginal Pan-Slav mother country" (*Urheimat, pra-rodina*) in which the ancestors of all the Slavic peoples are supposed to have started their historical life. Such generalizations cannot give any help to the historian, but may rather obscure the issue. Jordanis, who wrote in the sixth century A.D., already knew three groups of Slavic tribes: the Venethi, the Sclaveni, and the Antes. Other names were mentioned by classical authors of earlier date for the tribes of South Russia, which may be considered the ancestral groups of the Sclaveni and the Antes. The information given by Herodotus (fifth century B.C.) on the Scythians and their neighbors has also to be taken into consideration in this respect. Any ethnological identification of the classical tribal and national names is very difficult, especially with regard to peoples, such as the Scythians and the Sarmatians, who united vast territories under their control. Their names may have covered not only the ruling tribes but likewise native tribes conquered by them. One must not think that each such invasion resulted in a general extermination of the native tribes which had settled in the country long before the coming of the conquerors. Part of them, in any case, were usually allowed to remain in the country after recognizing the authority of the invaders. Thus after the coming of the Scythians, some of the proto-Slavic tribes may have remained on the fringe of the steppes, while other groups of them were probably pushed north to the forest zone. As to the period of the Sarmatian domination we have more positive evidence that some of the ancestral groups of the Russian tribes were already in the Pontic steppes under Sarmatian control.

Keeping in mind the above considerations we must assume that the ancestral groups of the Slavs originated partly in the forest zone and partly in the steppes, and that the process of their formation was both protracted and very involved. As we have mentioned already, from the point of view of the historian there is no sufficient evidence—and no need, either—to postulate the existence of an aboriginal Pan-Slav people at the dawn of Russian history, or that of an aboriginal Pan-Slav mother country. On the contrary, the evidence supplied by early authors, though scarce, is rather for the existence in ancient times of several—at least, three—groups of proto-Slavic tribes, differing one from another. Each of these must even in remote antiquity have spoken its own dialect and had its peculiar customs. Each, moreover, controlled its own territory. We may tentatively call these three the West Slavic, Middle Slavic, and East Slavic groups. We may conjecture that about the time of Christ's birth the abodes of the West Slavs were in the regions of the middle and upper Vistula River; the settlements of the Middle Slavs stretched from the Carpathian Mountains to the middle Dnieper; while the clans of the East Slavs spread along the northern fringe of the steppes, over the area which was to be known from the seventeenth century on as the Left Bank Ukraine and Slobidshina (the provinces of Kharkov, Kursk, Poltava, Voronezh).[1] Some East

1. Since in all archaeological publications prior to 1917 and even in some of those

Slavic groups probably expanded even more to the south, toward the region of the lower Don River.

There is no archaeological evidence for supposing that the above-mentioned Slavic groups were merely newcomers to the territory they occupied in the first century A.D. On the contrary, the evidence points rather to a certain continuity of culture in this territory for the millennium from 500 B.C. to A.D. 500.[2] We may thus conclude that the ancestral groups of the Slavic tribes settled in this area at least as early as 500 B.C.

Linguistic relationship and similarity of culture do not of course necessarily presuppose racial kinship. Tribes belonging to the same "linguistic area" or the same "cultural sphere" might be different in race or belong to different anthropological types. History offers abundant examples of one people accepting both the language and the culture of another. Thus at the time of the expansion of the Roman Empire the Kelts and Iberians in Gaul and Spain respectively adopted the language of their conquerors—the Latin tongue, out of which modern French and Spanish evolved. No less striking is the case of the Persian language, which after the conquest of Iran by the Arabs underwent a complete change. Not only were Arabic words accepted wholesale, but the very structure of the Persian tongue was profoundly influenced by the Arabic in spite of the fact that Persian is an Indo-European language, and Arabic a Semitic one. Russian history likewise cautions us against a hasty identification of language unity with race unity. It is well known, for example, that the Norsemen who became the ruling class in the Kievan state of the ninth and tenth centuries rapidly assimilated themselves with the natives by accepting the Slavic tongue. An interesting example of a social group united by culture and language, although built up out of variegated racial elements, is the Russian nobility. Some of the oldest Russian noble families derive their ancestry from the Alan and Varangian chiefs; others have Polish, Lithuanian, Ukrainian, German, Swedish, Mongol, Tatar, Armenian or Georgian blood. All these heterogeneous elements merged together because of their acceptance of the Russian tongue and Russian culture. Similar

which have appeared since that date the topography of the sites is adapted to the old administrative divisions of the Russian Empire, we shall have on many occasions to refer to the boundaries of the old provinces.

2. Gotie, pp. 15 f., 26 ff.

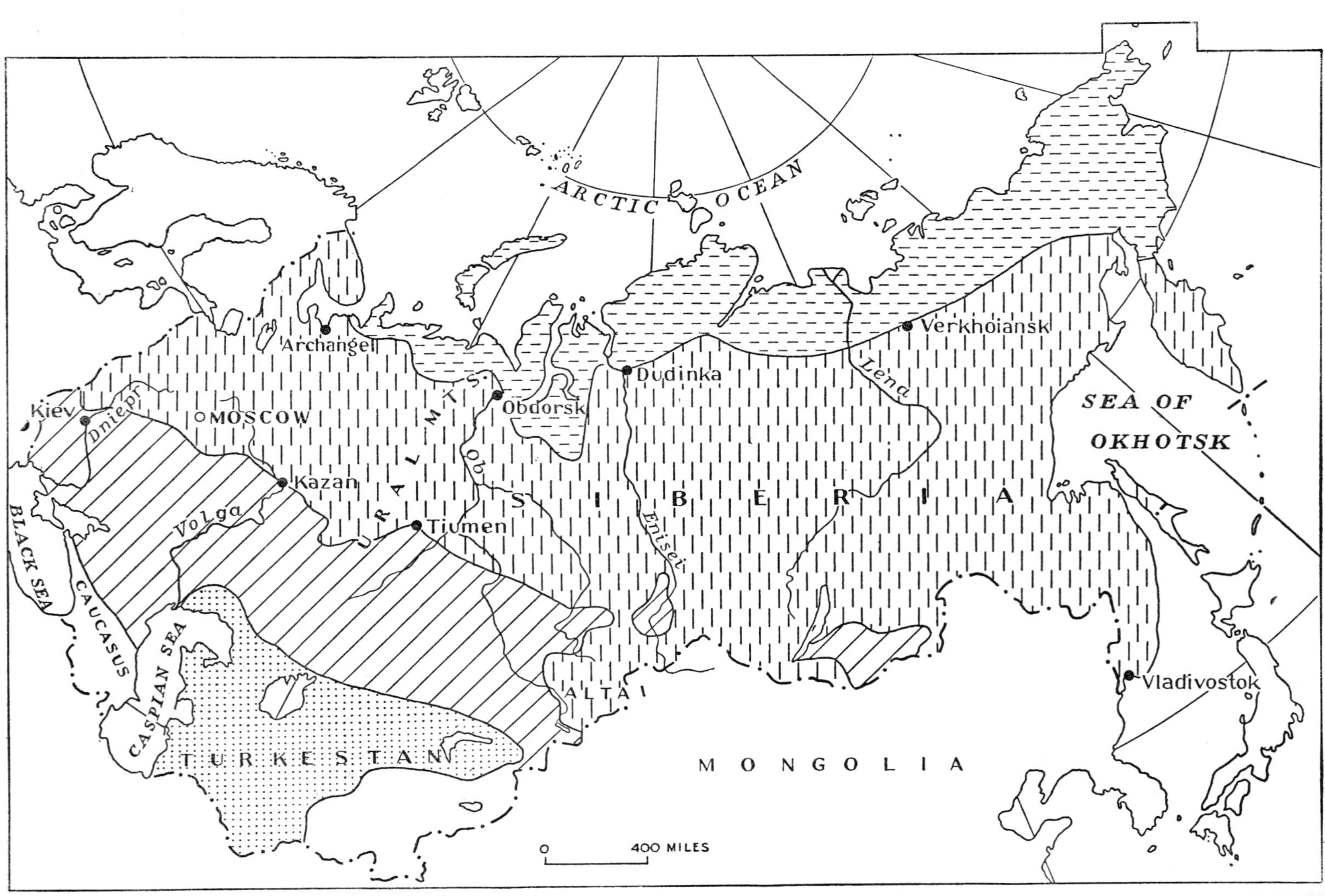
ARCTIC OCEAN
SEA OF OKHOTSK
Archangel
Verkhoiansk
Dudinka
Obdorsk
Lena
URAL MTS.
Kiev
Dniepr
MOSCOW
Kazan
Tiumen
Ob
Enisei
SIBERIA
Volga
BLACK SEA
CAUCASUS
CASPIAN SEA
TURKESTAN
ALTAI
MONGOLIA
Vladivostok
0
400 MILES

processes may have taken place in the earliest times. The Antes, whom the historians of the sixth century A.D. consider the strongest tribe among the Slavs, were ruled by Iranian clans, probably from the second century A.D. By the time of Procopius their language was, however, Slavic.

While thus recognizing the controversial nature of the subject, we may still suppose, with all due reservations, that the aboriginal Slavic tribes belonged basically to the Caucasian race, distinguished by its physical features from the Mongolian. Each of the three proto-Slavic tribes had different neighbors, however, and so was subject to admixture of different foreign ethnic features. The West Slavic group must have had some intercourse with the Baltic (Lithuanian) tribes in the north and the Germans in the west. The Middle Slavic tribe was probably in close relations with the Thracian tribes of Transylvania and the Balkans. The East Slavic group was more open to intermixture with the nomadic and seminomadic tribes of the steppes—and their name was legion. Tribes of Thracian, Keltic, Iranian, Gothic, Ugrian, Turk, and Mongol stock chased each other over the steppes in endless succession. Each must have left some trace in the country.

To sum up the argument, it is some of the aboriginal Middle and East Slavic tribes that may be considered the ancestral group of the Russian people. These early Slavs were settled chiefly on the fringe of the steppe zone, although some sections of them established themselves more to the north, in the forests, while other groups descended south into the steppes. Agriculture must have constituted the main pursuit of the people: those in the forests occupied themselves with hunting and apiculture; those in the south were cattle breeders. Since fish was abundant in the rivers, fishing was likewise an important means of subsistence. Thus the early East Slavs were familiar with river life; they made boats by hollowing out tree trunks. Such was their skill with boats that whenever they happened to descend to the shores of the Sea of Azov and the Black Sea they did not hesitate to venture on open water. The diversity of their natural background and economic conditions resulted in the early formation of different types of economic and social organization among the people. Clans or family communes of the zadruga[3]

3. The zadruga commune has survived in Yugoslavia until recently. It is of the "large family" type, at least three generations living together. There is an extensive literature on the zadruga. Among the recent publications see V. Popovic, *Zadruga* (Sarajevo, 1921); *idem*, "Zadruga: teorija i literatura," *SZM*, *33-34* (1921-22); Z.

type must have prevailed among groups whose chief occupation was agriculture. Hunting or fishing associations presented another type of social unit, while those who ventured south into the steppes and were used by Sarmatian chieftains as warriors were probably organized into military communes of the later Kozak type.

The area of the early expansion of the Middle and East Slavs coincides approximately with what later became known as Ukraine. By the eighth century A.D. they had spread over a much more vast territory, which is now usually called European Russia but may perhaps be better called western Eurasia, the term "Eurasia" comprising the areas of European and Asiatic Russia put together.[4] Western Eurasia may thus be considered the first, or combined ancient and medieval, stage of Russian expansion, and Eurasia as a whole its second and final stage.

In a sense, western Eurasia already in ancient times formed the general geographic background for the development of the East Slavs, even though at that time they actually occupied only the south of it. Geographically and economically the south was interdependent with the north, then as now. In order to approach the early history of the East Slavs we have therefore to study their prehistoric background within its larger geographic frame. While the population of western Eurasia in prehistoric times was scarce, the country was not a desert. Man had lived in it for several thousands, or rather tens of thousands, of years before Christ. It was in this remote antiquity that the foundation of his occupations were laid all through the territory of western Eurasia; by adjusting himself to the natural conditions of the country man created his early economy, and cultural traditions were gradually formed to be passed on to his descendants.

Scattered widely over the Eurasian plains, the settlements of prehistoric man were not isolated one from another. Relations of both peaceful and warlike nature were established between various groups, both in the primitive "pre-clan" (*dorodovoe obshchestvo*)

Vinski, *Die Südslavische Grossfamilie* (Zagreb, 1938); P. E. Mosely, "The Peasant Family: The Zadruga," *The Cultural Approach to History,* ed. by C. E. Ware (New York, 1940), pp. 95-108. Another article on the Yugoslav zadruga by P. E. Mosely is forthcoming in the *Slavonic and East European Review* and, as I understand, he is preparing a comprehensive monograph on the subject. Cf. also Vernadsky, *Zvenya,* pp. 87-90.

4. See my *History of Russia* (2d ed. Yale University Press, 1930), Introduction; and *Political and Diplomatic History of Russia* (Little, Brown and Co., 1936), chap. i.

period, according to the terminology of Soviet scholars, and in the period of more organized clan life. Migrations and wars took place; tradesmen followed in the wake of the warriors. Probably the rivers served at that time as the main commercial highways, and it is characteristic that most of the prehistoric sites so far discovered by archaeologists are located on or near the river banks. The intercourse of various groups was not limited to local trade. It is rather striking that in those ancient times commercial highways of international importance were established and the tribes of western Eurasia were thus to a certain extent connected with adjacent countries.

The agriculturists of the middle Dnieper established connections with those of Transylvania and the Balkans. Commerce spread far to the south and east. Wares of Caucasian type were brought both to the Dnieper and the upper Volga regions; painted pottery of the middle Dnieper area of this period shows a striking similarity to the pottery of Turkestan, Mesopotamia, and China. As was the case in the later period, the Pontic steppes were open to the inroads of the nomadic tribes of central and eastern Eurasia. As a matter of fact, these steppes were merely an extension of the Eurasian steppes. There is no doubt that long before the coming of the Scythians the latter's predecessors used the steppe zone for their migrations. It was of great significance that the steppe road from China to the Black Sea skirted such provinces of ancient civilization as Iran and the Caucasus, the cultural background of which was in Mesopotamia. Through the peoples of the steppes these old hearths of culture radiated their light far to the north. In the second millennium B.C. the inhabitants of the upper Volga region shaped their stone axes according to the pattern of the bronze axes of the Caucasians and ornamented their pottery with designs of Caucasian type. Since the Caucasian culture of this epoch was influenced by the Hittite civilization, patterns and designs of Hither Asia used to find their way to the north of Russia.

The student of Russian history cannot disregard the interplay of economic and cultural forces which took place in the territories of Russia long before the beginning of Russia proper. It was in this prehistoric period that the "living space" of the Russian people was formed. Some knowledge of this background is essential for an understanding of the main trends in early Russian economic and political history.

2. *Historiographic Remarks.*

The student of the history of the ancient Orient—Asia Minor, Mesopotamia, and Egypt—has at his disposal written sources for a period of more than three millenniums before the birth of Christ. The student of classical antiquities—Greece and Rome—may use the epic poems, the tradition of which goes up to the beginning of the first millennium B.C., while for the second half of the same millennium there is already a wealth of epigraphic and literary sources. The student of German history has a firm foundation in the works of Caesar and Tacitus, of the first centuries B.C. and A.D. respectively.

The student of Russian history is in a much more difficult position. Tacitus was one of the first authors to mention the Slavs, but he does so only casually. It is in the works of Jordanis and Procopius, historians of the sixth century A.D., that we first find real attempts to describe the life of the Slavs. To be sure, there is considerable information concerning the peoples who lived in the Pontic steppes for several centuries B.C.—the Scythians and the Sarmatians—in the works of a number of classical authors, starting with Herodotus (fifth century B.C.). Chinese chronicles likewise convey some data on the Eurasian nomads. However, the evidence as to the proto-Slavic and early Russian tribes subject to the Iranian nomads which we can extract from all these reports is scant and tentative. Things are even less bright with regard to written sources in Slavic. We may admit that the Russians had some rudiments of literature as early as the seventh and eighth centuries, using the Greek or some other kind of adapted alphabet. It is only when we come to A.D. 860, however, that "Russian characters" are mentioned, and what kind they were is still debated. However, soon after this, and probably on the basis of these early "Russian characters," a more elaborate Slavic alphabet was shaped by Constantine the Philosopher (St. Cyril, apostle of the Slavs); this was the so-called Glagolitic script (*Glagolitsa*); either simultaneously or a little later, but not later than the end of the ninth century, another Slavic alphabet was devised, the so-called Cyrillic script (*Kirillitsa*).[5] It was only thereafter that the art of writing spread widely among the Slavs, including the Russians. The first Russian chronicle was written in Kiev in the eleventh century A. D.; we know it in the early twelfth century ver-

5. See Chap. VIII, Sec. 5 and 6 below.

sion which was preserved in some later compilations, of the fourteenth and fifteenth centuries. The earliest known monument of Russian epigraphy is the so-called Tmutorokan Stone, dated 1068.

The earliest documents of Russian foreign relations—the Russo-Byzantine treaties of the tenth century—are translations from the Greek. The translations were made at the time of conclusion of each treaty, but the originals have been lost, so that what we have are later copies, though they seem to be accurate. The ancient Russian code of laws—the *Pravda Russkaia*—was written down in the eleventh century, but the oldest known manuscripts of it are again of a later period—thirteenth to fifteenth centuries. The oldest known Russian deeds are of the twelfth century.

Thus we see that Russian written sources are available only for the period since the tenth century, and that the foreign documentary evidence starts, for all practical purposes, only as late as the sixth century A.D., and is incomplete. In view of this situation the student of the ancient period of Russian history has to depend chiefly on archaeological evidence. While archaeology is of immense importance for the study of classical history as well as that of the ancient Orient, it is even more vital when it comes to early Russian history. It is only on the foundation of archaeological discovery that the history of the beginnings of Russia can be built up at all. It is unfortunate for the development of Russian historical science that Russian archaeology is so comparatively young. Only recently have attempts been made to connect the archaeological evidence with that of the literary sources and to use archaeological data from the point of view of Russian history.

In addition to archaeological research, linguistic data may be of great help to a historian. Unfortunately, no inscriptions or documents of any kind have been found prior to the appearance of the Greeks on the northern shores of the Black Sea (seventh century B.C.). For the Scythian period we have a number of Greek inscriptions; however, they bear either on the Greek colonies or on the Scythians, but not on the native tribes. We have therefore no linguistic key to the objects found by the archaeologists. Thus the archaeological material on the ancient Russians is mute from the point of view of a historian. As a result, it is no easy task to identify even tentatively that part of the finds which may refer to the life of the forbears of the Russian Slavs, especially since there must have been so much influence of adjacent peoples on the early Slavic culture.

The evidence points to the existence, on the territory where the Slavs later thrived, of a homogeneous "cultural sphere" lasting from around 500 B.C. to about A.D. 500. But it is only tentatively that we may identify this "cultural sphere" as the "proto-Slavic cultural sphere." Such identification is no more than a hypothesis, plausible though it may seem.

In view of the paramount importance of archaeology for Russian historical study it will not be amiss to give here a brief outline of the development of archaeological research in Russia. Ancient burial mounds with their wealth of gold and silver long ago attracted the attention of treasure hunters. Peter the Great was the first of the Russian rulers to understand the importance of such finds for science. He accordingly issued several ukases (1721-22) urging local governors to buy and to collect gold and silver objects of the kind for preservation in museums. It is in this way that the first collection of Siberian antiquities was established in the museum of the Academy of Sciences (1725).

About the same time the governor of Astrakhan, V. N. Tatishchev, a noted historian, compiled an elaborate manual for collecting materials on archaeology and ethnology. Tatishchev's plan was partly realized by the Academy of Sciences, several members of which traveled extensively all over Russia and explored the location of important mounds and ancient sites in South Russia and Siberia. The travels of Pallas, Lepekhin, Gmelin, and Rychkov, brought valuable results. Following Tatishchev's example some local governors showed their interest in archaeology as well. In 1763 the governor of the New Russian Territory (*Novorossiia*), A. P. Melgunov, ordered the excavation of what is known as the Litoi Kurgan, about twenty miles west of Elisavetgrad. A number of gold and silver objects of the Scythian period were found and sent to the Academy of Sciences, whence they were transferred to the Hermitage Palace museum. The Hermitage has since become the central depository for similar finds from South Russia. It was the Scythian and classical art objects of South Russia that chiefly attracted the attention of Russian archaeologists in the first half of the nineteenth century.

In the beginning of that century the academician Keler explored and described some of the monuments of the ancient Bosporan kingdom on the Kerch Strait. Excavations were conducted in Kerch itself from 1817 to 1835 by the French émigré Paul Dubrux, who enlisted the interest and support of the Kerch chief of police, Stempkovskii. In 1826 the governor general of the New Russian Territory, Count M. S. Vorontsov, approved Stempkovskii's project of establishing a museum of antiquities in Kerch. This museum, opened in the same year, became an important local center of archaeological research. It may be noted incidentally that the museum was destroyed by the British during the Crimean War (1855), but restored soon after. Near Kerch, in 1831 Dubrux and Stempkovskii excavated the Kul-Oba Kurgan, one of the most important Scythian mounds. Presently, in the 1840's, the city of Odessa assumed an active role in promoting archaeological research. In 1844 the valuable *Commentaries* (*Zapiski*) of the Odessa Society of History and Antiquities began to appear.

The capital of the empire, St. Petersburg, lagged somewhat behind. In 1846 an "Archaeological and Numismatic Society" was founded there, but it was not until 1865 that this group became really active under the new name of the "Imperial Archaeological Society." The most important event in the progress of archaeological studies in Russia was the organization in 1859 of the Imperial Archaeological Commission, which before long assumed the leading role in directing and coördinating research in Russia. Among the prominent members of this commission who were active in the beginning of the twentieth century the names of N. P. Kondakov, N. I. Veselovskii, M. I. Rostovtzeff, Count A. A. Bobrinskoy, and B. V. Farmakovskii may be mentioned here. After the Russian Revolution the commission was reorganized as the Institute of the History of Material Culture, recently merged with the Academy of Sciences. The Archaeological Commission sent to South Russia a number of expeditions, during which both Scythian and Sarmatian mounds as well as the sites of ancient Greek cities were excavated.

We may see that during most of the nineteenth century the work of Russian archaeologists centered around antiquities of the classical period. This was in a sense natural for the first stage of development of archaeological science in Russia, the finds in this field being so much more spectacular. Gradually, however, the antiquities of the Stone Age likewise began to attract the interest of scholars, though those interested in this period were at first less numerous than their colleagues who excavated the Scythian mounds. Count A. S. Uvarov may be called the pioneer of Stone Age studies in Russia. He was also the founder of the Moscow Archaeological

Society (1864). Several Stone Age sites were excavated by him and his associates in central Russia in the 1870's. In 1881 Uvarov's book on the archaeology of Russia was published, based chiefly upon the results of his own excavations. No less important with regard to the study of the Stone and Bronze Age culture were the results of excavations undertaken in the period between 1880 and 1917 by a number of Russian and Ukrainian scholars, including V. B. Antonovich, N. F. Beliashevskii, V. V. Khvoiko, E. R. von Stern, F. K. Volkov, Count A. A. Bobrinskoy, V. A. Gorodtsov, A. A. Spitsyn, and others. Most of the objects found in central Russia have been kept in the Moscow Historical Museum; for those found in Ukraine, the Kiev Archaeological Museum is an important depository. Several local museums both in the north and in the south likewise have valuable collections. Archaeological exploration in Siberia also achieved significant results, being centered chiefly around local museums of which the most important are those at Irkutsk (founded, 1805; enlarged, 1851; burned down, 1879; restored, 1882), Tobolsk (1870), Minusinsk (1877), and Krasnoiarsk (1889).

Since the revolution of 1917 archaeological studies have received even more attention, the explorations assuming a more organized form. The Institute of the History of Material Culture at the Academy of Sciences is one of the leading institutions in the field. The Academy of Sciences of the Ukrainian S.S.R. in Kiev supervises archaeological research within Soviet Ukraine. The State Historical Museum of Moscow has organized a series of archaeological expeditions in various parts of the Russian Socialist Federated Soviet Republic. Some local museums are very active as well. The most striking discoveries of the last two decades are in the field of paleolithic sites, but to both neolithic and bronze culture considerable attention has likewise been paid.

The first noteworthy attempt to use archaeological evidence for the study of Russian history was made by I. E. Zabelin in his book, *The History of Russian Life* (1876-79).[6] Even more ambitious was the plan adopted by V. M. Florinskii for his study, *The Aboriginal Slavs* (1895-98).[7] These two works, while interesting for the time of their publication, are now hopelessly antiquated. It was M. I. Rostovtzeff, in his book, *Iranians and Greeks in South Russia*

6. J. E. Zabelin, *Istoriia Russkoi Zhizni,* Vols. I-II (Moscow, 1876-79).

7. V. M. Florinskii, *Pervobytnye Slaviane,* Vols. I-II (Tomsk, 1895-98).

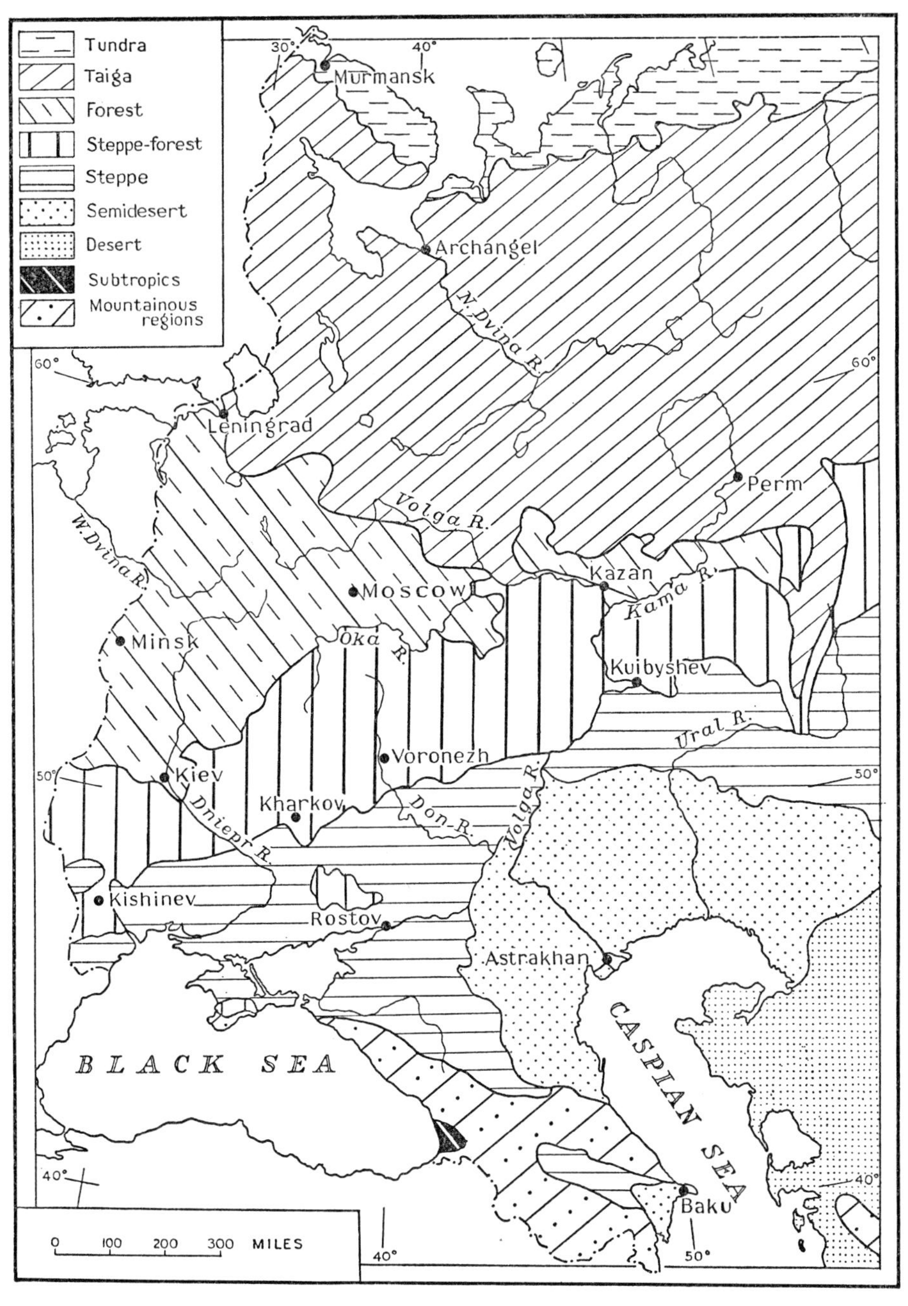

LANDSCAPE ZONES OF THE EUROPEAN PART OF U. S. S. R.

(1922), who first approached the problem of the connection between Russian archaeology and Russian prehistory along modern lines. A good survey of the archaeological material from the point of view of the student of Russian history was published in 1925 by Yu. V. Gotie (*Studies in the History of Material Culture of Eastern Europe*). Valuable archaeological studies have appeared in the course of the last two decades in the *Bulletin* (*Izvestiia*) of the Academy of the History of Material Culture. This is now replaced by *Brief Communications* (*Kratkie Soobshcheniia*) of the Institute of the History of Material Culture at the Academy of Sciences, into which the former Academy of the History of Material Culture was reorganized. Since 1936 a special archaeological review, *Sovetskaia Arkheologiia,* has been published with chief emphasis on the Stone Age. Some attention to current archaeological research is given in the *Journal* (*Vestnik*) *of Ancient History,* started in 1938. A. V. Artsikhovskii's general outline of archaeological research (*Introduction to Archaeology,* 1940) may also be mentioned here.[8]

3. *The Paleolithic Era.*[9]

The first excavations to reveal the sites of settlement of paleolithic man in Russia and Ukraine were undertaken in the 1870's. In 1873 was discovered the site at the village Hontsi (Gontsi) on the river Uday (Poltava Province). Four years later Count Uvarov explored the site in the Karacharov Ravine which descends to the Oka River. These two expeditions gave a good start to the exploration of the remnants of paleolithic culture in Russia, and in the period between 1877 and 1917 several sites were excavated. As we have already mentioned,[10] the field has been more systematically studied since 1917. New discoveries are now being made almost every year and before long the picture will be even more clear.

Archaeological science itself was developed, especially in its early stages, chiefly around the material of European findings—those

8. A. V. Artsikhovskii, *Vvedenie v arkheologiiu* (Moscow, 1940)—inaccessible to me. Cf. S. Kiselev's review of this book in *VDI,* No. 2 (1940), pp. 132-134.

9. M. Boule, *Les Hommes fossiles* (Paris, 1923); M. S. Burkitt, *The Old Stone Age* (Cambridge, 1933); Efimenko; Gotie, *Ocherki,* chaps. i-ii; Menghin; G. Merhart, "The Palaeolithical Period in Siberia," *AA,* XXV (1923); H. Obermaier, "Sibirien: Palaeolithikum," *RL, 12* (1928), 55-57; "Paleolit S.S.S.R.," *GA, 118* (1935); B. E. Petri, "Sibirskii Paleolit," *IUT,* V (1923) (volume of Plates [Irkutsk, 1927], inaccessible to me); L. Sawicki, "Materialy do znajomosci prehistorji Rosji," *PA,* III (1926-27).

10. See Sec. 2, above.

made in France, Germany, and Scandinavia. It is on the basis of this material that the classification of items of the Stone Age culture as well as the chronology of stages of culture was at first defined. To what extent such classification and chronology may be applied to Eurasian material is a problem which has not yet been sufficiently clarified. Even if we use the traditional terminology we must bear in mind that it may not be perfectly applicable to the archaeology of Eurasia.

In the study of paleolithic culture much depends upon the results of geological research. The chronology and classification of the strata offered by geologists are likewise not definitive, but still the data of geology are on the whole much more reliable than those of archaeology. Geological science has been built up upon a wider geographic background, since exploration in that field has long been conducted on an international scale. In Eurasia likewise, geological exploration began long before archaeological research. The Stone Age sites discovered so far on the territory of both Cisuralian (European) Russia and Siberia may be referred to the Quaternary period: to wit, the middle and upper strata of the Pleistocene. From the point of view of the historian it is remote antiquity, since it has to be measured in millenniums or even tens of millenniums.

The geographic background was in this remote epoch entirely different from that of our times. At the beginning of the Quaternary most of western Eurasia was covered with ice. The geologists postulate the sequence of three or four ice ages, divided by periods of intermission during which the glacier receded. During each ice age gigantic glaciers spread from Scandinavia to the south and southeast, covering the whole of north and central Russia. At the time of the greatest expansion of the glacier its southern fringe reached the line which might be drawn from the Carpathian Mountains to Kiev on the Dnieper River, and thence to Orel; from Orel it went in a curve to Voronezh and beyond it eastward to the Volga River, then up the Volga to the mouth of the Kama River and further north across the northern section of the Ural Mountains toward the mouth of the Ob River in Siberia. The southern Ural region was by that time covered by water. The huge lake of the Southern Ural was connected with two other lakes out of which later the Caspian and Aral Seas were formed.

Even after the glacier finally began to recede northward, around 4000 B.C., traces of it were long noticeable all over the country.

A spacious lake was formed in the northwestern section of Russia, of which Lake Ladoga and Lake Onega are but small remnants. In the south, as the glacier gradually retired and the ice fringe thawed, muddy torrents were formed, discharging into the Black Sea which by that time spread over its present shore northward to the steppe area. It is out of these torrents that the later rivers Dnieper, Don, Volga, and others originated. It was in the postglacial period that the basic subsoil of central and southern Russia and Ukraine, known as loess, was formed; a kind of granulated argillaceous loam of light gray color. The loess soil emerged only gradually from the cover of ice. While receding, the glacier deposited on its fringes what is known as the moraine, consisting of stones polished by water as well as granite boulders. Probably the climate of the areas recently freed from the cover of ice was cold, like the climate of present-day sub-polar areas. Such a climate was favorable to the expansion of the mammoth and it appears that this creature was in the postglacial period widely spread over the whole of western Eurasia. Gradually the climate became milder, but there were intervals when the glacier expanded again and a cold wave spread south. It is generally accepted that during the so-called Magdalenian period[11] the climate became colder again. When the climate had become definitely milder the southern plains were covered by ample vegetation, and gradually an upper stratum of humus was formed over the loess; it is in this way that the famous "black soil" (*chernozyom*) originated in the steppes of southern Russia and Ukraine.

It was only in the south that man could live during the glacial period. The man of the Middle Paleolithic, the so-called Mousterian period,[12] was still at a low level of cultural development. He was, however, already able to start fire. His abode was chiefly in caves or under protruding rock edges. Hunting was the main source of his sustenance, supplying him with both food and garments. His chief tool was the hand ax (*coup-de-poing*), a lump of flint of which one end was sharpened and the other rounded or left blunt. It could serve as a cleaver or an ax. This tool had no handle and was to be held in the clenched fist. For hunting a wooden spear, the head of which was sharpened by burning, was used. With the help of these weapons man was able to kill wild buffaloes, horses, and deer, as well as to fight beasts of prey, even the cave lion and the cave bear. This

11. From the Stone Age site at La Madelaine, Dordogne, France.
12. From the Stone Age site at Le Moustier, Dordogne, France.

was probably a period of primitive communism. The average hunting band or horde may have consisted of twoscore men.

Several Stone Age sites discovered in Russia belong to the Middle Paleolithic period. Such are certain caves in the Crimea, as for instance Volchy Grot, Kiik-Koba, Shaitan-Koba; the site at Ilskaia in the Kuban region; and the site on the bank of the Derkul River where it discharges into the Donets. During the excavations of these sites flint tools, bones of animals killed by man, and occasionally parts of human skeletons were found. Judging from those found in Kiik-Koba, the men who lived in the Crimean caves of those times were of the Neanderthal type.[13]

From the culture of the Middle we now turn to that of the Upper Paleolothic strata, known in western archaeology as the Aurignac-Solutré culture.[14] The settlements of this epoch were apparently of a more permanent nature than those of the preceding period. Dwellings were dug in the ground; earth walls were faced with boards or stones; the roof was probably made of wattles. As to tools and weapons, the sharp flint blade fixed on a short handle and the javelin with a flint spearhead are characteristic. The flint chisel was likewise an important tool. Other tools and utensils were made of bone or staghorn. Horn was sometimes ornamented by drawings, figures of deer or some other animal. Statuettes representing women were made of mammoth tusks. As in the preceding period, hunting was man's chief occupation.

Among the Stone Age sites of western Eurasia belonging to the Upper Paleolithic strata of the Aurignac and Solutré type, the following may be mentioned here: the Siuren cave in Crimea; Borshevo, Gagarino, and Kostenki in the Don basin; Mezin in the Dnieper region. The paleolithic settlement at Malta, in the region of Irkutsk, Siberia (situated on the river Belaia, a tributary to the Angara River), reveals a similar culture.[15]

At the end of this period the climate changed from mild to cold. During the following period, that of the Magdalenian culture, both vegetation and the animal world had to adjust themselves to the cold wave. It was the age of the reindeer. Human habits underwent

13. Efimenko, p. 178 f.

14. From the sites discovered at the Aurignac cave, Haute Garonne, and Solutré cave, Saône-et-Loire; both in France.

15. The Malta site is among many other Stone Age sites of central Siberia which are in the area to be flooded on completion of the power dams being developed on the Angara River in connection with the electrification of this region.

deep changes accordingly. Reindeer hunting and fishing were the main sources of man's subsistence at that time. The usual device for catching fish was that of damming brooks and rivulets with a barrier of stones at the time of spawning. Large fish among those thronged above the dam were then harpooned. On their hunting and fishing expeditions the people of those times probably led a wandering life, following the migration of the reindeer. Temporary dwellings were used in the intervals between migrations. For winter, dugouts served as shelters. In summer outside shelters were built to protect the hearth from rain. Platforms with remnants of hearths have been found, for example, at the Kirillova and Borshevo sites. Near some of the sites, pits were excavated containing bones of animals and various refuse (Karacharovo and Kostenki sites). Flint was less used in this period than before; bone, reindeer horn, and mammoth tusk were now the prevalent materials out of which utensils were prepared. A javelin with carefully sharpened bone spearhead was the standard weapon for hunting. There was a greater variety in utensils and ornamented ware. Some of the art objects had apparently religious meaning.

According to the types of objects found, the following Eurasian Stone Age sites may be classified as belonging to the Magdalenian period: Kostenki and Borshevo in the Don region; Karacharovo on the Oka River; Kirillova, at Kiev; Hontsi, in Poltava province; Novgorod-Seversk; Suchkino, near Rylsk;[16] Studenitsa on the Dniester; Tomsk and other sites in the basin of the Ob and Irtysh; Afontova Hill near Krasnoiarsk; Verkholenskaia Hill near Irkutsk. It is to be noted that some at least of the sites of this period are situated near the sites of the preceding epoch, which points to a certain continuity of settlements.

4. The Neolithic Age.[17]

The receding of the glacier opened to man the areas of central and northern Russia. As we have seen, the northernmost sites of the upper Paleolithic period were discovered on the banks of the Oka River. Remnants of the neolithic culture, or that of polished stone tools, have been found both in the north and south of Russia,

16. S. N. Zamiatin, "Pervaia nakhodka paleolita v doline Seima," *IIM, 8* (1940), 96-101.

17. V. G. Childe, *Danube in Prehistory* (Oxford, 1929); *idem, The Dawn of European Civilization* (New York, 1925); Ebert, chap. ii; Gotie, *Ocherki,* chaps. iii-v.

and in Ukraine and Siberia; not to mention the Caucasus, where the culture was no less old, and developed with larger strides because of its proximity to Mesopotamia and Iran. Burial grounds of neolithic man, his dwellings and workshops, have been excavated in various localities, and casual finds of tools and weapons such as axes, hammers, and arrows, are even more extensive. Judging from the topography of the neolithic finds within the forest zone, man of those times settled chiefly on river banks. As to the steppe zone, the burial mounds of the nomads were often situated far inland on the watersheds, which perfectly agrees with their habits as we know them, for they established their roads mainly along the watersheds.

Chronologically, the spread of neolithic culture over the territory of Russia may be referred to the end of the fourth or the beginning of the third millennium B.C. The face of the land must have been greatly changed by comparison with conditions of the ice age. The effects of the latter were long felt, however. The contours of the seashores shrank only gradually before assuming their present shape. Lakes were spread over the country. The climate, while milder than in the Magdalenian period, was still colder than that in our times. Both flora and fauna came closer to that familiar to us, but species unknown to our times were still in existence. Even in the twelfth century A.D. the primitive aurochs (*tur*) was still abundant in the Russo-Ukrainian steppes, while the academician Gmelin saw in Ukraine a wild horse (*tarpan*) as late as the eighteenth century.

New forms of social organization—by clans—came into being during the Neolithic Age, as well as new branches of man's economic activity such as agriculture and cattle breeding. Man's spiritual life must likewise have assumed new expressions. The elaborate ritual of burial which we know from the finds indicates the development of the idea of continuity of life beyond the grave. People must already have formed some definite system of religious beliefs, of which the ritual of burial was but a partial expression. Material culture made considerable progress as well. Man's polished stone tools of the Neolithic Age present evidence of his considerable skill in crafts. Not only flint but also other kinds of stone were wrought. New types of tools and weapons were produced. The finds of flint and bone arrowheads prove that the bow was already invented. This was to be for ages to come the most practical weapon for both hunting and war. The art of ceramics also made a noticeable advance. Various designs for the ornamentation of earthenware were used in the different regions; some of them primitive, others fairly elaborate. This variety in ornamentation is of primary importance for the student of archaeology since the types of decoration may serve as a gauge for comparing pottery of different "cultural spheres," as well as for establishing interrelations between them. Such differences in ornamentation also serve as tentative landmarks for the chronology of finds.

Since in a number of burial grounds of the Neolithic Age human skulls and skeletons have been found, it is possible to obtain some notion of the anthropological types of the population of that era. It appears that at least two races were then living in western Eurasia, one of them brachycephalic and the other dolichocephalic. Judging from skeletons found in Kherson province, the height of the people living there was no more than 169 centimeters; excavations in Kiev provinces disclosed bones of taller men, around 185 centimeters in height.

Comparison of the main neolithic finds in Eurasia enables the student to distinguish several cultural spheres existing in that territory. We shall first characterize briefly the so-called Anau culture in Turkestan. It was in Turkestan that the main types of culture of the Eurasian nomads met and cross-influenced each other.

The Anau culture.[18] The site of Anau is near Merv. The main work of archaeological exploration there was done in 1903 by an American expedition headed by R. Pumpelly. Three main cultural strata were explored. The Anau I stratum is referred by O. Menghin to around 3500 B.C.; Anau II represents the period around 2500 B.C.; and Anau III may be dated 2000 B.C. Even in the first period the Anau people were not only hunters but agriculturists as well. Barley and wheat were the staple crops. The ox and the sheep were domesticated long before the Anau II period, while pig, goat, dog, and camel appeared only in Anau II. Dwellings were made of clay bricks. The inventory of stone tools is rather poor: chiefly chisels and graters. The pottery, on the other hand, is quite remarkable. The pots are handmade and carefully fired. Many of them are painted in red and black; the ornamentation is mostly in brown. Spindle whorls, which were found in all strata, are evidence of an early development of the art of weaving.

18. See Menghin, pp. 303-308, 429-430; R. Pumpelly, *Explorations in Turkestan* (Washington, D. C., 1908).

It is noteworthy that painted pottery similar to that of the Anau has been found both in China (in Kan-Su and Honan provinces) and in Ukraine.

The Tripolie culture.[19] The culture of painted pottery in the basin of the middle Dnieper River in Ukraine is known as the Tripolie culture, from the site at Tripolie, province of Kiev, where the first important discovery of this type was made. Ornamental pottery is one of its prominent features. There are specimens both of painted pottery and of earthenware with incised ornament. The design was geometric; both spiral and meander patterns were widely used. When men, animals, or plants were represented, they also were adapted in contour to the geometric style. The Tripolie pottery is in some respects similar both to the Anau pottery and to that of the Balkans.

Judging from the remnants of the Tripolie culture its people were agriculturists who were, however, also familiar with cattle breeding. A large number of Tripolie sites have been excavated since the 1880's, chiefly in the area of the Right Bank Ukraine.[20] A characteristic feature of these sites is the so-called "platforms" (*ploshchadki*) reinforced with baked clay. These platforms are mostly of square shape; their width is from 5 to 13 meters and their length from 6 to 18 meters. They were found at a depth of from 0.2 to 1 meter under the present surface of the ground. The function of these platforms has long been a puzzle to archaeologists. Until recently the consensus of opinion was that the platforms were part of the burial grounds; now, on the basis of recent excavations, it is accepted that most of them were foundations of houses. These were themselves probably wooden frame houses, the wall frame being filled with clay, and for that reason little was preserved of them except the foundation. In several cases, however, the lower parts of the timberwork have been discovered. As to the roof, it was probably a gabled one with two sloping surfaces filled in with wattles.

19. Ebert, chap. ii; V. V. Khvoiko, "Kamennyi vek srednego Pridneprovia," *TAS*, XI, *1* (1899); *idem*, "Nachalo zemledeliia i bronzovyi vek v srednem Pridneprov'e," *TAS*, XIII, *1* (1905); E. Yu. Krichevskii, "Tripolskie ploshchadki," *SA*, VI (1940), 20-45; T. Passek, *La Céramique Tripolienne* (Moscow-Leningrad, 1935); T. Passek and B. Bezvenglinskii, "Novye otkrytiia Tripolskoi arkheologicheskoi ekspeditsii," *VDI*, IV (1939), 186-192; E. von Stern, "Doistoricheskaia grecheskaia kultura na yuge Rossii," *TAS*, XIII, *1* (1905); *idem*, "Südrussland: Neolithikum," *RL*, *13*, 34-50.

20. The terms, "right bank" and "left bank" Ukraine, meaning right or left of the Dnieper River if one looks downstream, are used to denote the portions of Ukraine west and east of the Dnieper River respectively.

Remnants of hearths have been found on several sites. Stoves were built of baked clay with a vaulted top. The height of the stove was from 1 to 1.5 meters. Pots and sundry pottery, bowls, clay figurines, bones of animals, grain, and heaps of refuse were found on many platforms. Some of the vases contained burnt human bones; these were apparently funeral urns. The platforms are usually situated in groups, each forming a settlement unit in itself. The plan of a typical settlement of the Tripolie type is very interesting. Buildings were arranged in two concentric circles, which must have facilitated the defense of the settlement in case of attack. In the settlement explored in 1938 at Kolomiishina, Kiev province, there were thirty-one buildings forming the outside circle, and eight making up the inside one. The diameter of the inside circle is 60 meters; there were no buildings inside it, this area apparently serving as a town square. Doubtless the settlement as a whole housed people belonging to the same clan or zadruga community.

In the late strata of the Tripolie settlements copper and bronze objects were found. It is thus apparent that before its downfall the Tripolie culture was evolving out of the purely neolithic stage. On the basis of tools and remnants of food found in sites of the Tripolie type we may obtain a pretty clear idea of the economic life of Tripolie man. His tools, such as axes, knives, and hammers, were made of stone or of bone. In later strata copper sickles were found, which points to gradual progress in the technique of agriculture. Several kinds of cereal grasses were apparently raised, such as wheat, millet, barley, as well as hemp. His food consisted chiefly of meat and bread cakes; flour was prepared by grinding grain by hand graters. A number of animals were domesticated—the sheep, the goat, the hog, and the dog; later on, the cow and the horse were added. The Tripolie people were apparently familiar with weaving, since a number of spindle whorls were found in the sites. Unfortunately no inscriptions of any kind were discovered which could throw light on the language of Tripolie man, and therefore the Tripolie people cannot be identified either linguistically or ethnologically.

The Culture of dolmens.[21] This so-called megalithic culture spread over the Crimean and Caucasian shores of the Black Sea. The

21. See Gotie, *Ocherki,* pp. 63-67; Minns, pp. 145-146. The word "dolmen" is derived from the Breton language: *dol,* "table," and *men,* "stone." Its coming into use is explained by the fact that dolmens were first studied in Brittany.

dolmen of the north Caucasian type is a building with walls of rough stones and a roof of flat stone slabs. It served as a house, not for the living but for the dead, who were deposited usually in a sitting position with legs stretched on the floor. Pots and various utensils were found placed at the side of the skeleton. In large dolmens several skeletons were found; these probably served as a burial vault for the whole family. In most cases dolmens were located in groups as if constituting a clan settlement of the dead. The origin of this culture is a moot question. During the late Neolithic and the early Bronze Age it expanded all over Hither Asia and the Mediterranean shores, reaching as far north as Brittany, Denmark, and southern Sweden. It seems most likely that the path of expansion of the dolmens in northern Caucasus and Crimea started in Transcaucasia. In this case we may presuppose a migration of the peoples who built the dolmens from Hither Asia to the North Pontic shores.

The Culture of painted skeletons.[22] The barrows of this cultural sphere are spread all over southern Russia and Ukraine, chiefly in the steppes. They are not high, usually from 1 to 2 meters. The corpse was placed in a cist in a contracted position and was always stained with red ochre; the inventory of the contents of the grave is poor, especially compared with Scythian mounds of the later period. Pottery is sometimes provided with cordlike ornamentation. Flint knives and axes were found in the graves, also battle-axes, the shape of which has a great similarity to the Scandinavian type of battle-ax.

While Tripolie man was an agriculturist, the man of the painted skeletons was primarily a herdsman. Hordes of these nomads must have controlled the Pontic steppes from the Dnieper River to the northern Caucasus. The horse they domesticated was of a primitive type; it is presumably represented on a silver vase found in the Maikop mound, of the North Caucasian area. It is possible that on the northern fringe of the steppes some tribes were gradually adapting themselves to agriculture. A number of agricultural tools was found by the archaeologist V. A. Gorodtsov in one of the sites of Kharkov province. This region served apparently as a bridge between the Tripolie culture and the steppe culture. In the Kharkov site referred to, painted pottery decorated in Tripolie style was discovered.

The Fatianovo culture.[23] This cultural sphere receives its name

22. Ebert, chap. ii.
23. Gotie, *Ocherki,* pp. 81-82.

from the site at the village Fatianovo, near Yaroslavl, where one of the typical finds is located. Its area lay in the basin of the rivers Oka and upper Volga, and it comprised the territory of the following Russian provinces: Tver, Yaroslavl, Kostroma, Nizhni-Novgorod, Vladimir, and Moscow. At the time of its greatest expansion the Fatianovo culture reached as far west as Smolensk and as far south as Michurinsk (Kozlov). Chronologically, its Stone Age period is referred to the end of the third and the first half of the second millennium B.C.[24]

In the oldest neolithic graves of the Oka region the dead were buried in shallow ditches without any tumuli. Graves found at Volosovo, near Murom, were dug under the roots of pine tree stumps, apparently to protect the contents of the grave from being washed away by rains. In the burial grounds of the later period—that of the Fatianovo type proper—the dead were deposited on a layer of charcoal. At the head and feet of the corpse, pots were placed upside down. Among the tools and utensils found in settlements of the Fatianovo type, carefully polished stone axes should be mentioned. Some of these axes, as well as ornamented vases with spheric bottom, point to an influence of North Caucasian patterns on the Fatianovo art.[25] As in the Tripolie area, copper and bronze objects began to appear in the later strata of Fatianovo neolithic culture. This process of transition, which in the Tripolie culture was interrupted by some catastrophe, in the case of Fatianovo culture was gradual and continuous. Of the bronze stage of the Fatianovo culture more will be said in the next section.

Western and central Siberia.[26] Both burial grounds and sites of settlement of the Neolithic Age were discovered in various localities of western Siberia: at Lake Andreev near Tiumen, on Chudatskaia Hill near Barnaul, and on the banks of the Ulagan River in the western Altai region. Several burial grounds of the neolithic type

24. The Fatianovo cultural area did not represent the northernmost expansion of neolithic man on the territory of Russia. Among the neolithic sites of the northern region, that on the banks of the Lake Ladoga, excavated in 1878 by A. A. Inostrantsev, may be mentioned. It is likewise to the Neolithic era that pictures carved on rocks in the Lake Onega area may be referred. See A. A. Inostrantsev, *Doistoricheskii chelovek poberezh'ia Ladozhskogo Ozera* (St. Petersburg, 1882); V. I. Ravdonikas, *Naskalnye izobrazheniia Onezhskogo Ozera* (Moscow-Leningrad, 1936).

25. See Sec. 5, below.

26. G. Merhart, "Sibirien: Neolithikum," *RL, 12,* 57-70; B. E. Petri, "Neoliticheskie nakhodki na Baikale," *MAE,* III (1916); *idem,* "Sibirskii Neolit," *IBG,* III (1926); S. A. Teploukhov, "Drevniia Pogrebeniia," *ME,* III, 2 (1927).

have been uncovered on the banks of Enisei River, of which that found on Afanasieva Hill near the village Bateni has been especially well studied. It may be dated around 2000 B.C. The cultural sphere to which it belongs is accordingly known as that of the Afanasieva culture. The bodies in the graves of Afanasieva type were laid out in trenches 1.5 meters deep, and the graves covered with stones. The skeletons were found in contracted position or in any case with bent legs. In some of the graves burnt human bones were discovered, an evidence of cremation. A number of poorly baked clay pots were found, most of them with conoidal bottom. The ornamentation is rather rough; in some cases it is executed by incising, in others by applying plaster. Some of the vases are coated with copper. Few tools or weapons were found, among them stone arrowheads and pestles, and bone needles. In the remnants of food, bones of fish, of the Siberian deer (*iziubr*), and wild buffalo, as well as those of some domesticated animals, such as horse, ox, sheep, were discovered. On the basis of these finds it is assumed that the man of the Afanasieva culture was familiar not only with hunting and fishing but with cattle breeding as well. It is characteristic that beads at the neck and wrists of many a skeleton were made of the shell of mollusks belonging to a species endemic in the region of the Aral Sea. The obvious implication is that in this period some kind of intercourse must have been established between people living in the Enisei region and those in the region of the Aral Sea. And indeed, some recent finds at Khoresm, south of the Aral Sea, show the similarity between the Afanasieva culture and the Kelteminar culture.[27] As the latter developed under the influence of the Anau culture, we may assume a certain unity of culture in Turkestan and Siberia in the late Neolithic and early Bronze Ages.

An interesting neolithic site was excavated at Biriusina, on the hilly banks of the Enisei River 45 kilometers south from Krasnoiarsk. In this locality the hills abound in calcareous caves, in some of which traces of settlement have been found. Both on the site of the Biriusina settlement and in adjacent caves a great number of stone tools were discovered, such as knives, chisels, and scrapers, as well as some bone tools: to wit, daggers, harpoons, needles, and awls. Since some of the chisels are of the paleolithic type we may conclude that the settlement had already existed in the Paleolithic

27. See Tolstov, pp. 156-159; *idem*, "Po sledam drevnei tsivilizatsii," *Izvestiia*, October 10, 1940.

period, and a continuity of local culture in this region may be surmised. Bones of the following animals were found at and around the Biriusina site: ox, goat, reindeer, moose, roe deer, horse, fox, and hare. Apparently hunting was the main occupation of the people. Five cultural strata are discernible, the upper one already containing some iron objects.

As to the neolithic burial grounds of the Baikal region they may be divided into two types, known from the names of characteristic sites as the Kitoi and the Glazov type. The Kitoi burial ground is situated on the left bank of the Angara River 5 kilometers from its confluence with the Kitoi. The dead were buried in shallow trenches without barrows; they were deposited in a contracted position lying on the back, and were stained with ochre. Necklaces of deer teeth and bird bones were placed on the forehead or attached around the neck. Nephrite axes, stone arrowheads and spearheads, bone harpoons and awls, and clay pots, were found in most of the graves. Graves of the Glazov type are more elaborate, each with a built-in cist of stone slabs. Above each, grave stones were piled forming a mound of conoid shape. The position of the skeletons in the graves is similar to that of the Kitoi graves but no traces of ochre were found. The inventory of stone tools is not rich. Copper knives were found in some of the graves.

Speaking generally, the technique of the Siberian Neolithic Age is on a comparatively high level. Arrowheads and some of the tools are of good craftsmanship. The stone was wrought both by polishing and sawing. Even such hard stone as nephrite was polished. Neat holes were bored in pieces of stone for the making of ornaments.

General remarks on the Neolithic Age in Eurasia. Certain conclusions of more general scope may be now drawn from our survey of neolithic finds in Eurasia. It is obvious that most of Cisuralian Russia as well as portions of Siberia were now inhabited. The economic life of neolithic man was more differentiated than that of the Paleolithic era. It was during the Neolithic Age that some of the fundamental types of man's economic activity were established, such as agriculture, cattle breeding, craftsmanship. Because of the diversity of natural background, different branches of husbandry prevailed in the various areas. In Cisuralian Russia the following three regions are important: the frontier zone of the forests and steppes in Ukraine, where agriculture and cattle breeding were developed; the region of the Oka and upper Volga, favorable to hunting and fishing—where, however, agriculture was also practiced; and the southern steppes, where the emphasis was on horse and cattle breeding. Rivers served as the main highways of commerce, the Volga playing an especially prominent role as a link between the North Caucasian cultural sphere and that of the upper Volga and Kama rivers. We have already had occasion to mention the fact that the commercial interrelations of the Neolithic era assumed a truly international character.[28] Indeed, the middle Dnieper region was connected with the Balkan area on the one hand and with the Caucasus on the other. Through the Caucasus the Oka-Volga region was open to the influences of Mesopotamian culture. And from the Volga-Kama region merchants must have penetrated western Siberia, and vice versa. People of western Siberia traded with those of Kazakhstan, and these in their turn found their way into the Caucasus. Thus the circle was completed.

The historian is naturally inclined to dwell on the political aspects of international economics. He may assume that economic interrelations between various neolithic provinces in Eurasia were in some cases accompanied by intense political and military struggle. Empires must have been formed and destroyed then as they were to be later on. However, due to the lack of written sources, nothing save mere hypotheses can be offered concerning the political history of neolithic Eurasia. A number of such hypotheses have been suggested for the interpretation of the archaeological material, but their validity can be questioned. It is pretty certain that the end of the third and the beginning of the second millennium B.C. must have been an important period in the development of the Indo-European peoples. Some of their important migrations must have taken place around that time. It is possible that the nomads of the culture of painted skeletons represented one stage in this process. It is likewise possible that the Hittites, whose language is related to the Indo-European family, passed, on their way to the Bosporus and Asia Minor, through the Pontic steppes, entering them from the east. All this is in the realm of mere surmise.

28. See Sec. 1, above.

5. *The Copper and Bronze Age.*[29]

The invention of the art of metallurgy brought about a new stage in the development of human civilization. Its importance can hardly be overestimated. Metallurgy developed first in the ancient centers of culture—Egypt and Mesopotamia—as early as the fourth millennium B.C. Thence the technique of smelting and forging metals spread to Transcaucasia and Asia Minor and further to the north and west, at a very slow pace at first.

Gold and copper were apparently the first metals used. Gold because of its scarcity served for ornaments only. Copper could be used more extensively for tools and vessels. Silver was introduced later than gold, and iron much later than copper (in the second half of the second millennium B.C.). Copper being too soft and heavy was not well suited for implements, but man soon learned to smelt it with tin. The alloy of copper and tin known as bronze is both lighter and harder than copper. Its invention brought about a gradual evolution of the "Copper Age" into the "Bronze Age."

Bronze first came into use in localities where beds of both copper and tin ore were discovered. As regards the Bronze Age culture of Eurasia, deposits of both metals had been known since ancient times in the Altai and Ural region as well as in Transcaucasia. Tin could also be imported from Asia Minor and Iran. It is possible that tin ore was available in northern Russia as well, namely, in the region of Lake Ladoga and Lake Onega; also in the Pechora basin.[30] There were no deposits of tin in middle or South Russia. Copper was, however, mined in the South Russian Donets basin.[31] But in general the territory of Cisuralian Russia offered a poor background for the development of the copper and bronze industry. Most of the copper and bronzeware found in this area must therefore have been imported from neighboring regions. As to commercial intercourse the Volga region, which is not so far from the Urals and is connected by a natural waterway with the Caucasus, was in a better position than Ukraine. On the whole, copper and bronze culture

29. V. G. Childe, *The Bronze Age* (Cambridge, 1930); Ebert, chap. iii; Gotie, *Ocherki,* chaps. vi-ix; Merhart; Radlov; Rostovtzeff, chap. ii; Tallgren, *Kupfer; idem,* "L'age du cuivre dans la Russie Centrale," *SMYA, 32,* 2 (1920); Teploukhov.

30. See A. V. Shmidt and A. A. Iessen, "Olovo na severe Evropeiskoi chasti S.S.S.R.," *GA, 110* (1935), 205 ff.

31. See n. 39, below.

expanded over the territory of Cisuralian Russia only gradually. At the time when inhabitants of the Caucasus were already familiar with the bronze industry, neolithic culture still held its ground in central Russia.

With these preliminary remarks, we may now turn to a survey of the spheres of copper and bronze culture in Eurasia. Let us start with the North Caucasian area which served as a bridge for the spread of copper and bronzeware to the Don and Volga regions.

The North Caucasian area.[32] Specimens of copperware have been found in some North Caucasian mounds that may be referred to the end of the third millennium B.C.; that is, to a period in which both Ukraine and central Russia were still in the Neolithic Age. To the North Caucasian area copper objects were first imported from Transcaucasia. It should be noted that the North Caucasus must have had commercial ties with Transcaucasia from time immemorial, while Transcaucasia itself was within the sphere of cultural influences coming from Asia Minor, Syria, and Mesopotamia. In the beginning of the second millennium B.C., Mesopotamia was controlled by Babylonian kings (Hammurabi, 1955-1913 B.C.), and in the second millennium the Hittites—whose language is close to the Indo-European family—became the leading power in Hither Asia. They created a strong empire in Asia Minor and Syria; culturally, they lived in the Bronze Age. By the end of the second millennium another kingdom arose in Transcaucasia, known as the Van kingdom or Urartu (Ararat). The kings of Urartu succeeded for several centuries in defending their independence from the Hittites on the one hand and from the Assyrians on the other. Because of the lively relations of the Urartu with other countries of Hither Asia the copper and bronze culture of Transcaucasia made rapid progress; and from Transcaucasia implements and weapons were exported to the North Caucasian area. Even later, when the art of metallurgy had developed in the Caucasus, copper and bronze weapons and tools made by native founders were in shape and design merely an imitation of Mesopotamian patterns.

The Caucasian Mountains are rich in metals. Copper lodes were known from remote antiquity. In the first millennium B.C. tin was

32. Gotie, *Ocherki*, chap. viii; F. Hančar, *Urgeschichte Kaukasiens* (Vienna, 1937) A. A. Iessen, "K voprosu o drevneishei metallurgii medi na Kavkaze," *GA, 110* (1935); Tallgren, "Kaukasus: Bronzezeit," *RL, 6* (1926), 264-267.

mined in the region between Mt. Elbrus and the sources of the Terek River in the middle of the Caucasus mountain ranges, and likewise in the region of Gandja in Transcaucasia. Due to importation of copperware as well as to the early development of native metallurgy, copper culture had established itself in the North Caucasian area by about 2000 B.C. The first period of the North Caucasian copper age is represented by the remarkable barrows of the Kuban region. According to M. Rostovtzeff the Maikop Barrow may be referred to the third millennium B.C.[33] A. A. Iessen dates it at the end of the same millennium.[34] The barrows at Novosvobodnaya (formerly Tsarskaia) must be somewhat later. The Maikop Barrow is 10.65 meters high. A circular enclosure of undressed stones was built at ground level under the tumulus. The trench was dug inside of the square enclosure, the bottom paved with pebbles, and the walls lined with wood. The grave was divided into three sections by wooden partitions. The skeletons were found in contracted position and were stained with red paint. A number of gold and silver objects of excellent craftsmanship were found in the chambers, among them over eighty stamped gold plaques with figures of lion and bull; it appears that such plaques were originally sewed on the clothing as ornament. Also discovered were gold and silver rings and beads; two massive statuettes of a bull, one of gold and the other of silver; and two golden and fourteen silver vases. Two engraved silver vessels are of particular interest. One is decorated with a mountain landscape. B. V. Farmakovskii has interpreted it as a representation of the Caucasus mountain range; in this case the engraving could be attributed to a native artist. However, the validity of the hypothesis has been questioned. The second vase is engraved with figures of animals, among them the primitive horse of the steppes. As to copper objects, five vases and ten tools and weapons were excavated, including a transverse battle-ax of the Mesopotamian type; a two-bladed ax-adz; two flat hatchets; two gouges; one large and one small dagger. In addition to these tools and to earthenware, attention may be called to beads of carnelian and turquoise as well as lapis lazuli and meerschaum. The gold and silver objects of the Maikop Mound were certainly imported from the south. As to copper tools, their origin is not so clear

33. Rostovtzeff, pp. 22-29.

34. Iessen, *GA*, *120*, 81. A. M. Tallgren refers the ensemble of the furniture of the Maikop Kurgan to B.C. 1660-1500, *ESA*, *5* (1930), 180; and *ESA*, *6* (1931), 144.

but it is likely that they also were imported. Sard and turquoise may have been brought from Iran; lapis lazuli from Afghanistan; meerschaum from Asia Minor.

The results of the excavation of the Tsarskaia barrows are less spectacular but no less important scientifically. The graves of these mounds are stone chambers of megalithic type built in the trench under the tumulus. Because of this feature, as well as because of the presence of stone tools together with copper ones, one may conclude that the culture of the Tsarskaia mounds is of transitional nature, the heritage of the Neolithic Age being still strongly felt. Fewer gold and silver objects were found in these mounds than in the Maikop Barrow. Copper tools, however, were more numerous; there were thirty-three in one mound and eight in another. According to A. A. Iessen, the complex of copper tools found in the Tsarskaia mounds may be considered typical of the Kuban region as a whole.[35] To this complex the following tools are referred by Iessen: the transverse ax, flat ax, burin, chisel, knife, small dagger, and socketed fork with two curved prongs which was probably used for grilling meat. Tools of this type were very likely of local production, being cast in stone or clay molds; flat axes, daggers, and some other tools were afterward trimmed by hammering.

In the finds referred to the middle of the second millennium B.C., bronzeware appears occasionally among the copper objects. Finds of this period have been as yet insufficiently studied, most of the objects excavated being kept in local museums such as the Kuban Museum at Krasnodar (formerly Ekaterinodar) and the Kabarda-Balkar Museum at Nalchik. Copper tools representing the North Caucasian culture of this period were undoubtedly produced on the spot. On the Kostromskaia site a local founder's hoard was excavated, consisting of cakes of raw metal ingots and broken tools. Two parts of a stone mold for casting bronze axes were discovered near the village of Zilch in the Vladikavkaz district. In the neighborhood of Koban in Ossetia several clay molds for casting axes and needles were excavated, also a crucible of clay.

By the end of the second millennium B.C. there had started in the North Caucasian area a flourishing period of the bronze culture, which was to last through all the first millennium B.C. Koban in Ossetia was the main center of this cultural sphere. Excavations were started in this locality at the end of the 1870's upon the initia-

35. Iessen, *GA*, *120*, 83 f.

tive of the Moscow Anthropological Society and the Society of Connoisseurs of Caucasian Archaeology. Since then Koban has attracted the attention of a series of Russian and foreign archaeologists, such as R. von Virchow, E. Chantre, J. de Morgan, Countess P. S. Uvarova, A. A. Ivanovskii, V. I. Dolbezhev, and others.

The *aul*[36] of Koban is situated at 30 kilometers from Ordzhonikidze (Vladikavkaz) near the Dergav gorge of the Gizel Don.[37] The slope of the mountain forms four terraces, on one of which lies the oldest burial ground. Its surface area is around 1.5 square hectares. The graves have the shape of stone chests built of unhewn slabs. Skeletons are always found lying in a contracted position with the hands raised to the head. The inventory of the Koban graves is rich and diverse. Heavy bronze axes have a characteristic shape, being narrow and curved with an oval shaft hole. Most of the axes are decorated with incised ornament, either linear or in representation of animals. The latter style includes outlines of deer, tigers, snakes, fish, and fantastic creatures. Bronze daggers of two kinds were excavated. Those of the first group had been cast whole, hilt and blade in the same mold. In the case of the second group blades were cast separately, the hilts being of bronze, bone, or wood. Hilts are often carved in the shape of animal heads. Blades are broad and double-edged, of the Mesopotamian type. Among other bronze objects needles, necklaces, fibulas, bracelets, pendants, and horsebits may be mentioned. Broad belts either of sheet bronze or textile with bronze plates deserve special attention, since they are similar to those in which deities and kings appear in Assyrian and Babylonian art. It is also interesting that in some later graves the bronze plaques on such belts are ornamented with inlaid iron. The ceramics of the Koban graves is less diverse than their bronzeware. Pots were made of black clay and fired. The ornamentation, of linear type, was by incision; the incisions were then filled in with white stucco matter.

Bronze tools of the Koban type were found in many localities of the North Caucasian area. There is no doubt that there were several local centers of the bronze industry. Founders and craftsmen worked on local ore and had in mind local needs. Thus in agricultural regions copper and bronze sickles were manufactured. In several sites of this area socketed celts were found, of the same shape as those

36. *Aul* in the language of the Caucasian Tatars and some other tribes means "village."

37. Don, in Ossetian, means "river."

excavated in Ukraine, central Russia and Finland. No mold for making such celts has so far been discovered in the North Caucasian area; it is possible that they were imported either from Ukraine or the Volga region.

The variety in the inventory of bronzeware in North Caucasian graves points to a considerable development of industry and trade. In some localities craftsmen and merchants must have constituted social groups of their own; the appearance of settlements of the town type was probably the result of such social differentiation. The bulk of the population lived, however, by agriculture and cattle breeding.

The Pontic steppes.[38] At the beginning of the second millennium B.C. copper tools and utensils make their appearance in the territory of Ukraine and the Don. Bronze items follow; by the middle of that millennium copper and bronze culture was well established in the Pontic steppes. While it was chiefly under the influence of North Caucasian standards, some Balkan connections may be surmised as well. Generally speaking, however, the Bronze Age culture in Ukraine was poorer than that of the North Caucasian sphere. Bronzeware was probably imported, but some of the copper tools must have been supplied by local industry. Old copper mines have been discovered at the village of Kalinovskaia near Bakhmut.[39] Some of the pits are 20 to 30 meters deep. In one of them a human skull and bones were found, permeated with copper oxide. In another, stone tools and bronze axes were unearthed. These probably served for extracting the copper ore. In the Dnieper region, where no copper ore was mined, founders' hoards consisting of scrap copper have been discovered; the metal was probably imported and then used for founding. Small tools only were produced in such cases.

As to the political and ethnic structure of the population of Ukraine, it apparently underwent radical changes in the first quarter of the second millennium. Around 1800 B.C., some major catastrophe must have occurred in the Dnieper region, such as an enemy invasion as a result of which the Tripolie people were partly annihilated and partly pushed out from their country. Who the conquerors of the Tripolie people were and where they came from is

38. Tallgren, *Pontide; idem,* "Südrussland: Bronzezeit," *RL, 13* (1929), 50-52.

39. V. A. Gorodtsov, "Rezultaty arxeologicheskikh issledovanii v Bakhmutskom uezde," *TAS,* XIII, *1* (1905).

open to discussion. According to A. M. Tallgren, they were of Indo-European race and came from the northwest. He supposes that after subduing the Tripolie area they continued their drive eastward until they reached the Kuban region.

The barrows left by the nomads who controlled the Pontic steppes in the middle of the second millennium B.C. are of the same type as those of the end of the third and the early part of the second millennium. The bodies of the dead were similarly stained with ochre. Some of the barrows of that period are higher than those of the preceding one. In some cases the dead were cremated. In addition to the grave-furniture, several hoards of weapons and art objects of this period have been excavated. One of the most remarkable is that found at Borodino, Bessarabia. Tallgren refers it to the period between 1300 and 1100 B.C. In his attempt to establish a comprehensive chronology and classification of the Pontic finds of the second millennium, Tallgren suggests that two stages should be distinguished in the development of the copper and bronze culture of the Pontic area: an elder stage, 1600-1400 B.C., and a younger, 1400-1100 B.C.

Among the types of weapons and tools characteristic of the first stage, shaft hole axes may be mentioned, some of which have a shape similar to the stone axes of southern Scandinavia; others resemble the Balkan or Caucasian axes. Small flat axes and scrapers of copper are of the Caucasian type. To the second period celts similar to those found in Finland and central Russia may be referred. Socketed spearheads of the Borodino hoard belong to the same type of craftsmanship. The contour of the blade of a typical Borodino spearhead is like a laurel leaf; the tube of the socket extends into the body of the blade as a midrib. Daggers, copper needles, and bronze rings and pins of the Borodino period have also been discovered in Ukraine and the Don areas. The finding of sickles is evidence of the role of agriculture in the life of the people of this period. Clay vases found in the mounds are made for the most part by hand. Ribbon, linear, and geometric patterns are used in ornamentation.

Central Russia.[40] The expansion of the copper and bronze culture in central Russia progressed at a much slower pace than in the

40. *Idem,* "Kultura bronzovoi epokhi v srednei Rossii," *IMO* (1914); Gotie, *Ocherki,* chap. ix; Tallgren, "Fatjanovo-Kultur," *RL, 3,* 192-193; Tallgren, *Kupfer.*

south. Most of the copper and bronze tools were imported. Some small implements such as needles were, however, cast in local shops from imported metal. Stone tools were still in use together with the copper and bronze ones. Some of the stone axes of this period seem to have been shaped in imitation of the imported bronze axes. The culture of central Russia of the second millennium was basically of the same Fatianovo type as at the end of the third millennium. The graves are in shallow trenches without a barrow. Built-in stone chambers of primitive type have been found in some of them. In such cases the skeletons are found in a contracted position with traces of ochre staining. Remnants of burnt ritual food have been discovered at some sites. Ornamented vases with spheric bottom, mentioned before,[41] are likewise characteristic of this Bronze Age extension of the Fatianovo culture. Comb ornamentation is prevalent; usually the neck of the vase only is ornamented. In the graves of the Moscow province vases with cord ornamentation were found. Copper and bronze axes are not numerous in the Fatianovo area. Some of the axes have curved butt ends. Copper and bronze gouges, awls, and sickles have likewise been found in some of the Fatianovo graves, as well as silver ornaments such as pendant temple rings. Dagger handles sometimes have the shape of an animal head.

A more developed stage of bronze culture is represented by the Seima burial ground, referred to the end of the second millennium B.C. This ground is situated in the region of the lower Oka River. Axes, celts, spears, and knives form the inventory of bronze tools of the Seima graves. Some of the axes are similar to those found in the Fatianovo area. One of the knives has a double-edge blade, the blade on the concave edge having a series of teeth to be used as a saw. Spearheads are similar to those of the Borodino hoard. It is noteworthy that flint knives and arrowheads as well as nephrite rings were found together with bronze tools. The pottery of the Seima graves is of good craftsmanship, most of the vases being of spheric shape with flat bottom. The neck and shoulders of the vase are usually decorated with comb ornamentation, similar to that of the Fatianovo vases.

Another remarkable burial ground of the Oka region is the so-called Later Volosovo, near Murom. In it iron tools were found together with the bronze, mute evidence of the transition of culture

41. See Sec. 4, above.

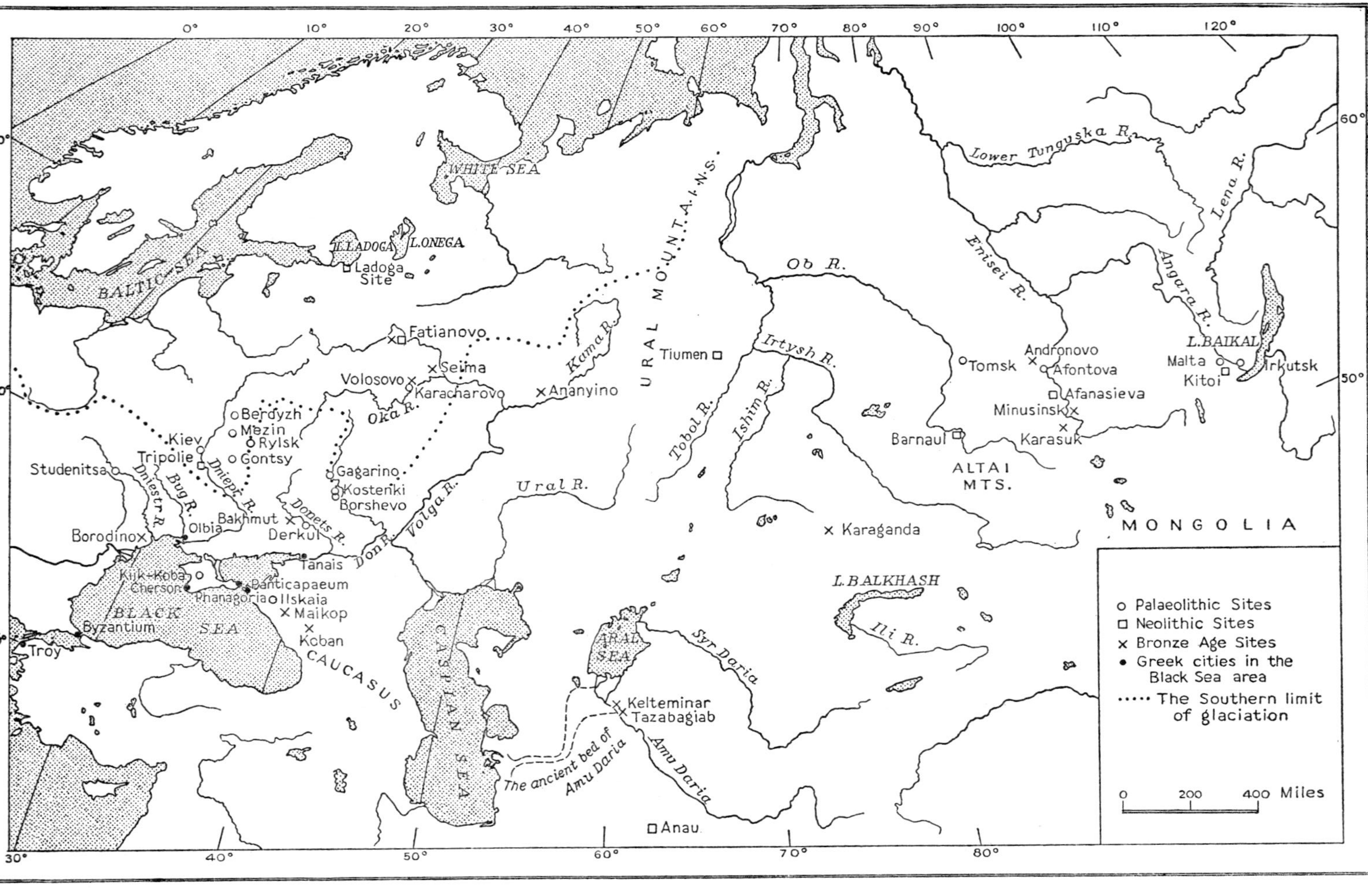

ARCHAEOLOGICAL MAP OF WESTERN AND CENTRAL EURASIA

from the Bronze to the Iron Age. Chronologically the Volosovo burial ground may be referred to the beginning of the first millennium B.C.

Judging from the central Russian finds of the second millennium, agriculture, hunting and fishing constituted the main fields of occupation. The similarity of some imported tools to those of Scandinavia (celts), as well as to Caucasian and Balkan types (axes, daggers, spearheads), is indication of the wide range of commercial relations of the central Russian area at this period; an area which extended to the Baltic Sea on the one hand, and to the Black Sea on the other.

Turkestan and Siberia.[42] As in central Russia, the copper and bronze culture in Siberia expanded at first but slowly. Not before 2000 B.C. did the people of Siberia begin to use copper tools. We have seen[43] that at the Afanasieva burial ground clay vases coated with copper were found which may be referred to that date. In view of the probability of commercial ties between Afanasieva and the region of the Aral Sea[44] it is possible that copper was imported from Kazakhstan. Kazakhstan in its turn was culturally connected with Khoresm. Since 1938 the Khoresm antiquities have been systematically studied by members of the archaeological expedition organized by the Institute of the History of Material Culture. The early culture of Khoresm, which is as we have seen[45] similar to the Afanasieva culture, is known as the Kelteminar culture. In the course of the second millennium B.C. Khoresm played an active role in the expansion of the so-called "steppe bronze" culture, one of the stages of which is now known as the Tazabagiab culture.[46] Khoresm now became one of the important junctions of cultural highways.

The culture which spread in the first half of the second millennium B.C. over the area of Kazakhstan and southern Siberia is known as the Andronovo culture, since the first typical burial ground excavated was that found near the village Andronovo, in the district of Achinsk. In Kazakhstan this type is represented by the burial grounds at the *sovkhoz* ("Soviet farm") Gigant, district of Karaganda, explored by P. S. Rykov, as well as those in the region of

42. A. M. Tallgren, "Sibirien: Bronzezeit," *RL, 12,* 70-71; *idem,* "Turkestan: Bronzezeit," *RL, 13,* 485-486.
43. See Sec. 4, above.
44. *Ibid.*
45. *Ibid.*
46. Tolstov, pp. 156, 159.

the Ural River excavated by M. P. Griaznov.[47] The inventory of the Andronovo grave furniture shows some similarity to the finds of the Seima culture. The tumuli over graves of the Andronovo type are usually low. They are often encircled by a low stone fence. Stone-slab cists or lumber chests served as burial chambers. The skeletons usually lie on the side with arms bent at the elbows and legs bent both at the pelvis and at the knees, with knees close to the body. Clay pots with flat bottom are abundant, being of the two following types: (1) of rough craftsmanship, decorated with impressed or incised ornamentation of simple patterns; (2) of fine craftsmanship, with convex and concave sides, decorated with geometric ornamentation such as triangles, diamonds, meander, and swastika. Both stone and copper tools were found in Andronovo graves. Among the former, scrapers and arrowheads may be mentioned, and among the latter, celts and daggers. Copper plates for belts as well as copper pendants inlaid with gold leaf were likewise found. Beads are of various materials: copper, sard, stone, animal teeth. In the remnants of funeral food bones of horse, ox, and sheep were discovered; in one of the graves the skeleton of a dog was fully preserved. The man of the Andronovo cultural sphere apparently had a number of domesticated animals and led a pastoral life.

By the end of the second and the beginning of the first millennium the area of Kazakhstan and southern Siberia became the home of a more developed copper culture, known as the Karasuk culture from the river Karasuk, tributary to the Enisei, where typical graves of the culture have been excavated (Bograd Region, district of Khakas). The funeral chambers in these graves are like those of Andronovo, faced and covered with stone slabs. The skeletons lie on the back. In some cases the burial customs included cremation. As in Andronovo graves, a great many clay vases were found, most of them with spheric bottom and high neck, of fine craftsmanship. The ornamentation is of grooved pattern. Copper tools are more numerous than in Andronovo graves. Copper celts and knives of a different shape, as well as pendants and finger rings, were found in abundance. At least part of them seem to have been produced locally. In the remnants of funeral food joints of mutton were discovered. One grave contained no skeleton but that of a dog, which

47. P. S. Rykov, "Raboty v sovkhoze Gigant (Karaganda)," *GA, 110* (1935), 40-48; M. P. Griaznov, "Pogrebeniia bronzovoi epokhi v zapadnom Kazakhstane," *Kazaki* (a symposium published by the Academy of Sciences), *Vol. II* (1927).

seems to be an evidence of dog worship. The dog may have been worshiped in its capacity of loyal guardian of flocks. Stone sculptures were discovered, some in the shape of a man's face, others in the shape of a ram's head. These were probably of totemistic character. The man of the Karasuk culture was, apparently, primarily a cattle breeder. The Karasuk culture expanded south and west of the Minusinsk area. Tools and vessels of the Karasuk type have recently been found both in Tannu-Tuva and in the Karaganda district, Kazakhstan.

By the ninth and the eighth centuries B.C. bronze tools and vessels began to appear in southern Siberia. The center of the copper and bronze culture of Siberia was in the Minusinsk area, which is rich in copper ore. Numerous mounds in the southern steppe zone of Siberia belong to the sphere of this so-called Minusinsk culture. It was in full bloom by the middle of the first millennium B.C., that is, in the period of the Scythian domination of South Russia. It will be dealt with, accordingly, in the next chapter.

Chapter II

THE CIMMERIAN AND SCYTHIAN ERA, 1000-200 B.C.

1. The Transition from the Bronze Age to the Iron Age.

If the invention of bronze contributed much to the progress of man's material culture, a no less important move forward was made with the introduction of iron into use. Both copper and bronze were adequate for vessels and utensils but not hard enough for tools and weapons. While a number of bronze swords have been found by archaeologists, they were probably used chiefly as rapiers, since bronze is too fragile to use for a striking edge. It was only after the sword had been created in iron that it became a redoubtable weapon. Similarly, with regard to agricultural tools, it was only with the invention of the iron plowshare that agriculture entered into a new stage of development.

As we have already seen,[1] iron came into use much later than bronze. It was known in Asia Minor and Mesopotamia from at least 1300 B.C. After 1000 B.C. the use of it penetrated into Koban, in the North Caucasian area. The earliest iron tools of both central Russia and Ukraine may be dated around 900 B.C. About this same time, iron was introduced into Greece. In central Europe the first Iron Age, known as the Hallstatt culture, established itself in the first half of the first millennium B.C. In the second half of the millennium a richer and more elaborate iron culture developed, known as the La Tène culture. Its standard-bearers were the Kelts. Around 500 B.C. the expansion of the Kelts to southeastern Europe started, and with it the spread of the La Tène culture. In the first quarter of the third century B.C. the Kelts reached western Ukraine, Bessarabia and the Balkan peninsula. As in the case of copper and bronze, iron was introduced only gradually into use. In many regions iron tools at first only supplemented the bronze. This was true in the development of the iron culture over the territory of Russia. While iron tools made their appearance both in central Russia and

1. See above, Chap. I, Sec. 5.

in Ukraine around 900 B.C., as we have seen, centuries were to pass before the coming of the real Iron Age to these areas.

It must be noted that natural conditions were more favorable in Russia for the development of iron industries than for copper and bronze. Iron deposits of the Dnieper basin lay too deep for exploitation by primitive techniques, but both in western Ukraine and in central and northern Russia there were plenty of surface or near-surface deposits of the ore, chiefly near lakes and in swamps. Both Slavs and Finns had barely started to use local iron ores by the beginning of the Christian era. The ore was at this time smelted by primitive methods, in ditches and pits. In the period of the Antes, in the fourth to seventh centuries A.D., the iron industry made considerable progress in the south and smelting furnaces were used.

At the beginning of the Iron Age the Pontic steppes were controlled by the Cimmerians, a people akin to the Thracians. In the seventh century B.C. the Cimmerians were replaced by the Scythians who migrated to South Russia from Kazakhstan. The Scythians represent certainly not the first wave of Eurasian nomads to reach the Pontic steppes from the east, but they are the first of which we have definite information. The Scythian march westward was to be followed in the course of time by numerous incursions of other nomads. It seems therefore logical to coördinate the plan of our brief survey of the cultural spheres of Eurasia in the Cimmerian and Scythian age with the direction of the principal migrations. We shall therefore deal first with Siberia and Kazakhstan, then turn to the Caucasus and Crimea, and afterward examine the archaeological background of the Pontic steppes and of central and northern Russia.

Siberia and Turkestan.[2] We may assume that in the first millennium B.C., as in the preceding millennium,[3] northern Turkestan and southern Siberia were closely connected culturally. Both lands still lived in the Copper and Bronze Age. It was the period of flowering of the Minusinsk culture, so called because the Minusinsk area—that is, the valley of the upper Enisei River—was one of its important centers. The Saian Mountains situated in this region are extremely rich in copper ore. Numerous mounds of the Minusinsk

2. Merhart; Radlov; Teploukhov. For a study of the barrows of the Scythian period in the lower Volga and Southern Ural area see B. Grakov, "Monuments de la culture scythique entre le Volga et les monts Oural," *ESA*, *3* (1928), 25-62. Cf. Rostovtzeff, *Skythien*, I, 447-494.

3. See Chap. I, Sec. 5.

type are scattered over the whole steppe zone of southern Siberia. They present evidence of considerable density of population. Cattle breeding, agriculture, and hunting were the main branches of the economics of the Minusinsk man.

The first stage of the Minusinsk culture may be referred to the eighth and the seventh centuries B.C. The mounds of this period are not high and are usually enclosed by a square stone fence. The burial chamber was built-in, either of stone slabs or of lumber. One or more bodies were deposited in each chamber. The funeral furniture consists of clay vases with grooved ornamentation and of bronze mirrors; copper and bronze daggers, knives, hatchets, arrowheads, awls, needles, and fishhooks were also deposited in the chamber. Of ornaments there are conical beads and hemispheric plates; ornamented bone combs were also found in many graves. Copper and bronze socketed celts are likewise characteristic of the sites of the Minusinsk type.

The second stage of the Minusinsk culture reached its full expression in the second half of the first millennium B.C. The mounds of this period are large and high; the enclosure is also usually of large stones, as before, and the sides of the square are oriented with the points of the compass. The burial chambers are very spacious, so that a number of corpses could easily be deposited. According to S. Teploukhov each chamber accommodated a whole family or even a clan. In the later mounds burial had been preceded by cremation. The burial inventory comprises clay vases, for the most part without ornament; copper and bronze hatchets, daggers, knives, punches, metal plaques, glass and jasper beads. Some of these objects are decorated with figures of deer, goat, and some other animal, drawn in a peculiar style: the eyes and nostrils of the animals as well as the ends of the feet and tails have a circular shape, shoulders and haunches protrude, ears are long and at times stick out to the fore. While the stylization is more marked than in the Scythian objects of South Russia, the basis of the ornamentation is similar.

The barrows of the Scythian age in Kazakhstan have been studied intensively in the last few years in connection with the archaeological exploration of Khoresm.[4] So far, however, less material has been published with regard to Kazakhstan than for the Minusinsk area. P. S. Rykov's excavations in the Karaganda district[5] have

4. Tolstov, pp. 155 ff.

5. Rykov, as in n. 47 to Chap. I.

brought evidence of the continuity of cultural development, since in several cases old graves of the Andronovo type were used again in the Scythian period.

The Caucasus and the Greek cities on the northern shores of the Black Sea.[6] While bronze held sway in Siberia during the Cimmerian-Scythian epoch, the Caucasus was rapidly entering the Iron Age. The earliest iron objects found in the Koban graves may be dated around 1000 B.C. The iron ornaments of Koban belts have already been mentioned.[7] Gradually various iron tools made their appearance in the North Caucasian area; these included axes, adzes, hoes, plowshares. Probably the earliest iron objects found in the Caucasus were imported from the Urartu kingdom, as was the case with early bronze. Later on, iron industries were developed locally. There are more than ten iron beds in Transcaucasia and the northern Caucasus which may be served as foundation for early local iron works. Two old iron foundries have been discovered recently (1928) in Chuber, Upper Svanetia.[8] Layers of slag had been left on the platforms and hillsides. A belt of forges was discovered on the slopes of the hill, with layers of slag all around. Each forge was coated inside with clay. The forge was filled with ore and fuel through a groove built of hewn stones cemented with clay. Iron forged in Chuber was of high quality as can be seen in the tools found there.

The Chuber iron forges must have already existed around 250 B.C., although the exact date of their origin is not known. Other similar forges in the Caucasus may have started even earlier. It is possible that the tradition of the Greek authors of the fifth and fourth century B.C. concerning the Chalybes, a people of blacksmiths, may refer to the Caucasian iron forgers. The art of forging iron must have been kept secret for a long time by the clans of forgers, in order to preserve their privileges. Therefore, while the tools they made were exported, their technique did not at first spread outside the Caucasus. It was the Greeks who became middlemen in the iron trade between the Caucasus and the northern Black Sea region. Numerous Greek colonies were founded along the northern shores of the Black Sea as early as the seventh century B.C., and some of them before long became quite prosperous. The cities lo-

6. See n. 16, below.
7. See Chap. I, Sec. 5.
8. B. E. Degen-Kovalevskii, "K istorii zheleznogo proizvodstva Zakavkazia, *GA, 120* (1935), 238-340.

cated on both sides of the Cimmerian Bosporus (Kerch Strait) were especially active in the Caucasian metal trade.

The Pontic steppes.[9] In the Cimmerian period the population of the Pontic steppes used chiefly bronze tools and ware, although iron tools were known from about 900 B.C. Later, the Scythians brought with them a peculiar culture of their own, which included both bronze and iron. Rich gold and silver ornaments were especially characteristic of this culture. Scythian kurgans (barrows) dating from the sixth to the third century B.C. are spread along the vast steppe zone from the Danube to the Ural River. Thousands have been excavated. Most of them are not high and their inventory is rather poor. Apparently those buried in them were common warriors, in some cases not even Scythians but representatives of tribes conquered by them. The graves of the Scythian kings and grandees are, on the contrary, extremely rich in gold and jewelry. The barrows over them are high. To the earlier group of these Scythian mounds belong the Litoi Kurgan, near Elisavetgrad between the Dnieper and the Bug rivers (excavated in the eighteenth century), and the Kelermes Kurgan in the North Caucasian area. Both may be referred to the sixth century B.C. It is apparent that as early as this the Scythian kingdom was already based, geographically, upon both the Dnieper and the Kuban regions.

The Seven Brothers Kurgan (*Semibratnii*) in the Taman region, at the delta of the Kuban River represents the middle ages of Scythian domination, in the fifth and fourth centuries B.C. Among the later Scythian kurgans, from the fourth to third centuries, the following may be mentioned here: Karagodeuashkh, in the North Caucasian area; Kul-Oba, near Kerch, Crimea; Chertomlyk, Alexandropol; and Solokha in the region of the Dnieper cataracts. Several big kurgans of the same period are situated between the southern bend of the Dnieper River and the Sea of Azov.

The location of the big kurgans is important for understanding the political geography of the Scythian realm. There were apparently three main centers in this realm, namely: the North Caucasian area, the Crimea, and the lower Dnieper region, especially the zone of the cataracts. This last zone corresponds to the region called by Herodotus the Gerrhoi. According to this historian it was here that the Scythians buried their kings. The Gerrhoi was a reserved area in which no foreigner was allowed. The main Scythian

9. See n. 16, below.

horde grazed their horses between the Gerrhoi and the sea to enforce the privacy of the royal kurgans. As a result, the Greeks had no precise information concerning the Gerrhoi region, and it is significant that Herodotus was not able to convey any data about the Dnieper cataracts. Obviously, none of his informers knew of them or in any case dared to talk about them. Thus all Herodotus could make out, from reports of local people in Olbia, was that the Dnieper was navigable only as far up as the Gerrhoi region.

The graves of Scythian chieftains contain usually a great number of gold and silver ornaments, and the bronze weapons found in these graves are likewise ornamented by gold plaques. Iron swords are occasionally found. Wives, slaves, and horses of the Scythian chief were usually buried with him. The so-called animal style is an outstanding feature of Scythian art. Metal bowls, bow cases, belts, sword hafts, horse trappings, and other various objects are ornamented with figures of animals, such as the panther, tiger, deer, horse, bull, and often with scenes of animal life. A beast of prey is usually represented as clawing a herbivorous animal. The Scythian animal style is somewhat akin to that of the Minusinsk culture, although more elaborate. The refinement of Scythian style is apparently the result of the contact of the Scythians with the Greeks in the Pontic steppes. First-rate Greek artisans were employed by Scythian kings, and in this way the steppe art was cross-fertilized by Greek techniques. Later this Greco-Scythian style influenced in its turn the development of Hellenistic art.

Ukrainian steppe-forest border zone. In this zone numerous kurgans of the Scythian age have been found, but the burial rites as well as the contents of the graves are somewhat different from the steppe kurgans. There are two types of burial in the steppe-forest border zone: inhumation and cremation. In the first case the body was laid in a deep ditch, the walls of which were reinforced with lumber. In the second case the ashes were simply deposited in a hole. Tools and weapons found in the kurgans of both types are mostly bronze but occasionally iron. Pottery is partly of the Scythian and partly of the Greek pattern. On sites near some of the kurgans, pits with grain have been discovered; thus apparently people practicing agriculture lived near by. For this reason A. A. Spitsyn[10] considers the kurgans in the region of Kiev, Kharkov, and Poltava

10. A. A. Spitsyn, "Kurgany Skifov—pakharei," *AK, 65* (1918).

as remnants of the civilization of the so-called Scythian-Plowmen.[11] It should be noted, however, that very few if any agricultural tools were found in the kurgans themselves. Bits and arrowheads are typical of the objects revealed. Hence, the people who buried their dead here are likely to have been horsemen and bowmen like the Scythians.

In the region to the northwest of the Ukrainian kurgans, and partly in the very region of the kurgans themselves, remnants of a different, non-Scythian culture have been discovered. This is the so-called culture of the funeral urns.[12] This cultural sphere covered a vast area comprising southern Poland, Galicia, and Volyn. Its southern boundary of expansion goes along the forty-ninth parallel of latitude. Two kinds of burial—inhumation and cremation—were practiced by the people. In the case of cremation, burned bones were deposited in an urn. Such urns, together with various potteries, were buried on clay platforms which were then covered with earth, without a tumulus. The platforms were not deep: around 1 meter under the surface. In the case of inhumation the platforms were built much deeper: from 1 to 3 meters beneath the surface. The corpse was deposited in an extended position lying on the back. Several pots were placed near the body. One of these usually contained lamb bones; occasionally a knife was thrust into the ground near by. The objects associated with the funeral urns are rather poor, especially as compared with those of the Scythian graves. Beads of cornelian, amber, glass, or shells, are found in abundance. Silver, bronze, and iron fibulas are likewise frequent, as well as belt clasps. Among other items, bronze needles, awls, rings, hairpins, and bracelets may be mentioned. Also knives and sickles.

The culture of funeral urns lasted in the area between the Carpathian Mountains and the middle Dnieper for many centuries. While its oldest monuments are referred to the Scythian period, other burial grounds of the same type may be ascribed to the beginning of the Christian era. In addition to the burial grounds, numerous remnants of old settlements (*gorodishche*)[13] belonging to the same cultural sphere have been excavated in approximately the same region. Agricultural tools, such as sickles and spades, as well

11. See Sec. 3, below, for the explanation of the term.

12. Gotie, pp. 8 ff.

13. *Gorodishche* is singular, and *gorodishcha,* plural. Both forms will be used hereafter. For a general characterization of the *gorodishcha* see A. M. Tallgren, "Gorodišce," *RL, 4,* 369-397.

as stone hand mills for grinding grain were found in most of the *gorodishche* sites. It is obvious that the people of this cultural sphere were agriculturists.

In view of the fact that the cultural sphere of the funeral urns partly coincides with the area of the kurgans of the steppe-forest borderland, it may be assumed that in this region two different ethnic or social groups cohabited for a number of centuries. One consisted of horsemen, the other of peasants. We have mentioned that in Spitsyn's view the kurgans of this area belonged to the so-called Scythian-Plowmen. If Spitsyn's conjecture is to be accepted, we may then say that these "Scythians" did not plow the land themselves but only controlled the neighboring peasant population and collected grain from them as tax in kind.

Northeast Russia.[14] The most interesting development in this area during the Scythian period was the blossoming of the so-called Ananyino bronze culture in the middle Volga and Kama area. It is named after the village of Ananyino, in Viatka province, where the first typical burial grounds were discovered. The culture belongs to the period from the sixth to the second century B.C.; that is, it coincides chronologically with the period of Scythian domination in the Pontic steppes. Judging from its remnants, the people who created it were chiefly hunters and fishermen. A great number of hunting and fishing tools, including harpoons, were found in the sites. Most of them were of bone, but some of bronze and iron. Bones of domestic animals as well as seeds of hemp were likewise found, which points to the possibility that part of the people at least practiced both agriculture and cattle breeding as subsidiary means of existence. The dead were either deposited in graves, in an extended position, or were cremated; in the latter case, a clay urn with the ashes of the deceased was buried in the grave. The Ananyino people seem to have been engaged in a brisk fur trade, exporting furs far away to the south.

Among ornaments of the Ananyino culture, bronze torques and bracelets displaying animal heads, as well as leather belts with bronze plates and buckles on them, are typical. Some are reminiscent of the Greco-Scythian art, showing especially close similarity to objects found in the Greek colony of Olbia, at the mouth of the

14. Gotie, *Ocherki,* chap. x; Tallgren, "L'époque dite d'Ananino dans la Russie orientale," *SMYA, 31* (1919); A. V. Zbrueva, "Anan'inskii mogilnik," *SA,* II (1937), 95-111.

Dnieper River. Designs of animals and birds follow the Caucasian patterns. Bronze knives are of the Minusinsk type, while iron knives are similar to those produced in the Koban area. It is obvious that the Ananyino people maintained commercial relations with various regions, and Ananyino itself was at the crossroads of important international commercial routes. The Volga riverway, connecting the Ananyino region with the Caucasus, was probably most important. In addition Greek merchants likewise used the overland road from Olbia to the middle Volga region.[15]

2. *The Cimmerians and the Scythians in South Russia.*[16]

For the history of South Russia in the first millennium B.C. not only archaeological materials but likewise some written sources are available. This epoch therefore belongs no longer to prehistory, but rather to ancient history. The establishment of numerous Greek colonies on the northern shores of the Black Sea not only resulted in promoting commercial relations between the Greeks and the Scythians but also enabled Greek scholars to observe conditions of life on the Scythian steppes. One of the foremost authorities on Scythia was Herodotus (*ca.* 484-425 B.C.). He not only collected information on the contemporary Scythian state and society, but was also interested in the history of both the Scythians and their predecessors, the Cimmerians. Later Greek geographers, as for example Strabo (*ca.* 63-23 B.C.), made much use not only of Herodotus' narrative but also other sources which have since been lost. The epigraphic material is likewise important. Numerous inscriptions on stone have been found at the sites of Greek cities on the Black Sea shore. They convey ample evidence of the life of these cities, and to some extent of their Scythian neighbors as well. Greek coins found both in Scythian kurgans and in these Greek city sites are also helpful.

In approaching the history of the Cimmerians and the Scythians the historian has first of all to face the problem of their ethnic background. This question, however, remains a moot one. While the peoples settled in South Russia are designated in various epochs by

15. Compare Sec. 3, below.

16. The basic works on the subject are the following: Minns; Rostovtzeff, *Iranians and Greeks;* Rostovtzeff, *Skythien.* See also G. Borovka, *Scythian Art* (London, 1926); M. Ebert, "Südrussland: Skythische Periode," *RL, 13,* 52-98; Kondakov, *Drevnosti,* I-II; Kondakov, *Ocherki,* chap. i; "Minns Volume," *ESA, 9* (1934); Rostovtzeff, *Animal Style;* Toll.

different names, we cannot be sure that every change of name corresponds to a migration of whole ethnic groups. It appears that from time to time new ruling clans seized control of the country, and while some of the former groups emigrated the bulk of the native population remained, only to receive an admixture of the newcomers' blood. South Russia was first organized politically by the Cimmerians (1000-700 B.C.), then by the Scythians (700-200 B.C.) and the Sarmatians (200 B.C.-A.D. 200); the Goths (A.D. 200-370) followed, to be replaced by the Huns (A.D. 370-454). In most cases, the bulk of the native population while recognizing the political control of the newcomers clung desperately to their old homes or settled again not too far from their former abodes. In their turn, each newly arrived group added a new ethnic touch to the variety already represented. Thus, above the original stock of the natives of South Russia, whom the late Nicholas Marr called the Japhetides, an ethnic superstructure of variegated nature was gradually built up, but on the whole there was a certain continuity of racial strains.

To return to the Cimmerians, one may assume that they constituted the country's ruling class only. The problem of their racial background is thus more limited than that of the ethnic foundation of the population of South Russia as a whole. Recently A. V. Bashmakov has suggested that the Cimmerians are akin to Circassians, a people in the North Caucasian area.[17] However, the opinion expressed earlier by M. I. Rostovtzeff may still be considered the authoritative hypothesis on the origins of the Cimmerians: namely, that they belong to the same ethnic group as the Thracians.[18] It is characteristic that several Bosporian kings bore Thracian names. Now it was in the region on both sides of Kerch Strait that people of Cimmerian ancestry are supposed to have remained even in the Scythian period, and the strait itself was known as the Cimmerian Bosporus. From the archaeological point of view, celts found in Bessarabia, that is, in the area of the aboriginal expansion of the Thracians, are similar to those found in the North Caucasian area, east of Kerch Strait. The Thracians belong linguistically to the Indo-European family. Therefore, the Cimmerians may be considered Aryans as well.

17. A. Baschmakoff [Bashmakov], *Cinquante siècles d'évolution ethnique autour de la Mer Noire* (Paris, 1937), p. 140.
18. Rostovtzeff, p. 39.

The Cimmerians must have controlled for some time the whole northern littoral of the Black Sea from the Dniester River to Kerch Strait. In the middle of the eighth century B.C. the main provinces subject to their domination were in the Crimea and in the Azov and Kuban regions. From there the Cimmerians spread to Transcaucasia and toward the end of the century attacked the kingdom of Van (Urartu). Later they concluded an alliance with the Urartu people against Assyria. They are mentioned in Assyrian sources under the name of Gimirrae.

In order to combat the inroads of the Cimmerians the Assyrian king Assurgadon concluded an alliance with the Scythians, whose abodes were then in Turkestan and Kazakhstan. The migration of the Scythians as well as some other nomadic peoples of central Eurasia may be explained by political events on the borders of China. From time immemorial the Chinese had waged a protracted struggle with the Eurasian nomads, whom they called "the northern barbarians." These barbarians later became known in China as Hiung-nu (the Huns). In the reign of the emperor Siouen, of the Chou Dynasty (827-782 B.C.) the Chinese succeeded in administering a series of crushing defeats to the nomads. As a result of this, the Hiung-nu turned west, and there started a general migration of the nomadic peoples toward the Caspian Sea. The Scythian migration must be considered one episode of this general shifting of the nomads toward the west. Herodotus says on one occasion that it was the Massagetae who pressed the Scythians.[19] In another section of his work, based upon an earlier source (Aristaeus' poem, of the sixth century B.C.) he mentions in this connection the Issedones rather than the Massagetae.[20] The Issedones themselves were pressed by the Arimaspians.

While the Scythians were retreating before their eastern neighbors, their horde was sufficiently strong to attack the Cimmerians, especially as they coördinated their effort with the Assyrians. It appears that under the violence of the Scythian onslaught the Cimmerians were cut in two parts. One group was stranded in the Crimea and the North Caucasian area, where they mixed with the native tribes known as the Sindians. The other group of Cimmerians retreated westward, and was finally defeated by the Scythians on the Dniester River. According to Rostovtzeff, a scene of the Scytho-

19. Herodotus, IV, 11.
20. *Idem*, 13.

Cimmerian war is represented on the Scythian bow case found in the Solokha Kurgan.[21] Two Cimmerians are represented fighting on foot with Scythian horsemen. One is fighting with battle-ax, the other with a dagger. The Cimmerians have the Aryan type of face while the features of the Scythians are rather of the Altaic type.

To what racial stock the Scythians belonged is a disputed question. Controversial opinions have been expressed on the subject by various scholars. Some—Neumann, for example—have considered the Scythians Mongols; others, such as Muellenhoff, Tomaschek, Rostovtzeff, have expounded the theory of the Iranian origin of the Scythians; while certain Russian scholars—Grigoriev, Zabelin, Ilovaiskii—suggest that they must have been of Slavic origin.[22] Each of these theories may have at least a grain of truth in it, since it seems likely that in many cases under the name "Scythians," tribes of various ethnic stock were meant. The ruling Scythian horde was probably of Iranian origin; some of the auxiliary hordes may have consisted of Ugrians and Mongols; and it is likewise not impossible that other groups known under the name of Scythians—as, for example, the Scythian-Plowmen—were of proto-Slavic stock. The names of Scythian kings quoted by Herodotus and some other writers are obviously Iranian. One has also to take into consideration that the Persians called the Scythians "Sacae." More specifically, the Sacae were the branch of Scythians which stayed in Turkestan even after the migration of other hordes to the Pontic steppes. And the Turkestan Sacae were undoubtedly Iranians.

In the course of the first half of the seventh century B.C. the Scythians broke down the resistance of the Cimmerians and spread their own rule from the Volga to the Dniester River. By the end of the century the Scythian state on the steppes had assumed definite shape. Their realm was but one in the long series of nomadic empires which replaced each other on the Eurasian steppes, and the Scythian Empire was not a centralized state. The authority of the king of the main horde was recognized by the chieftains of the lesser hordes, but the chief king was not an absolute ruler. The Scythian state was rather a confederation of powerful nomadic clans. Both socially and legally it was a state based upon clan law.

Cavalry was the main arm of the Scythian military organization. Scythian horsemen, as later the Sarmatians, used a saddle, which

21. Rostovtzeff, p. 40, and Table XXI.

22. See Minns, pp. 35 ff.; M. Vasmer, "Skythen: Sprache," *RL, 12,* 236-251.

gave them a decided advantage over western cavalry, since neither the Greeks nor the Romans used saddles. Whether the Scythians had stirrups, is uncertain. On the vase found in the Chertomlyk Kurgan there is a picture of a saddled horse, and in it a thong hanging from the girth looks like a stirrup leather. No iron stirrups have been found, however, in Scythian graves. Incidentally, as to the western peoples, it was only after the coming of the Avars in the sixth century A.D. that stirrups began to be used by the Frankish cavalry.[23] The bow was the most dangerous weapon of the Scythian horseman. The Scythian bow being short (around 2.5 feet) with a double curve was well adapted for shooting from horseback.[24] Arrows were made of wood or of reed; arrowheads were of bronze, although occasionally stone, bone, and iron arrowheads are found in the kurgans. The range of the arrows was over 400 feet. The bow case or *gorytus* as it was called by the Greeks, was made of wood or of leather, and was more often than not richly ornamented. The bow case of a Scythian chieftain was covered with gold or silver plates ornamented—through incising or bas-relief—with drawings representing military scenes. In addition to the bow the Scythian warrior used also a bronze or iron sword, and a dagger. Typical Scythian tactics consisted in attacking the foe at different places simultaneously with small cavalry detachments. After the first skirmish the Scythian horsemen took to flight in order to lure the enemy army deep into their country, where it was easy to encircle and destroy it. The unsuccessful campaign of the Persian king Darius as described by Herodotus may be considered the classical example of Scythian war tactics.[25]

The Scythian Empire may be described sociologically as a domination of the nomadic horde over neighboring tribes of agriculturists. The Khazar State (seventh to tenth centuries A.D.) as well as the Mongol Golden Horde (thirteenth to fifteenth centuries A.D.) were to be built up on the same pattern. The Scythians of the main horde were typical nomads. Horse breeding was the foundation of their way of life. They lived in tents fixed on carts. Such a cart had four or six wheels and was drawn by two or three pairs of oxen. Boiled meat and mare's milk constituted the essentials of their diet. The clothing consisted of a cowl, caftan, and trousers. Considerable at-

23. See Chap. V, Sec. 2.
24. See F. E. Brown, "A Recently Discovered Compound Bow," *AIK, 9* (1937), 1-9.
25. See Sec. 6, below.

tention was paid to the belt, which was of leather and adorned with ornamented metal plates. Women wore a loose dress (*sarafan*) and a high headdress (*kokoshnik*).

While the majority of the Scythians were cattle breeders and nomads, some, and in any case most of the native tribes controlled by them, were agriculturists. It is known that grain was exported from Scythia to Greece in great quantities. The clothing of the agricultural people was probably of the same pattern as that of the Scythians themselves. As to the religious beliefs of the Scythians they presented a mixture of Iranian and Alarodian cults. The supreme male god of the Scythians corresponded to the Persian Ahuramazda; he was often represented on horseback. On the other hand, a feminine deity, the Great Goddess or the Mother of Gods was worshiped. Herodotus also mentions the Scythian cult of the sword.

The main horde was known as the Royal Scythians. Herodotus says that these were the best and the strongest, and that they considered the others their slaves.[26] The Royal Scythians lived "on the other side" (i.e., eastward) of the river Gerrhos, spreading as far east as the Sea of Azov and as far south as the Taurida.[27] According to F. K. Brun's conjecture,[28] which is very plausible, the Gerrhos River should be identified as the Konka, or Konskaya, a river part of which discharges into the Dnieper from the east opposite Nikopol, while a maze of other channels run parallel to the Dnieper, following its eastern bank as far south as the mouth of the Ingulets. Thus we may say that the main area of the Royal Scythians was in northern Tauria.[29] It is significant that a great number of rich kurgans have been found there. However, the Royal Scythians must also have controlled the right bank of the Dnieper, since several big kurgans are likewise located between the Dnieper and the Bug.

Close to the Royal Scythians and to the seashore roamed another

26. Herodotus, IV, 20.

27. We prefer to use here the pseudo-classical name "Taurida" instead of the modern "Crimea," since the latter came to general use only after the Mongol period. The name Crimea is to be derived from the Turkish word *qirim* (hence the Russian *krym*), which means "fosse" and refers more specifically to the Perekop Isthmus, the old Russian word *perekop* being an exact translation of the Turkish *qirim*. A. D. Godley's suggestion the "name [Cimmeria] survives in Crimea" (*Herodotus* in "The Loeb Classical Library," II, 213, n. 1) is inacceptable.

28. Brun, II, 47-48.

29. By northern Tauria, the steppe section between the southern bend of the Dnieper River and the northeastern shore of the Sea of Azov is meant; by Taurida, the Crimean peninsula itself.

horde, called by Herodotus the Scythian-Nomads.[30] Their abodes were between the mouth of the Ingulets and the Perekop Isthmus. According to the historian they neither plowed nor sowed. West of them, between the Ingulets and Ingul rivers lived the Scythian-Georgoi (agriculturists), whom the Greeks also called the Boristhenitae[31] from the name of the river Boristhenes, as the Dnieper was known at that time. Part of them mingled with Greek settlers, and were known as "Half-Greeks" (*Mixhellenes*)[32] West of the Scythian-Agriculturists, in the lower Bug region, were the abodes of the Callippidae whom Herodotus terms Helleno-Scythians. North of the Callippidae, in the northern section of the Bug basin, lived the Alazones.[33]

According to Herodotus, the way of life of both the Callippidae and the Alazones was similar to that of the Scythians, except that they sowed cereals and ate bread as well as onion, garlic, lentils, and millet. West of the Callippidae, on the lower Dniester, were the abodes of the Tyritae. West of these the Getae lived on the lower Danube, and the Agathyrsae in Transylvania. Both the Getae and the Agathyrsae must have belonged to the Thracian ethnic group.

South of the area of the Royal Scythians, in the Taurida Mountains, lived the Tauri, a warlike people inclined to brigandage. The Maeotians were the closest neighbors of the Royal Scythians to the southeast. Their name is connected with that of "Lake Maeotis" (the Sea of Azov). They controlled the steppes between the lower Don and the lower Volga, as well as the eastern shores of the Sea of Azov and the Kuban region in the North Caucasian area. The Maeotians are considered the remnants of the native tribes who survived through both the Cimmerian and the Scythian period. They had a peculiar social organization, since the women dominated the tribal life. Theirs was a matriarchal society. It was the Maeotian matriarchate which gave birth to the Amazon legend, widely spread among the Greeks and recorded by Herodotus.[34] Among the Maeotian tribes, the Sindians and Sauromatae may be mentioned here. The former lived in the Azov-Kuban area, and the latter on the lower Don and lower Donets rivers.

30. Herodotus, IV, 19.
31. *Idem,* 18.
32. Minns, p. 461.
33. Herodotus, IV, 17.
34. *Idem,* 110-117.

The Scythian domination secured peace for western Eurasia for about three centuries. The *Pax Scythica* had great importance in promoting trade and bringing prosperity not only to the Scythians themselves, but likewise to the other tribes under their control. It was the Greeks who profited most by the favorable trade conditions. Among the Greek cities which sprang up on the northern shore of the Black Sea like so many mushrooms, the following were the most prominent: Olbia, at the mouth of the Bug; Chersonese (Cherson)[35] in Crimea, near present-day Sevastopol; and Panticapaeum, modern Kerch, on the Cimmerian Bosporus (Kerch Strait). The Greeks bought slaves, cattle, hide, furs, fish, timber, wax, and honey in Scythia; in exchange they sold textiles, wine, olive oil, and sundry items of art and luxury. The mouths of the big rivers like the Dniester, Bug, Dnieper, and Don were used by the Greeks as their commercial bases, from which they sent caravans inland. How far north the Greek merchants ventured to travel is not well known. In any case, only the lower course of the Dnieper River was known to them; Herodotus conveys no word of the Dnieper cataracts. The Don and Volga riverways were apparently better explored by the Greeks. Herodotus mentions the town of Gelon, deep inland toward the northeast. It was probably situated on the lower Don or on the Donets River. Judging from the fact that in the Kama region objects produced in Olbia have been found, we may assume that there were lively commercial relations between the Ural area and Olbia. Apparently goods from Olbia were transported overland to the lower Don, then shipped upstream to the spot where the Don comes closest to the Volga; from there they were hauled over the portage and shipped farther up the Volga and Kama rivers. It may be added that the Don-Volga riverway was also important in relation to the Caucasus-Ural trade. The Greek city of Tanais, at the mouth of the Don, was an important station for transshipping goods coming from the Caucasus by sea via Kerch Strait to river boats to be sent northward.

35. Chersonese is a transcription of the original name, but about the third century A.D. a shorter form, Cherson, came to use, which prevailed in the Byzantine period. The short form will be used hereafter.

3. The Greek Colonies on the Northern Shores of the Black Sea.[36]

As we have already mentioned,[37] the Greek cities on the northern shores of the Black Sea played an important role in the development of international commerce, serving as a link between the Mediterranean basin and Eurasia. In that sense they were the forerunners of the Genoese and Venetian cities on the Black Sea which played the same role in the Mongol period of the thirteenth to fifteenth centuries A.D. From the sociological point of view there was, however, a great difference between the ancient Greek and the medieval Italian cities. The latter were mere commercial factories, while the role of the former was not limited to a commercial function. Some Greek cities of the Scythian period were full-fledged communities in which not only commerce, but art and crafts flourished, while agriculture achieved a high level in the neighboring regions. Thus the Greek cities of the period became important cultural centers in more than one aspect. They were, moreover, closely bound to the cities of Greece proper as well as to those of Asia Minor, remaining part of the Hellenic world at large. They served therefore as a bridge between the Hellenic world and the Scythians. Greek artists and artisans executed orders for Scythian kings and magnates, adapting themselves to Scythian artistic demands. Thus a new artistic style, which may be called the Greco-Scythian style, was created, which in its turn influenced the development of Greek art in the later, so-called Hellenistic, period.

Most of the Greek towns on the north shore of the Black Sea were founded by colonists coming from Miletus, Clazomenae, and other Greek cities in Asia Minor. In the sixth century B.C. the Greeks of Asia Minor recognized the authority of the Persian king. This resulted in a favorable position of the Greek cities with regard to international commerce. The Persian kingdom was what may be called a "world empire," stretching from the Aegean Sea in the west to the Indus and Jaxartes rivers in the east. It included such old provinces as Asia Minor, Transcaucasia, and Mesopotamia, and continued the cultural traditions of the Hittites, Urartu and Assyro-Babylonians.

The Greek cities of the coast of Asia Minor served as a link be-

36. Minns; Rostovtzeff; *Olvia* (Ukrainian Academy of Sciences, Kiev, 1940); "Zhebelev Volume," *SA, VII* (1941).

37. See Secs. 1 and 2, above.

tween Hither Asia, the Mediterranean basin, and the Pontic steppes; while the Greek cities on the northern shores of the Black Sea were like so many outposts of the older cities of Asia Minor. The Greek merchants of Olbia, Cherson, and the Cimmerian Bosporus served as middlemen in the trade intercourse between the Persian kingdom and the Scythians. In the fifth century B.C. most of the Greek cities on the Aegean littoral emancipated themselves from the authority of Persia. It was now Greece proper and particularly Athens which became the leading force. During the century from 477 to 377 the Black Sea commercial routes were controlled, both economically and politically, chiefly by Athens, in spite of the fact that at the end of the fifth century the power of Athens was considerably weakened by the Peloponnesian War. Generally speaking, the conditions for the development of the Black Sea cities were less favorable in the period of Athenian hegemony than in that of the Persian rule.

From the historical point of view the Bosporan kingdom on Kerch Strait, which lasted from the sixth century B.C. to the sixth A.D., was in a sense the predecessor of the Russian principality of Tmutorokan, of the ninth to eleventh centuries A.D. There were several Greek cities in the kingdom, on both sides of Kerch Strait. They were founded in the seventh and the sixth centuries B.C. Most of them were probably built on the sites of older native settlements of the Cimmerian period. The first Greek cities east of Kerch Strait were founded by colonists from Caria. Later, new settlers came from Miletus. These established themselves on the Crimean side of the strait. The city of Panticapaeum, which became the capital of the Bosporan kingdom, was originally a Milesian colony. Economically the Bosporan kingdom was based on trade between Asia Minor and Transcaucasia on one hand, and the Azov and Don regions on the other. Among the goods shipped from Transcaucasia, metal and metal ware played an important role. Fish and corn came in return from the Don and Azov areas.

Originally, the city of Panticapaeum had an aristocratic constitution. In the fifth century B.C. it became the capital of a monarchy. The Bosporan kingdom was the result of a necessary compromise between the Greek newcomers and the native tribes, the Greeks not being numerous enough to colonize the whole country. They stayed chiefly in the cities. On the other hand, local Japhetide and Iranian tribes generally known as the Sindians and Maeotians were in the majority outside of the cities and were reluctant to let the Greeks rule them. Some clashes took place, and finally a local magnate belonging to a native but thoroughly Hellenized family seized the rule and proclaimed himself king of the Sindians and Maeotians under the name of Spartocus I (438/7-433/2 B.C.). While he was recognized as king by the native tribes, the city of Panticapaeum accepted him only as *archon* ("chief"). Actually he had full power even over the Greeks and controlled the army administration through a *chiliarchos* ("commander of a thousand," cf. *tysiatskii* in Medieval Russian).

After the establishment of monarchical government in the Bosporus, the country became strong enough to protect itself against the inroads of the Scythians and other steppe tribes. In some cases the Bosporan kings paid tribute to the Scythians instead of going to war. They could afford to buy them off, since the kingdom was fairly prosperous. Trade in grain was the foundation of its economic stability. The Bosporan kings attempted to monopolize this line of trade in the eastern areas of the Black Sea. According to a treaty of friendship with Athens (434/3 B.C.) the Bosporan king was to supply Athens with grain. After a protracted struggle with the city of Heracleia, King Leucon (389/8-349/8 B.C.) conquered the important port of Theodosia, thus securing monopoly of the grain trade. As a result, the Bosporan kingdom became in the fifth and fourth centuries the main granary of Greece. In Leucon's reign 670,000 *medimna* (around 22,000 tons) of grain were exported annually to Attica, which amounted to half of the whole Attic import of grain.

Next to these cities, Cherson was the most important Greek center in the Crimea. This was the longest-lived of the early Greek colonies there. It was still prosperous in the Byzantine period. In the tenth century A.D. Cherson, known as Korsun in Russian medieval chronicles, was for some time controlled by the Kievan princes. It was originally a colony found by Heracleia, which in its turn had been a colony of Megara. Heracleia was founded in 599 B.C. The exact date of the founding of Cherson is unknown; Herodotus does not mention it. Documentary evidence of Cherson starts with the fourth century B.C. In this century the oldest city wall was built.

The geographic location of Cherson was less favorable than that of the Bosporan cities, since it was remote from the Azov and the Don areas. On the other hand, it was better protected from the inroads of the nomads and its harbor facilities were excellent. Also, it was closer to the southern shore of the Black Sea than any other north-shore city, which was a great advantage for maintaining regular commercial relations with Asia Minor. Like most of the other Greek cities of the northern shore, Cherson entered into close relations with Athens at the time of Athenian supremacy. Athenian influences were strong in the life and art of the city until the middle of the fourth century B.C., after which Chersonian vases, gold ornaments, terra cotta, etc., come close to the standards of Asia Minor.

With regard to its political organization, in the Scythian period Cherson was a democracy. All power belonged to the people's assembly, and all public officeholders were elected. Actually, more important questions were first discussed by the city council and then reported to the assembly. An interesting inscription of the third century B.C. has been found containing the text of the oath required of any Chersonian official. It bound him not to violate the democratic order, and to convey no information either to a Greek or to a "Barbarian" which could be detrimental to the interests of the city. Many a citizen owned fields and vineyards outside the city walls; these were sometimes rented out, in other cases it was the owner himself who tilled the land. The city controlled all the western littoral of the Crimean peninsula and part of the fertile steppes inland in its northern section.

Northwest of the Crimea the leading role belonged to Olbia, "city of the Boristhenites," which was situated at the mouth of the Bug River and controlled the whole of the Bug-Dnieper estuary. The city was thus in a favorable position as regarded the commercial ways which led inland to the north. It will not be amiss to mention here that the Dnieper estuary likewise played an important role in the commercial intercourse between Kievan Russia and Byzantium. The Russo-Varangian princes attempted to control firmly the mouth of the Dnieper, which offered a suitable station for the *Rus* merchants on their way to Constantinople. The Russians established their settlement in the Dnieper estuary at Oleshie. Geopolitically, Oleshie then played a role similar to that of Olbia in earlier times.

Olbia, a colony of Miletus, was founded in the second half of the seventh century B.C. Originally it must have been a fishing village. Fish constituted even later an important item of its trade. Agriculture was developed as well. Olbia had the closest bonds with the Scythian world of all the Greek colonies. She paid tribute to the Scythian kings and enjoyed their protection in return. Her merchants shipped their goods inland up the Bug and the Dnieper rivers. In addition, Olbia was the starting point of the great overland caravan route to the Volga and Kama regions to the northeast.[38]

Olbian Greeks had constant intercourse with the neighboring natives, which resulted in a considerable exchange of mutual influences in art, handicrafts, ways of life, etc. In the fifth and the beginning of the fourth century B.C. the city had friendly relations with Athens. In the period of Macedonian predominance Olbia's relations with the Greek mainland were not so fortunate. Around 330 B.C. the city was besieged by Zopyrion, Alexander the Great's viceroy in Thrace. In order to unite all its people against the invaders the Olbians adopted radical measures: natives were given citizenship and the slaves were freed. A number of inscriptions dated at the beginning of the third century B.C. throw some light on economic conditions in Olbia. As seen from some of them, a wealthy citizen by the name of Protogenes lent the city 1,000 gold coins, partly without interest, for buying grain. In addition he supplied himself with 2,500 *medimna* of wheat, at a reduced price.

Like Cherson, Olbia was a democracy. Prior to 330 B.C. only Greeks among the inhabitants of the city enjoyed political rights, including that of voting in the assembly.

4. The Northern Neighbors of the Scythians.

In his list of the peoples living north of "the market of the Borysthenites" (i.e., Olbia) Herodotus mentions among other tribes the Callippidae and the Alazones.[39] The Alazones lived probably in the middle Bug region. "Above the Alazones there live the Scythian-Aroteres (Plowmen). Above them the Neuri live, and the country north of the Neuri as far as we know is not settled at all."[40] In another section of his work Herodotus says that the river Tyras (Dniester) starts from a big lake which serves as a boundary between the Scythians and the Neuri.[41] At present there is no big lake at the source of the Dniester, though there are several small lakes and swamps near the upper part of the Zbruch, one of its tributaries. One must take into consideration, however, that in the times

38. See Sec. 2, above.
39. *Ibid.*
40. Herodotus, IV, 17.
41. *Idem*, 51.

of Herodotus—that is, around twenty-five hundred years ago—the face of the country may have differed considerably from what it now shows. There were more woods, the rivers were much deeper, and many lakes were still left from the glacial age which later turned to swamps. In any case we may assume that, according to Herodotus, the southern boundary of the Neuri country crossed the Dniester somewhere in its middle or upper course. Of the Neuri themselves Herodotus has little to say. He characterizes their customs as "Scythian." On the authority of Greek travelers in Scythia he tells a story about them, to which he personally does not give much credit. He was told by his informants that each Neurus turns to a wolf for several days every year and then turns back to a man.[42] The story apparently reflects the superstition of werewolves, which must have been popular among the Neuri as it was later on in Ukrainian folklore. According to popular belief, the sorcerer in order to turn a man into a wolf lets him don a wolf's hide, and pronounces magic spells. It is possible that one of Herodotus' informers was present at some sorcerer's incantation, in the success of which he was led to believe. It is also possible that the tale which reached Herodotus was the result of the fact that in winter the Neuri clothed themselves in wolfskins, which they may very easily have done. Combining the insufficient geographic data on the Neuri with the story of werewolves, and referring to Ukrainian folklore, one may tentatively locate the Neuri in northern Podolia and Volynia. If this is correct, the country of the Neuri may be characterized from the archaeological point of view as part of the area of the funeral urns.[43] The culture of the funeral urns lasted about a millennium, 500 B.C. to 500 A.D. We know that in the first centuries A.D. this area was settled by the Slavs. It seems quite probable that they were there in the last centuries B.C. as well.

Is it possible, on the ground of the above considerations, to identify the Neuri of Herodotus as Proto-Slavs? Such an identification was first suggested by Safarik, then accepted by both Niederle and Minns.[44] It was pointed out that in Galicia (as well as in Poland) one may find such names of rivers and settlements as Nur, Nurets, Nurchik. In the Middle Ages, the region between the middle course of the Visla and the western Bug was known as the Nur Land.[45]

42. *Idem*, 105.
43. See Sec. 1, above.
44. Safarik, I, 116 f.; Niederle, I, 266; Minns, p. 102.
45. Gotie, p. 28.

However, it is only in the western part of the proto-Slavic area that we may locate the abode of Herodotus' Neuri. Therefore, even if we consider the Neuri as Proto-Slavs, they represent but one of several proto-Slavic tribes. In the search for other such tribes among the peoples mentioned by Herodotus, some scholars have mentioned the Budini, whose very name, according to Niederle, sounds Slavic.[46] Various opinions have been expressed as to the geographic location of the Budini. Niederle would place them in the middle Dnieper region, while Minns allows them the middle Volga area.[47] In order to interpret correctly Herodotus' words about the Budini we have to take into consideration that Herodotus, or rather his informant, when speaking of the Budini takes his bearings from the south northward, starting with the Sauromatae. The latter lived in the region of the lower Don and the lower Donets rivers. The abodes of the Budini were, according to Herodotus, "above" the Sauromatae.[48] Consequently, we may assume that they lived on the upper Don or upper Donets. He says that they live in a locality covered by wood of a different kind. This may point to the right bank of the middle Donets, between the present towns of Izium and Slaviansk since this region from the point of view of soil and vegetation presents an island of woods wedged in between the steppes. If our surmise is correct it would mean that the Budini lived in the easternmost part of the original territory of proto-Slavic expansion. Between the area of the Neuri (in northwestern Ukraine) and the area of Budini (in northeastern Ukraine) there remains the area of the middle Dnieper (i.e., central Ukraine). It is in this central area that the "Scythian-Plowmen" may be located.

We have seen[49] that the Scythian-Plowmen were probably a tribe of horsemen controlling the neighboring peasant population. These horsemen may have been conquerors coming from outside, but they may also be thought of as a group of native squires who adopted Scythian ways and habits of life. It seems quite likely that either the Scythian-Plowmen[50] or the peasants controlled by them, or both, belonged to the proto-Slav ethnic group. It goes without saying that all the above considerations are of a hypothetical nature only.

46. Niederle, I, 275-285; IV, 24.
47. Niederle, IV, 24; Minns, p. 104.
48. Herodotus, IV, 21.
49. See Sec. 2, above.
50. On the Scythian-Plowmen see Spitsyn, as in n. 6, above; also, V. Shcherbakivskyi, "Zur Agathyrsenfrage," *ESA, 9* (1934), 208.

In Herodotus' list of tribes bordering upon the Scythians the name of the Neuri is followed by those of the Androphagi ("Cannibals") and Melanchlaeni ("Black Robes"). It is supposed that both tribes belonged to the proto-Finnic group. According to Herodotus the Androphagi were "a peculiar tribe, not at all Scythian. Of all men the Androphagi have the wildest customs; they recognize no justice and have no laws; they lead a migratory life; their garments are similar to the Scythian; their language is quite different; they alone of all these tribes are cannibals."[51] It has been suggested that the Androphagi may be considered the ancestors of the Mordvians (Mordva).[52] The name, Mordva, may be derived from the Iranian *mard,* "man." Mordva would mean men, speaking collectively. The exact location of the Androphagi is a doubtful question. According to Herodotus the traveler coming from the south had to go up the Dnieper River and then cross a desert.[53] Tallgren has suggested that the abodes of the Androphagi were along the bank of the Desna River, north of present-day Chernigov.[54]

East of the Androphagi lived the Melanchlaeni. They also, according to Herodotus, were not a Scythian tribe. He says: ". . . the Melanchlaeni wear black garments from which their name is derived; their customs are similar to the Scythian."[55] The Melanchlaeni are considered the ancestors of the Finnish tribes Meria and Cheremissians. Tallgren places them north of Voronezh.[56] Still more to the east—in the Volga region and beyond the Volga—the abodes of the Thyssagetae and the Iyrcae may have been located. It seems that these two tribes must have lived in a more distant region than those previously mentioned. Herodotus says that between the Budini and the Thyssagetae there is a desert which takes seven days to cross.[57] One must also remember that in the time of the invasion of the Persian king Darius,[58] the Scythians asked assistance of all the neighboring tribes except the Thyssagetae and the Iyrcae. Apparently there was no direct connection between these two tribes and the Scythians. We may tentatively locate the Thyssagetae in

51. Herodotus, IV, 106.
52. Minns, p. 104.
53. Herodotus, IV, 18.
54. Grousset, p. 42.
55. Herodotus, IV, 107.
56. Grousset, p. 42.
57. Herodotus, IV, 22.
58. See Sec. 6, below.

the region of the middle Volga and Kama rivers, and the Iyrcae in Bashkiria, southern Ural area. The Iyrcae may be identified as the Iugra, or Ugrians.[59]

5. The Eastern Neighbors of the Scythians.

The Pontic steppes, which were occupied by the Scythians in the course of the seventh and sixth centuries B.C., are but the western extension of the long zone of Eurasian steppes which stretch eastward almost to the Amur River. Together with the adjacent zone of deserts to the south, the steppe zone served from time immemorial as a huge reservoir of nomadic tribes which from time to time inundated the border regions of old civilized countries such as China, Iran, and the Mediterranean area. The Scythians themselves came to the Pontic steppes from beyond the Volga River. Other nomads later followed suit in their westward thrust from central Eurasia to the Mediterranean basin. In the second century B.C. the Sarmatians replaced the Scythians in South Russia. Beginning in the fourth century A.D. the nomadic world of Eurasia was in a state of almost perpetual flux, one wave pressing westward after another. In the fourth and fifth centuries Turkish and Mongol tribes such as the Huns took the lead, followed by the Avars—"Western Turks"—and Khazars in the sixth and seventh centuries, the Patzinaks from the ninth to eleventh centuries, and the Cumans in the eleventh and twelfth centuries. The climax came with the Mongol invasion of the thirteenth century. Thereafter the westward drive of the nomad tribes gradually subsided, the last wave being that of the Kalmyk migration to the lower Volga in the seventeenth century. The student of Russian history has to watch carefully the development of trends in the Eurasian nomadic world, since without some knowledge of these developments many an event in the history of Russia proper can never be sufficiently understood and evaluated.

The causes of the westward drive of Eurasian nomads were manifold. In some cases it may have been the result of climatic changes. Increased dryness affected the cattle pasturage and forced the nomadic peoples to look for new fields. In other cases the migration may have been caused by political and military factors. Repulsed from the boundaries of China or Iran, the nomads went farther west in search of less protected countries to loot. In the case of a reverse

59. Minns, p. 107.

suffered by some nomadic tribe in China, and after the consequent retreat, it would fall on its next western neighbor; the latter being compelled to make room for the newcomers would move west in their turn, and so on. An expansionist wave may also be the result of certain domestic changes within a tribe or group of tribes—changes in their social and political organization. A number of tribes and clans would occasionally merge under the dictatorship of some outstanding military leader, who limited the autonomy of clan elders. Such was the case with the rise of Chingis Khan. Economic motives, such as a desire to control the transcontinental commercial highways, supplied another driving force to the policy of a conqueror of the steppes. It must be emphasized that the creation of a nomadic empire, not only in the case of Chingis Khan but in some other cases as well, was the result not of a mere chain of casual events but of an ambitious policy of imperial expansion. Such expansion required always a complete coöperation between the leading clan and the whole tribe or group of tribes. The empire built on such a foundation was never stable, however. Clan elders who at first gave their full support to the Great Khan (Kagan), would later try to secure privileges of their own. A struggle between the more influential tribal and clan chiefs would develop, resulting in the formation of what was called by the late Vladimirtsov "nomadic feudalism."[60] The interplay of these centrifugal forces would then rapidly destroy the unity of the empire.

Let us now survey briefly the nomadic tribes who roamed the Eurasian steppes and deserts east of the Ural River in the time of Herodotus. The information relating to them supplied by Herodotus is rather vague. Strabo says somewhat grudgingly that "the early Greek authors used to call peoples living beyond the Caspian Sea in some cases the Sacae, in other cases the Massagetae, without being able to make any reliable statement concerning them."[61] The evidence of the Greek writers may be to some extent supplemented by information drawn from Chinese chronicles. These are considered pretty reliable from the time of the ninth century B.C.

It is still Herodotus' report with which we are obliged to begin. We have seen[62] that in one part of his narrative he says that the

60. B. Ya. Vladimirtsov, *Obshchestvennyi stroi mongolov* (Leningrad, 1934).
61. Strabo, XI, 6, 2.
62. See Sec. 2, above.

Massagetae drove the Scythians westward. In another place, instead of the Massagetae he mentions in the same connection the Issedones. The latter, he explains, were themselves pressed by the Arimaspians. In addition to the Issedones and the Arimaspians Herodotus places east of the Don River the "Scythian-Apostates"[63] and the Argippaei. To that list of the eastern peoples the Sacae may be added, part of whom belonged to the Fifteenth province (satrapy) of the Persian kingdom according to Darius' division of satrapies.[64]

By comparing Herodotus' information with the evidence supplied by other authors we may tentatively locate the above-mentioned peoples in the following way. The "Scythian-Apostates" must have lived in the Akmolinsk area, northern Kazakhstan. They had split from the "Royal Scythians" and did not follow them to the Pontic steppes. They may most properly be called the Eastern Scythians. As to the Issedones, we must distinguish between their original home and the country to which they later migrated. According to A. Herrmann, they must have originally lived in the region of the river Isset, a tributary to the Tobol.[65] The very name of the people must be connected with that of the river. Subsequently the Issedones migrated to the southeast, probably to eastern Turkestan (Sin-Kiang). The home of the Argippaei was probably in Jungaria, and that of the Arimaspians at the foot of the Altai Mountains. The Massagetae lived in Turkestan. The Sacae lived closer to India, probably in southern Turkestan.

Let us now attempt to determine the racial affiliations of at least part of these tribes. The Sacae belonged undoubtedly to the Iranian family. The Eastern Scythians were probably likewise Iranians; they may be considered the ancestors of some of the Sarmatian tribes. The Argippaei may have been Mongols. Herodotus describes them in the following words: "It is said that they are all bald from birth, both men and women; they are snub-nosed and have protruding cheekbones; they speak a language of their own, but their garments are of Scythian pattern."[66] The Arimaspians, because of their geographic location, may be considered ancestors of the Turks:

63. Herodotus, IV, 22.
64. *Idem*, III, 93.
65. A. Herrmann, "Issedoi," *PW*, *18* (1916), col. 2244.
66. Herodotus, IV, 23.

it was in the Altai region that the Turkish State was founded in the sixth century A.D.[67]

The problem of the Massagetae is more involved. Herodotus says, "the Massagetae wear garments similar to the Scythian; their way of life is likewise close to that of the Scythians. They go into battle either on horseback or on foot since they are skillful warriors in either way. Bows and spears, but also battle-axes are their weapons. They use gold and copper . . . but no iron and no silver."[68] The assortment of weapons used by the Massagetae merits attention. The bow was a characteristic weapon of the Scythians, the spear, that of the Sarmatians, and the battle-ax that of the Cimmerians. Thus the Massagetae seem to have combined the weapons of various tribes. It may be, therefore, that they themselves were of various ethnic stocks. The Cimmerians as we have seen[69] were akin to the Thracians. May not some Massagetian clans be considered an eastern branch of the Thracians, mixed with some Iranian elements? The very name "Massagetae" seems significant from this point of view since one of the Thracian tribes in the Balkans was known as the Getae.[70]

A similarly composite ethnic group, for which there is some evidence in Chinese sources, existed about the same period in the province of Kan-Su, western China. Two peoples were living there in close contact: the Yue-chi and the Tokhars. The former seem to have dominated. While the Tokhars are considered an Iranian tribe, the Yue-chi belonged, judging at least from their language, to the western branch of the Indo-European family. It is the language of the Yue-chi which is commonly known as the Tokharian; it is closer to the Keltic and the Latin than to either Slavic or Iranian.[71] Both

67. Recently Mr. Benveniste has suggested that the Arimaspians must have been Iranians; he reconstructs the name as *Ariamaspa* ("Friends of horses"). See Grousset, p. 37, n. 3.

68. Herodotus, I, 215.

69. See Sec. 2, above.

70. On the Massagetae see Minns, p. 111 f.; Grousset, p. 37, n. 3; Markwart "Skizzen zur geschichtlichen Völkerkunde von Mittelasien und Sibirien," *Festschrift für Friedrich Hirth* (Berlin, 1920), p. 292. According to Markwart, the name Massagetae (*massjage-ta*) means "fishermen."

71. On the Tokharian and Yue-chi problem see Charpentier; S. Feist, "Der gegenwärtige Stand des Tocharerproblems," *Festschrift für Friedrich Hirth* (1920), pp. 74-84; Haloun; Herrmann; R. Grousset, "Les études historiques et l'Orientalisme," *RH, 181* (1937), 1-39; E. Schwentner, "Tocharica" and "Neue Tocharische Literatur," *ZVS, 65* (1938), 126-133 and 266-273; E. Sieg, W. Siegling, and W. Schultze, *To-*

the Yue-chi and the Tokhars later on, at the beginning of the Sarmatian period, moved from Kan-Su to Turkestan and played an important role in the history of Turkestan and some adjacent countries. We shall meet them, accordingly, later.

6. Glimpses of the Political History of Scythia.

Our information on the political history of the Scythians is both casual and incomplete. Herodotus mentions a few names of Scythian kings, so that it is possible to build up a fragmentary genealogy. But of the policies of these kings we know little.

Having crushed the resistance of the Cimmerians and occupied the zone of the steppes from the Volga to the Danube River, the Scythians became interested in promoting trade relations with adjacent countries, particularly to the south. The Greek cities on the northern littoral of the Black Sea thrived on Scythian trade; most of them, however, had to pay a certain tribute to the Scythians who offered their protection in return. Of the neighboring tribes, those living in the Don area—the Budini, the Geloni, and the Sauromatae—were apparently to a certain extent also dominated by the Scythians. All of them supported the Scythians against King Darius in 512 B.C. On the same occasion the Neuri, the Androphagi, and the Melanchlaeni proclaimed their neutrality, which was much resented by the Scythians who administered severe punishment to these neutrals after Darius' departure from Scythia.

The main problem of the domestic policy of the Scythian kings was probably the just distribution of grazing areas between the main horde and the lesser hordes, so that the interests of each horde with regard to horse and cattle breeding would be sufficiently protected. It seems probable that the Scythian state was led not by one king but by two—as was the case with the Hiung-Nu and the Turks—or even more. Describing Scythian preparations for defending their country against Darius, Herodotus mentions three Scythian kings or rulers (Scopasis, Idanthyrsus and Taxacis). Each of them

charische Grammatik 1931); Tarn, chap. viii. According to Haloun (p. 316), the name Yue-chi must have been pronounced *Zgudja,* which may be compared with *Ashkuzai,* the name of the Scythians in Assyrian. It should be emphasized that the Tokharian problem is a very involved one and is far from being solved. There is a considerable divergence of opinion on it, and a number of scholars are now inclined to identify the Yue-chi with the Tokhars. It seems certain in any case that the Yue-chi group consisted of at least two different tribes, whatever their respective names may have been.

ruled his own horde, while each horde in its turn consisted of several sections (cf. Turkish *ulus*) and clans (cf. Turkish *iurt*), headed by tribal and clan princes and chiefs. This complicated aristocratic system was welded together by the authority enjoyed by the royal house, of which we may judge from the care with which the royal tombs were kept.[72]

Due to their intercourse with the Greeks in the Pontic cities, part of the Scythians became gradually subject to the influence of Greek civilization. Herodotus' story of the Scythian king Anacharsis is very characteristic in this regard. Anacharsis went traveling in Greece and spent some time studying in Athens (at the end of the seventh or the beginning of the sixth century B.C.). Since the majority of the Scythians opposed any innovations, Anacharsis upon his return to Scythia was killed by his brother Saulius, who may be called the leader of Scythian die-hards. The story of Anacharsis repeated itself later in the person of Scyles, son of King Ariapithes. This prince was likewise executed.

Around 512 B.C. Scythia was invaded by the armies of Darius, king of Persia. Darius' starting point was Chalcedon on the Bosporus.[73] A pontoon bridge was built, on which his army crossed the Bosporus and headed north through Thrace. Simultaneously, his fleet was sent to the Black Sea to meet the overland army at the mouth of the Danube River. On his way to the Danube he conquered the Thracian tribe of the Getae. When his army reached the river, Darius ordered another pontoon bridge to be built there, which was left under the guard of the Ionian Greeks, his vassals. His main army then entered Bessarabia on its way to Scythia proper. It was at this juncture that the Scythians asked their northern and eastern neighbors for assistance, as mentioned above.[74] Since some of them refused any help the Scythians decided not to meet the Persians in regular battle, but to divide their forces into three sections and to retreat inland, driving away their cattle, burning the grass, and wrecking the wells. This became the classic example of the "scorched earth" strategy, used by the Russians against Napoleon in 1812, and against Hitler in A.D. 1941.

Herodotus' account of the campaign is detailed, but we do not

72. See Sec. 2, above.

73. The Thracian Bosporus, not to be confused with the Cimmerian Bosporus, or Kerch Strait.

74. See Sec. 4, above.

know how far it is reliable. His informant must have heard stories of it from old people who themselves could not have been eyewitnesses of the events and only conveyed what they heard from men of the previous generation. On the basis of Herodotus' report, the course of Darius' campaign may be reconstructed along the following lines: The Persians crossed the Pontic steppes from the mouth of the Danube eastward to the Don or Donets River. After burning the city of the Budini they turned first north and then west. In this way they went through the countries of the Melanchlaeni, the Androphagi, the Neuri, and the Agathyrsae. Finally they retreated back south to the lower Danube. Assuming that this was Darius' route, the whole campaign must have lasted much more than the sixty days during which, according to Herodotus, the Ionians pledged to guard the Danubian bridge. These latter, however, stayed beyond the appointed term and were still guarding the bridge when Darius finally appeared with the remnants of his forces. The whole campaign was a failure. While the Scythians at first showed no resistance, they began to harass the Persian troops as soon as they were compelled to retreat. According to Herodotus, Scythian agents urged the Ionians guarding the bridge to desert, but while they wavered at first the majority finally decided to stay. Thus Darius succeeded in bringing back to Thrace at least some of his army.

Recently, M. I. Rostovtzeff has offered a new interpretation of the true meaning of Darius' Scythian campaign.[75] In this scholar's opinion, the warrior-king was not bent upon conquest and did not intend to destroy and subjugate the Scythian Empire. His objective was only "to make an impressive raid into the Scythian kingdom as a proof of Persian power, and to deal one or two heavy blows at the Scythian army." Rostovtzeff believes that Darius succeeded in his enterprise. Exception may be taken to this view, and it appears that if Herodotus exaggerated Darius' failure, Rostovtzeff has gone rather to the other extreme. It may be that the Persian monarch was willing to be content with reconnoitering only, but his losses were probably more serious than he anticipated, and anyway the results of the reconnaissance were far from cheering since it showed the tremendous strength of the Scythians. Following in the wake of Darius' retreat a detachment of Scythians raided the Thracian Chersonese (modern Gallipoli). The failure of Darius himself and

75. Rostovtzeff, p. 84.

his son and successor, Xerxes, to conquer Greece in a series of campaigns which lasted from 490 to 479 B.C., as well as the subsequent protracted war between the Persians and the Greeks, prevented the possibility of any further aggressive action by the Persians against the Scythians.

It was only with the foundation of the Macedonian kingdom in the middle of the fourth century B.C. that the Danubian border of Scythia was again menaced. In the last year of the reign of Philip of Macedon his son, the famous Alexander, in pursuing the Thracian tribes of the Triballi and the Getae occupied Peuce Island and crossed the Danube northward (335 B.C.).[76] This campaign proved again to be but a reconnoitering operation, since first the death of his father and then troubles in Greece diverted Alexander's attention from the Danube. He then concentrated his efforts on the struggle with the Persian kingdom. His grandiose eastern campaign (334-325 B.C.) resulted in breaking the power of the Persians, with the consequent Hellenization of the whole of Hither Asia. What interests us in this connection is Alexander's attempt to conquer the northeastern corner of the Iranian world—southern Turkestan. After crushing the main Persian army the great general pursued its remnants up to the banks of the river Oxus (Amu-Daria) and established his control over Bactria (the region of modern Balkh). He then founded a city on the Jaxartes River (Syr-Daria) which was to serve as the outpost of Hellenism in Turkestan. The city was called "Alexandria the Farthest" (modern Khodjent).[77] Alexander's campaign beyond Jaxartes proved a failure, however. The Sacae offered desperate resistance and the king lacked time to undertake aggressive operations on a large scale. He left the business unfinished and turned to India instead. Thus we see that Alexander started his struggle with the northern Iranians by a lightning blow across the Danube (against the Scythians) and completed it by building a fortress on the Jaxartes (against the Sacae).

Alexander attached much importance to the organization of his new eastern provinces, Bactria and Sogdiana. In order to secure his authority he sent thither thousands of Greek and Macedonian colonists. In Bactria alone twelve new towns were founded, in which over fourteen thousand Greeks and Macedonians settled. Thus Hellenism established itself firmly in Turkestan, and the new Hellene

76. W. W. Tarn, "Alexander: the Conquest of Persia," *CAH, VI,* 355.
77. Tarn, Alexander, pp. 392-393.

cities of Bactria were to play the same role in the cultural development of the Transcaspian area as the older Greek cities in the Black Sea region. After the death of Alexander (323 B.C.) his empire was divided among his generals, known as the "Successors" (*Diadochi*). His Turkestan possessions were included in Seleucus' kingdom, which stretched from the Syrian littoral of the Mediterranean Sea eastward to the Indus River. In the middle of the third century B.C. the Bactrian viceroy proclaimed himself an independent ruler and thus the Greco-Bactrian realm came into being, which may be compared, in its historical role of bringing together the Greeks and Iranians, with the Bosporan kingdom.[78]

Let us now turn to developments in the Danubian region. At the time of Alexander's Persian campaign, his general Zopyrion crossed the Danube and invaded Scythia. He succeeded in getting as far as Olbia but then had to retreat, was defeated, and perished with most of his troops, probably somewhere in Bessarabia.[79] In the beginning of the third century B.C. Lysimachus, one of Alexander's successors, undertook a campaign against the Getae, during which he crossed the Danube and moved into the Dniester region. His army was, however, surrounded by the Getae, whom apparently the Scythians were supporting. Lysimachus was taken prisoner (291 B.C.).[80] Several years later the western part of Scythia was threatened by the invasion of the Kelts, known also as the Gauls. Beginning in 284 B.C. the Kelts ravaged Thrace, and some of their bands raided western Ukraine and Bessarabia as well.[81] They left some traces in the toponymics of these regions. For example, the name of the town Bârlad in Moldavia derives, according to Jacob Bromberg's conjecture, from the name of the Keltic tribe Britolagi (Britogalli).[82] The name of the city of Galich (Halich) in Galicia may likewise be connected with the Gauls (Galli), as also the name of Galicia itself.

78. On the Greco-Bactrian kingdom see V. Bartold, "Greko-Baktriiskoe Gosudarstvo: ego rasprostranenie na severo-vostok," *AN* (1916), pp. 823-828; Rostovtzeff, *Hellenistic World*, pp. 542-551; Tarn, chap. iii; Trever, *Pamiatniki.*

79. Minns, pp. 459-460; Tarn, Alexander, p. 394; Tarn, "The Heritage of Alexander," *CAH*, VI, 464.

80. Minns, p. 123; Tarn, "The New Hellenistic Kingdom," *CAH*, VII, 82. Subsequently, Lysimachus returned from captivity and took active part in the wars of the Diadochi. He fell in battle with Seleucus in 283 B.C.

81. Braun, pp. 164-172; Hrushevskyi, I, 113-114; H. Hubert, *Les Celtes*, (Paris, 1932), 2 vols.; Niederle, I, 303-318; E. Rademacher, "Kelten: Archaeologie," *RL, 6*, 281-300; Zeuss, pp. 170-175.

82. Bromberg, p. 470.

While the western borders of Scythia were harassed by the Kelts, its eastern portion was menaced by the Sarmatians who were pushing from beyond the Volga. At the beginning of the third century B.C. the Sarmatians approached the eastern banks of the Don River, and by the end of the century had already crossed the Don westward. Pressed both from west to east, the Scythians were able to hold, until the beginning of the second century B.C., only the central part of their former empire. They now concentrated in the steppes of northern Tauria and the Crimean peninsula. Their tents moved close to the Greek cities of the Bosporan kingdom. The Kul-Oba Kurgan near Kerch remains a monument of this drive of the Scythians deep into the Taurida.

Chapter III

THE SARMATO-GOTHIC EPOCH, 200 B.C.-A.D. 370.

1. Summary of the Chapter. Sources and References.

THE pressure of the Sarmatians in the direction of the Pontic steppes assumed momentum in the third century B.C. This was a period of unrest in the entire eastern Iranian, or Sacian, world. While the Sarmatian tribes began to move westward from Kazakhstan, the Parthians rebelled in Iran against the Hellenistic rule of the Seleucids (248 B.C.). This westward drive of the Sarmatians, which started in the third century B.C., was accelerated in the following century by the general migration of the peoples of middle Eurasia. The Huns, defeated by the Chinese, retreated westward and drove the Yue-chi farther west to Turkestan. The Yue-chi in their turn pushed from Turkestan the tribes which had settled there previously. All this contributed to the Sarmatian migration to the Pontic steppes. In the first half of the second century B.C. the Sarmatians crushed Scythian resistance and replaced the Scythians as overlords of South Russia.

While there is no consensus of opinions with regard to the ethnic stock of the Scythians, the Sarmatians may be considered Iranians without any doubt. Like the Scythians, they were a nomadic people of horse and cattle breeders. There was even less unity between their hordes than in the case of the Scythians. Both in military organization and in tactics, the Sarmatians differed considerably from their predecessors in South Russia. There was likewise a difference in the respective artistic style of these two peoples.[1] The international situation had also changed considerably. We have already mentioned the Parthian uprising against the Seleucids. The Parthians were not only able to obtain independence, but gradually extended their control to Mesopotamia. For the next four centuries, the Parthian kingdom was to play the leading role in the history of Hither Asia. Si-

1. See Sec. 3, below.

multaneously, the Hellenistic world was menaced from the west by the Romans. By the beginning of the Christian era not only Greece proper but also that part of the Hellenized East not conquered by the Parthians was obliged to recognize the supreme authority of Rome. As early as the first century B.C., Roman and Parthian troops clashed in Mesopotamia, and the Roman infantry proved helpless before the Parthian horsemen. It was with the utmost difficulty that the Romans succeeded in barring to the Parthians access to the Syrian coast. As to the Black Sea region, Roman authority was gradually expanding. Several legions were stationed on the lower Danube to beat off Sarmatian attacks. Roman garrisons were likewise stationed in the Greek cities of the Crimean peninsula. Thus, along the vast arc from the lower Danube to the Euphrates River, the Romans carried on a protracted struggle with the Iranians. Simultaneously, the Roman fortified frontier line—the *limes*—in the north was menaced by the drive of the Teutonic tribes. At the end of the second century A.D. the Goths skirted the Roman boundaries and, in the first half of the third century, established their power in the Pontic steppes. Various Sarmatian tribes which had occupied this region before the coming of the Goths were partly conquered and partly pushed away.

At the time when the domination of the Sarmatians over South Russia was replaced by that of the Goths, the Parthian dynasty of the Arsakids who ruled in Iran and Mesopotamia was overthrown by the Persian clan of the Sassanids (A.D. 223). In this way the ascendancy of the steppe Iranians—the Sarmatians and the Parthians—came to a close simultaneously in the Pontic region and the Hither East. However, while in South Russia it was the Goths who replaced them as rulers, in Iran and Mesopotamia one Iranian group was superseded by another. The fourth century A.D. witnessed important new upheavals in the international setting. The emperor Constantine founded a second capital of his realm on the Thracian Bosporus, where on the site of the old Greek town of Byzantium a new sumptuous city was built, known as Constantinople (now Istanbul). Subsequently the Roman Empire split into two parts—the West and the East. It is the Eastern, or Byzantine Empire, which has a greater importance for our subject matter. The eastern emperors were interested in both the Pontic shores and the Levant, and their diplomats watched closely all important developments in the steppe world to the north and took necessary measures accordingly. Because of this, Byzantine diplomacy became one of the important factors in the history of South Russia.

An event of paramount importance for that history was the invasion of the Huns, around A.D. 370. The aftermath of this invasion will be dealt with in the following chapter. Here we must emphasize the importance of the Sarmato-Gothic epoch as a whole for the formation of the East Slavic tribes. It is in this period that the tribe of the Antes came to the fore, which, as we suppose, was originally controlled by Alanic clans, some of the latter being known as the Rukhs-As (the Light As). It seems probable that it was from their name that the name Rus[2] should be derived. In any case it is with the Antes that Russian history proper has its beginning.

The amount of both archaeological and historical evidence available for the student of the period is perhaps more adequate than for previous ages. However, there are still many gaps not covered by the sources. As for the preceding time, the history of the south can be better illustrated by the sources available than that of the north. Archaeological evidence remains supreme for this period as it was for the earlier one. The contents of the barrows of the Sarmatian period excavated by archaeologists are not less instructive than those pertaining to the Scythian age. Recently a number of remarkable kurgans of the Sarmatian time have been discovered in the Altai region as well as in northern Mongolia. Their inventory contributes much to the understanding of the various shades of the animal style in nomadic art. Later on, the Goths accepted the Sarmatian polychromatic style, with some modification, and in their subsequent drive to the west spread it all over Europe.

As to the so-called "funeral fields" of the Slavic area west of the middle Dnieper, there are no marked changes in grave furniture for this period as compared with the preceding one. Numismatics has greatly assisted the work of the archaeologist, especially as to the dating of the finds. A number of Roman, Parthian, Sassanian and other coins have been found in several of the barrows excavated.

As to the epigraphic material, in addition to the Greek inscriptions as before, the expansion of the Roman Empire on the lower Danube and on the Black Sea, in the first century B.C. and the first two centuries A.D., supplies the historian with a number of important data contained in various Latin inscriptions.

2. The *s* in "Rus" is to be pronounced softly (***Rus'***).

Turning now to the literary evidence, we may refer to the following Greek and Latin historians and geographers, whose works are especially useful for our purposes: Strabo (63 B.C.-A.D. 23), Pliny (A.D. 23/24-79), Tacitus (A.D. *ca.* 55-*ca.* 120), Ptolemy (second century A.D.), and Ammianus Marcellinus (b. A.D. *ca.* 330, d. at the end of the fourth century A.D.). For the history of the Goths in South Russia (second to fourth centuries) the chief authority is Jordanis, whose account was written in the middle of the sixth century A.D., that is, much later than the events he describes. Jordanis made extensive use of Cassiodorus' work, the manuscript of which was subsequently lost. Both Cassiodorus and Jordanis were able to use some remnants of contemporary evidence, chiefly through oral tradition.

The events of central Asia, which have such importance for the understanding of the causes of the westward drive of both the Sarmatians and the Huns, are best traced in the Chinese chronicles, of which the following three are especially valuable for our purpose: (1) the *Shi-ki* ("Historical Records"), started at the end of the second century B.C., completed between 74 and 49 B.C.; (2) the *Ch'ien Han Shu* ("History of the Former Hans"), compiled in the first century A.D.; and (3) the *Heou Han Shu* ("History of the Later Hans"), compiled in the second quarter of the fifth century A.D. The chapter of each of these chronicles dealing with the "western countries" (chiefly Turkestan) is now available in Russian, English, French, and German translations.

The flowering of the Islamic (both Arabic and Persian) historical literature started of course much later than the period to which this chapter refers, but some important bits of information bearing on this period may be found in the later works of Arabic writers as well.

The use of the data supplied by both comparative linguistics and historical ethnology is likewise essential for our purpose, especially for such problems as the early civilization of the Slavs and the Finns, and their intercourse with the Iranians of South Russia.

The material supplied by the primary sources has not received equal historical interpretation with regard to all aspects of the period. There are problems which have been rather fully explored, for example, the history of the Sarmatians for which the research done by M. I. Rostovtzeff has been of primary importance. German scholars have naturally paid much attention to the history of the

Goths. The problem of the origin of the Slavs has been investigated chiefly by Slavic scholars. The standard work is the *Slovanské Starožitnosti* ("Slavonic Antiquities") by Lubor Niederle.

As to the reconstruction of the history of South Russia as a whole in the period of the Sarmatians and the Goths, Rostovtzeff's book on the Iranians and Greeks quoted above[3] must again be cited. A useful attempt at a general survey of both archaeology and history, not only of South Russia but of the northern sections of Russia as well, has been made by Yu. V. Gotie. In addition to the work quoted earlier[4] we must mention here his *Iron Age in Eastern Europe*, published in Russian in 1930.

2. *Central Eurasia in the Sarmatian Age.*[5]

The original home of the Sarmatians was in the vast area of steppes and deserts east of the Ural River and the Caspian Sea. Their westward migration was a long-drawn-out process of about two centuries' duration, during which period even the clans of the Sarmatians which were on their way west did not completely lose contact with their kinsmen in the east. Therefore the study of the Turkestan and Altai civilizations is essential for a better understanding of the history of the Sarmatian states in South Russia. As in earlier times, there was in the Sarmatian period a certain unity of the "steppe culture" of Kazakhstan, Northern Turkestan, Altai, and Mongolia. We have seen that the so-called Minusinsk bronze culture had its counterpart in Turkestan.[6] In the course of the third and second centuries B.C. the peoples of the steppes became acquainted with iron and iron tools. In the first century B.C. and the first century A.D. the material culture of the Turkestan and Mongolian nomads shows a remarkable progress, partly the result of the growth of commerce along the great overland highway which led from China to the Mediterranean area. Furs were exported southward from Siberia, and silk eastward from China. Iron weapons and gold ornaments were conveyed north from Bactria; the Altai became an important mining center.

The nomadic chiefs accumulated immense wealth, and part of the treasure of each was usually buried with him after his death. The

3. See Chap. I, Sec. 2.
4. *Ibid.*
5. Grousset; McGovern.
6. See Chap. I, Sec. 5.

grave of a renowned chieftain consisted of one or more funeral chambers secured by wooden walls. Such a chamber was dug deep under the surface of the earth, and a huge kurgan built over the grave. A number of the kurgans belonging to this period were opened and robbed by treasure hunters in the seventeenth and the eighteenth centuries. Some, however, remained either hidden or only partly broken; while others have been but recently discovered by Soviet archaeologists. Thus for example, M. P. Griaznov excavated in 1929 a large kurgan in the eastern Altai known as the Pazyryk Kurgan.[7] This kurgan may be dated at the end of the second or the beginning of the first century B.C. It appears that the grave had been partly robbed soon after the funeral, but not troubled afterward. It was found in a frozen condition. Close to the grave the bodies of ten horses were discovered, each with saddle and trappings. The heads of two of the horses were covered by masks. One of them, a leathern one, represents the head of a deer. The other, made of felt, has the shape of a griffin. In Griaznov's opinion the deer mask is evidence for Nicholas Marr's theory that the deer was used for riding before the horse. The horse trappings are ornamented with the designs of human and animal heads. The saddles and covers are embellished with leather plates designed to represent fighting animals.

Likewise of considerable interest is the Shiba grave in the middle Altai, excavated by M. P. Griaznov in 1927.[8] It had also been partly robbed, but what remained in it is valuable enough. Several mummified bodies were found, each covered with garments of fur, leather, or silk. Wooden and metal plates ornamented in animal style were also preserved. Among other things, a piece of Chinese lacquer bowl was found which, judging by the pattern, may be dated between 86 and 48 B.C.

A number of graves of the beginning of the Christian era were excavated in 1923-25 in Noin-Ula, Mongolia, by the P. K. Kozlov expedition.[9] They bring further evidence concerning the intercourse of the steppe nomads with China. Chinese silk fabrics, lacquer, gold, jade, and bronzeware, as well as coins, were among the things found

7. M. P. Griaznov, "The Pazirik Burial of Altai," *AJA, 37* (1933), 30-44.

8. M. P. Griaznov, "Fürstengräber in Altaigebiet," *WPZ* (1928), 120-123.

9. P. K. Kozlov, S. A. Teploukhov, and G. I. Borovka, *Kratkie otchety ekspeditsii po issledovaniiu severnoi Mongolii* (Leningrad, 1925); K. V. Trever, "Excavations in Northern Mongolia (1924-1925)," *GAM,* III (1932).

in these graves. Among the native goods, remarkable woolen carpets may be mentioned, which are adorned with mosaic appliqué work of quilted woolen stuff. The patterns represent fighting animals, such as the elk and the wolverine; the yak and the tiger. These animal scenes are comparable to some compositions of Greco-Scythian art, such as the deer and the griffins of the Chertomlyk vase, the *phalaron* of the Starobelsk treasure, etc. No less interesting are some pieces of woolen fabric found at Noin-Ula. They are embroidered with wool threads of variegated colors; the design represents men on horseback. Their dress and hairdress are of Scythian type. The ornamentation of the fabrics is of Grecian pattern. Thus Noin-Ula grave goods show that the Eurasian steppe culture was influenced by both Chinese and Hellenistic patterns.

Through the archaeological evidence, a fairly accurate idea of the wealth of the nomadic chieftains as well as the wide range of their commercial interests may be obtained. We are thus better able to understand the inside story of the rise and development of nomadic states. Accumulated wealth in the hands of some able chieftain would expand his popularity among neighboring clans; his participation in international commerce would supply him with both additional wealth and information concerning the political situation outside his own *ulus*. He would then enter the path of military adventure, and if his first moves were successful, would start the ball rolling. Such was the pattern of steppe imperialism from the early Sarmatian chieftains to Attila and Chingis Khan.

Turning to the more detailed story of nomad migrations in central Eurasia in the second century B.C. and after, we must begin with the so-called Hiung-Nu nomads and their attacks on China. It seems probable that the main horde of the Hiung-Nu was Turkish, which means that the Hiung-Nu of the Chinese chronicles were basically of the same stock as the Huns who invaded Europe at the end of the fourth century A.D.; therefore, for the sake of convenience, we shall call the Hiung-Nu of the Sarmatian age "Huns."

Taking advantage of the troubles in China at the end of the third century B.C. the Huns intensified their inroads into China proper and adjacent territories. They became especially dangerous when their smaller hordes were united under the strong leadership of Modun. In 177 B.C. the Huns invaded simultaneously China and Kan-Su, which province was then occupied by the Yue-chi.[10] In China

10. Cf. Chap. II, Sec. 5.

they met strong resistance. Since 202 B.C. a new dynasty known as the Han had controlled the land, and before long the authority of the imperial power had been greatly strengthened.

While the Huns were repulsed from China on this occasion, they administered a crushing blow to the Yue-chi. A second campaign against the Yue-chi (around 165 B.C.) was even more successful. As a result of these reverses the state of the Yue-chi was broken up, and they split into two groups. The smaller of the two, known as the Little Yue-chi, migrated southward to Khotan. The larger group, known as the Great Yue-chi, drove westward. According to information gathered by the Chinese envoy Chang-Kien, the army of the Great Yue-chi numbered from 100,000 to 200,000 mounted archers. Reaching Jungaria, they defeated the Osuns and subsequently pushed the Sacae southward from Semirechie. For about two decades the Yue-chi controlled the Semirechie area, until they were again attacked by the Huns, around 140 B.C. The Huns acted in the name of the Osun prince who had fled to them, asking them for protection, when his people were first overcome by the Yue-chi. Unequal to face another attack from the Huns the Yue-chi left Semirechie and moved southwest to Fergana, from which they again dislodged the Sacae. Even after their first encounter with the Yue-chi, part of the Sacae had migrated to Kabulistan. From there the Sacae penetrated into the Punjab in the Indus valley.[11]

Meanwhile the Yue-chi conquered the province of Sogdiana, and their chieftain pitched his tent on the northern bank of the Oxus River. It was here that he received the above-mentioned Chinese envoy in the year 128 B.C. Bactria became the next objective of the Yue-chi. The resistance of the Greco-Bactrian troops was of no avail, and the Greco-Bactrian realm thus came to its end. From Bactria the Yue-chi invaded Iran proper, where they clashed with the Parthians. While the latter were able to keep control of the western section of Iran, the invaders conquered the eastern provinces. Subsequently, treading in the footsteps of the Sacae, they penetrated into the Punjab. The realm of the Yue-chi now included Bactria, eastern Iran and the Punjab. It became known as the Indo-Scythian kingdom.

The "Indo-Scythian" civilization was subjected to strong Hel-

11. On the wars and migrations of the Yue-chi see Herrmann; McGovern, chaps. v and vi; Tarn, chap. vii.

lenistic influences. While the Yue-chi destroyed the Greco-Bactrian realm they assimilated to a certain extent its Hellenistic culture and continued its traditions in art and handicraft. As to religion, the Indo-Scythian kings accepted Buddhism, which was then still dominant in northwestern India. Thus a new style in religious art was created, known as the Greco-Buddhic. The vicissitudes of the Yue-chi attract our attention not only on behalf of this mysterious Indo-European people itself but chiefly because of their close historic connection with the Iranians. Even when still living in Kan-Su the Yue-chi were united with an Iranian tribe which the Greek writers called the Tokhars (Tochari). Though their language was different from that of the Tokhars, it has become customary to refer to the Yue-chi language as Tokharian. Following their migration to Turkestan they again mixed with the Iranians. Some students of the Yue-chi problem suggest that at the time of their appearance in eastern Turkestan they were known as the Arsi.[12] This name may be compared with that of the Aorsi, one of the major Sarmatian tribes.[13] It is possible that while, as a result of all the various migrations of the second and the first centuries B.C., the main body of the Aorsi moved westward to the Volga and Don areas, part of the tribe remained in Turkestan. More apparent, however, is the connection between the Yue-chi and another Sarmatian tribe, the Alans. In the Chinese chronicle known as the *History of the Later Hans* and completed in the fifth century A.D., it is stated that the area of the Alans was previously called Antsai (*An-ts'ai*).[14] The province of Antsai is first mentioned in the report of the Chinese envoy Chang-Kien in 128 B.C. It was probably situated near the Aral Sea. Since Chang-Kien did not visit this land personally, he must have collected his information about it from the Yue-chi. I consider it possible that the very name of the province, Antsai, is Tokharian, to be derived from the Tokharian word *ant* which meant "plain," "lowland." If so, the people *Ant* (Anti, Antes) were so called because they lived on plains, or steppes.[15] The name of a Russian tribe, *Poliane,* may be mentioned in this connection: from *pole,* ("field").

The people of Anti are first mentioned in western sources by the Latin geographer Pomponius Mela whose work was written around

12. The problem of the name Arsi is very involved. See Tarn, p. 284 f.
13. See Sec. 3, below.
14. *History of the Later Hans* (*Heou Han Shu*), chap. 118, *TP,* VII (1907), 150.
15. Vernadsky, *Origins,* p. 60 f.

A.D. 44. According to his information the Anti lived somewhere "above" the Hyperboreans and the Amazons.[16] Pliny, who completed his *Natural History* in A.D. 77, likewise mentions the Anti.[17] The Greek authors of this period do not mention them, but we may take it that the same people is meant by the Greeks under the name of Asii ("Ασιοι), Asaei ('Ασαῖοι) or Assaei ('Ασσαῖοι).[18] The Asii may be identified as the As ("Asy" or "Iasy" of the Russian chronicles), that is, the forefathers of the Ossetians. The As were otherwise known as the Alans. Now, as we have seen, the Chinese chronicles identify the Alans as the Antsai. It follows that the Anti of the Latin authors and the Asii of the Greeks were different transcriptions of the same name. The contraction of the name Ant into As may be explained from the phonetical laws of the Greek language (compare πᾶσι from παντσι[19]). On the authority of Chang-Kien's report we may surmise that around 127 B.C. the Ants or As lived in the vicinity of the Aral Sea, that is, in present-day Kazakhstan.

We have now to turn our attention, in the same connection, to the people of Osun (Wu-sun) in Jungaria who were conquered by the Yue-chi around 160 B.C. According to the Chinese chronicles the Osun had blue eyes and blond hair.[20] These features seem to indicate that they were of Aryan stock; it seems probable that they were one of the Sarmatian tribes, possibly another branch of the Alans, and from this point of view the Chinese description of the appearance of the Osun may be compared with Ammian Marcellinus' account of the Alans.[21] It is significant that according to Strabo there existed another form of the name Asii: Asii or Asiani ("Ασιοι ἢ 'Ασιανοί).[22] The form "Asiani" seems to be especially close to the name Osun. Jarl Charpentier, accepting the identification of Asii as Osun, remarks that the name As had a parallel form Os which was preserved in the name of the Ossetians.[23] Therefore the Os, or Osun, of Jungaria must have been a branch of the As, or Ant, of Kazakhstan. While the problem is rather involved, one conclusion

16. Pomponius Mela, I, 13.
17. Pliny, VI, 35.
18. Strabo, XI, 8, 2; Ptolemy, V, 9, 16; Stephanus of Byzantium, *s.v.* 'Ασσαῖοι.
19. Vernadsky, *Origins*, 61.
20. Charpentier, p. 358.
21. See Sec. 3, below.
22. Strabo, XI, 8, 2. The reading, ἢ ασιανοί instead of πασιανοί, as in printed editions, is by Haloun, p. 244. Tarn, however, accepts πασιανοί (Tarn, p. 284).
23. Charpentier, p. 359 f.

in any case may be drawn from the preceding argument: the As, or Antes, lived in the second century B.C. in southern Kazakhstan and possibly even in Jungaria.

We have now to take into consideration that both the As of Kazakhstan and the Os of Jungaria were in close contact with the Yue-chi after the latter's invasion of Turkestan. Trogus' mention of the "Asian kings of the Tokharians" (*reges Tocharorum Asiani*)[24] is very significant. It appears that at this time an Alanic clan ruled over the Yue-chi. If so, we may suppose that later on some groups of the Yue-chi joined the Alans in their westward movement. We may also assume some contact between the Tokharian and the Alanic languages.

3. The Sarmatians in South Russia.[25]

The migration of the Sarmatians to South Russia was not an event of such cataclysmic force as the later invasions of the Huns, the Avars, and the Mongols proved to be. The pressure of the Sarmatians was gradual and it was likewise only gradually that the Scythians ceded ground to the newcomers. As early as the third century B.C., the center of the Scythian Empire shifted from the region of the Sea of Azov to the Dnieper. Around 179 B.C. the Sarmatians, as reported by Polybius, started their inroads into the Scythian possessions in northern Tauria.[26] By the middle of the second century B.C., the Scythian Empire broke down. Part of the Scythians joined the newcomers and recognized their authority. Others went west, crossed the lower Danube, and occupied the Dobrudja, where they were able to hold their ground for a comparatively long period. This area became known as "Little Scythia" among the Greek and Latin writers.

The replacement of the Scythians by the Sarmatians at first affected painfully the life of the people and economic relations in the north Pontic area. However, when the period of fighting was over, the Sarmatians succeeded in securing peace and stability and in restoring commercial contacts between the steppe people and the

24. Trogus, "Prologus Libri XLII."

25. M. Ebert, "Südrussland: Sarmatische Periode," *RL, 13,* 98-114; Kondakov, *Drevnosti,* II; idem, *Ocherki,* chap. i; Rostovtzeff, *Animal Style; idem, Centre; idem, Iranians and Greeks; idem, Sarmatae; idem, Skythien; idem, Zhivopis.*

26. Polybius, XXV, 6, 13.

Greek cities on the littoral. Being a nomadic nation like the Scythians, the Sarmatians depended economically on neighboring peoples for supplies as regarded products of agriculture and handicrafts. Therefore, like the Scythians, they took special pains to sponsor commercial intercourse with their neighbors and to protect the commercial highways. Among the agricultural peoples controlled by the Sarmatians, Slavic tribes in the Ukrainian area should not be overlooked. For the development of handicraft and industries, besides the Greek cities on the Pontic littoral, the rise of town settlements in the North Caucasian area may be mentioned. As we have seen[27] some Sarmatian chieftains, even before their migration to South Russia, accumulated immense wealth by patronizing international trade. The transcontinental commercial highway from China to Turkestan was the backbone of the commercial imperialism of the steppe leaders. By moving to the Pontic steppes the Sarmatian chieftains were now able to connect the transcontinental trade route with the maritime commerce of the Black Sea region.

As in the preceding period, the Pontic Greeks played an important role as middlemen between the steppe peoples and the Mediterranean world. But now the role of the Bactrian Greeks in the Transcaspian region became even more important, nor is the influence of Parthian art to be overlooked.[28] As a result of all this, there is a considerable difference between the Scythian style and the Sarmatian style in art and handicrafts. In M. Rostovtzeff's words, "The Sarmatian animal style is at once vigorous and savage and highly refined and stylized." [29] Its foundation was laid by native artists of central Eurasia. Gradually the design of animal contours became rather conventional, as if intended chiefly for the purpose of ornamentation. An important feature of the Sarmatian style was its polychromy, achieved by means of the wide use of precious and semiprecious stones for incrustation.

Generally speaking, Sarmatian antiquities have been less systematically studied than the Scythian, and it is only now that, due chiefly to M. Rostovtzeff's works, the characteristics of the Sarmatian artistic style and its reflections in Chinese art are being

27. See Sec. 2, above.

28. On Parthia and Parthian civilization see Rostovtzeff, *Sarmatae,* especially pp. 124-130; W. W. Tarn, "Parthia," *CAH,* IX, chap. xiv.

29. Cf. Rostovtzeff, *Sarmatae,* p. 103.

better understood. Beginning in the east, remnants of Sarmatian culture have been recently found in Khoresm.[30] Prior to this, a number of important Sarmatian barrows were excavated in the Orenburg region, of which those at Prokhorovka may be mentioned here. Another group of Sarmatian mounds was found in the region of the Volga Germans, east of the middle Volga. No less important are the Sarmatian barrows of the North Caucasian area in the Kuban basin. The so-called Buerova Mogila on the Taman Peninsula may be referred to the third century B.C.; the findings at Siverskaia, southwest of Krasnodar, to the second century B.C.; the Zubov barrow northwest of Armavir, and one of the Armavir Kurgans, to the first century either B.C. or A.D.; some of the barrows on the banks of the Kuban River, such as those near Tiflisskaia and Ust-Labinskaia, to the second century A.D. Barrows and grave sites of the Sarmatian period have also been found in Ukraine, both east and west of the Dnieper. The furniture of some of them is stylistically very close to the Kuban group. Such is the case, for example, with the Selimovka find in Izium district, Kharkov province, and the Tsvetna find in Chigirin district, Kiev province. It is likewise to the Sarmatian period that the famous Novocherkassk treasure belongs, with its gold diadem and other precious jewels. It may be tentatively dated in the first century A.D.

With the exception of the Novocherkassk hoard, Sarmatian graves are less rich in gold jewelry than the Scythian. Another difference between the two periods is that horse sacrifice was apparently no longer popular, since no complete horse skeletons have been found in any of the typical Sarmatian barrows of South Russia. The men's graves are usually well furnished with armor and weapons. Iron helmets, breastplates, swords, lances, and iron and bronze arrowheads are abundant, as are horse trappings, among them silver- or gold-plated phalarae. Items of ornament such as torques, bracelets, garment and belt plaques and buckles of silver, sometimes of gold wire, are also abundant. There is of course even more variety in the ornaments found in women's graves, which include necklaces, bracelets, earrings, strings of pearls, and fibulas; gold and silver perfume bottles are also characteristic.

In addition to grave furniture, wall paintings in some of the tombs

30. Tolstov, p. 160.

excavated near Kerch, of the first century B.C. and the first two centuries A.D., are of great assistance for the study of the Sarmatian culture. From these pictures and the contents of the graves, as well as from literary sources, one may draw a fair idea of the Sarmatian way of life and of their army. Heavy cavalry constituted the mainstay of Sarmatian military might. This was recruited from the flower of the nobility. The Sarmatian horseman wore a helmet and either a coat of mail or a leather coat. His chief weapons were a long spear and a long iron sword. Tacitus comments that hardly any army could withstand the charge of Sarmatian cavalry unless the latter were handicapped by terrain and weather.[31] On a rainy day or on swampy ground Sarmatian horses would slip and fall under the burden of their heavily armored riders. In battle the bulk of the heavy cavalry was usually put in the center of the front line, while the two flanks were entrusted to light cavalry. The warrior of such a flank squadron had no heavy armor; he handled bow and arrows instead of spear and sword. The horsemen of the light cavalry were drawn from what we may call the petty gentry or the lower middle class of Sarmatian society.

There was even less unity in the Sarmatian political organization than in that of the Scythians. At best we may think of a federation of Sarmatian tribes, but even this federation must have been rather loose. The migration was by single tribes. The first to appear in the Pontic steppes were the Iazygians. The Roxolani followed; then the Siracae, and the Aorsi. The Alans were the last comers. According to M. I. Rostovtzeff, the Iazygians were not a Sarmatian but a Maeotian tribe, which was pushed out of the Don area westward as the result of the Sarmatian drive.[32] However, the names of the two Iazygian kings mentioned by the historian Dio Cassius (A.D. 150–235) sound definitely Iranian.[33] Therefore we may suppose that even if the Iazygians were not a purely Sarmatian tribe their ruling clan must have been of Iranian stock. After crossing the steppes of South Russia in their movement westward, the Iazygians settled for about two centuries on the shore of the Black Sea between the mouth of the Dniester and the lower Danube, in the region roughly corresponding to that which later became known as Bessarabia. In the

31. Tacitus, *Historiae,* I, 79.
32. Rostovtzeff, *Sarmatae,* pp. 92-93.
33. Dio Cassius, 71, 16; cf. Miller, p. 86.

Middle Ages this region was called *Ugol* (the "corner") in Slavic, which was transcribed into Greek as Ὄγγλος. The Tatars referred to it as Budjak, which is a translation of the Slavic term.[34] In this way the Iazygians were close to the country of Dobrudja, where the remnants of the Scythians had settled after being pushed out of South Russia. Subsequently, with the expansion of the Roman Empire on the Danube the Iazygians came in touch with the Romans, which may explain the fact that we find more information in Roman sources about the Iazygians than about other Sarmatian tribes.

The Romans had plenty of trouble with the Iazygians as they tried to fend them off from the former's Danubian provinces. In the second quarter of the first century A.D. the Iazygians moved to the Pannonian steppes, between the Tisa River and the middle Danube. The Roxolani settled down to the east of the Iazygi, occupying the steppes between the Dnieper and the Don. The first part of the name Roxolani may be derived from the Iranian *rukhs* which means "light." Thus the name Roxolani obviously meant "the light Alani."[35]

The Roxolani formed some sort of alliance with the Iazygians and supported the latter's drive against the Romans in several instances. After the removal of the Iazygians to the middle Danube the Roxolani were their successors in the "Corner" on the lower Danube. We are indebted to Strabo for a description of the typical attire of a Roxolan warrior.[36] Strabo's statement has been corroborated by recent archaelogical evidence.[37]

East of the Roxolani on the lower Don River were the abodes of the Aorsi. Their name may be derived from the Iranian *ors* or *uors* which means "white."[38] Next to the Aorsi to the southeast of the Sea of Azov the Siracae established themselves. They centered round the Kuban valley that was the old haunt of the Sindians. Part of the latter were probably pushed south to the seashore and up into the mountains. The remainder no doubt pledged allegiance to the newcomers. By the end of the first century A.D. both the Aorsi and the Siracae must have recognized the Alans as their rulers.

34. Barsov, pp. 96-97; Niederle, IV, 159; see also Chap. V, n. 139.
35. Miller, p. 86.
36. Strabo, VII, 3, 17.
37. Rostovtzeff, *Sarmatae*, p. 101.
38. Miller, *Sledy*, p. 235.

We now come to the Alans. As has already been mentioned, they were the last to appear in South Russia and consquently had to occupy the eastern portion of the territory. From about the end of the first to the end of the fourth century A.D. they controlled the steppe area at the Sea of Azov from the lower Don to the lower Volga and to the foothills of the Caucasus Mountains. Gradually they spread north to the upper Don and Donets region, entering the mixed forest-steppe zone.

We have said[39] that in the second and the first centuries B.C. the Alans played an important role in the political life of Turkestan. It seems probable that some of their clans remained east of the Caspian Sea even after the main horde migrated westward. By the end of the fourth century A.D. the western Alans must still have kept their oriental ties alive.

Says Ammianus Marcellinus: [40] "The Halani . . . inhabit the measureless wastes of Scythia. . . . In another part of the country [i.e., east of the Don River] . . . the Halani mount to the eastward, divided into populous and extensive *gentes;* these reach far into Asia, and, as I have heard, stretch all the way to the river Ganges, which flows through the territories of India and empties into the Southern Ocean."

It is obvious that Ammianus has here in mind the Indo-Scythian realm of the Yue-chi; we must recall in this connection that according to Trogus the ruling dynasty of the Yue-chi was Alanic.[41] Because of the close connection between the Alans and the Yue-chi we may suppose that, in their turn, some Yue-chi detachments penetrated to South Russia together with the Alans. It is quite possible that some of the Alanic clans of South Russia were of Yue-chi origin.

According to Ammianus the Alans, like the other Sarmatian tribes, were typical nomads: "They have no huts and care nothing for using the plowshare, but they live upon flesh and an abundance of milk, and dwell in wagons, which they cover with rounded canopies of bark and drive over the boundless wastes." [42] Ammianus' comment upon the appearance of the Alans is especially interesting,

39. See Sec. 2, above.

40. Ammianus Marcellinus, XXXI, 2, 13 and 16. The trans. here and subsequently cited is by John C. Rolfe, in "The Loeb Classical Library," slightly revised at some points.

41. See n. 24, above.

42. Ammianus Marcellinus, XXXI, 2, 18.

in connection with the Chinese remarks upon the appearance of the Osun.[43] "Almost all the Halani are tall and handsome, their hair inclines to the blond (*crinibus mediocriter flavis*), by the ferocity of their glance they inspire dread, subdued though it is. They are light and active in the use of arms. In all respects they are like the Huns, but in their manner of life and their habits they are less savage."[44]

In the religion of the Alans, as well as of other Sarmatian tribes, the worship of the Iranian God-Horseman, to be identified as Ahuramazda or Mithra, played apparently the most important role, but the veneration of the Great Goddess of the Scythian age was likewise continued.[45]

It should be noted that with the spread of the authority of the Alans over vast territories their name began to be applied not only to the Alans proper but to a number of tribes of different stock conquered by them. In Ammianus' words: "By repeated victories they gradually wore down the peoples whom they met and like the Persians incorporated them under their own national name."[46] Among other tribes controlled by the Alans were some Slavic tribes, and at least one of them, the Antes, assumed the name of their new rulers: for Antes, as we have seen,[47] was the name of one of the Alanic tribes in Turkestan. In the same way, after the Alans established their rule in northern Caucasus they likewise must have incorporated some of the native tribes into their state. Thus the Caucasian tribe of Ossetians, or Os, alias As, are probably of mixed Alano-Japhetide origin.

The native tribes of the North Caucasian area conquered by the Alans were well acquainted with iron forging. Subsequently the Alans themselves developed considerable skill in forging weapons, and the tradition was later kept alive by the Antes.

43. See Sec. 2, above.
44. Ammianus Marcellinus, XXXI, 2, 21.
45. M. Rostovtzeff, "Bog-Vsadnik," *SK, 1* (1927), 141-146.
46. Ammianus Marcellinus, XXXI, 2, 13.
47. See Sec. 2, above.

4. *The Bosporan Kingdom and the Greek Cities on the Northern Shores of the Black Sea.*[48]

The troubled period of struggle between the Scythians and the Sarmatians in South Russia (third and second centuries B.C.) affected painfully the life of the Greek cities in the Taurida. Receding slowly before the drive of the Sarmatians, part of the Scythians retreated to the Taurida, where they mixed with the native tribe of the Tauri to become known as the Tauro-Scythae. By the end of the second century B.C. the Tauro-Scythae were compelled to recognize the supreme authority of the Sarmatian tribe of the Roxolani. The independence of Cherson and Panticapaeum, as well as of the other Greek cities in the Taurida, was now seriously threatened.

Unable to rely upon their own forces, the Greeks of the Taurida were obliged to look for assistance to some outside quarter. The nearest power they could think of was the kingdom of Pontus on the south shore of the Black Sea in Asia Minor. In the third and second centuries B.C. this kingdom was merely one of the second-rate Hellenistic states of the Near East. Its rapid ascent started at the end of the second century B.C. with the accession to the throne of Mithradates VI (113 B.C.).[49] The new king was a man of powerful vitality and great ambition, the creation of a world monarchy being his ultimate goal. The request for assistance on the part of the Taurida Greeks excellently suited his plans of extending his control over the northern shores of the Black Sea, in order to get access to the vast resources of South Russia.

Mithradates was consequently pleased to send to the Taurida one of his best generals, Diophantes, with a brigade of well-trained hoplites six thousand strong. It was high time to stop the advance of the Tauro-Scythae if Cherson was to be saved from them. The Tauro-Scythae were led by the energetic Palakus, son of the Scythian king Skilurus; both father and son were vassals of the Roxolani and their combined possessions stretched from the Taurida to Olbia. Having received news of the landing of Diophantes' troops

48. Minns; Rostovtzeff, *Iranians and Greeks; idem,* "The Bosporan Kingdom," *CAH,* VIII, chap. xviii; *idem, Hellenistic World,* especially pp. 585-587 and 594-602; *idem, Roman Empire, passim; idem, Skythien; idem, Zhivopis.*

49. M. Rostovtzeff and H. A. Ormerod, "Pontus and Its Neighbors," *CAH,* IX, chap. v; see also Rostovtzeff, *Hellenistic World,* chap. vii.

near Cherson (110 B.C.), Palakus asked his suzerain Tasius, king of the Roxolani, for help. The latter sent some troops to the Taurida, but they were no match for Diophantes' hoplites. The war was fought in the hilly region of the southern Crimea where the Roxolani had no room to deploy their cavalry. Diophantes not only succeeded in beating off their attack on Cherson but compelled them to retreat north, after which he subdued the Tauri (108 B.C.). Having secured the safety of Cherson, Diophantes moved his troops to the eastern part of the Crimean peninsula in order to remove the Scytho-Sarmatian danger from Panticapaeum. As the price of their "liberation from the Barbarians" both Panticapaeum and Cherson were obliged to recognize the royal authority of Mithradates. In this way Mithradates became king of the Bosporus while Cherson, which had not previously been a part of the Bosporan kingdom was now drawn into it (106 B.C.).

With the establishment of control over Taurida, Mithradates was now involved in the network of intricate diplomatic intrigues of the Mediterranean world, since before long a protracted struggle developed between himself and Rome.

After experiencing many vicissitudes of fortune Mithradates lost most of his dominions and had to fall back upon the Bosporus as his last stand. But the arm of Rome reached him even there, and Roman diplomacy succeeded in sponsoring an uprising of the natives against him led by his own son, Pharnaces. The old king had no alternative but suicide (62 B.C.).

Pharnaces in his turn was killed by the native chieftain Asander, who was recognized by Rome as the "archon" of the Bosporus. In order to legalize his authority in local public opinion Asander married Pharnaces' daughter Dynamis, after which he assumed the royal title (41 B.C.). The period of Asander's reign spelled a lull in the troublesome history of the Bosporan kingdom.

However, in 16 B.C. new troubles began, probably not without some further intrigue by Rome, where the growing authority of Asander was looked upon with some suspicion, as a result of which Roman support was promised to a rival chieftain. The following years brought much unrest, and changes on the throne. The troubles were partly the result of the clash of interests between the Greeks, the Maeotae, and the Sarmatians, and partly due to the personal ambitions of Queen Dynamis who married each new pretendant to the throne in turn. It was only under the rule of Aspurgos, probably Dynamis' fourth husband,[50] that things quieted down.

After Dynamis' death (7 B.C.) Aspurgos married a Thracian princess. Their son Cotys (king from A.D. 49) was the founder of the new Bosporan dynasty, which was more connected both culturally and personally with the Thracian and the Iranian than with the Greek world. Life at the court of the Bosporan monarchs was rapidly assuming new aspects, and some later Bosporan coins portray the ruler in the heavy dress of an Iranian king.[51]

Rome gave her full support to both Cotys and his successors, since the control of the northeastern corner of the Black Sea had great strategic value for the Roman emperors. The Taurida served as an advance post which enabled them on one hand to watch the movements of the nomads in the South Russian steppes and on the other to protect the rear of their operations in Transcaucasia.

The invasion, first of the Goths in the third century A.D., and then of the Huns in the fourth century, severed for some time the political ties between the Bosporus and the Empire and it was only in the age of Justinian I (527–65) that the Empire (now known as the Byzantine) was again able to restore its control in Panticapaeum, which subsequently assumed the new name of Kerch.

The economic foundation of the Bosporan kingdom was of the same type as in Scythian times. Wheat was the staple product. It was both raised locally and imported from the steppes beyond the Sea of Azov. Grain constituted likewise the chief item of export. The king himself was the biggest dealer in grain. A number of lesser dealers had their offices in Panticapaeum. Members of the native aristocracy had large land estates in the neighborhood of the city where they usually spent their summers living in the traditional tents of nomads, supervising their field workers and ready to protect them in case of any raid from the north.

There was a considerable artisan population in the cities, engaged in various handicrafts. The Hellenistic civilization was gradually losing ground with the people. Greek was still spoken but chiefly as an official language. Iranian dialects were replacing it in the homes. Greek costume likewise gave way to Iranian fashions. As to religious life, the cult of the Heavenly Aphrodite, representing the

50. Rostovtzeff, "Queen Dynamis," *JHS, 39* (1919), 103.
51. See Rostovtzeff, p. 159.

Great Goddess of Asia Minor, was especially popular. From the end of the first century A.D. the influence of Judaism became noticeable due to the influx of Jewish settlers. Christianity came much later—around the fourth century. The formation of a strong Judaic community on the Bosporus was to have important repercussions in the future, since it formed the background for the expansion of Judaism among the Khazars in the eighth and the ninth centuries, of which more will be said later.[52]

The whole political structure of the Bosporan kingdom underwent profound changes. Former democratic institutions disappeared leaving few traces. The government became known as the "Sublime Porte" and assumed a bureaucratic character not unlike that of the Persian kingdom or the Byzantine Empire. Civil administration was separated from the military, the former headed by a "Protector of the Realm" (ὁ ἐπὶ τῆς Βασιλείας), and the latter by a "Commander of the Thousand" (χιλίαρχος).

We turn now to Cherson. As we have seen, at the end of the second century B.C. Cherson together with Panticapaeum recognized the authority of Mithradates VI. Later on, Roman control was established over the whole of the Taurida, and Cherson received a "charter of freedom" from Rome which meant that she became autonomous with regard to the Bosporan kingdom (24 B.C.).

It was Rome who now assumed the task of protecting Cherson from her enemies. When in the course of the first century A.D. pressure from the nomads again became menacing, a Roman general from the Danubian provinces came to the rescue of Cherson (A.D. 62). The city became an outlying Roman fort and the Roman navy used its harbor as a base for its galleys.

Under the Roman protectorate the economic life of Cherson developed fairly well, agriculture remaining its foundation. The period of the second and third centuries A.D. was one of moderate but steady progress. The troubles of the fourth and fifth centuries checked economic expansion and made the task of defense paramount. We shall see in due course that the city was able to adapt herself to the new political conditions and maintained her authority for a few centuries more.

As to the spiritual life of the population, the early penetration of

52. See Chap. VII, Sec. 6, and Chap. VIII, Sec. 5.

Christianity was the most important factor. Cherson was used by the Roman administration during its struggle against Christianity as a place of exile for some outstanding Christian leaders, and by the time of Emperor Constantine's edict granting recognition to the Christian church (A.D. 312) there was already a strong Christian community in the city.

While both Cherson and the Bosporan kingdom were able to hold their ground throughout the Sarmatian period, Olbia was less fortunate. Around the year 50 B.C. the city was plundered by the Getae, a Thracian tribe. It was later restored and recognized the authority of Rome, being included in the Roman province of lower Moesia (end of the second century A.D.). The Goths plundered it again in the third century. Under such circumstances it is small wonder that the city was never able to recover its former prosperity of Scythian times.

5. *The Legacy of the Iranian Age in Russian History.*

The Iranian period was one of fundamental importance for the subsequent development of Russian civilization. Indelible traces of Iranian influence still exist on the map of Russia, since in numerous instances the geographic names, of South Russia especially, are derived from the Iranian language. We likewise find derivatives from the Iranian in the languages of both the Slavs and the Finns, in various terms of household and husbandry. Moreover, as we shall see,[53] it was the Iranians who laid the foundations of the political organization of the Eastern Slavs.

The art of old Russia was likewise permeated by Iranian motifs. In the Russian folk (peasant) art and handicrafts, Iranian traditions have been kept almost to our own day.

Aside from their immediate contact with both the Slavs and the Finns, the Iranians occupying the steppes of South Russia served also as an intermediary link between the Greek and the Persian civilizations on the one hand and the peoples of central and northern Russia on the other.

It was due to the facilities of commercial intercourse established through the Bosporan kingdom that objects of both Parthian and Sassanian origin found their way north up the Volga River, which

53. See Secs. 7 and 8, below.

explains for example the fact that so many silver dishes of Graeco-Bactrian and Sassanian craftsmanship have been found in the southern Ural region.[54]

Let us first examine the toponymic traces left by the Iranians in Russia.[55] The name of the river Don is characteristic. *Don* means "water," "river" in Ossetian (*dan* in old Iranian). The name Dunai (Danube) is from the same root. Likewise, the first part of the names Dnepr (Dnieper) and Dniestr (Dniester) are derived from the root *don.* According to Pliny, the Scythians called the river Tanais (Donets-Don) "Sin."[56] This is another Iranian word for "river." A. I. Sobolevskii suggests that the name Tsna (Sna) is derived from "Sin." There are several rivers named Tsna: a tributary of the Volga, a tributary of the Msta, two tributaries of the Dnieper, and a tributary of the Vistula. The name of the Tor, a tributary of the Donets, is to be derived from the Iranian root *tur,* "to drive." The Russian verb *proturit* ("to drive off," "chase away") comes from the same root. This is also one of the components of the name Trubezh, a river tributary to the Dnieper. The old name of the Dniester, Tyras (τύρας in Greek transcription), belongs to the same group. The name of the Styr, a tributary of the Pripet, may be compared with the Ossetian *styr* ("great," "strong"). In another dialect it becomes *khtyr,* cf. Akhtyrka, Kharkov province. The name of the river Khalan, a tributary of the Oskol which in its turn is a tributary of the Donets, reflects the tribal name of the Alans (Halani, in Ammianus Marcellinus' transcription).

The companion tribal name, As, has been preserved in many local names in South Russia, as will be later shown in a different connection.[57] The old name of the town of Sudak in the Crimea, Sugdaea, is derived from the Iranian adjective *sugda* ("pure," "sainted").[58] It is probable that the name Ros (alias Rus) also dates from the Iranian period. The Volga River is called Rhos (Ῥῶς) by an anonymous Greek author of a geographic treatise compiled in the fifth century A.D.[59]

Some of the Arabic and Persian writers of the ninth and tenth

54. Ya. I. Smirnov, *Vostochnoe Serebro* (St. Petersburg, 1905); Trever, *Pamiatniki.*
55. Cf. Sobolevskii, I-II; Vasmer, *Iranier.*
56. Pliny, VI, 20.
57. See Chap. IV, Secs. 6 and 8.
58. Miller, *Sledy,* p. 240.
59. Latyshev, I, 295; cf. Smirnov, p. 8.

centuries A.D. call the Don River the "Russian River" (*nahr ar-Rusiya*).[60] According to Narbut the Oskol, a tributary of the Donets, was known in old times as Ros.[61] One of the tributaries of the Dnieper is called Ros even now. In a Russian geography of the seventeenth century, the so-called *Book of the Great Delineation* (*Kniga Bolshomu Chertezhu*), Rusa, a tributary to Seim, is mentioned.[62] It seems probable that the name Rsha (Orsha) is likewise connected with the name Ros: Orsha, a tributary of the Dnieper; Rsha, in the old Chernigov principality; and Rsha, a tributary of the Sula. As a special group, rivers with the name of Ros or Rus in the northwestern area may be mentioned. According to Narbut, a middle section of the river Nieman was in old times known as Ros; also the right channel of the lower Nieman. A tributary of the Narev and a tributary of the Szesczup are also called Ros.[63]

The origin of the name Ros, or Rus, is not definitely established. Some students of linguistics derive it from the conjectural Aryan *ronsa,* meaning "moisture," "water." [64] Hence allegedly the Russian word *rosa* ("dew"). Personally, I incline to a different explanation of the name. As we have seen,[65] the Sarmatian tribes of Aorsi and Roxolani spread as early as the second century B.C. over the area of the Volga, Don, Donets, and Dnieper rivers. The names of these tribes may be derived from the Iranian words *ors,* or *uors* ("white"), and *rukhs* ("light"). It seems fairly plausible that some rivers in the area of expansion of these tribes should become known under the tribal names of the settlers. However, the possibility of the dual derivation of these names must also not be overlooked. The Iranian tribal name may have been rationalized by the native Slavs with the help of their own language (Ros from *rosa*). Dual origin of certain names and terms occurs very often in the folklore of various peoples, and especially in Russian folklore. Neither the Roxolani nor the Aorsi could possibly have reached as far as the Nieman and Vistula, but there may have been some commercial intercourse between the Ros people of the upper Donets and the lower Dnieper basin on

60. It must be noted that some scholars referred the "Russian River" of the Oriental authors to the Volga, and not to the Don. Cf. Minorsky, pp. 41, 75, 216-218, 316.

61. Gedeonov, II, 421.

62. Kniga, p. 91.

63. Gedeonov, II, 421.

64. F. Knauer, "Der russische Nationalname und die indogermanische Urheimat," *IF, 81* (1912-13), 67-70.

65. See Sec. 3, above.

one hand, and the Nieman and the Vistula basin on the other; which may have resulted in the expansion of the name Ros to the north. Still, it seems more probable that names such as Ros and Rus appeared in the northern region in a later period, that of the Goths or even of the Varangians.

From the traces of Iranian culture found in the toponymics let us now turn to vocabulary.[66] A number of Russian and Ukrainian words, such as *khata* ("house"), *sharovary* ("loose pants"), *topor* ("ax"), *sobaka* ("dog"), were borrowed from the Iranian. In my opinion, it is likewise from the Iranian that the old Russian word *smerd* ("man of lower class," "peasant") is to be derived, cf. Iranian *mard* ("man"). We have mentioned previously,[67] that some Yue-chi (Tokharian) detachments may have penetrated to South Russia together with the Alans. In this connection it should be recalled that the Russian vocabulary has at least one word apparently borrowed from the Tokharian, to wit, *slon* ("elephant"), cf. the Tokharian *klon.*[68]

The dependence of the Russian vocabulary upon certain Iranian and possibly Tokharian roots is interesting not only from the point of view of linguistics, but also because of its implications as to the path of cultural progress. It is obvious from the above examples that the cultural legacy of the Iranian period manifests itself in various aspects of the life of the early Slavs and Rus, as expressed in dwelling (*khata*), dress (*sharovary*), tools (*topor*), domestic animals (*sobaka*), social organization (*smerd*). We may assume that it was likewise through the Iranians that the old Rus became acquainted with the Near-Eastern measures of length and weight.[69] The measures of weight common to the whole Near East in the Sarmatian period were based upon the Babylonian, and there is a close coordination between the old Russian and the Babylonian systems of weight. Thus the old Russian "large *grivenka,*" later known as the Russian pound, corresponded to the Babylonian mina, and the Russian *pud* to the Babylonian talent.

Old Russian measures of length are equivalents of the so-called Philetaeric scale which was adopted in the Hellenistic realm of

66. See Melioranskii, I-III; Miklosich, I, III-IV; Vernadsky, *Zvenya,* p. 16 f.

67. See Secs. 2 and 3, above.

68. The parallel was suggested to me by the late Edward Sapir.

69. N. T. Beliaev, "O drevnikh i nyneshnikh Russkikh merakh protiazheniia i vesa," *SK, 1* (1927), 247-288.

Pergamon, Asia Minor, in the third century B.C. The Pergamene measures start with the "finger" (0.5 of the Russian *vershok*). The "step" of the Pergamene scale is equal to the Russian *arshin*. The Russian *sazhen* corresponds to the Pergamene "rod." Following the spread of Roman control over the Near East, Pergamene measures of length were somewhat coördinated with the Roman scale, and thus a Pergamene "mile" was established to comprise 1,000 steps. It is interesting to note in this connection that while in modern times the Russian *versta* comprises 500 *sazhen*, the old Russian *versta* was equal to 1,000 *sazhen*.

Let us now turn to the tradition of the Iranian period as reflected in Russian folk art. The problem is very involved. There cannot be any doubt that some patterns of this folk art, such as the embroidery work, show a striking similarity to Iranian motifs; however, we must bear in mind that Iranian motifs could have penetrated into Russian folk art at a later time through some intermediary patterns, whether western or oriental. The intermediary links in the development of Russian folk art have not as yet been sufficiently studied.

Altogether, however, we may suppose that the foundation of Russian folk art was laid during the Iranian period. Let us take, for example, the clay toys of Russian peasant art.[70] The chief subjects represented are: woman, the horse—as well as some other animals, the bull, deer, goat, and bear—and the bird. Man is portrayed very rarely and only as an appendage to the horse. The repertory of subject matter is certainly not accidental. It may be explained as a legacy from pre-Christian times, more precisely from the period of Iranian control over the Slavs. The horse, the bull, the goat, and the bear, all played an important role in the rites and mythology of the ancient Slavs. The bird had a special significance in Iranian mythology.[71]

The exclusive place of woman in the subject matter of old Russian toys is likewise to be explained by the ancient Irano-Alarodian cult of the Mother Goddess; otherwise the Great Goddess.[72] The worship of feminine deities by the Scythians is mentioned by Herodotus.[73] It is characteristic that clay figurines similar to the later Russian toys have been found in some of the old Kievan burial sites

70. See L. A. Dintses, *Russkaia glinianaia igrushka* (Moscow-Leningrad, 1936).
71. See Sec. 8, below.
72. Rostovtzeff, pp. 33-34, 72-73.
73. Herodotus, IV, 59.

(*gorodishcha*). Among the subjects of these figurines, woman, the horse, and the bird play an important role. The sites in question may be dated from the sixth to the thirteenth centuries A.D. Similar figurines were found in the Gnezdovo funeral sites at Smolensk, of the seventh to tenth centuries.[74] Some such figurines—as one bird found at Toporok in the upper Volga region—were undoubtedly used in pagan rites and ceremonies, possibly as symbolic offering. Others may have been used as amulets.

The image of the Great Mother of Iranian times is likewise a prominent motif in old Russian embroidery.[75] The woman, in these embroideries, is always represented standing in the center of the picture, always facing the onlooker in the characteristic Parthian manner. In the upper part of the typical picture two swastika symbols are usually placed, representing obviously the sun and the moon. The horses which are usually embroidered on either side of the woman have apparently also a symbolic meaning, since there are usually swastika signs beneath their hoofs. In some cases deer are represented instead of horses; occasionally, the lion and the panther occur. Such embroideries form interesting parallels to certain objects of Scythian and Sarmatian art. The famous gold plaque of the tiara from the Karagodeuashkh Kurgan, as well as the fragments of a drinking horn—the *rhyton*—from Merdjany in the Kuban region, may be mentioned here.[76] Dacian votive plaques of the second and third centuries A.D. are also interesting in this connection.[77]

6. *The Western and Northern Neighbors of the Sarmatians.*

With the invasion of the Sarmatians the proportion of Iranian stock in the population of the Pontic steppes was greatly increased. However, the ethnic composition of the native population underwent no complete change. It was the Scythians who had to bear the brunt of the blow. Even they were not all expelled or exterminated; as we have seen, part of them were allowed to remain in the Taurida after recognizing the authority of the Roxolani. Having taken from the

74. Dintses (as in n. 70), p. 29 f.
75. Gorodtsov.
76. Rostovtzeff, Plate XXIII. See also Rostovtzeff "Predstavlenie o monarkhicheskoi vlasti v Skifii i na Bospore," *AK, 49* (1913), 9 ff.
77. Gorodtsov; Rostovtzeff, "Une tablette votive thraco-mithriaque du Louvre," *AIM, 13* (1933), 385-408.

Scythians their control over the native tribes in South Russia, the Sarmatians had no intention of exterminating them. Part of these tribes had to move to less fertile regions to make room for the newcomers; others, on the contrary, took advantage of the disintegration of the Scythian realm to take possession of better lands. After a while a certain balance of tribes was established, only to be upset later on by the invasions of the Goths.

Among the names of tribes of Sarmatia as mentioned by contemporary Latin and Greek authors we may find some which have been familiar from Herodotus' time. Whether the tribes themselves are identical with those mentioned by Herodotus is hard to tell, because in many cases, authors of the third or fourth century A.D. used the ancient historians' names for the sake of keeping up the classical tradition. However, in addition to the tribal names mentioned by Herodotus, new names appear in the historical and geographical literature of the Sarmatian period.

In his famous book on Germany, written in A.D. 98, Tacitus mentions three tribes as located "between the Germans and the Sarmatians," to wit: the Peucini (alias Bastarnai), the Venedi, and the Fenni.[78] Tacitus himself is not certain whether these tribes are to be classified as German or Sarmatian. In the case of the Bastarnai he is inclined to consider them Germans—which is also the opinion of modern scholars. As to the Venedi, he likewise points to features in their way of life which relate them to the Germans rather than to the Sarmatians. The Venedi, remarks Tacitus, build houses, use shields, move about on foot; all this is different from the habits of the Sarmatians who live in tents and on horseback. It is now accepted that Tacitus' Venedi must be considered Slavs. According to Tacitus they lived between the Peucini and the Fenni. The latter are undoubtedly to be identified as the Finns. According to Tacitus the Finns were exceedingly wild and poor. While he knew of the Finns only by hearsay, his remark that Finnish arrowheads are made of bone and not of iron is corroborated by archaeological evidence, which shows that his informants were fairly reliable.

For the brief survey of the peoples and tribes "between the Germans and the Sarmatians" which follows we may use Tacitus' plan: that is to start with the region of the lower Danube, then turning to western Russia, and finally to the Finnish north.

78. Tacitus, *Germania,* 46.

The region of the lower Danube was, from the second century B.C., controlled by the German tribe of Bastarnai who dominated over the neighboring Thracian tribes. Of the latter only the Getae and the Daci kept a certain degree of autonomy. Around 50 B.C. the Getae, as we have already mentioned,[79] raided Olbia. When the Roman Empire extended its boundaries to the Balkan peninsula, the Romans were faced with the problem of protecting the banks of the Danube from the inroads of the Germans, the Daci, and the Sarmatians. In the course of the first century A.D. they were on the defensive. At the end of this century, however, because of the constant inroads of the Daci, Emperor Trajan decided to send troops across the Danube to destroy the enemy forces at their bases. Two campaigns (A.D. 101–2 and 105–6) proved sufficient to crush the resistance of the Daci, and Dacia became a Roman province. In addition to Roman garrisons stationed at strategic points, agricultural colonists were settled in the new province. As a result, the Latin tongue began to spread rapidly among the population of Dacia as was the case in both Spain and Gaul under similar circumstances. It is to the Roman colonization of the Balkans in the second and third centuries A.D. that the origins of the Rumanian language are to be referred.

Dacia remained a Roman province for less than two centuries. Even as early as the year 174 Emperor Marcus Aurelius had to admit the German tribe of Vandals into the northwestern part of Dacia, and provide them with land. In the middle of the third century Dacia became the object of numerous inroads by the Goths and the Gepidae. In 268 the emperor Probus decided to abandon the province and began its evacuation by moving one hundred thousand Bastarnai to Thrace. Probus' successor Aurelianus ordered the Roman troops back to the southern bank of the Danube, which became again the boundary of the Empire. The retreat of the army gave the signal for the exodus of Roman colonists, most of whom likewise moved to Thrace.

From the peoples of the region of the lower Danube, let us now turn, following Tacitus, to the tribes of the Vistula basin: the Venedi or Venethi. They were undoubtedly Slavs; we may identify them more precisely as the western branch of the Slavs. The area occupied by the Venedi in the first and the second centuries A.D.

79. See Sec. 4, above.

may be defined as Galicia, Volynia, and Little Poland. According to Jordanis, who wrote in the sixth century, the "populous race of Venethi" dwelt on the northern slopes of the Carpathian Mountains, at the source of the Vistula River; they occupied "a great expanse of land."[80] As peoples kindred to the Venethi Jordanis mentions the Sclaveni and the Antes. These two represent the eastern branches of the Slavs, and will be dealt with later.[81] From the archaeological point of view the territory of the Venedi should be connected with the area of the fields of funeral urns.

To the northeast of the Venedi Jordanis places the Aestii,[82] a people of Baltic (Lithuanian) origin not to be confused with the Ests, a Finnish tribe. Among the Finns, Jordanis mentions the Thiudos (*Chud* in Old Russian), the Merens (Russian *Meria*), and the Mordens (Russian, *Mordva*).[83] The boundaries of expansion of the various tribes of the northwest were thrown into confusion by the migration of the Goths.[84] In the first century A.D. the Goths, coming from Scandinavia, settled in the basin of the lower Vistula River. They are mentioned in turn by Pliny,[85] Tacitus,[86] and Ptolemy,[87] and their intrusion into the lower Vistula area must have resulted in migrations of the native tribes. Part of the Aestii had apparently to move further east. In the second half of the second century A.D. the Goths migrated farther south, to the Dnieper and the Black Sea region. Their march must have disturbed additional sections of both the Venedi and the Balts.

In the middle of the fourth century the Gothic king Ermenrich (A.D. *ca.* 350–70) attempted to conquer most of the tribes of central and northern Russia. Among the peoples he subdued, Jordanis notes the three above-mentioned Finnish tribes (Thiudos, Merens, and Mordens), as well as the Aestii, the Venedi, the Sclaveni, and the Antes. Unable to withstand Ermenrich's attack, the Venedi and the Sclaveni retreated farther to the north. It was probably at this juncture that a tribe of the Sclaveni migrated from the middle

80. Jordanis, Sec. 34. This and subsequent quotations in English are adapted from C. C. Mierow's translation.

81. See Sec. 7, below.

82. Jordanis, Sec. 36.

83. Jordanis, Sec. 116. For the identification of "Thiudos," "Merens," "Mordens" see Zeuss, pp. 688-689; cf. Mommsen, p. 165.

84. The standard work on the history of the Goths is L. Schmidt's *Ostgermanen.*

85. Pliny, IV, 99.

86. Tacitus, *Germania,* 43.

87. Ptolemy, III, 5, 8.

Dnieper area up the Dnieper River, to settle finally around Lake Ilmen.[88] As a result of this northern march of the Sclaveni, the Balts were cut into two sections: a western one, between Polotsk and the Gulf of Riga, and an eastern one, located in the region of the upper Oka River. The tribe of the Galindi, known to the Russian chronicles of the twelfth century as the Goliad, must be considered the remnants of the eastern section of the Balts.[89]

7. *Eastern Slavs in the Sarmatian Period.*

In the preceding paragraphs we have offered a brief survey of the western and northern neighbors of the Sarmatians, in the order in which these tribes are mentioned by Tacitus. We have dealt with the western branch of the Slavs known to Tacitus as Venedi. No other Slavic tribe is mentioned by him, because their abodes from his point of view were within the boundaries of Sarmatia proper, and he consequently did not differentiate those tribes from the Sarmatians. Yet for our purpose it is the eastern Slavic tribes which must command our full attention.

The Gothic historian Jordanis mentions three main groups of the Slavs, calling them the Venethi, the Sclaveni, and the Antes, respectively.[90] He also adds that single Slavic tribes and clans are also known under various other names. Another historian of the sixth century, Procopius of Caesarea, was interested in the Slavs only in so far as they came into contact with Byzantium. For this reason Procopius omits the Venedi and speaks only of the Sclaveni and the Antes (Antae). According to this writer both Sclaveni and Antes were originally known under a common name, as the Spori. Procopius derives this from the Greek root σπορ which means "dispersion" (cf. "diaspora").[91] The explanation is hardly valid, but the name deserves attention. "Spori" may be compared with the name Spoli or Spali, a people of the Pontic steppes mentioned by Jordanis; [92] the name is given as Spalei by Pliny.[93] According to Pliny the Spalei used to live in the basin of the Tanais River (Donets-Don). The

88. M. Vasmer, "Die aelteste Bevoelkerungsverhaeltnisse," *Geistige Arbeit* (November 5, 1937), p. 2.

89. Vasmer, *Beitraege,* I.

90. Jordanis, Sec. 34.

91. Procopius, VII, 14, 29.

92. Jordanis, Sec. 28.

93. Pliny, VI, 22.

name of the tributary of the Donets, the Oskol, seems to reflect that of a people mentioned by both Pliny and Jordanis (Oskol or Ospol).[94] According to Jordanis' narrative the Goths attacked the Spali after having crossed a big river, presumably the Dnieper.[95] Moving eastward from the region of Kiev, the Goths must next have reached the Oskol and Donets region, and it is thus in the Oskol area that they must have encountered the Spali.

We must now take into consideration that Procopius places the tribes of the eastern section of the Antes "above" the Utiguri, that is, north of the Sea of Azov, presumably in the Donets-Don region.[96] Thus the eastern branch of the Antes lived in the sixth century in about the area where the Goths met the Spali in the second century. The obvious conclusion is that the eastern Antes were, topographically at least, the successors of the Spali. There is also an interesting linguistic parallel between the names Spali and Antes, with regard to their respective semasiology. The Slavic word *ispolin* ("giant") is to be derived from the name Spoli.[97] On the other hand, the old Anglo-Saxon word *etna* ("giant") seems to be a metathesis of the name *enta* (Antes).[98] It is probable that by Spali, or Giants, the Donets Slavs meant the Alanic tribe which occupied the Donets basin in the first century A.D. and established its control over the natives.[99] We may recall in this connection that in the Mingrelian language the word *alan* means "strong," "brave," [100] which is close to the Slavic *ispolin* ("giant"). The name of the Alanic clan of Spoli, or Spali, may have later applied to the native Slavic tribes controlled by the Alans. In this way, Procopius' information that the Slavs were originally known as Spori may be explained.

Let us now turn to the Antes. We have seen[101] that this was

94. Dr. R. Jakobson, while accepting my identification of the Spori as Spali, has expressed his doubts as to the validity of the parallel Oskol—Ospol (see Dr. Jakobson's letter to me of February 2, 1942). Irrespective of the problem of the linguistic affiliations, there is every reason to connect geographically both the Spali and the eastern Antes (As) with the Oskol region. Cf. also the name Askal, mentioned by Ibn-Fadhlan (see Chap. VI, Sec. 3).

95. See Sec. 9, below.

96. Procopius, VIII, 4, 9.

97. Berneker, I, 434.

98. Cf. *Beowulf*, I, 2979; A. Olrik, *Ragnarok* (Berlin & Leipzig, 1922) pp. 475 ff.; Vernadsky, *Goten*, p. 15.

99. See Sec. 3, above.

100. Abaev, p. 833.

101. See Sec. 2, above.

another form of the name As, or Alans. While Pliny and Pomponius Mela (first century A.D.) mention the Anti, Ptolemy (second century A.D.) renders the name as Ἄσιοι and Stephen of Byzantium (fifth century A.D.) as Ἀσσαῖοι. We may suppose that the Antes, or As, came to the Azov region at the time of the general migration of the Alans, in the first and second centuries A.D. Later on, they were known to the Russian chroniclers as Asy or Iasy (the modern Ossetians). The As are likewise mentioned by a number of medieval travelers, among others by Rubruquis.[102] Since the As or Alans spread early to the Taurida as well, it is no wonder that we find the name Antas in one of the Kerch inscriptions of the third century A.D.[103] We now recall Ammianus Marcellinus' statement that the Alans incorporated the peoples whom they conquered under their own national name.[104] Thus the group of Slavs conquered by the As may have assumed the name of their new rulers. We may thus explain why, at the time of Jordanis and Procopius, the name Antes was applied to the eastern branch of the Slavs.

That both Jordanis and Procopius speak of the Antes (or Antae) rather than the As, may be likewise elucidated if we remember the form "Antas" of the Kerch inscription. The transmutation of the Ἆς into Ἄντες is in full accord with the phonetic laws of the Greek language, cf. γίγας, plural γίγαντες. It is noteworthy that in modern Greek, from the plural γίγαντες a new singular has been formed: γίγαντας. Likewise, from the original Ἆς first the plural Ἄντες may have been formed, and then as a secondary derivation, the singular Ἄντας.[105] Thus Procopius' Antes should be considered a Slavic tribe controlled by the Alanic clan of As. In other words, the Antes were Aso-Slavs. In Procopius' time they were divided into two branches: the eastern, in the Donets region; and the western, in Bessarabia. Jordanis knows only the western Antes. According to his information, they lived at the bend of the Pontic shore between the Dniester and the Danube.[106] It was in this locality that the Goths attacked the Antes around 376.[107] We may assume that they had settled there long before the Gothic attack.

102. See Vernadsky, *Origins*, p. 62.
103. *IPE*, II, No. 29; cf. Ἄντης ἀνήρ, Agathias, III, 21, p. 275.
104. Ammianus Marcellinus, XXXI, 2, 13.
105. Vernadsky, *Origins*, p. 63.
106. Jordanis, Sec. 35.
107. See Chap. IV, Sec. 2.

In Langobard annals of the seventh century, for which some older traditions were undoubtedly used, a country of Anthaib is mentioned through which the Langobardi are supposed to have marched on their way from the Baltic to Pannonia.[108] It has been suggested that the name Anthaib should be explained as the Land of the Antes.[109] The reference to Anthaib is not quite clear, however.[110] The Langobardi could hardly have ever reached either the lower Dnieper or the Southern Bug. Still, there is nothing against the surmise that at the time they were in Transylvania they may have entered into negotiations with the Antes and sent envoys to them. Such intercourse between the Langobardi and the Antes might have taken place at any time between the end of the second and the beginning of the fourth century A.D. Thus, if we give any credit to the Langobard tradition, we may conjecture that the Antes, or rather their western branch, settled in the Bug region not later than in the third century A.D. and possibly earlier. In my opinion, the settlement of the Antes in the Bug region may be referred to the period of the Alanic migration, that is to the second century A.D.

The two groups of the Antes, as mentioned before, were probably in older times more closely connected. The western or Bug group occupied the region between the Dnieper and the Bug, while the eastern, or Donets group, settled in the region between the Dnieper and the Donets. The junction of the two groups was probably in the cataract section of the Dnieper River. The Gothic invasion, cutting between the two Antic groups, separated them from each other, but later on they got in touch once more.[111] As we know,[112] one of the clans of the Iranian Antes or As was known as the Light As (Rukhs-As). Later, the Slavic tribes subordinated to the Rukhs clan must have assumed this name. In the list of tribes conquered by Ermenrich,[113] we find the name Rocas (Rogas). This is probably another transcription of the name Rukhs-As (Roc-As). Another tribe mentioned by Jordanis which may bear on the problem is that of the Rosomoni.[114] According to Jordanis the Rosomoni re-

108. "Scriptores Rerum Langobardorum," *MGH* (1878), pp. 3, 54.
109. Niederle, IV, 72-73.
110. Cf. Muellenhoff, p. 98.
111. See Chap. IV, Sec. 8.
112. See Sec. 3, above.
113. See Sec. 8, below.
114. Jordanis, Sec. 129.

volted against Ermenrich shortly before the Hunnic invasion. It is possible that the name in Jordanis' record, if not mutilated by oral tradition, is another form or pronunciation of the name Roxolani.[115] The original *Rukhs* might in some local dialects, Slavic among others, sound as Rohs, Ross, or Rus, in the light of which the origins of the Greek ʽΡῶς and Slavic Rus may be understood.

Let us now turn to the Sclaveni. If the Antes lived in the Donets and the Bug regions, and the Venedi in the upper Vistula region, it may be suggested that the Sclaveni originally occupied the territory between them: that is, the area between the Carpathian Mountains and the middle Dnieper, chiefly in the Kiev region. A section of the Sclaveni, as we have seen, due to pressure by Ermenrich went north and ultimately settled around Lake Ilmen. The bulk of the Sclaveni must have remained, however, in their old abodes, being subject to the Goths and later to the Huns. By the end of the fifth century they started their migration to the lower Danube.

Two other tribes which were possibly likewise of Slavic origin—the Navari and the Borani—lived in the region of the Sea of Azov. Ptolemy (second century A.D.) locates the town of Navar (Ναύαρσν) in the basin of the river Karkinit,[116] which may perhaps be identified as either Utliuk or Tokmak in northern Tauria.[117] According to V. F. Miller, the name Navar derives from the Iranian *nau* ("boat");[118] consequently we may conclude that the Navars were boat builders and seamen. Since neither the Iranians nor the Turks ever showed inclination for shipping or navigation, the Navars may be considered Slavs rather than either Iranians or Turks. The Borani are mentioned in some sources of the Gothic period (third century A.D.) as daring seamen.[119] They lived somewhere in the lower Don region. The name sounds Slavic—*boran,* now spelt *baran,*

115. See, however, Hrushevskyi, I, 497. Markwart (pp. 365 f.) suggests the connection between the name Rosomoni and the name Hros cited by Zechariah the Rhetor. On the Hros see below, Chap. VI, Sec. 8.

116. Ptolemy, III, 5, 13.

117. According to Latyshev's reconstruction of Ptolemy's map, the Karkinit discharges into the Black Sea west of the Perekop Isthmus, but there is actually no river comparably large in that locality; we may suppose therefore that the river Ptolemy had in mind discharged into the Sea of Azov.

118. Miller, *Sledy,* p. 242.

119. See Sec. 9, below. It must be noted that while Zosimus has "Borani" (Βορανοί) in the *Chronicon Paschale* (I, 57) the name reads "Borades" (Βοράδες); cf. also Vasiliev, pp. 4-5.

means "ram" in Russian. It is interesting that Plutarch mentions a hill Brixava on the river Tanais (Donets-Don) and comments that the name means "Ram's Frontlet" in the native tongue.[120] According to V. F. Miller, the name Brixava is Iranian, meaning "Ram's Horn."[121]

8. Some Data on Slavic Civilization in the Sarmatian Period.

We have said that the material culture of an ancient people may be best studied in the light of the archaeological evidence. In the case of the ancient Slavs the difficulty is that our information is so scarce and nebulous, especially with regard to the Scythian period. Even for the Sarmatian period it is difficult to locate precisely on the map the various Slavic tribes mentioned in the sources, and it is therefore hard to differentiate Slavic antiquities from those of other peoples. The problem is especially tangled when it comes to the border zone between forest and steppes, and even more so in the steppe zone itself.

In the western section of the Ukrainian forest-steppe border zone, the so-called Culture of Funeral Urns, which started in the Scythian period, continued to hold ground in the Sarmatian period as well. Roman coins of the second century found in Kiev region point to the development of commercial relations between the Right-Bank Ukraine and Dacia. An examination of the inventory of the sites (*gorodishcha*) of the Kiev, Chernigov, and Poltava regions shows that the people of this area were agriculturists as in the earlier period.[122] Since the culture of these sites is of a somewhat different nature from that of the west Ukrainian "Fields of Funeral Urns," we may assume the existence of two different tribes, or groups of tribes, both probably of Slavic stock and both agriculturists, one living west of Kiev, and the other to the east. The former was under the influence of West Slavic, German and Roman culture, while the latter was strongly affected by Iranian civilization. Linguistic evidence may be used to supplement the archaeological data. As we have seen, according to Tacitus, the Slavs in contrast to the Sarmatians "build houses" (*domos figunt*).[123] The type of Slavic house in

120. *Plutarchi Libellus de fluviis,* XIV, 4; cf. Latyshev, I, 502.
121. Miller, *Sledy,* p. 241.
122. Gotie, pp. 6 ff.
123. Tacitus, *Germania,* 46.

the steppe-zone differed from that of the forest-zone. In the steppes it was a frame structure plastered with clay (the Ukrainian *khata*). In the forest-zone it was a log cabin (the Russian *izba*). While the word *khata* is of Iranian origin,[124] *izba* according to some students of linguistics is to be derived from the German *Stube*. It is more likely, however, that *izba* is a purely Slavic word, being a contraction of *istopka* ("a heated house," "house with stove").[125]

In order to illustrate more fully with the data of linguistics the life of the East Slavs in ancient times, caution is necessary in selecting from the Russian and Ukrainian vocabularies words that are really old. The safest way is of course to consider only words which are common to all or most Slavic languages, since these must have originated in the very ancient period of Slavic history.[126] The following is a list of such words referring to various aspects of private and public life.

(1) Buildings and household furniture: *dom* ("house"), *izba* ("log cabin"), *klet'* ("storeroom" or "small barn"), *stol* ("table"), *lavka* ("bench").

(2) Food and beverages, kitchen implements: *khleb* ("bread"), *miaso* ("meat"), *muka* ("flour"), *drozhzhi* ("yeast"), *testo* ("dough"), *pivo* ("beer"), *mëd* ("mead"), *kvas* ("near beer"); *chasha* ("bowl," "cup"), *nozh* ("knife"), *lozhka* ("spoon").

(3) Agriculture: *orati* (Ukrainian and Old Russian "to plow"), *ralo* ("plow"), *kosa* ("scythe"), *serp* ("sickle"), *borona* ("harrow"), *voz* ("cart"), *koleso* ("wheel"), *seiat'* ("to sow"), *semia* ("seed"), *rozh* ("rye"), *zhito* (in Ukrainian, "rye"; in Czech, "wheat"), *ovës* ("oats"), *proso* ("millet"), *lën* ("flax"), *konoplia* ("hemp").

(4) Orchard and vegetables: *ogorod* ("orchard," in old Russian, "vegetable garden"), *ovoshch* ("fruit" in Old Russian, "vegetables"), *iablonia* ("apple tree"), *grusha* ("pear," "pear tree"), *sliva* ("plum," "plum tree"), *orekh* ("nut"), *bob* ("bean"), *gorokh* ("peas"), *luk* ("onion"), *repa* ("turnip").

(5) Cattle breeding and dairy; poultry: *byk* ("bull"), *vol* ("ox"), *korova* ("cow"), *telia* ("heifer"), *kon'* ("horse"), *boran* ("ram"), *ovtsa* ("ewe"), *vepr* ("boar"), *porosia* ("pig"), *runo*

124. Berneker, I, 386. cf. Wanstrat, p. 59. Ugrian origin has also been suggested.
125. Berkener, I, 436-438.
126. See A. S. Budilovich, *Pervobytnye Slaviane*, I-II (Kiev, 1878-1882).

("fleece"), *volna* ("wool"), *moloko* ("milk"), *syr* ("cheese"), *maslo* ("butter"); *gus'* ("goose"), *kuria* ("chicken"), *utka* ("duck"), *yaitso* ("egg").

(6) Apiculture: *pchela* ("bee"), *bort'* ("beehive"), *mëd* ("honey"), *vosk* ("wax").

(7) Hunting and fishing: *lov* (Old Russian for "hunting"), *luk* ("bow"), *strela* ("arrow"), *bobr* ("beaver"), *kunitsa* ("marten"), *volk* ("wolf"), *olen'* ("deer"), *ryba* ("fish"), *uda* ("angle"), *nevod* ("dragnet"), *okun'* ("perch"), *losos'* ("salmon"), *shchuka* ("pike"), *ugor'* ("eel").

(8) Metals and forging; weapons: *zoloto* ("gold"), *serebro* ("silver"), *med'* ("copper"), *zhelezo* ("iron"), *kovat'* ("to forge"), *molot* ("hammer," "sledge"), *mech* ("sword"), *kopie* ("spear"), *sekira* ("ax," in Russian especially "battle-ax"), *shchit* ("shield").

(9) Handicraft and trade: *tkat'* ("to weave"), *priazha* ("yarn"), *polotno* ("linen"), *gonchar* ("potter"), *torg* ("market"), *miera* ("measure"), *lokot'* ("ell").

(10) Social organization; types of settlement: *pravda* ("justice," "truth"), *zakon* ("law"), *vlast'* ("power"), *rod* ("clan"), *plemia* ("tribe"), *voisko* ("army"), *selo* ("village"), *gorod* ("town"; originally "burg," "castle").

All the words in the above list must have been present in the Slavic vocabulary in the Sarmato-Gothic period if not earlier. They interest us here not from the linguistic point of view but because of their implications with regard to the history of the Eastern Slavs. A people's vocabulary reflects its culture. The words in the above list are so many terms of early Slavic husbandry, technology, and social institutions. They may help us to understand better the evolution of the people's life.

We have now to compare the linguistic with the archaeological data. As we have seen,[127] in ancient sites and burial grounds of the Ukrainian forest-steppe and steppe zone, numerous agricultural tools, pieces of house furniture, spools, etc., have been found together with grain and bones of domestic animals. Combining this with the linguistic evidence we come to the conclusion that the culture of the East Slavs must have reached in the Sarmatian period a comparatively high level.

127. Chap. II, Sec. 1.

The East Slavic arts and handicrafts were under obvious Iranian influence.[128] The existence of such old Slavic words as *gudba* ("music"), *gusli* ("psaltery"), *bubny* ("tambourine"), is evidence of the musical propensities of the people. There is a characteristic tale in Theophylactus' chronicle (of the beginning of the seventh century), which shows that the Byzantines considered the Slavs a highly musical people.[129] Recording the events of one of Mauricius' Danubian campaigns, the chronicler mentions the appearance of three Slavic envoys coming from a distant country. The envoys told Mauricius that their people did not care for either war or weapons and only enjoyed playing the cither.

As to the religion of the ancient Slavs, it has been described by Procopius in the following words:[130]

> They believe that one god, the maker of the lightning, is alone lord of all things, and they sacrifice to him cattle and all other victims; but as for Fate, they neither know it nor do they in any wise admit that it has any power among men, but whenever death stands close before them, either stricken with sickness or beginning a war, they make a promise that, if they escape, they will straightway make a sacrifice to the god in return for their life; and if they escape, they sacrifice just what they have promised, and consider that their safety has been bought with this same sacrifice. They reverence, however, both rivers and nymphs and some other spirits, and they sacrifice to all these also, and they make their divinations in connection with these sacrifices.

The original stratum of Slavic religion presumably consisted of worship of the clan ancestors and the forces of nature.[131] The worship of the forefather (*prashchur*) left a trace in the invocation now used by children in some games, *chur menia* ("let my forefather help me"). As to the worship of natural forces, Russian folklore supplies ample evidence to corroborate Procopius' information that the ancient Slavs reverenced rivers. The worship of lightning also mentioned by Procopius was particularly elaborated, and the god

128. See Sec. 5, above.

129. Theophylactus, VI, 2, 10.

130. Procopius, VII, 14, 23. (This and subsequent quotations from Procopius in English are according to H. B. Dewing's trans.)

131. On the religion of the ancient Slavs see Mansikka, Religion; Niederle, Zivot, II, 1.

of thunder Perun is mentioned in Russian chronicles. The religious beliefs of the East Slavic tribes must have been considerably influenced by Alarodian and Iranian cults. The worship of the Great Mother has already been mentioned.[132] The veneration of the mythical bird (or rather, bird-dog) Senmurv, which played an important role in old Iranian cosmogony,[133] was apparently likewise widely spread. According to Pahlavi texts Senmurv was a primeval bird whose function consisted in guarding the "Tree of All Seeds" and spreading the dry seeds over the water so that they might return to the soil with the rain. In a sense, then, Senmurv was a genius or deity of fertility. There is a picture of Senmurv on a plaque found in the Seven Brothers Kurgan (*Semibratnii*) in the Taman region.[134] The creature represented has the body of a dog, a pair of wings, and two heads, one of a dog and the other of a swan. In the representations of Senmurv of the Sassanian period, it resembles a winged dog rather than a bird. There is for this period no evidence of the veneration of Senmurv among the Proto-Slavs, but we may surmise it by inference from the existence of such worship in later times.

While Perun was a masculine deity, similar to the Teutonic Thor, the Great Mother was of course feminine. It must be remembered in this connection that the social organization of some of the pre-Sarmatian tribes of the Azov region, such as the Sauromatae, was of matriarchal type.[135] Were not some of the eastern proto-Slavic tribes originally organized along matriarchal lines? Traces of matriarchal customs may be found in old Russian folklore, especially in some of the *byliny*, as well as in the Kievan Code of Laws known as the Rus Law (*Pravda Russkaia*).[136]

9. The Goths in Ukraine.[137]

In the first century A.D. the Goths lived on the Baltic shores at the mouth of the Vistula River.[138] In the course of time the popula-

132. See Sec. 5, above.
133. Trever, *Senmurv,* pp. 293-328.
134. Kondakov, *Drevnosti,* II, Fig. 103 (p. 119); Trever, *Senmurv,* p. 313. On the Seven Brothers Kurgan see Chap. II, Sec. 1.
135. See Chap. II, Sec. 2, above.
136. Cf. Shcherbakivskyi, *Formatsiia Ukrains'kogo Narodu* (Podiebrady, 1937).
137. The basic work on the Goths is by Schmidt; see also Braun; Gotie, pp. 17-21; Rostovtzeff, pp. 216-218, and Index, *s.v.* Goths; Vasiliev.
138. See Sec. 6, above.

tion grew, and the country did not afford sufficient food. In the second half of the second century A.D. the majority of the tribal leaders decided that their people should move south in search of more fertile land.[139] One tribe, however, that of the Gepids, preferred to stay in their old haunts. The Gepids migrated south only later, in the third century A.D. when they settled in northern Dacia.[140] Jordanis describes the hardships the Goths encountered in their march, in crossing swamps and bogs[141] which may be identified as those of the upper Pripet basin. A spearhead with a runic inscription found near Kovel may be considered a monument of this Gothic drive.[142] Some time after crossing the swamps they approached a large river. According to Jordanis they were by this time already in Scythia, in a locality which they called Oium.[143] F. Braun suggests that this name is to be derived from the Gothic word *Aujom,* a "waterside country."[144] However, L. Schmidt has offered a different explanation of the name. He compares "Oium" with the German word *Aue* which means "meadow," "field."[145] The name Oium may thus mean "steppe-country." The "large river" mentioned by Jordanis must have been the Dnieper. The steppe zone starts on the right bank of the Dnieper, south of Kiev. Thus it seems probable that the Goths reached the Dnieper near Kiev.

To follow Jordanis' narrative, the Goths started to cross the river (i.e., Dnieper at Kiev) by a bridge, but before all of them succeeded in crossing the bridge broke and they were thus divided into two groups. While a part of them remained on the right bank of the Dnieper, those who had already crossed the river rushed farther east and attacked the tribe of Spali[146] who, as we have already seen,[147] must have lived in the region of the upper Donets River. After defeating the Spali the Goths turned south to the Sea of Azov and then invaded the Taurida. A section of them eventually crossed the Cimmerian Bosporus (Kerch Strait) and penetrated to the

139. See Jordanis, Sec. 26.
140. Schmidt, pp. 529 ff.
141. Jordanis, Sec. 27.
142. Schmidt, p. 199.
143. Jordanis, Sec. 27.
144. Braun, p. 245.
145. Schmidt, p. 199.
146. Jordanis, Sec. 28.
147. See Sec. 7, above.

mouth of the Kuban River on the Caucasian shore of the Black Sea. As for the group of Goths that remained on the right bank of the Dnieper, it subsequently moved down the Dnieper to the Black Sea and spread west along the coast, eventually reaching the mouth of the Danube. By the middle of the third century the Goths controlled the whole northern coast of the Black Sea.

It must be mentioned in this connection that the Goths were followed in their march from the Baltic to the Black Sea by another Teutonic tribe, that of the Heruls.[148] The Heruls, probably a much less numerous tribe than the Goths, settled in the region of the lower Don, seizing the old Greek colony of Tanais at its mouth. Still another Teutonic tribe, the Burgundians, are mentioned in some sources as having their abodes near the Heruls.[149] Actually only a small band of the Burgundians migrated to the Sea of Azov, while the bulk of the tribe settled in the middle of the third century along the banks of Main River in western Germany.

The Goths did not at first form any centralized state in South Russia, each tribe keeping to itself. The Gothic tribe which settled in Bessarabia was known as the Tervingi (Forest-People, cf. the Russian Drevliane) or the Visigoths. The Taifali stayed further west, in the Lesser Wallachia. The Greutungi (Steppe-People, cf. the Russian Poliane), also known as the Ostrogoths, were the strongest tribe among the eastern Goths. The Taurida group of Goths subsequently became known as the Trapezite Goths[150] from the Crimean mountain, Chatyr-Dag, which has the shape of a table (*trapeze* in Greek). By the middle of the third century A.D. the Goths were already harassing Roman possessions south of the Danube. In 251 the emperor Decius set forth against them but his army was surrounded by enemy forces and he himself perished in battle. In the second half of the third century the Goths put to sea, and their maritime expeditions did even more harm to the Balkan and Aegean provinces of the Roman Empire than their overland depredations.

While the Goths, as a Scandinavian nation, might be expected to have seafaring traditions in their blood, it should be noted that the initiative in the third century series of maritime expeditions on the

148. On the Heruls, see Schmidt, pp. 548 ff.

149. Schmidt, p. 131.

150. The Trapezite Goths were formerly referred to as the Tetraxite Goths. The manuscripts give either reading. See Vasiliev, pp. 57-69.

Black Sea belonged not to the Goths, but to the Borani.[151] In the year 256 a number of small Boran boats sailing from the mouth of the Don crossed the Sea of Azov and appeared at the Kerch Strait. The Bosporan authorities hastened to make a friendly agreement with the Borani and supplied them with seagoing ships. The Boran flotilla then cruised along the Caucasian shore of the Black Sea and attacked Pitiunt (modern Pitzunda). The attack was a failure, however. In the next year the Borani put to sea once more, this time reinforced by the Goths. The allies first approached Phasis (near Poti) where they tried to plunder the temple of Artemis, in which attempt they were frustrated. They then turned to Pitiunt and this time succeeded in taking it; they also seized a number of ships in the Pitiunt harbor by which they reinforced their own flotilla. They then headed toward Trebizond, which they took by a surprise night attack. The unfortunate city was thoroughly sacked, and the Borani and the Goths returned home with their ships heavily laden with booty and prisoners.[152]

News of the Trebizond raid spread rapidly among the Goths, both eastern and western. The group of them which controlled the mouth of the Dniester now decided to start a navy of its own. In the winter of the year 257-58 ships were built for them by prisoners and native workers at Tyras (Akkerman). In the spring of 258 the Dniester Goths' flotilla put to sea, cruising along the western coast of the Black Sea. Their army set forth simultaneously overland. Passing Tomi and Anchial, the Gothic flotilla entered Phileat Bay, northwest of Byzantium. The overland troops came to the same point. Seizing all the boats available from local fishermen, the entire company was now able to embark. Their expanded flotilla entered the Bosporus and plundered a number of coastal towns, among others Chalcedon, Nicea, Nicomedia.[153] In their subsequent maritime expeditions of the years 262 and 264, the western Goths raided the littoral of Thrace, Bithynia, and Cappadocia.[154] In 267 the eastern Goths put to sea once more, this time in collaboration with the Heruls. For this expedition five hundred boats were built at the mouth of the Don. The Heruls and the Goths crossed the Black Sea, broke through the Bosporus in spite of the attempt of Roman

151. See Sec. 7, above.
152. Zosimus, I, 31-33.
153. *Idem*, 34-35.
154. Schmidt, pp. 214-215.

guard boats to stop them, plundered Cyzicus, as well as the islands Lemnos and Skyros, and then attacked both Athens and Corinth. Under the leadership of Dexippus, a prominent historian of that time, the Athenians offered desperate resistance to the invaders. Nevertheless the latter sailed home with large booty.[155]

The success of this expedition stirred the Dniester Goths to new action. During the whole winter of 267-68 the Dniester shipwrights were busy building boats. According to Zosimus, six thousand boats were built, probably an exaggerated figure; however, the boats may have been small.[156] Both maritime raid and overland campaign were undertaken. Men of various tribes took part in the expedition, as for instance the Heruls, Ostrogoths, Visigoths, Gepids, and the Kelts or "Keltions." In the so-called *Easter Chronicle,* of the seventh century, we find the remark that the Keltions are identical with the Sporades,[157] and, as we know, by Spori or Sporades Procopius meant the Slavs.[158] Accordingly, we may surmise that Slavs took part in the expedition as well. The flotilla easily broke through the Bosporus and the Dardanelles and raided both Salonika and the Athos peninsula. The army was less successful, being defeated at Naissus (Niš) by the troops of the emperor Claudius.

While it was the initiative of the Borani that set the Goths and the Heruls to building up their Black Sea navy, in the organization of their army the Goths were much indebted to the Sarmatians, with whom they were in a close intercourse. Although the Goths had pushed the main body of Roxolani and some other Sarmatian tribes out of the western section of the Pontic steppes, a part of these Sarmatian tribes remained on the spot and recognized the suzerainty of the Goths, as did the East Slavic tribes. Relations between the Goths and the Alans were on the whole friendly. It was only at the time of Ermenrich's aggressive policy that the Rukhs clan of the Alans revolted. While originally the Goths fought on foot, after their migration to South Russia they were obliged to go on horseback, since only horsemen had any chance in steppe warfare. Gothic cavalry consisted of men of the upper classes, the common people continuing to supply foot troops. The cavalry was organized along the Sarmatian pattern as regards both tactics and

155. *Idem,* pp. 215-216.
156. Zosimus, I, 42.
157. *Chronicon Paschale,* I, 57.
158. See Sec. 7, above.

armament, except that the Goths did not use the long spear of the Sarmatians. Gothic belt clasps were of Sarmatian style. Gothic arts and handicraft at large showed more and more similarity to Sarmatian standards.

Conditions of life in the steppes gradually affected the social organization of the Goths as well. Originally their organization had been similar to that of other Teutonic tribes. The people consisted of three classes: freemen, the half-free, and slaves. Only the first group represented the nation politically. The armed freemen of each tribe or clan constituted the tribal assembly which elected tribal chiefs, known as dukes, judges, or *konungs*. Due to the formation of cavalry squads, the class of freemen was now divided into two sections: the horsemen and the foot. Since the importance of cavalry in the Gothic army was rapidly growing, the horsemen considered themselves the flower of the nation. Thus an aristocratic social regime was gradually replacing the old democratic way of life. All the higher offices of the army and administration were filled by horsemen. The next step was their receipt of grants of land from the duke. Thus a landed nobility came into being among the Goths, which gradually assumed feudal-like authority over the peasant population. The position of the natives, Slavs among others, must have been precarious indeed.

With regard to the spiritual culture of the Goths, their conversion to Christianity in the course of the third and the fourth centuries was of paramount importance. It appears that the Azov and Crimean Goths were the first to be affected by Christianity, with the teachings of which they became acquainted through the Caucasian and the Trebizond Greeks taken prisoners during the raids of the years 256-57. As a result, the Christian missionaries who ventured to preach among the Goths came from Asia Minor and Jerusalem, and not from Constantinople. At the end of the third and the beginning of the fourth century Christianity began to spread among the Visigoths as well. Bishop Theophilus of the Goths took part in the First Ecumenical Council at Nicea in the year 325. His see was probably in Bessarabia.[159] The next bishop of the Visigoths was the famous Ulfila or Wulfila (311-86) who translated the New Testament into Gothic. In the subsequent strife between the Orthodox and the Arians Ulfila joined the Arians, and consequently Arianism became

159. Vasiliev, p. 18.

the denomination of the Visigoth.[160] As to the Crimean Goths, they remained loyal to Orthodoxy.

The Goths were among the first German tribes to be converted to Christianity, and since they received their new faith from the Greeks their terminology in ecclesiastical matters was influenced by the Greek. Later on, the Gothic ecclesiastical terms were adopted by other German tribes, and there are still in the German several ecclesiastical terms reflecting their Greek origin. Such are, for example, the German *Kirche* ("church"), from the Greek κυρικόν ("the house of God"), *Bischoff* ("bishop"), *Pfaffe* ("pope," "priest"), *Pfingsten* ("Pentecoste"), etc.[161]

In the middle of the fourth century the East Gothic tribes formed a strong federation headed by one of the tribal chiefs, Ermenrich, who was elected king of the Ostrogoths (*ca.* 350-70). After consolidating his authority over the East Gothic tribes Ermenrich began to subdue the neighboring non-Gothic peoples, some of which were already under Gothic control. Ammianus Marcellinus characterizes Ermenrich as follows: ". . . a most warlike monarch, dreaded by the neighboring nations because of his many and varied deeds of valor."[162] According to Jordanis, Ermenrich's first campaign was against the Heruls, a Teutonic tribe settled in the Azov region. Their duke was killed in the battle, and the people accepted Ermenrich as their ruler.[163] Some time later, probably around 362, Ermenrich must have conquered what remained of the Bosporan kingdom at Kerch Strait. While Jordanis does not mention this event it is known from other sources.[164] Having enforced his authority in the southeast, Ermenrich turned to the northwest, undertaking a campaign against the Venedi. In order to penetrate to the land of the Venedi—that is to the region of the upper Vistula River—the Ostrogoths had to cross either the land of the Sclaveni (that is, the Kiev region), or the land of the Antes (that is, the southern Bug region). Jordanis says that both the Sclaveni and the Antes recognized Ermenrich's authority.[165] Part of the Sclaveni must have migrated north on this occasion.[166]

160. Schmidt, pp. 234 ff.
161. Dopsch, II, 197.
162. Ammianus Marcellinus, XXXI, 3, 1.
163. Jordanis, Sec. 116.
164. Vasiliev, pp. 22-23.
165. Jordanis, Sec. 119.
166. See Sec. 7, above.

The war against the Venedi ended in Ermenrich's victory. The Venedi were poorly armed and could rely only upon their numerical superiority. *Sed nihil valet multitudo inbellium,* remarks Jordanis.[167] The Venedi were conquered without much difficulty, whereupon the Aestii (Balts) likewise recognized Ermenrich as their suzerain. Ermenrich's kingdom now stretched from the Black Sea to the Baltic. Jordanis gives the following list of tribes recognizing the suzerainty of the Ostrogothic king: Golthescytha, Thiudos, Inaunxis, Vasinabroncae, Merens, Mordens, Imniscaris, Rogas, Tadzans, Athaul, Navego, Bubegenae, and Coldae.[168] Out of this list we have already identified[169] the Thiudos as the Chud of Russian chronicles, the Merens as Meria, the Mordens as Mordva, and Rogas (Rocas) as Rukhs-As. The first three were Finnish tribes, the last an Alano-Slavic. The Navego were probably Iranians or Irano-Slavs; their name may be derived from Iranian *nava,* "new," cf. the Ossetian *naeu-aeg.*[170] "Inaunxis" is apparently not an ethnic name but a definition of the "Thiudos"; the Vasinabroncae may be identified as the Ves of the Russian chronicles.[171]

While some Slavic tribes were first conquered by Ermenrich, others had been subdued by the Goths long before. Generally speaking, the close connection between the Goths and the Slavs in South Russia lasted for about two centuries, from the end of the second to the last quarter of the fourth century. It is small wonder that words of Gothic origin appeared in the Slavic language and vice versa. The following Slavic words are considered of Gothic origin:[172] *kniaz* ("prince"), from the Gothic *kuni* ("clan elder"); *peniazi* ("money"), from the Gothic *pannings; polk* ("armed people," "regiment"), from the Gothic *volk; shlem* ("helmet"), from the Gothic *hilms.* On the other hand, the Gothic *meki* ("sword") may be derived from the Anto-Slavic *mech.* The corresponding German word is *Schwert.* Antic swords are mentioned in the *Beowulf.*[173] It

167. Jordanis, Sec. 119.

168. *Idem,* Sec. 116.

169. See Sec. 7, above.

170. Cf. Miller, *Sledy,* p. 242. Perhaps it is possible to connect Jordanis' "Navego" with Ptolemy's "Navari" (see Sec. 7, above).

171. Mommsen, pp. 165-166. "Thiudos Inaunxis" is interpreted as "the Chud in the Aunus [Olonets] region"; "Vasinabroncae" as "the Ves in the Biarmia region." Cf. Zeuss, pp. 688-689; Muellenhoff, p. 74. See also J. J. Mikkola, "Die Namen der Völker Hermanarichs," *FUF,* XV (1922), 56-66.

172. See Vernadsky, *Goten,* p. 14.

173. *Beowulf,* v. 1679.

is likewise characteristic that many of the Gothic kings and princes had names which sound Slavic rather than Teutonic.[174] Thus Ermenrich's successor had the name Vithimir; a grandson of his was called Vidimer. Vidimer's brother's name was Valamir (cf. the Slavic name Velemir). Later the same process of Slavization of personal names was to apply to the Scandinavian rulers of Rus (of the ninth and subsequent centuries). The first Varangian princes had Norse names, such as Riurik, Oleg, Igor. Igor's son, however, took a Slavic name—that of Sviatoslav (reigned 964-72).

174. Jordanis, *passim.*

CHAPTER IV.

THE HUNNO-ANTIC PERIOD, 370-558.

1. *Preliminary Remarks.*

THE invasion of the Huns, which like the migration of the Sarmatians in the preceding period was caused by ethnic upheavals in middle Eurasia, had far-reaching historical consequences for the further development of both western Eurasia and Europe proper. It was the Huns who started the "Great Migration of the Peoples" (*Voelkerwanderung*), as it has been called. The Alans were first to receive the impact of the Hunnic drive, and the Heruls, Burgundians, and Goths soon followed. The retreat of these peoples before the oncoming Huns resulted, in turn, in moving other German tribes from their places, and since all of them at one time or another rushed against the boundaries of the Roman Empire, the latter were bent or even at places pierced. Some Germans were allowed to enter the confines of the empire peaceably on condition that they would help to protect the imperial boundaries against other "barbarian" tribes pushing from the east or north. In other cases they forced their way into Roman provinces. Both those who came as the emperor's allies and those who came openly as his foes alike claimed control of the provinces they occupied. For some time every tribe seemed to be in constant motion, pushing farther and farther south and west. The Visigoths and the Alans skirting the Danubian boundary invaded first southern Gaul and then Spain, whence the Alans eventually penetrated into Africa and settled in the environs of ancient Carthage. The Ostrogoths stopped for several decades in Thrace and Illyricum and then seized Italy.

Following at the Germans' heels, the Huns established themselves in Pannonia on the middle Danube. Attila's campaigns smashed at both Rome and the Germans. In this maelstrom most of the western provinces of the Roman Empire were gradually overrun by various German tribes, and finally the Herul Odoacer seized control of Rome itself (476). It was now the New Rome, that is, Constantinople, which became the capital of the empire, or rather of what remained of it. Actually, only the eastern part survived, and from Latin it changed to Greco-Byzantine. But for many centuries to come Constantinople still preserved her prestige as Imperial City—*Tsargrad,* in Slavic.

As part of its international impact the Hunnic invasion introduced far-reaching changes in the position of the Anto-Slavic tribes. By destroying the power of the Ostrogoths, the Huns prevented the possibility of Germanization of the Anto-Slavs in South Russia. Moreover, the remnants of the Iranian tribes in South Russia were likewise weakened. A considerable part of the Alans moved westward following the exodus of the Goths. As a result, the role of the Iranian element in the life of the As or Antic tribes decreased while Slavic influence increased. The age of the Hunnic invasion is thus, in a sense, the period of emancipation of the East Slavs not only from Gothic but from Iranian control as well. Drafting the Slavic detachments into their army and using them as auxiliaries during their campaigns, the Huns taught militarism to the Anto-Slavs.

Following the death of Attila (453) the Hunnic Empire split into several *ulus*. From Pannonia its hordes now retired eastward to the Pontic and Azov steppes where they gradually became known as Bulgars. With the weakening of Hunnic power the Slavic tribes—both the Antes and the Sclaveni—emerged as an independent force. In the sixth century the Slavs pressed upon the Danubian border of the Roman (now Byzantine) Empire. Bands of Slavs infiltrated not only into Thrace and Illyricum but into Greece proper. In this way intercourse started between the Slavs and the Greco-Roman world; inimical at first, but in time partly friendly as well.

Slavic detachments were incorporated in the imperial army and in it from time to time Slavic generals occupied leading posts. Thus the process of gradual Slavization of the Byzantine Empire began, while in Bessarabia and Ukraine the first Slavic state—that of the Antes—was being organized. The rise of the Antic state was endangered, beginning in 558, by the invasion of a new nomadic horde, also coming from central Eurasia: that of the Avars. Byzantine diplomacy immediately attempted to use the Avar newcomers as the empire's allies against both the Hunno-Bulgars and the Slavs. The device was successful, but for a short while only, since before long the Avars turned their arms against the empire itself.

Only the most important sources of the period may be mentioned here. Any list of contemporary historical works must open with the name of Ammianus Marcellinus (330-*ca.* 400), an officer of the Roman army who participated in a number of eastern campaigns and was well acquainted with the events he described. By birth he was a Syrian Greek, but he wrote in Latin. The Hunnic invasion is dealt with in Book XXXI of his *History.* Of the Greek writers of the fifth century Zosimus and Priscus must be mentioned. Zosimus wrote a *Modern History* covering the period from A.D. 270 to 410. He was a resident of Constantinople, occupying an important position in the administration of finance, and was quite familiar with the policies of the government of the East Roman Empire. Priscus, a lawyer and professor of philosophy, was a native of Pania in Thrace. He served as secretary to the senator Maximinus on the latter's embassy to Attila in 448, and wrote a valuable report of this mission; of which, however, only excerpts are known. The two outstanding men among sixth century historians are Jordanis, whom we have already met,[1] and Procopius of Caesarea (b. at the end of the fifth century, d. after 560). Like Ammianus Marcellinus, Procopius took part personally in most of the military campaigns he described. He had the important position of chief of the chancellery of the Byzantine commander-in-chief, Belisarius. By origin Procopius was a Palestine Greek, and by character a double-faced Levantine. He glorified Justinian in his book *On the Buildings,* and calumniated the same emperor in his *Secret History* which of course was not in circulation until the emperor's death. In his main work, however—the *History of Justinian's Wars*—Procopius' attitude is much more objective and his description of the chief events is detailed and accurate. On the whole, Procopius was a great historian, and his work is especially valuable for our purpose since he was the first author to convey more or less adequate data on the Slavs. Another important work in this respect is *A Manual of Warfare* ("Strategicon") of the end of the sixth century by Mauricius, whom some scholars have been inclined to identify as the emperor Mauricius (582-602). It was in any case written during Mauricius' reign. The author of the *Manual* is naturally interested in the methods of warfare of potential enemies of the empire, among them the Antes and the Sclaveni.

A trustworthy source for the history of the events of the first half of the sixth century is the chronicle by the *comes* Marcellinus (not to be confused with Ammianus Marcellinus), written in Latin in the

1. See Chap. III, Sec. 1.

first years of Justinian's reign. It will not be amiss to mention here that down to the reign of Mauricius Latin was the official language of the imperial administration. Marcellinus was Justinian's secretary previous to his accession to the throne, and thus had ample opportunity to use official documents for his chronicle. Marcellinus' brief notes are therefore at times more valuable than a lengthy narrative by a less informed writer would be.

The chronicle of John Malalas, an Antiochean Greek who wrote between 528 and 540, is of a quite different nature. Malalas means "orator" (*rhetor*) in Syriac, but judging both from his style and the lack of organization in the contents of his book it does not seem likely that the author was actually a *rhetor,* that is, a professor of eloquence. It is much more likely that he was a monk of little erudition. He offers a popular outline of world history from the Creation. From the point of view of a student of Byzantine literature Malalas' chronicle has a special value since it is one of the first works in that literature to be written in popular dialect instead of the classical Greek. Only the last part of the chronicle is interesting to us, since he records there some contemporary events. Malalas' work has been preserved in an abridged form, but the text may be reconstructed to some extent with the help of an early Slavic translation of it, as well as from quotations by later Byzantine authors.

In addition to Greek and Latin historical works, the importance of Syriac literature should not be overlooked. The chronicle of John of Ephesus (sixth century) contains valuable, although brief, notes on the Slavic invasion of the Balkan peninsula. The original of this chronicle has not been preserved in full but some of its lost sections may be restored from a later historical compendium—the chronicle of Michael, the Jacobite Patriarch of Antioch (twelfth century). Another Syriac work worth mentioning is the *Church History* attributed to Zechariah the Rhetor, written around A.D. 555; it contains excerpts, in Syriac translation, from the Greek chronicle by Bishop Zechariah of Mitilene, which was set down around A.D. 518. The Greek original has been lost.

As to the archaeological evidence, much material bearing on the period has been excavated in South Russia, but has not as yet been sufficiently classified. It is only recently that attempts have been made to segregate the antiquities of the Antes from the accumulated stores of grave furniture and other finds of the period.

All events of the Hunno-Antic period have not been studied, in modern historical literature, with equal attention. Until recently the history of South Russia has been interpreted only so far as its study seemed important for the history of the Byzantine Empire or of the German tribes. While Edward Gibbon's (1737-94) famous book, *The Decline and Fall of the Roman Empire,* is naturally out of date it has not been superseded by any general work of the same range and scope. Of the more recent literature, A. A. Vasiliev's and G. Ostrogorsky's general outlines of Byzantine history should of course be mentioned first. For more detailed information the reader may be referred to I. A. Kulakovskii's and J. B. Bury's valuable works. Josef Markwart's study *Osteuropäische und Ostasiatische Streifzüge* (1903) still keeps its paramount value for the history of the Khazars, Bulgars, Magyars, etc. There are two recent outlines of the history of nomadic empires, one in French by R. Grousset, the other in English, by W. McGovern.

It was the late D. I. Ilovaiskii who first recognized the importance of the Hunnic period from the point of view of the student of Russian history.[2] He has, however, oversimplified the issue by identifying the Huns with Slavs. The importance of the Antic background for Russian history has been aptly emphasized by D. Odinets in his little book on the origins of the East Slavic state.[3] Recently, much attention has been paid in Soviet publications to the Antes. Among pertinent studies, B. A. Rybakov's article on the Antes is especially valuable (1939). Finally, the author's own studies on the Antes published in 1938 and 1939 may be mentioned here.

2. *The Hunnic Invasion and the Gotho-Antic War.*

We have already dealt with the role of the Huns in the history of China and middle Eurasia and their struggle with the Yue-chi.[4] Under the Han Dynasty (202 B.C.–A.D. 220) China's power was in the ascendancy, and the Huns suffered severe reverses. In the course of the first century A.D. the Chinese conquered Eastern Turkestan and extended their protection to the overland caravan route from China to the Mediterranean, which was of paramount importance for the silk trade. Pressed by Chinese armies the Hunnic

2. D. I. Ilovaiskii, *Razyskaniia o nachale Rusi* (Moscow, 1876; 2d ed., 1882); cf. Moshin, *Vopros,* pp. 367-368.

3. D. Odinets, *Vozniknovenie gosudarstvennogo stroia u Slavian* (Paris, 1935).

4. See Chap. III, Sec. 2.

hordes retreated north and west. One of them stopped in the region of Lake Balkhash. It was only in the second half of the third century A.D., when troubles started in China itself, that the Huns became bolder again and renewed their attacks on ancient empire.

At the beginning of the fourth century A.D., after a series of defeats administered by the Huns to Chinese troops, the Chinese Government was compelled to let a section of them enter the boundaries of the Chinese Empire; these Huns were accepted as auxiliaries and settled in the border area by the same arrangement as certain German and Sarmatian tribes on the borders of the Roman Empire. However, in the middle of the fourth century the Huns were in their turn attacked from the northeast by tribes presumably of Manchu origin, whom the Chinese chronicles call Sien-pi and Zhen-Zhen (Zhuan-Zhuan). It appears to have been the pressure of these tribes which resulted eventually in the westward migration of the Huns. The easternmost Hunnic horde, retreating before the Manchus, pushed the neighboring horde westward, and the shock was finally transmitted to the Balkhash horde. Part of the Balkhash horde migrated to Turkestan, where they became known as the Ephtalite Huns.[5] The main horde rushed further west, skirting the northern shores of the Caspian Sea and eventually penetrating to the lower Volga region. Not later than A.D. 360, the Huns crossed the Volga and attacked the Alans.

There is great diversity of opinion with regard to the ethnic composition of the Hunnic horde.[6] Some scholars considered them to be Mongols (Pallas, Bergman, Baer, Neumann, Howorth); others Ugrians (St-Martin, Claproth, P. P. Semenov); still others Slavs (Zabelin, Ilovaiskii, Florinskii); and some, Turks (Kunik, Vambery, Radlov, Aristov). It is now more or less generally accepted that the main Hunnic horde was of Turkish stock; it was, however, joined by Ugrians and Mongols as well, and in the last stages of its drive it also included some Iranian and Slavic tribes.

The Huns were a nomadic people. Ammianus Marcellinus says:

> No one in their country ever plows a field or touches a plow-handle. They are all without fixed abode, without hearth, or law, or settled mode

5. Grousset, pp. 110-115; McGovern, pp. 404 ff.

6. On the Huns, aside from Grousset and McGovern, as well as works quoted by them, see A. A. Alföldi, "Funde aus der Hunnenzeit und ihre ethnische Sonderung," *AH, 9* (1932); K. Inostrantsev, "Hun-nu i Gunny," *Zhivaia Starina, 10* (1900); Kondakov, *Drevnosti,* III; Toll.

of life, and keep roaming from place to place, like fugitives, accompanied by the wagons in which they live; in wagons their wives weave for them their hideous garments, in wagons they cohabit with their husbands, bear children, and rear them to the age of puberty. None of their offspring, when asked, can tell you where he comes from, since he was conceived in one place, born far from there, and brought up still farther away.[7]

On the Hun warriors Ammianus' comment is as follows:

. . . They are almost glued to their horses, which are hardy, it is true, but ugly, and sometimes they sit them woman-fashion and thus perform their ordinary tasks. From their horses by day or night every one of that nation buys and sells, eats and drinks, and bowed over the narrow neck of the animal relaxes into sleep so deep as to be accompanied by many dreams.[8] . . . They are so hardy in their mode of life that they have no need of fire nor of savory food, but eat the roots of wild plants and the half-raw flesh of any kind of animal whatever, which they put between their thighs and the backs of their horses, and thus warm it a little.[9] . . . They fight from a distance with missiles having sharp bone instead of their usual points [i.e., of metal], joined to the shafts with wonderful skill, then they gallop over the intervening spaces and fight hand to hand with swords, reckless of their own lives; and while the enemy are guarding against wounds from the sabre-thrusts, they throw strips of cloth plaited into nooses over their opponents and entangle them.[10]

From Ammianus' description we may surmise that he dealt mainly with the Mongol detachments of the Hunnic horde. The Mongol type of face seemed so weird to both the Greeks and the Romans that they believed its features were the result of a surgical operation performed on the cheeks of every Hunnic child. ". . . The cheeks of the children are deeply furrowed with the steel from their very birth, in order that the growth of hair, when it appears at the proper time, may be checked by the wrinkled scars, they grow old without beards and without any beauty, like eunuchs." [11] Apollinaris Sidonius, an author of the fifth century, makes a similar statement.[12]

7. Ammianus Marcellinus, XXXI, 2, 10.
8. *Idem,* 2, 6.
9. *Idem,* 2, 3.
10. *Idem,* 2, 9.
11. *Idem,* 2, 2.
12. Apollinaris Sidonius, "Panegyricus dictus Anthemio Augusto," verse 245 ff. It should be noted that some deformation of skulls—of a different nature than that described with regard to the Huns by Ammianus and Sidonius—was a habit widely spread among the Alans, see *RL, 13,* 109.

Let us now turn back to the story of the Hunnic invasion. We have said that the Alans were the first to bear the brunt of the Hunnic attack. They were not able to withstand it. A section of them surrendered outright and was incorporated into the Hunnic army. Another section moved to the North Caucasian area to reinforce those of their blood who had penetrated there long before.[13] Finally, a considerable group of the Alans retreated north to the upper Donets region, which had been likewise controlled by the Alans and Aso-Slavs even before the Hunnic invasion.

After the defeat of the Alans it was the Ostrogoths who had to face the Hunnic onslaught. King Ermenrich personally led his army against the Huns. But the Ostrogoths proved no match for them, either. Their army was crushed and Ermenrich himself fell in battle (A.D. *ca.* 370). According to Ammianus Marcellinus, the king committed suicide.[14] According to Jordanis, he was fatally wounded by two warriors of his own army.[15] These two, says the chronicler, were brothers who had been seeking an opportunity to avenge the death of their sister, executed earlier at Ermenrich's order. They belonged to the tribe of Rosomoni, one of those previously conquered by Ermenrich. The Rosomoni, as we have seen,[16] may be identified as the Roxolani; that is, the Rukhs-As. If this tale is true, then it is probable that personal revenge was not the only motive of the brothers, but that they acted on the advice of the As, or Alans, who by this time had recognized Hunnic authority. We may believe that it was a case of revolt of the Rukhs-As against the Ostrogoths, and that they hailed the Huns as their saviors.

Following Ermenrich's death, a part of the Ostrogoths and the Heruls recognized the authority of the Hunnic khan. Small groups of both tribes followed the group of Alans who had retired to the North Caucasian area; a strong band of Ostrogoths settled in the Taurida, probably as Hunnic vassals. The remnants of the main body of the Ostrogothic people started their retreat to the west in the direction of the lower Dnieper River. Groups of both Heruls and Burgundians from the Azov region joined the retreat. The Ostrogoths elected a new king to replace Ermenrich. He belonged to the Amali clan and his name was Vinitharius, according to Jor-

13. See Chap. III, Sec. 3.
14. Ammianus Marcellinus, XXXI, 3, 2.
15. Jordanis, Secs. 129-130.
16. See Chap. III, Sec. 7.

danis;[17] Ammianus, however, gives his name as Vithimir.[18] This sounds rather Slavic.[19] It is possible that the new king had two names, one Gothic and the other Slavic.

As soon as the retreating Ostrogoths reached the Dnieper they realized that the way for further retreat westward was barred by the Antes who lived in the Bug region. This was what we call the western group of the Antes.[20] It appears that the Antes refused to let the Ostrogoths pass through their land, and so a war started between them. According to Jordanis the Ostrogoths were defeated in the first encounter, but later on succeeded in crushing Antic resistance. Enraged by the stubborn opposition of the Antes, King Vithimir applied terror. The captured Antic king Boz (Bus) was crucified together with his sons and seventy Antic chiefs (*primates*).[21] Boz' fate served as the subject of epic songs, and even at the time of Prince Igor's campaign in A.D. 1185, Gothic girls still sang of the times of Bus.[22]

Since the western Antes defeated by Vithimir were a branch of the Aso-Slavic people, it was quite natural for the eastern Antes to intervene in favor of their kinsmen. We have already mentioned that together with other As or Alans the eastern Antes had become by this time vassals of the Hunnic khan. They could now act only with the latter's permission. This must be taken into consideration in evaluating Jordanis' statement that after the defeat of the western Antes by Vithimir, the Huns set forth against the Ostrogoths led by their khan in person.[23] Ammianus Marcellinus does not mention the Huns at all in this connection but speaks only of a war between the Alans and the Ostrogoths. If we try to coördinate these two reports, we must conclude that Ammianus' information was the more precise. It seems quite probable that the khan sent against the Ostrogoths not his main Hun horde but his Alanic vassals, particularly as the Alans must have been themselves eager to avenge their kinsmen, the western As. It is characteristic that Ammianus, whose outline of these events is very brief, makes no distinction between the western and eastern As or Alans but mentions in a general way

17. Jordanis, Sec. 246.
18. Ammianus Marcellinus, XXXI, 3, 3.
19. Cf. Chap. III, Sec. 9.
20. See Chap. III, Sec. 7.
21. Jordanis, Sec. 247.
22. *Slovo,* pp. 25-26. See, however, Vasiliev's comment (Vasiliev, pp. 139-140).
23. Jordanis, Sec. 248-249.

a war between the Alans and the Goths. It is obvious that for Ammianus Vithimir's attack on the western Antes was but an episode of the Alano-Gothic War as a whole.

He says: "After his [Ermenrich's] demise Vithimir was made king and resisted the Halani for a time. . . . But after many defeats which he sustained, he was overcome by force of arms and died in battle.[24]"

The final battle between the Alans and the Ostrogoths took place at the river Erak (now called Tiligul), [25] around A.D. 375. Jordanis, using probably some old saga, describes this battle as an archery duel between the king of the Huns (i.e., Alans) and the king of the Ostrogoths. The former kills the latter with his arrow.[26] According to Jordanis the name of the king of the Huns (i.e., in this case, of the Alans) was Balamber. A similar name was later borne by a Gothic chieftain, grandson of Vithimir: Βαλάμερος in Greek transcription, according to Priscus;[27] Valamir, according to Jordanis.[28] Balamber is probably a retransliteration into Latin of a Greek transcription (Βαλάμερος) of the name Valamir. This name, in turn, is probably of Slavic origin (cf. the Slavic Velemir).[29] In view of the close symbiosis of the Alans and eastern Slavs there would be nothing striking in the fact that the ruler of the Alans had a Slavic name.

3. The Great Migration and the Westward Expansion of the Alans.

The defeat of the Ostrogoths by the Alans prepared the ground for a further drive of the Huns against the Goths. The Alans played the role of the Hunnic vanguard. After the successful action of the vanguard, the main army of the Hunnic khan—that is, the Hunnic horde proper—was set in motion. The Ostrogoths had no alternative but to retreat farther west to the banks of the Dniester River. There they built up a fortified camp and attempted to make a determined stand. Vithimir's youthful son Viderich was now elected king of the Ostrogoths. In his name two chiefs took charge of affairs: Alatheus and Sarfac. The latter name sounds Iranian rather than Gothic.

24. Ammianus Marcellinus, XXXI, 3, 3.
25. N. Zupanić, "Prvi nosilci etnickih imen Srb, Hrvat, Čeh," *Etnolog,* II (1928), 74 ff.
26. Jordanis, Sec. 249.
27. Priscus, IV, 28.
28. Jordanis, Sec. 252.
29. Cf. Chap. III, Sec. 9.

The turn of events in the Pontic steppes also affected the Visigoths, for whom the Dniester then served as eastern frontier. Their ruler, whose title was "Judge" and whose name was Athanarich, decided to oppose the onslaught of the Huns and concentrated his army on the western bank of the river. The Visigoths, however, did not join forces with the Ostrogoths; the two armies acted independently. The Huns were quick to take advantage of this lack of unity and coordination between their enemies. They decided to deal with the Visigoths first. Crossing the river by night the Huns attacked Athanarich's camp without warning. The Visigoths retreated in utter disorder to the line of the river Pruth, but were unable to make a stand even there.[30]

Before long, disorganized bands of Visigoths appeared on the northern bank of the Danube River imploring the Roman officials to let them enter Thrace in order to settle there.[31] The Ostrogoths followed, and likewise camped on the bank of the Danube awaiting their fate. The emperor Valens agreed to accept the Goths into the empire, intending to keep them as auxiliary troops for the protection of its border lines. He made two conditions, however: the Goths were to send hostages to Constantinople and must pledge to surrender their weapons to the Roman officials before crossing the river. The hostages were duly sent, but only a small part of the weapons were yielded, since the Greek officials proved ready to let any Goth keep his arms for a small bribe. The crossing was poorly organized; there was an insufficient number of boats, and no food stores had been prepared on the southern bank of the Danube—famine consequently broke out among the Visigoths, who crossed first. The imperial commissars took advantage of the situation by offering bread to "barbarians" who would surrender their womenfolk and children into slavery.

Finally the starving and exasperated bands of Visigoths revolted and rushed into Thrace, looting everything in their path (autumn of 376). The Ostrogoths, who crossed the Danube without waiting for permission from the imperial commissars, followed suit. Thus the Eastern Empire had to face a Gothic invasion. In the autumn of 377 a bloody but indecisive battle took place between the Visigoths

30. Ammianus Marcellinus, XXXI, 3, 4-8.

31. For the following see Ammianus Marcellinus, XXXI, 5-13; Jordanis, Secs. 131-138; Schmidt, pp. 257 ff.

and Roman troops at Marcianople. The Visigoths suffered heavy losses and, not relying on their own forces, called on both the Ostrogoths and the Alans for assistance. The emperor Valens personally led his troops against the combined forces of "barbarians." The decisive battle was fought at Adrianople. The Ostrogothic and Alanic cavalry broke the lines of the Roman army, and in the following confusion the Visigoths cut to pieces most of the Roman infantry. The emperor himself perished in the battle (August 9, 378).

It was with great difficulty that the new emperor, Theodosius I, one of the outstanding military leaders of the epoch, succeeded in reëstablishing the Roman army and in detaching the Alans from the Goths. After the former had left for the north, the latter were brought to some degree of submission and acknowledged themselves allies of the empire (*foederati*). As such the Visigoths received lands for settlement in Thrace and Macedonia, and the Ostrogoths in Pannonia (380).

Meanwhile the Huns, having pushed the Goths from Bessarabia, did not move farther and left the Alans to take care of Dacia. Before long the main Hunnic horde recrossed the Dniester to the east, and for some time stayed in the Pontic steppes between that river and the Volga. The Huns also paid much attention to the North Caucasian area and gradually established their control there. The bands of Alans, Ostrogoths, and Heruls who sought refuge in this area after 370 were now compelled to recognize the suzerainty of the khan of the Huns. In 395 the Huns penetrated to Transcaucasia and even raided Syria.[32]

On the west the Alans, acting as vassals of the Hunnic khan, cleared Dacia of the remnants of various German tribes who had previously settled that region, such as Visigoths, Taifals, Gepidae, Burgundians, etc. Most of them now moved farther west to the area of the middle Danube; some groups recognized the authority of the Alans. The main Alanic horde now established itself in Bessarabia and Moldavia, and the river Pruth became known as the "Alanic River."[33] It is possible that to this period may be referred the foundation of Yasy (Iași), "city of the As," i.e. of the Alans. It is mentioned as the "Market of the As" (*Asskyi Torg*) in Russian

32. Nicephorus Kallistus, XVI, 26; cf. Deguignes, I, 2, p. 294.

33. "Lanus" in Isidore of Seville, *Etymologiae,* IX, 2, 94.

chronicles of the fourteenth century.[34] The Alans, however, did not confine themselves to Dacia. Before long some groups of them, supported at times by the Huns, ventured to the area of the middle Danube. Not later than 380 an Alanic band crossed the river Tisa and got in touch with the Iazygians whose abodes were at that time between the Tisa and the Danube, as well as with the Vandals, who were settled in Pannonia west of the middle Danube.

While the Alans tended at the end of the fourth century to expand westward, their masters the Huns showed no interest in any offensive drives of their own into Europe. On the contrary, they proved quite willing to negotiate with the Roman Empire. The emperor Theodosius I (379–95), and subsequently Stilicho, ruler of the western section of the empire (395–408), did not miss the opportunity of establishing friendly relations with the redoubtable nomads. Twice in the beginning of the fifth century (in 402 and 405) the Huns and the Alans helped Stilicho to repulse attacks by certain German tribes.[35] It was only due to the wise policies of Theodosius and Stilicho, who persistently cultivated friendship with the Huns, Alans, and Goths, that the empire was able to survive the turbulent decades of the end of the fourth and the beginning of the fifth century. By drafting "barbaric" detachments into the imperial service, these rulers succeeded in transfusing healthy young blood into the senescent veins of the empire.

From the military point of view the barbarians presented much better material for soldiers than the demoralized natives. Fortunately for the empire, there was still enough gold in the treasury; also part of the barbarian troops were supplied with land instead of money. Thus "the Goth, the Hun, and the Alan joined the ranks of the army and relieved one another as sentries." [36] Some of them came to occupy high positions in the imperial army and administration. Stilicho himself was a Vandal by birth. The emperor Gratian of the western section of the empire had a predilection for the Alans, out of whose numbers a special guard regiment was formed. Gratian habitually wore Alanic garb and girded himself with Alanic weapons.[37] The Alanic guard regiment was not abolished even after

34. There was another migration of the Alans to Moldavia in the thirteenth and the fourteenth centuries, and the foundation of the city of Yasy is usually referred to that later period. Cf. Kulakovskii, *Alany*, p. 66.

35. *Idem*, p. 29.

36. L. Pacatus Drepanius, *Panegyricus Theodosio Augusto dictus*, Chap. 32.

37. Kulakovskii, *Alany*, pp. 26-27.

his death (383). *Comites Alani* are mentioned in the Notitia Dignitatum of the beginning of the fifth century.[38]

We have seen that Alanic bands appeared on the banks of the middle Danube as early as the year 380. The influx of the Alans into Pannonia continued in later years, until by the beginning of the fifth century there was already a considerable horde of them concentrated there. In 406 this Alanic horde joined the Vandals in their drive to Gaul. The further campaigns of the west Alanic horde bear on the history of Europe and, as we shall presently see, Africa, rather than that of Russia. However, they must to some extent interest the student of Russian history as well. Of all the peoples who invaded South Russia in the Sarmato-Gothic and Hunnic periods the Alans struck deeper roots in Russia, and entered into closer coöperation with the natives—especially with the Slavs—than any other migratory tribe. It was, as we know, by the Alanic clans that the Slavic tribes of the Antes was organized, and we may assume that there were Antic (Aso-Slav) and Rus (Rukhs-As) units even in the west Alanic horde. The western expansion of the Alans was thus, in a sense, the first Russian invasion of Europe.

At the time of the coming of the Alans and the Vandals, Gaul was in a chaotic state.[39] A considerable part of the country was still at least nominally under Roman rule, sustained by the help of legions recalled from Britain. These legions were not strong enough, however, to stop the invasion of the various German tribes. The Franks penetrated into the northwestern part of Gaul, while the Burgundians followed in the wake of the Alans and the Vandals. Before long the Alanic horde which had entered Gaul split into two sections. One, led by Goar, made an agreement with the local Roman authorities. The other, led by Respendial, remained loyal to the Vandals. The latter clashed with the Franks and would have perished had not Respendial's Alans helped them. Still the impact of the Frankish attack resulted in further migration of the Vandals. In 409 they moved to Spain, accompanied by Respendial's warriors. The allies had little trouble in conquering this country, which they divided between themselves (411). The Alans received as their share the provinces of Lusitania and Cartagena. The name of the town Antia which is listed in the manual of the anonymous geographer of

38. *Notitia Dignitatum* (ed. Seeck), *Occident,* VI, 130.
39. For the following see Bury, I, 185 ff.

Ravenna[40] may be noted as evidence of the Alano-Antic colonization of Spain in this period.

Let us now return to the fortunes of Goar's Alanic horde.[41] Goar made some effort to revive Roman authority in Gaul, for which purpose he entered into an agreement with the Burgundians. A Gallo-Roman officer, Jovinus by name, was proclaimed emperor upon Goar's initiative (412). However, before Jovinus had sufficient time to strengthen his power a new barbarian horde broke into Gaul, that of the Visigoths. We have seen that in the beginning of the reign of Theodosius I the Visigoths were settled in Macedonia and Thrace as allies of the empire. They proved to be very troublesome allies indeed, especially under the leadership of the energetic Alaric who was elected their king in 395. It was not long before Alaric launched raids on both Greece and Italy. Stilicho, ruler of the western portion of the empire, had to apply all available measures of protection to keep the Visigoths in check, but in 408 he was murdered by an assassin, and there remained no one to stop Alaric. The Visigoths invaded Italy in force and finally plundered Rome itself (410). Soon after, Alaric died and his successor Ataulf agreed to leave Italy in peace on condition that he should be entrusted with the administration of Gaul.

In the spring of 412 the Visigoths crossed the Alps and occupied southern Gaul in the name of Emperor Honorius. The position of the pretender Jovinus sponsored by the Alans became precarious. He failed to make an agreement with the Visigoths and was finally arrested and executed (413). Ataulf's next move was to appoint an emperor of his own in Gaul, a certain Attalus. A troubled period followed. In 414 the Visigoths attacked the town of Burdigal (now Bordeaux). Paulinus, Roman prefectus of Burdigal, escaped to a neighboring town from which he sent a messenger to the king of the Alans (probably Goar) asking him for assistance. A strong Alanic detachment was then sent by the king to protect Paulinus, and the Visigoths retreated.[42]

In 416 they invaded Spain and attacked the combined forces of the Alans and the Vandals. For two years the Visigoths pushed their enemies to the south, and in 418 they administered a crushing defeat to the Alans near Tartes (now Cadiz). The king of the Alans,

40. *Rav. An.*, IV, 45 (p. 82).
41. Kulakovskii, *Alany*, p. 35.
42. *Idem*, p. 36.

Addac, was slain in battle, and the Alanic horde was smashed to such a degree that its remnants now merged with the Vandals.[43] The latter's ruler assumed the title of king of the Vandals and Alans. In 427 both the Vandals and the Alans migrated to north Africa and settled in the area of Carthage (now Tunisia).[44] The kingdom of the Vandals and Alans in Africa lasted for over a century, until Justinian's reign.

4. The Hunnic Empire on the Danube.

We have had occasion[45] to mention that the Alans played the role of the Hunnic vanguard in the regions of the lower and middle Danube (Dacia and Pannonia respectively). The drive from Pannonia to Gaul in 406 seems to have been undertaken by the Alans independently of the Huns. However, connections were probably not severed between the Alanic horde which went west and that which remained in Dacia. Even after the migration of the western branch of the Alans to Africa, the western and eastern Alans kept in touch with each other and thus became middlemen between Attila, khan of the Huns, and Gaiseric, king of the Vandals and Alans.

Soon after the migration to the west of the Alans from Pannonia the Huns themselves moved westward. It is to be noted that the migration of the Visigoths to Gaul,[46] left even more room for newcomers in the area of the middle Danube. The steppes of this area were well fitted for nomadic ways of life, for which reason various nomadic hordes had been attracted to Pannonia long before the coming of the Huns. Pannonia was also important from a strategic point of view, since it presented a convenient base of operations against both the Balkans and Italy. It was only natural that the Huns should become interested in this area. By 420 a strong Hunnic horde had established itself in the steppes of the middle Danube region. It consisted of three *ulus,* each headed by a khan of its own. One of the three khans, Roila (Rugila) was considered the chief khan. The two other khans were probably his brothers; their names were Mundjuk and Oktar, respectively.[47]

43. *Idem,* p. 41.
44. See Gautier, *Geiserich* (Frankfurt a. M., 1934).
45. See Secs. 2 and 3, above.
46. See Sec. 3, above.
47. Bury, I, 272 and 278; Kulakovskii, I, 262.

The governments of both Rome and Constantinople tried to keep friendly relations with the Huns. Constantinople agreed to pay yearly "presents" to the khan. Rome sent to his headquarters a young officer of the Guards, Aetius, as a hostage. Aetius spent several years at the court of Khan Roila and succeeded in winning his friendship as well as that of some influential Hunnic chiefs. All this proved very useful to him afterwards, when he returned to Rome. Aetius' ambition was to rule the empire as Stilicho had before him, and even more than Stilicho he reckoned on friendly relations with the Huns for his own rise to power. After Emperor Honorius' death (423) Aetius supported the candidacy of a certain John, a civil servant. At Aetius' request Khan Roila promised to send to Italy a strong army of the Huns and Alans. The army came too late, however; John had already been defeated by supporters of the boy Valentinian, a nephew of the late Honorius. The Constantinople government sent an auxiliary corps of troops to promote Valentinian's cause. The commander of this corps was Ardabur, an Alan by birth. Because of his Alanic connections, Ardabur succeeded in reaching an agreement with Khan Roila's expeditionary force.[48] There was no battle, and Aetius was granted a pardon. He returned to Rome and gradually restored his influence with the Roman court.

While friendly relations between the Huns and Rome were thus reestablished, the Huns were suspicious of the schemes of the Constantinople government. In 424 the emperor Theodosius II agreed to pay 350 pounds of gold as a yearly tribute ("presents") to the khan.[49] On the other hand Theodosius hired several Hunnic detachments as auxiliary troops, which was contrary to his agreement with the khan. Roila therefore protested and demanded that all Huns in the imperial service be dismissed and extradited to him. This the Constantinople government refused to do and Roila consequently sent his Hunnic and Alanic troops into Thrace.

The source evidence for this Hunnic invasion is scant and somewhat confused. The event is mentioned but briefly by the church historians Socrates[50] and Philostorgius.[51] The patriarch Proclus (434–47) devoted one of his sermons to the Hunnic invasion.[52] In it

48. Philostorgius, XII, 13; Olympiodorus, frg. 46; Socrates, VII, 23.
49. Bury, I, p. 271.
50. Socrates, VII, 43.
51. Philostorgius, V, 26.
52. See Nicephorus Kallistus, XIV, 37.

he recalled Ezekiel's prophecy concerning the prince of Rosh and Meshech.[53] It is just possible that Proclus was induced to think of the Biblical Rosh by the presence of the Ros or Rus (Rukhs-As) in Roila's army. In that case his sermon would contain the first mention of the Aso-Slavic Ros (Rus) in Byzantine literature.[54]

In the midst of the campaign Roila died (433 or 434) and the Huns retreated to elect a new khan. The co-khan Mundjuk's sons, Attila and Bleda, were elected to replace Roila, and it was Attila who assumed actual power.[55] Attila was one of those indomitable world conquerors who from time to time succeeded in uniting the nomadic tribes into a mighty empire. Like Chingis Khan, he was not only a military genius but also a statesman of great ability. While ruthless when at war, Attila was not cruel by nature. He was of dark complexion, with small, deep-set eyes, a flat nose, and a thin beard. His calm dignity and fierce aspect impressed all who came in touch with him, and one tribe after another recognized him as their ruler. The pattern of Hunnic success was similar in most cases. First a speedy military defeat was administered to the enemy; diplomatic negotiations followed with the object of binding him firmly to the Hunnic horde. The personal influence of the great khan then completed the task of breaking the will of the former enemy.

In his negotiations with Constantinople Attila at first proved inclined to peace rather than to war. In 434 his envoys met those of the emperor Theodosius in a field near the bank of the Danube, at the mouth of the Morava River. According to the Hunnic custom, the envoys of both sides remained on horseback during the conference. The provisions of the treaty were hard for the empire. The emperor agreed to extradite all the Huns he had previously accepted into the imperial service and not to enlist any more; not to support any nation against the Huns; to allow Hunnic merchants free access to the border towns; and to double the annual tribute from 350 to 700 pounds of gold.[56] By this treaty Attila gained an important

53. Ezekiel, 38. 2.

54. On the interrelation of the Biblical name, Rosh, and the Greek, Rhos (Ῥῶς) see A. Florovskii, "Kniaz Rosh u proroka Iezekiila," *Sbornik v chest' na V. N. Zlatarski* (Sofia, 1925), pp. 505-520. Cf. also M. Siuziumov, "K voprosu o proiskhozhdenii slova Ῥώς, Ῥωσία, Rossiia," *VDI,* II (1940), 121-123. Neither of the above scholars refers to Proclus' sermon.

55. The chief source evidence on Attila is Priscus' *Gothic History,* preserved in fragments only; see also Jordanis' *Getica,* pp. 178-228, 254-258. Cf. Bury, I, chap. ix; Kulakovskii, I, 261-277.

56. Kulakovskii, I, 264.

advantage over the court at Constantinople, and now, feeling that the position of the Huns in the Balkans was quite secure, he was free for action elsewhere. His attention turned eastward, where his main objective was to consolidate Hunnic power in the North Caucasian area.[57] As a result, the threat to Constantinople was removed for some seven years.

While the court at Constantinople had pledged not to enlist Huns in its army, the government of Rome, due to the friendly relations between Aetius and the Hunnic chieftains, enjoyed the assistance of both the Huns and the Alans in its struggle against the Germans. It was with the help of the Hunnic and Alanic auxiliary troops that Aetius was able to carry through the war against the Burgundians and the Visigoths and to repulse the latter from Narbo in southern Gaul (435–39). Aetius thereupon allotted lands for settlement in the Narbonese district to the Alanic chieftain Sambida and his horde (439).[58] The Marselian priest Salvianus, who wrote between 439 and 451, comments on these Alans as impudent people but less treacherous than the Goths.[59] A year later (around 440) another Alanic chieftain, Eochar, received for his horde lands in Armorica between the lower Loire and Seine rivers.[60] The name Eochar may be derived from the Ossetian language: *ieukhar* means "millet-eater" in Ossetian.[61] It is recorded in the *Gallic Chronicle* (*ca.* 440) that while settling in their new lands the Alans met with considerable native opposition; which was, however, crushed.[62] The name of the river Don, a tributary of the Vilaine, may be considered a relic of Alanic colonization in Armorica.[63]

57. *Idem,* 265.

58. Kulakovskii, *Alany,* p. 38. Attention should be called in this connection to the name Alagne, a locality in the department of Aude (Longnon, *Noms,* p. 133). Cf. the name *Khalan'* in South Russia, see Chap. III, Sec. 5.

59. Salvianus, *De Gubernatione Dei,* VI, 64; cf. Kulakovskii, *Alany,* p. 40.

60. Kulakovskii, *Alany,* p. 38.

61. Miller, p. 96.

62. *Chronica Gallica,* A.D. 441; cf. Kulakovskii, *Alany,* p. 38.

63. "Don (le) ou L'Uldon," *La Grande Encyclopédie, 14,* 882; Gregory of Tours mentions a certain *Ulda fluvius* which Auguste Longnon corrects to *Uldus* and which he identifies as l'Oust (Lognon, *Geographie,* p. 159). "Uldon" is probably abridged from "Ulaen-Don"; *ulaen,* in Ossetian, means "wave." For other traces of the Alanic settlement in the toponymics the name "Allaines" (Eure-et-Loir) may be mentioned (Longnon, *Noms,* p. 133). For archaeological evidence see L. Franchet, "Une Colonie scytho-alaine en Orléanais au V-me siècle," *Revue Scientifique,* February 8 and 22, 1930.

Let us now turn back to the Huns. We have mentioned that soon after his treaty with Emperor Theodosius (434) Attila led his main horde to the Caucasus. By 440 he succeeded in establishing complete control over the North Caucasian area and was ready to return west to collect the tribute due him from the court of Constantinople, which was slow in paying. The position of the East Roman Empire was at this time rather precarious. Theodosius' main army was on the Persian frontier; another armed force had been dispatched to Sicily to prepare for an attack on Gaiseric's possessions in North Africa. The Danubian frontier was left practically without protection.

Since Attila was in friendly relations with both Gaiseric and the Sassanian shah Yazdagard II, he was well aware of the disposition of imperial troops. There was apparently a close coördination of action between the three rulers—Attila, Yazdagard, and Gaiseric—which resulted in Attila's taking care of the Danubian theater of war. In 441 Hunnic cavalry squadrons appeared again on the banks of the Danube. Taking by assault the fortresses of Singidun (now Beograd) and Viminacium, they rushed south through the valley of the Morava River and before long reached Naissus (Niš), after which they turned east along the Constantinople road and penetrated as far as the Thracian Chersonese (Gallipoli) without meeting any serious resistance on the part of Roman troops. The Huns seemed now to be in position to storm Constantinople itself, but when the emperor sued for peace Attila agreed to negotiation. As a matter of fact, the city was protected by a strong garrison, to reinforce which the government had called troops from both the Persian frontier and Sicily, and had in addition hired a band of those warlike Anatolian mountaineers, the Isaurians. According to the provisions of the treaty (A.D. 443) the emperor agreed to surrender the deserters and to pay the arrears of tribute amounting to 6,000 pounds of gold.[64]

In the following year Attila removed from power his brother Bleda and became the supreme ruler of all the Hunnic hordes from the Caucasus to the Danube. The Hunnic Khanate thus became the most powerful state of its time, and Attila's court the center of international politics and intrigues. Alans, Greeks, Germans, and Romans were among the khan's assistants. One of his secretaries was

64. Bury, I, 275; Kulakovskii, I, 267-268.

a Roman nobleman sent to him by Aetius, and Aetius' son spent some time at Attila's court in the capacity of a hostage. From the report of Priscus, who was secretary of the imperial embassy of 448,[65] we have a pretty clear idea of what Attila's court was like. His headquarters had grown into a veritable town protected by wooden walls. Inside the walls were numerous wooden buildings, some of them a type of huge log cabin and others covered with carved boards. Attila's own palace, built on a hill, was also of log cabin type but very spacious. Near by the palace of his chief wife and the houses of his adjutants were situated, and at some distance storehouses and other service buildings, among them a stone bathhouse.

During his journey from Constantinople to Attila's headquarters Priscus met several Greeks, formerly prisoners of war but now enjoying full freedom. They told Priscus that life was easier in Attila's realm than within the Roman Empire. They especially liked the absence of any taxation. While the population of the empire suffered from the extortions and abuses of the tax collectors, Attila imposed no taxes at all upon his subjects. He had no need to bother with taxation, since his treasury was always full from the proceeds of war booty as well as from the Byzantine tribute.

The Hunnic army was a formidable force. Its main body, as was the case with all the nomadic peoples, consisted of cavalry. As cavalrymen the Huns and their vassals the Alans knew no equal. But it appears that the Huns, as later the Mongols, were also well versed in military engineering. They had engines for breaking even the strong stone walls of Roman fortresses. It is possible that the Huns first became acquainted with siege machinery in China. It is likewise possible that after Attila's agreement with Yazdagard (440) the latter may have sent him some of his Persian engineers. And there is no doubt that when the Huns penetrated the Roman fortified line along the Danube they must have obtained full knowledge of Roman military engineering devices. Roman engineers, both prisoners and deserters, may have been employed to build siege machinery for the khan. According to Priscus' description of the siege of Naissus,[66] they used high movable platforms protected by parapets made of boughs and covered with hides. Archers were placed upon them, and they were then driven close to the city walls. When the

65. Priscus, frg. 8; English trans., Bury, I, 279-288.
66. *Idem,* frg. l-b.

enemy soldiers, under a terrific hail of arrows and other missiles, abandoned the ramparts, rams and ladders were moved in close to the walls and gates of the city, which was then before long taken.

It seems probable that aside from the Alanic units there were Slavic detachments in the Hunnic army. The Slavic language must have been widely used in Attila's state. According to Priscus, when the Byzantine embassy crossed the Danube on its way to Attila's headquarters, local people treated the Greeks with a beverage which they called μέδος which is certainly the Slavic *mëd* ("mead"). The embassy servants were offered another kind of beverage, made of barley, which was known as κάμος—that is, the Slavic *kvas*.[67] One more Slavic word is mentioned by Jordanis: *strava* ("funeral banquet").[68]

5. *The Last Years of Attila's Reign.*[69]

Attila's court was always filled with foreign agents, some of them bona fide diplomatic representatives, others spies and saboteurs, even would-be assassins. To counteract their activities Attila was obliged to build up an intelligence service of his own. A characteristic story concerning this interplay of spying and intrigue is told by Priscus. In 448 Attila sent as his envoy to Constantinople Edecon, a German sincerely devoted to him. When Edecon arrived at the capital he was approached by Vigila, a Goth in the service of the empire, who attempted to bribe him to murder Attila. The scheme was engineered by an influential Byzantine courtier, the eunuch Chrysaphius, whose agent Vigila was. Edecon pretended to be interested in the suggestion. Chrysaphius' next move was to include Vigila as an interpreter in the staff of the Byzantine diplomatic mission sent to Attila, of which the senator Maximinus was chairman and Priscus secretary. Vigila took along with him a bag of gold intended for Edecon as the price of his assistance in the organization of Attila's murder. According to Priscus, neither he nor Maximinus knew anything of the business. Maximinus' mission arrived safely at Attila's headquarters. Vigila meant to hand the gold to Edecon, not immediately upon the arrival of the mission but when Maximinus had completed the parleys and was about to start home. But since Edecon remained loyal to Attila, Vigila's plan went wrong.

67. *Idem*, frg. 8.
68. Jordanis, Sec. 258.
69. Bury, I, 258-296.

The khan ordered him searched, and his bag of gold was seized as evidence of his scheming. Attila was at first about to order his execution but then changed his mind and offered to let him go for a ransom of 50 pounds of gold. Vigila's son was dispatched to Constantinople to collect the money, and until his return Vigila was kept under arrest. Upon receipt of the ransom money Attila freed Vigila but now demanded the extradition of the eunuch Chrysaphius. Theodosius was forced to offer the khan still another sum of gold to secure Chrysaphius' safety.

While Constantinople was sending more and more gold to Attila, as to Rome, the khan was considering a marriage plan. It appears that the initiative in this matter was taken by the ambitious Princess Honoria, sister of Emperor Valentinian III. Fearing to lose his throne as a result of Honoria's intrigues her brother decided to marry her to some courtier loyal to him, and in 450 she was forcibly engaged to an old senator whom she despised. It was at this juncture that Honoria made a bold move: she secretly dispatched her trusted eunuch to Attila to hand him her engagement ring and ask for his protection. Attila was quick to grasp the potential political advantages he might draw from the marriage, and immediately sent envoys to Rome asking for Honoria's hand and half the empire as dowry. Emperor Valentinian declined, however, to accept Attila as a brother-in-law. Honoria was put under arrest. Until this time Aetius, actual head of the Roman Government, was as we have seen[70] an "appeaser" with regard to the Huns. Now, however, there seemed no alternative to war, and Aetius started preparations for it with all his energy.

While Aetius' previous policy had been to defeat the Germans with the help of the Huns, he now attempted to obtain German support against them. He succeeded in forming a powerful coalition in which the Visigoths, the Burgundians and the Franks agreed to participate. On his own part, Attila was likewise active in the diplomatic field. He succeeded in breaking the unity of the Franks, and while the elder of the two brother-rulers supported Aetius, the younger went over to Attila's side. While the Visigoths were Aetius' allies, the Ostrogoths joined force with Attila. Gaiseric, king of the Vandals and the Alans, likewise entered into an agreement with Attila.

The war of 451 was fought in the fields of Gaul. The campaign started with a race of both Aetius and Attila toward the fortified

70. See Sec. 4, above.

city of Aureliana (Orleans) which was held by Sangiban, ruler of the Alanic horde settled in Armorica.[71] Attila hoped that Sangiban would surrender the city and go over to the Huns with his Alans. Things turned out differently, however, since it was Aetius who reached Orleans first, bringing the Visigoths with him. The Alans submitted to Aetius somewhat reluctantly.

Attila then by-passed the city on the north and stopped on the "Campus Mauriacus," near present-day Troyes. It was here that the famous Battle of Nations took place in June 451.[72] On Attila's side, beside the Huns and the eastern Alans, were the Gepids, the Ostrogoths, the Heruls, and a section of Franks. Aetius' forces consisted of Roman legions (recruited chiefly from the Gauls and the Germans), the Visigoths, the Burgundians, the Franks, and the unreliable Armorica Alans. The battle was bloody but indecisive. Since the main part of the field remained under control of the Visigoths, Aetius boasted that victory was his. He did not, however, resume the attack on the next day. After a while Attila led his horde back to Pannonia while the Visigoths retreated south to Toulouse.

The Hunnic danger was not over, and in the autumn of 451 Attila started preparations for an invasion of Italy. The position of that country was desperate. While Aetius was able to mobilize the Visigoths for the defense of Gaul, he did not dare call them to Italy lest they occupy it themselves. In the spring of 452 the khan began his Italian campaign. He led his troops through the mountain passes of the Julian Alps meeting no resistance, and surrounded Aquileja. Taking this fortress after protracted siege, he went on to Milan. Here he met Roman envoys—Pope Leo and two senators. After conferring with them, Attila called the campaign off and returned to Pannonia.

The Romans attributed the great warrior's retreat to the intercession of Saints Peter and Paul. Centuries later Raphael immortalized the meeting between the khan and the Pope in a painting in the Vatican. There may, however, have been contributing reasons for Attila's decision. Due to the poor harvest of the previous year, famine and plague had spread over Italy. Byzantine troops in Illyria threatened to break the Hunnic lines of communication. No peace treaty was signed, and Attila did not withdraw his claims to Honoria's hand. But he decided for the present to strike at

71. See Sec. 3, above.
72. Lot, pp. 107-108.

Byzantium instead of Rome. In the midst of preparations for a campaign against Constantinople, he celebrated his nuptials with the young German beauty, Ildico. On the morning after the wedding night Attila was found dead (453). It is not known whether he died from a stroke or was poisoned by his bride, as rumor had it.[73]

6. The Azov Region, the Taurida, and the North Caucasian Area in the Fourth and the First Half of the Fifth Century.

In the preceding survey of Hunnic history we have concentrated our attention on the westward expansion of the Huns and have only casually mentioned their Caucasian campaigns. However, we must remember that economically the strength of the Hunnic Khanate depended on control of the Pontic steppes, through which the western extension of the great Eurasian overland route[74] reached the Danube. An important side extension of this route branched off from the Azov region southward to Transcaucasia, and control of this branch was one of the objectives of the Hunnic drive in the Caucasus.

Unfortunately we have little information on the economic life of the Azov Region, the Taurida, and the North Caucasian area in the Gothic and early Hunnic periods. We may only surmise that at this time, as in the preceding and subsequent periods, the Azov region was the gateway of trade between the Russian north and the Levant, and that furs constituted an important item of this trade. According to Jordanis it was the Onoguri, a Magyar tribe under Hunnic authority, who specialized in the fur trade in the fifth and sixth centuries.[75] Commercial relations between the Azov-Tauric region and the Levant had their counterpart in the expansion of Christianity in the Taurida and adjacent areas. The missionary and the merchant came together, as has often been the case in history.

The ethnic composition of the population in the area we are now studying was diverse. Widely different tribes were united under the political control of the Huns. There were some remnants of aboriginal tribes, such as the Maeotians;[76] also some Greeks, descendants of the Greek colonists of the Scythian period; remnants of the German tribes, such as the Goths and the Heruls; numerous Alanic

73. See J. Moravcsik, "Attila's Todt in Geschichte und Sage," *KCA*, II (1926).
74. Cf. Chap. III, Sec. 3.
75. Jordanis, Sec. 37.
76. See Chap. II, Sec. 2.

communities partly mixed with the native tribes of the North Caucasian area, as for example the Kasogians (Circassians). As we know, part of the Alans, or As, had mixed with the Slavs (the Antes). Thus, when we find evidence concerning the As or the Antes, it is not always clear whether the Iranians, or the Slavs, or mixed Irano-Slavic tribes are meant. Generally speaking the Iranian element was more pronounced among the eastern than among the western Antes. After the migration of the Alanic horde from Dacia to Spain and Africa, the Iranian element must have been running low among the Bessarabian Antes, so that they eventually became practically pure Slavic tribes.

The As and Antes in the Azov region and the Taurida continued to represent a symbiosis of the Iranians and the Slavs. Among the As of the North Caucasian area (the Ossetians) the Iranians were predominant, although there may have been, even there, Slavic communities as so many enclaves in the Iranian territory. In the Don area Iranian and Slavic communities coexisted probably from the beginning of the Christian era; most of them survived the Hunnic invasion and continued to exist as late as the twelfth century, at the beginning of which the Russian prince Yaropolk, son of Vladimir Monomach, waged war against the Yasians (the As) on the lower Don.[77] In the Greek inscriptions found on the site of the old city of Tanais, and generally referred to the third century A.D., names of Iranian origin are frequently mentioned.[78] Such for example are Φίδας (cf. Ossetian *fida,* "father"); Φούρτας (Ossetian *furt,* "son"); Μάδακος (Ossetian *mada,* "mother"); Λείμανος (Ossetian *liman,* "friend," "dear"); Σόρχακος (Ossetian *surkh,* "red"); Ῥάσσογος (Ossetian *rasog,* "pure," "clean," etc.).

We must recall that the Roxolani (Rukhs-As) penetrated into the Taurida as early as the second century A.D.[79] In the course of the second and the third centuries the Alans-As reached the southern littoral of the Tauric peninsula. In the year 212 they founded the city of Sugdaea (now Sudak).[80] The old Greek town of Theodosia became known in the Sarmato-Gothic period as Abdarda, an Iranian name meaning "Seven Sides." [81] Judging from the names of Iranian

77. Hyp., col. 280.
78. Miller, *Sledy,* pp. 242 ff.
79. See Chap. III, Sec. 4.
80. Cf. Chap. III, Sec. 5.
81. Miller, *Sledy,* pp. 239-240.

origin in the Panticapaeum (Kerch) inscriptions of this period there must have been plenty of Alans among the inhabitants of this city.[82] The following may be mentioned in this connection: Phidas, Liman, Pharnac, etc.

There is also some toponymic evidence of the expansion of the As in the steppes of the northern Taurida: several villages within the former Eupatoria and Perekop districts have "As" as their name or a part of their name. Such are: As, Biuk-As, Kuchuk-As, Terekli-As, etc. There also is a river As in the northern part of the peninsula.[83] The name of the Gothic city of Doras, or Dory (Eski-Kerman), may be approached from the same angle. *Dor* means "rock" in Ossetian; Doras—Dor-As, the Rock of the As (cf. Dar-i-Alan, "The Gate of the Alans" Daryal). The form Dory may be considered an abridgment of Dor-i-As.

Another group of the As lived on the Caucasian side of the Bosporus. Here again, names of Iranian origin in the Anapa and Taman inscriptions may be cited as evidence; such, for example, as Kars, Tsavag, Kopharn, Alexarth, etc.[84] The ancient name of the Kuban River Antikites[85] may likewise refer to the Antes, or As, in its first part. Later on, when the Kasogians (Circassians) replaced the Antes on the banks of the Kuban River, they accepted the name of the river as their own. Adyge, which is a variation of Antike (Antikites), is another name of the Circassians.[86] To complete the picture, the name of the hill Assodag (As-Dag) in the Kuban delta, near Taman, may be mentioned here.[87] According to Ibn-Rusta, an Arabic author of the tenth century, one of the prominent clans of the North Caucasian As was known as Rukhs-As ("the Light-As").[88] It is probably from the name of this clan that the town Malorosa, mentioned by the anonymous geographer of Ravenna[89] of the seventh century, derives its name. *Mal* means "swamp," "bog," in Ossetian.[90] Thus, Malorosa would mean "the Bog of the Ros" (Rukhs). In

82. *Idem,* pp. 243, 248.

83. A. I. Markevich, "Geograficheskaia nomenklatura Kryma," *TO,* II (1928), 12; Vasmer, *Iranier,* p. 70.

84. Miller, *Sledy,* pp. 246, 247, 257, 259, 261; cf. Vasmer, *Iranier,* pp. 31 ff.

85. Strabo, XI, 2, 9.

86. Marr, *Sostav,* pp. 45 and 52.

87. Goertz, I, 79 f.

88. Minorsky, p. 445.

89. Rav. An., IV, 3 (p. 45).

90. Miller, *Slovar,* p. 787.

the Ravenna manual Malorosa is mentioned among the Bosporan towns, as close to Cimmerium. The latter was situated on the Taman side of the Kerch Strait, and it seems certain that Malorosa was likewise somewhere in the Kuban delta, near Phanagoria, perhaps at Temriuk. Incidentally, Phanagoria is not mentioned by the Ravenna geographer at all. The Kuban delta is swampy throughout; thus the first part of the name, Mal-, fits well with local conditions.

In the third century A.D. the Goths fought their way into the Taurida.[91] At first they occupied only the mountainous central section of the peninsula, but later they attempted to establish their control over the whole of it. Around 362 they conquered Panticapaeum, which had been the capital of the kingdom of the Bosporus. Some fifteen years after this event the Huns made their appearance in the Taurida. In the winter of 377 or 378 a division of them crossed the frozen Kerch Strait from the Caucasian to the Crimean side. These Huns belonged probably to the horde which later became known as the Utiguri.[92] They drove the Goths back to the central part of the Crimean peninsula; the Huns themselves did not stay long in the Crimea, but, crossing the Tauric steppes and the Perekop Isthmus, joined the main Hunnic horde at the mouth of the Dnieper River.

After departure of the Huns the Goths must have gradually extended their control to the eastern part of the peninsula once more. In any case, around the year 400 Bosporus (Kerch) was once more under their authority, as we may judge from John Chrysostom's correspondence.[93] We have already seen[94] that by the beginning of the fourth century Christianity was already firmly established in the Taurida. The oldest Christian community in the Crimea was that of Cherson. At the First Ecumenical Council in Nicea (325) the Taurida was represented by two bishops: Philip of Cherson, and Cadmus of Bosporus. It is probably to the latter's eparchy that the Gothic parishes belonged. Later, the Gothic congregation was for some time under the immediate authority of the Patriarch of Constantinople. John Chrysostom was favorably inclined to the Goths and assigned them a church in a suburb of Constantinople where they were allowed to have service in their own language. Around

91. For the following see Vasiliev, pp. 21 ff.; and Kulakovskii, *Tavrida,* pp. 38-39, 54 ff.

92. See Sec. 7, below.

93. John Chrysostom, "Epistola XIV," *PG, 52,* col. 618; cf. Vasiliev, p. 33.

94. See Chap. III, Secs. 4 and 9.

the year 400 John consecrated the first bishop of the Tauric (Crimean) Goths, Unila. His see was probably in Bosporus (Kerch). Unila died in 404, and nothing is known of his immediate successors. The see of the Gothic bishop was later located in Dory (Eski-Kerman).

7. The Downfall of the Hunnic Empire.

After Attila's death the power of the Hunnic Khanate was divided among his sons, of whom none inherited his father's administrative abilities. The moment seemed propitious for a revolt on the part of the subjugated peoples. A coalition of German tribes was formed in which the Gepids, the Rugii, and the Heruls joined. The Ostrogoths kept aloof from the struggle. One of Attila's sons, Ellak, attempted to crush the rebellion but his forces proved insufficient for the task. His army was defeated and he himself perished in the battle (454).[95] By this defeat the unity of the Huns was broken. The remnants of Ellak's horde moved east of the Carpathian mountains. Two of the remaining sons of Attila, Dengizik and Ernak, with their clans, made Dacia and Bessarabia their headquarters for some time. A tribe of Alans previously settled there now had to cross the Danube and move into the Dobrudja. This tribe was ruled by King Candac whose secretary was an Ostrogoth, Paria, grandfather of the historian Jordanis. Aside from the Alans, several Hunnic bands likewise penetrated to the right bank of the Danube and received land allotments as allies of the empire.[96]

In the last years of the reign of Marcian (d. 457) and in the first half of the reign of his successor Leo I, the direction of Byzantine policy was in the hands of Aspar, whose father was an Alan and whose mother was a Gothic girl.[97] Through his Alanic and Gothic connections Aspar was familiar with the movements of the Hunnic hordes in the Danubian area. One of his lieutenants, the army commander in Thrace—Anagast by name—was a "Scythian" according to the evidence of the chronicles.[98] By the fifth century the term "Scythian" had become rather indefinite, meaning a northern barbarian at large. Later it was occasionally used to denote

95. Jordanis, Secs. 259-261; Schmidt, p. 268 f.

96. Jordanis, Sec. 265.

97. On Aspar see Tillemont, pp. 409-414; O. Seeck, "Flavius Ardabur Aspar," *PW*, 2, cols. 607-610.

98. John of Antioch, frg. 205 (*Exc. Ins.*, p. 129).

Slavs. In this case it probably stood for an Antas. Anagast is a typical Antic name.

In spite of the dismemberment of Attila's empire, the Hunnic danger was not yet over. In 468 Dengizik and Ernak sent their envoys to Constantinople to demand the opening of the Danubian markets to their merchants. When the demand was denied, Dengizik crossed the Danube and invaded Thrace. The Huns were, however, defeated by Anagast's troops and Dengizik himself was killed in battle. Anagast sent the khan's head to Constantinople, where it was paraded through the capital's thoroughfares and then fixed on a pole in the Wooden Circus.[99]

The war was not over, since more Huns crossed from Dacia. It was only with the utmost effort that Aspar and Anagast succeeded in crushing the bulk of the late Dengizik's horde. Its remnants re-crossed the Danube and retreated eastward following the lead of Ernak, the younger khan, who had not supported his brother in his attack on Byzantine possessions.[100] It is significant that of the two victorious Byzantine generals one (Aspar) was an Alan, and the other (Anagast) an Antas. There must have been hundreds of Alans and Antes in the retinues of each of them. In a sense, the Danubian war of 468–69 was a war of the Alans and the Antes against their former lords, the Huns.

As a result of Aspar's victory and the Huns' retreat to the east, Dacia and Bessarabia were thrown open for Slavic colonization. It is even possible that the Slavic drive to the lower Danube region was partly the result of a deliberate scheme on the part of Byzantine diplomats. To oppose one barbarian tribe to another was a traditional method of Byzantine diplomacy in its constant effort to secure the northern borders of the empire. As we have seen, Aetius applied this method early in the fifth century,[101] and we shall see[102] that in the sixth century the Byzantine government first made an agreement with the Avars against the Bulgaro-Huns, later attempted to use the Bulgars against the Avars, and so on almost indefinitely. Aspar

99. Priscus, frgs. 36, 38, 39; *Chronicon Paschale,* I, 598; *Marcellinus, s.a.* 469.

100. I am ready to accept in its essence J. Bromberg's thesis that "the Protobulgarian Huns lived between the end of the fifth century and the arrival of the Avars only near the Azov Sea and *not* in the Balkans or in Transylvania" (Bromberg, p. 58). Mr. Bromberg is preparing a comprehensive monograph on the subject.

101. See Sec. 3, above.

102. See Chap. V, Sec. 2.

appears to have planned now to settle the Slavs on the lower Danube in order to avert the Hunnic menace. It is also possible that he felt he might need their support in his struggle for power within the empire itself. One must take into consideration that Aspar was at the time about to revolt against the emperor Leo.[103] The latter's son-in-law Zeno commanded the Isaurian guard regiment, which remained loyal to Leo, and Aspar was hastily mustering his followers to overcome the Isaurians. It is in this connection that he may have thought of the Slavs.

In 471 Aspar and two of his sons were invited to Leo's palace under a suitable pretext and there the intriguing statesman and his eldest son Ardabur were treacherously murdered.[104] The younger son, Patricius, also known as Patriciolus, was wounded but succeeded in escaping. One of the commanding officers of Aspar's retinue, Ostrys, attempted to storm the imperial palace in order to avenge his chief's murder. His detachment, however, was prevented by the Isaurians from entering the palace, and Ostrys fled to Thrace.[105] Judging from his name, he was either an Alan or a Slav.[106]

The subsequent fate of Anagast is unknown. In any case, the Alano-Gothic retinue of Aspar was disbanded, and it was the Isaurians who now became the emperor's chief support. After Leo's death (474) his son-in-law Zeno who commanded the Isaurians, was proclaimed emperor.

Zeno's position was at first rather precarious, due to the opposition of the Goths settled in Thrace. Only after their main body moved to Italy (488) could the Byzantine Government consider itself safe from the Gothic danger, but now a new threat had developed, that of the Hunno-Bulgars. It was Zeno himself who called the Huns (by this time already known as the Bulgars) back to the Balkans; his idea was to use them against the Goths. An auxiliary Hunnic squadron arrived in 482 and proved at first quite useful to the Byzantines. However, not long after Zeno's death (491) the Huns ran amuck and began to raid Thrace (493, 499,

103. Bury, I, 318-320; Kulakovskii, I, 351-354.

104. Nicephorus Kallistus, XV, 27.

105. Malalas, pp. 371-372; cf. *Exc. Ins.*, p. 161.

106. F. I. Uspenskii, who considers Ostrys a Slav, derives his name from the Slavic adjective *ostryi* ("sharp") (Uspenskii, I, 389). I suggest the derivation of the name from the Ossetian *stur,* "great," "big." Cf. Miller, *Slovar,* p. 1131.

504).[107] It is quite probable that they were joined by Slavs on at least some of these raids. Comes Marcellinus, whose chronicle is one of our best sources for the period, calls the raiders of 493 "Scythians."[108] He may mean either Huns or Slavs or both under this antiquated name, but it is more likely that he means Slavs, since the Huns now usually appear under the name of Bulgars.

The two main Hunno-Bulgar tribes of this period were known as the Kutriguri and the Utiguri. The Bulgar horde which subsequently settled in the Balkans in the course of the seventh and eighth centuries was of Utiguri stock, and since the Bulgar khans of those centuries considered themselves the descendants of Ernak,[109] we may conclude that it was Ernak's horde which became known as the Utiguri horde. Ernak, as we know, moved eastward from Bessarabia during or after his brother Dengizik's war with Byzantium. It is probable that the Utiguri spent several years in the lower Dnieper region, after which they entered the north Crimean steppes through the Perekop Isthmus; they did not settle in the Crimea, however, but drove through the peninsula from northwest to southeast until they reached the Bosporus (Kerch Strait), which they crossed in order to settle in the Azov-Taman region. The Utiguri drive from Bessarabia to Taman may be considered historically a return to their old abodes, since their route was the same as that of the section of the Hunnic horde which crossed Kerch Strait westward on the ice in the winter of 377.[110] Only now the move was in the opposite direction. It is quite possible that at the time of the first, or westward, drive some Utiguri *ulus* remained in the Azov-Taman region, so that the Utiguri were now rejoining their kin. While crossing the Crimean steppes they came into contact with the Crimean Goths, part of whom followed them to the Taman side of the strait. These Goths, settled on the eastern shore of the Sea of Azov, are sometimes more specifically called the Trapezites (Tetraxites).[111]

The Kutriguri, or the remnants of Dengizik's horde, followed the lead of the Utiguri in their eastward drive. By the end of the fifth century they roved between the bend of the lower Dnieper and the Sea of Azov, controlling likewise the steppes of northern Tauria

107. Kulakovskii, I, 468.
108. Marcellinus, *s.a.* 493.
109. Runciman, pp. 279-281.
110. See Sec. 6, above.
111. Vasiliev, pp. 57-69; cf. Chap. III, Sec. 9.

and of the Crimean peninsula as far east as Bosporus. The area occupied by the Kutriguri thus corresponds to the area of the old Scythian kurgans.[112] The Byzantine authorities in the southern Crimea became worried by Kutriguri pressure and in 488 the governor of Cherson decided, with the emperor Zeno's approval, to restore the walls and towers of Cherson which had been destroyed by an earthquake eight years before.[113]

Besides the Utiguri and the Kutriguri there was a third Hunnic horde in the North Caucasian area, the Sabiri or Saviri (Sabeiroi). The Sabiri appear to have extended their authority over various Ugrian (Magyar) tribes who came to the area in the second half of the fifth century from the Ural region. Among these Ugrian tribes, the Onoguri[114] and the Saraguri may be mentioned here, the latter to be identified as the White Ugrians of the Russian *Primary Chronicle*.[115]

Notwithstanding the inroads of the barbaric tribes in the Crimea, Christianity was making steady progress there. The bishops of both Bosporus and Cherson attended the church councils at Ephesus and Constantinople (438–451).[116] Several Christian funeral cave chambers—a kind of catacomb—were excavated in the nineteenth century in the outskirts of Kerch. In the catacomb dated 491 an Alanic couple had been buried, as may be seen from the names in the inscription (Savag and Phaisparta).[117]

Little evidence is available as to the commercial role of Bosporus (Kerch) in the fifth and the first half of the sixth century. In one of the Kerch inscriptions bearing on the time of Justinian I,[118] a functionary with the title of *comes* is mentioned. There were in the Byzantine bureaucracy of the time *comites* of various ranks and functions. Some took care of the collection of customs duties (later such officers were known as *commerciarii*). According to Kulakovskii it is to this group of civil servants that the *comes* of the Kerch inscription must be referred.[119] If so, it would point to a considerable volume of trade transactions in Bosporus. As has been

112. See Chap. II, Sec. 2.
113. Vasiliev, pp. 43-47.
114. See Moravcsik.
115. Vernadsky, *Lebedia,* pp. 183-186.
116. Kulakovskii, *Tavrida,* p. 56.
117. *Idem,* pp. 57-58.
118. See Sec. 10, below.
119. Kulakovskii, *Tavrida,* p. 59.

already mentioned,[120] furs must have constituted an important item of this commerce.

8. The Antes from the End of the Fourth to the Middle of the Sixth Century.

While references to the Antes have been made on several occasions in preceding sections, it is now time to reconsider the Antic problem and to attempt to draw a general picture of the expansion of the Antes and their civilization. Such a picture cannot be complete, owing to the gaps in our source evidence. We have already seen[121] that in the Sarmato-Gothic period there were two groups of the Antes, one in the region of the upper Donets, the other in the region of the lower Bug River. A number of them must have penetrated to the Crimea together with the Alans.[122] Following the Alano-Gothic war of 375, a section of the Antes may have moved to Bessarabia as a part of the general Alanic drive. At the end of the fifth and the beginning of the sixth century, when the Sclaveni started to move south to the region of the lower Danube, the Antes may have occupied part of the area formerly settled by the Sclaveni in the Kiev and Volynia regions; there is, however, no definite evidence for such a surmise. Generally speaking, the Antes occupied hardly any continuous territory of large size, and it would be difficult to define precisely the boundaries of the Antic expansion.

Following the Hunnic invasion, and especially the subsequent dismemberment of the Hunnic Empire, the ethnic and political situation in the Pontic steppes was somewhat confused. Alanic and Slavic communities were hemmed in by many Turkish and Ugrian tribes. According to Procopius' evidence the Dniester River was the *eastern* boundary of the Bessarabian group of the Antes.[123] As to the Donets group, they were now cut off from the sea by the Hunno-Bulgar hordes. Nevertheless, a number of Antic settlements must have continued to exist both in the region of the lower Don and in the North Caucasian area, where the Antes were mixed with the As, or Alans.

The above considerations may be to a certain extent confirmed by the data of toponymics and archaeology. We have already seen

120. See Sec. 6, above.
121. See Chap. III, Sec. 7; cf. Sec. 2, above.
122. See Sec. 6, above.
123. Procopius, VII, 14, 32-33.

that the name As is reflected in many names of localities in South Russia.[124] In view of the close connection between the As and the Antes we may assume that in certain cases the name As was used to mean the Antes as well. The problem is indeed rather involved. From our point of view the Antes may always be called the As, since they were Slavs ruled by Alanic clans. On the other hand, the As are not always to be identified as the Antes since in many cases they were pure Iranians without any admixture of Slavic blood. Such were the North Caucasian As, or the Ossetians. In the Kuban delta region as well as in the Crimea we may assume the existence of both Iranian and Slavic As (i.e., Antes). Therefore the names of some of the Crimean localities derived from the name "As" may be considered an evidence of the Antic expansion. In this connection the names of the town of Kichkas (Kuchuk As) on the lower Dnieper, and the city of Yasy in Moldavia, may likewise be mentioned. It appears that the island of Berezan in the Dnieper estuary was also known as Aas.[125]

An attempt to study the archaeological background of the Antes was first made by the late A. A. Spitsyn.[126] His conclusions were tentative especially since he did not include Alanic antiquities in the field of his study. Spitsyn first approached his subject from the topographical point of view. In his opinion the territory settled by the Antes extended from the region of the lower Dniester to the upper Donets River. The group of antiquities of the sixth and the seventh centuries wrought in the same style and found within the alleged territory of Antic expansion should be identified as Antic antiquities, according to Spitsyn. He thus refers to the Antes a number of treasure hoards of the period, found in various locales in the provinces of Kherson, Kiev, Chernigov, Poltava, Ekaterinoslav, Kharkov and Voronezh. Spitsyn's conclusions have been recently confirmed and developed by B. A. Rybakov.

According to Rybakov,[127] the territory settled by the Antes stretched from the lower Danube to the Donets River. The following group of antiquities of the fifth, sixth, and seventh centuries found within this territory may be considered Antic according to

124. See Sec. 6, above; also, Chap. III, Sec. 7.

125. So called in the Russian "Life of St. Aetherius," *Zhitiia Sviatykh* by St. Dmitri of Rostov, March 7, quoted by Brun, I, 92.

126. A. A. Spitsyn, "Drevnosti Antov," *ANORS, 101* (1928), 492-495.

127. Rybakov, pp. 320-323.

Rybakov: digitate and plain fibulas, pendants, moon-shaped ornaments, square metal plates, metal earrings of coarse grain; bracelets with widening ends; spiral eyes (for hook and eye); massive belt clasps; one-sided combs of a peculiar type, with high ornamented back; temple rings, etc. Most of these things are made either of bronze or silver, but some are of gold. To this list swords of Antic type should be added. In another connection Rybakov himself mentions Antic swords of the seventh century.[128]

The above list will probably be considerably revised and enlarged, if and when a systematic parallel study of Antic and Alanic antiquities is undertaken. A convenient archaeological site for starting such a study would be Verkhni Saltov on the upper Donets River.[129] The settlement at Verkhni Saltov was an important commercial station in the trade between northern Russia and the Azov region. Objects excavated are referred to the period between the sixth and the ninth centuries, but in all probability the As settlement here was founded long before the sixth century. Subsequently, Verkhni Saltov was occupied by the Magyars, and then probably by the Swedes. Hence the contradiction in the opinions of various scholars who have studied the antiquities of Kharkov province, where Verkhni Saltov is situated. The Swedish scholar T. Arne refers to some antiquities found in this province as Swedish.[130] The Magyar archaeologist N. Fettich has defined some of the Saltov objects as Magyar.[131] Thus, some things found in and around Verkhni Saltov may be Swedish, others Magyar, and still others Alanic (As, Antic).

According to Rybakov the center of Antic civilization was in the region of the middle Dnieper, in Kiev and Chernigov provinces; to the east the Antic area comprised the regions along the rivers Desna, Seim, Psiol, Vorskla, and reached the Don near Voronezh; southward, it extended to the lower Dnieper. It must be noted that Rybakov makes no distinction between the boundaries of expansion of the Antes in the earlier period (the fifth and the first half of the sixth century) and in the later period (second half of the sixth, and the seventh century). Approaching the problem from the point of view of general historical background, we may suppose

128. *Idem*, p. 337.

129. Gotie, pp. 58-62; A. M. Pokrovskii, "Verkhne-Saltovskii mogilnik," *TAS*, XII, *1* (1905); V. A. Babenko, "Novye sistematicheskie issledovaniia Verkhne-Saltovskogo mogilnika," *TAS*, XIV, *3* (1911).

130. Arne, pp. 57-59.

131. Fettich, p. 188; cf. Zakharov, pp. 67 f., p. 73.

that the lower Bug region and Bessarabia were the area of the earlier Antic civilization. It was only later that its center shifted north, to the Kiev region. As Rybakov himself suggests, some antiquities of the Antes are similar to the antiquities of Byzantine cities on the northern Pontic littoral. This is evidence of the close connection between the Antes and the Greeks; such a connection is most easily explained if we assume that at least some of the Antic settlements were close to the Black Sea. It also points to the existence of Alano-Antic communities in the Crimea.

While agriculture seems to have been the mainstay of Antic economy, cattle breeding was likewise well known to the Antes. In the Byzantine and Syriac sources we find references to the stores of millet and vegetables in the settlements of the Antes;[132] to Antic fields along the Danube;[133] and to herds of cattles and horses.[134] The Antes seem to have settled by clans or large families of the zadruga type, and to have paid great attention to making their settlements inaccessible to their enemies. "They live in woods and swamps, between rivers and lakes; their settlements have many exits for escaping in case of danger."[135] Recently, several sites of old settlements have been excavated in Ukraine which may be referred to the Antes.[136] Such are the Gochevo *gorodishche* of the sixth and seventh centuries on the bank of the Vorskla River, etc. Remnants of a Slavic (Antic) settlement have been likewise found in Borshevo.[137] The ground plan of an Antic *gorodishche* of the Borshevo or Gochevo type consists of a large central circle around which dugouts are placed; the settlement is provided with many exits. This fits well with Mauricius' description. The dugouts in the *gorodishcha* of this type are square, 5 by 5 meters; in the center of each there was a clay stove, and along the walls, earthen benches. Near the hut were pits for storing food; millet grain and bones of domestic animals (cow, pig, sheep, goat) have been found in such pits.

Let us turn now to the political and social organization of the Antes. Procopius calls it a democracy. "For these nations, the Sclaveni

132. Mauricius, XI, 5.

133. To be more precise, Menander speaks of the "Slavic" fields in this case. Menander, frg. 48 (p. 99).

134. Procopius, VII, 14, 22; John of Ephesus *apud* Michael Syrus, ed. Chabot, p. 380; cf. Markwart, p. 483.

135. Mauricius, XI, 5.

136. Rybakov, pp. 323-325.

137. See Chap. I, Sec. 3, on the older cultural strata of Borshevo.

and the Antae, are not ruled by one man, but they have lived from ancient times under a democracy, and consequently everything which involves their welfare, whether for good or for ill, is referred to the people."[138] According to Mauricius, "both the Sclaveni and the Antes live in freedom and do not let anybody subjugate them. . . . They have no supreme power but always quarrel one with another."[139] The picture of the political organization of the Antes as given by both Procopius and Mauricius is not complete, however, since we know from other sources that certain groups or communes of Antes were headed by chieftains wielding considerable authority. Thus, as we have seen,[140] at the time of the Alano-Gothic War of 375 the Antes were led by King Boz and seventy grandees.[141] Menander likewise mentions the "archons" of the Antes.[142]

Since (in our opinion) the Antes were Slavs organized by Iranians (Alans), the Antic ruling clan must have been of Iranian origin. It is characteristic that the names of Antic chieftains as recorded in the chronicles are in many cases Iranian or half-Iranian. Such are, for example, the names Ardagast,[143] Peiragast,[144] Kelagast.[145] These names are compound. The second part of each, "-gast," is also known as a separate name from a Kerch inscription (Γάστης).[146] It may be either Iranian, Keltic, Thracian, or Slavic, but the fact that it was used in the Bosporan kingdom shows that it was in any case assimilated by the Iranians. Some Slavic names followed the same pattern, as for example Dobrogast.[147]

When during the Hunnic period the Antes began to take part in distant campaigns, some of their chieftains did not fail to seize the opportunity of enriching themselves with war booty and prisoners of war, which must have considerably enhanced their social prestige. It is probably to such successful Antic chieftains that some of the treasure hoards found in the Russo-Ukrainian forest steppe zone should be referred. One such hoard was found in 1927 near the village Bolshoy Kamenets, Lgov Region, Kursk province; most

138. Procopius, VII, 14, 22.
139. Mauricius, XI, 5.
140. See Sec. 2, above.
141. Jordanis, Sec. 247.
142. Menander, frg. 6 (p. 5).
143. 'Αρδάγαστος (Theophylactus, I, 7, 5; VI, 7, 1; VI, 9, 1).
144. Πειράγαστος (Theophylactus, VII, 4, 13).
145. Κελαγαστός (Menander, frg. 6).
146. Vasmer, *Iranier*, p. 37.
147. Δαβραγάστης (Agathias, III, 6)

of the objects from this hoard are now in the Armory at Moscow.[148] Among them a silver jug with embossed relief, partly gilded, may be mentioned here. It is of Greek craftsmanship and has the stamp of a Constantinople shop. Judging from its style it may be tentatively dated A.D. 400. The famous Pereshchepino hoard,[149] found in 1912 and since then kept in the Hermitage, may also be considered as part of the treasury of an Antic chieftain. The date in this case is seventh century.

9. Byzantium, the Antes, and the Bulgars in the First Quarter of the Sixth Century.

We have already mentioned[150] that at the end of the 460's a leading Byzantine statesman, Aspar, seems to have been interested in promoting Antic colonization in the lower Danube region. Aspar's assassination (471) and the subsequent change in Byzantine policy prevented a Byzantino-Antic *rapprochement* at the time. After Aspar's death it was upon the Isaurians that the imperial government called for support, and after the emperor Leo's death the commander of the Isaurian guard regiment, Zeno, ascended the throne. In Zeno's reign (474-91) the Byzantine Government tried to keep friendly relations with the Huns, as a result of which the latter, now called the Bulgars, appeared again on the lower Danube and probably subordinated to themselves such Sclavenian and Antic communes as may have settled in that region by that time.

The death of Zeno resulted in a drastic change of imperial policy. Leading men in the Byzantine administration had had enough of the lawlessness of the Isaurian military dictatorship, and according to their advice Zeno's widow Ariadne (who was Leo I's daughter) proclaimed the *silentiarius* Anastasius as the new emperor.[151] Anastasius, who reigned from 491 to 518, was a mature and experienced administrator. His first move was to break the arrogance of the Isaurians. By his order, Zeno's property was confiscated and his brother arrested and deported, while the bread ration of Isaurian soldiers considerably cut, resulting in a mutiny of the entire Isaurian

148. L. A. Matsulevich, "Pogrebenie varvarskogo kniazia," *GA, 112* (1934).

149. Count A. A. Bobrinskoy, "Pereshchepinskii klad," *MAR, 34* (1914). Some of the archaeologists refer the Pereshchepino findings to the Avars, *AH, 18* (1936), 59 ff.

150. See Sec. 7, above.

151. On Anastasius see Bury, I, chap. xiii; Charanis; Kulakovskii, I, 432-521.

guard regiment. While the revolt in the capital was quickly crushed, years were to pass before the Isaurians in Asia Minor were pacified.

Taking advantage of the civil war in the empire and perhaps called upon by the Isaurians for assistance, the Hunno-Bulgars, probably reinforced by the Antes, invaded Thrace (493). As we have already mentioned,[152] in Comes Marcellinus' chronicle these invaders are called Scythians. Six years later the Bulgars (this time so called in Marcellinus' chronicle) again raided Thrace and administered a crushing defeat to the Byzantine army (499). In 502 another Bulgar inroad took place. Three years later trouble sprang up in the region of the middle Danube where a commander of the *foederati* troops, Mund, revolted against the empire.[153] John Malalas considers him a Gepid;[154] Comes Marcellinus, a Getian.[155] Marcellinus' information is usually very reliable, but unfortunately the meaning of the name Getian is rather vague for this period. The original Getae or Getians were Thracians.[156] By the sixth century their descendants had already mingled with various newcomers. Following the classical tradition Jordanis calls the Goths, Getae.[157] In this particular case, however, Jordanis describes Mund not as a Getian but as a tribesman of Attila, that is, a Hun.[158] Ennodius in his panegyric of Theodoric, the Ostrogoth king of Italy, refers to Mund as a Bulgarian[159]—that is, likewise a Hun. Thus Mund was either a Hun or a Getian, and in any case he was not a Goth. The contradiction in the sources concerning him may be explained by the fact that while he was a Hun, he headed a "Getic" revolt. But who could be meant under the name of Getians in this case? Quite possibly the Slavs.[160]

It must be taken into account that the situation on the Danubian frontier of the empire was, in the first half of the sixth century, quite favorable for the gradual infiltration of Slavs into these regions. It was not regular army regiments that were stationed along

152. See Sec. 7, above.
153. Bury, I, 460.
154. Malalas, p. 450; cf. Theophanes, p. 218.
155. Marcellinus, *s.a.* 505.
156. See Chap. II, Sec. 2.
157. *De Origine Actibusque Getarum* is the title of Jordanis' work on the history of the Goths. In his terminology Jordanis follows Cassiodorus.
158. Jordanis, Sec. 301.
159. Ennodius, p. 278.
160. Cf. Vasiliev, *Slaviane*, pp. 407-408.

the banks of the Danube for the protection of the imperial frontier, but chiefly companies of the *foederati* recruited from various barbaric tribes, the Slavs among others. When a brigade of *foederati* stayed for years in the same province, its commander came to feel himself not so much a Byzantine officer as an autonomous border ruler. At an auspicious moment he would demand that the emperor appoint him a *strategos* ("general"), or a *magister militum* ("master of the soldiers"), with full authority over the troops and the civilian population of his province. If refused, he would revolt against the emperor. Such was probably the course of events in Mund's case, and such it was to be later on in the cases of Vitalian and Pseudo-Chilbudius. It must be added that the native population usually supported such revolts wholeheartedly since they hoped to get rid of the imperial tax collectors.

While Mund's rebellion was eventually put down, the emperor, Anastasius, understood very well its dangerous implications and decided to play safe and assure better protection to his capital city and its outskirts against further eventualities. He therefore ordered a fortified line, the so-called Long Wall, to be built from Derkos on the Black Sea to Selymbria on the Sea of Marmora. This wall was completed by the year 512, its length being about fifty miles.

In 514 a new crisis took place which affected the empire much more painfully than Mund's rebellion. This time it was Vitalian, comes of the *foederati* in Scythia Minor (Dobrudja), who started the revolt. According to John Malalas, he was a Thracian,[161] a term which had by now lost any definite ethnic connotation and must be understood geographically: a native of Thrace. The name "Thracian" became thus a synonym of the term, Getian. In the *Church History* by Zechariah the Rhetor Vitalian is identified as a Goth.[162] Comes Marcellinus calls Vitalian a Scythian, but at the same time, commenting on the assassination of a Byzantine general by one of Vitalian's adjutants, says that he was killed "with a Getic knife."[163] By this he obviously means that he was killed by order of a Getian; and since it was by Vitalian's order that the general was killed, it follows that Vitalian was a Getian.

We may consider Vitalian either a "Getian" or a Goth, or possibly a descendant of both "Getic" and Gothic ancestors. Who were

161. Malalas, p. 402; cf. *Exc. Ins.*, p. 169.

162. Zacharias Rhetor, p. 136.

163. Marcellinus, *s.a.* 512.

Vitalian's ancestors? We know that his father's name was Patricius or Patriciolus. In this connection we may recall that the name of one of Aspar's sons was likewise Patriciolus or Patricius.[164] Was not Vitalian Aspar's grandson?[165] If this can be credited, it explains, much in Vitalian's mentality: his self-assurance and his imperious tone in his parleys with the Constantinople Government. One has, however, to note that while Aspar was an Arian, Vitalian is a champion of Orthodoxy. But it is quite possible that after Aspar's death his son Patricius (in whom we see the father of Vitalian) may have abandoned Arianism and been converted to Orthodoxy.[166] If we identify Vitalian as Aspar's grandson, we should agree that in his veins was both Gothic and "Getic" (Alanic) blood. In any case it is plain that Vitalian was closely connected with the native population of the Dobrudja, which was in part Alanic and in part possibly Antic as well.

Vitalian revolted after the emperor, Anastasius, had ordered the *magister militum* for Thrace Hypatius to stop payment of his, Vitalian's, salary and to cut the pay of his *foederati* brigade. The order appears to have been issued after the emperor had received from his spies some unfavorable information concerning Vitalian. Actually, the imperial order itself accelerated events and brought about the civil war. From the very beginning of his revolt Vitalian attempted to build his program on a broad ideological foundation. He proclaimed that his chief objective was the protection of the purity of the Orthodox faith against the Monophysitic tendencies of Anastasius.[167] This announcement secured to him the support of the Orthodox clergy both in Constantinople and in Rome. As to his personal role, Vitalian demanded that the emperor appoint him the master of the soldiers (*magister militum*) of Thrace. Such an appointment seemed assured, and the custodian of the provincial treasury at Odyssos (Varna) felt it his duty to surrender to Vitalian all its funds. With the help of these funds Vitalian had no difficulty in gathering an army of about fifty thousand men which he led to Constantinople, meeting no resistance. The Long Wall proved of no

164. See Sec. 7, above.

165. Such an identification was made by both Tillemont, p. 414, and Gibbon, IV, 207, but rejected—without any statement of reasons—by Mommsen, *Hermes*, VI (1872), 349, n. 1.

166. In any case we know that Patricius promised to abandon Arianism on the occasion of his being made Caesar (Kulakovskii, I, 353).

167. On the religious policy of Anastasius see Charanis.

avail and before long Vitalian's soldiers appeared before the walls of the city itself. Vitalian did not have a strong enough force to storm the capital, however, and he therefore proved ready to negotiate a truce, by the provisions of which Anastasius was to refer the dispute in religious matters to the Pope for his decision. While Vitalian was not appointed military governor of Thrace, the former governor was dismissed, both Vitalian himself and his adjutants receiving liberal gifts from the emperor.

Following the conclusion of peace Vitalian returned to Dobrudja. The agreement was not to last long, since the emperor had no intention of keeping the truce. To the newly-appointed governor of Thrace secret instructions were given to arrest Vitalian as soon as things quieted down. Vitalian received word of this plan and decided to strike first. One of his adjutants, the Hun Tarrak, killed the governor. When news of this assassination was received in Constantinople, the emperor Anastasius called an emergency meeting of the state council, and Vitalian was proclaimed a public enemy. An army of eighty thousand men was sent into the field under the command of the former *magister,* Hypatius. To counter this threat Vitalian called to his assistance a band of Hunno-Bulgars from beyond the Danube, and with their help raided the Byzantine camp at Odyssos. The imperial troops were badly beaten and Hypatius himself taken prisoner.

Vitalian now set forth for Constantinople for the second time. He now had a navy at his disposal—a fleet of some two hundred Danubian river boats. Recalling the traditional skill of the Slavs in navigation[168] we may guess that most of these boats were manned by Danubian Slavs. Since Constantinople was in danger of complete blockade, the emperor had no alternative but to make peace with Vitalian on the latter's conditions. These were as follows: an imperial decree on Orthodoxy to be issued; bishops who had been dismissed because of their refusal to compromise with the Monophysitic party to be restored to their sees; Vitalian to be appointed master of the soldiers (*magister militum*) of Thrace and to receive 5,000 pounds of gold as indemnity.

While the emperor had to agree to these provisions, he did not mean to keep them. The historian Theophanes Confessor ascribes to Anastasius the following words on this occasion: "There is a law which orders the emperor to lie and to violate his oath if it is neces-

168. See Chap. III, Sec. 9.

sary for the well-being of the empire."[169] Vitalian on his part was suspicious of the emperor and attempted to find new allies in case of any future eventuality. More likely than not it was at his instigation that the Sabiri Huns made their incursion into the Pontic provinces of the empire, in 515.[170] Whether Anastasius had any definite information concerning negotiations between Vitalian and the Sabiri, or only suspected some contact between them, he apparently decided to play safe and in 516 Vitalian was removed from his command as master of the soldiers. Instead of obeying the imperial order Vitalian led his forces to Constantinople for the third time, using again both his army and navy. According to the chronicler John Malalas there were Goths, Huns, and Scythians among these soldiers and sailors.[171] It seems probable that by "Scythians" the Slavs were meant. This time the campaign was a failure for Vitalian. The imperial troops were led by a courageous and skillful general, Justin, who like Vitalian himself was a Thracian by origin, but not a "Getian"—that is, not an Alan nor, contrary to Safarik's opinion, a Slav.[172] The imperial navy was under the command of Marinus, the minister of finance, who made use of a chemical compound invented by Proclus the Athenian (probably a mixture of liquid sulphur and naphtha) to set the enemy's ships on fire.[173] This or a similar device was later to be known as the "Greek fire." By it Vitalian's fleet was destroyed, after which his overland army retreated in disorder (516). Some of his adjutants were taken prisoner and executed. Vitalian himself succeeded in getting back to Dobrudja.

While Vitalian had lost any hope of success and thereafter held his peace, his last campaign in spite of its failure roused the Danubian "Getians"—in this case definitely Slavs—to new action. In 517 huge bands of them invaded both Illyricum and Macedonia, devastating the country, holding wealthy burghers to ransom, and

169. Theophanes, p. 161.

170. Charanis, pp. 63-64.

171. Malalas, p. 405; cf. *Exc. Ins.*, p. 169.

172. Safarik, p. 160 f.; cf. A. A. Vasiliev, "O slavianskom proiskhozhdenii Iustiniana," VV, *1* (1894), 469-492.

173. Malalas, p. 403; cf. *Exc. Ins.*, p. 169. Proclus the Athenian was probably the famous Neoplatonist. Charanis, p. 64, n. 52, denies the identification on the ground that Proclus the Neoplatonist died "in 482" (484, according to *PW*, *28*, col. 1760). However, Proclus might, before his death, have passed on his formula to some of his pupils and one of the latter's words spoken in the name of the late philosopher may have been cited by Malalas as Proclus' own.

demanding large indemnities from the cities they were unable to seize.[174] In his narrative of these events the chronicler Comes Marcellinus refers to Jeremiah's prophecy concerning the lightning arrows coming from the north.[175] It must be noted that Marcellinus' statements are usually very concise and matter-of-fact, without literary adornment. In this case he may have quoted Biblical parallels under the influence of Proclus' sermon of 434.[176]

Soon after this "Getian" inroad the emperor Anastasius died at the ripe age of 88 (518). In spite of all adversities he had succeeded in completely rebuilding the Byzantine financial administration, so that by the time of his death a cash surplus to the amount of 320,000 pounds of gold was accumulated in the imperial treasury. His successor was Justin I, the general who defeated Vitalian in 516. Justin began his reign by repelling the Slavs, who were pushed north across the Danube and kept quiet during the whole of his reign (518-27).[177]

As a measure of precaution Justin decided to lure Vitalian from his Dobrudja refuge to Constantinople so as to prevent any possibility of another revolt on his part. Vitalian was granted amnesty and appointed consul, which required his personal appearance at the capital. He was received with honors by both Emperor Justin and the heir apparent, Justinian, who was Justin's nephew. Within a short time, he was murdered. The historian Procopius in his *Anecdota* (*Historia Arcana*, "Secret History") accuses Justinian of ordering the assassination.[178] However, the *Secret History* is not a reliable source in personal matters; it is quite possible that Vitalian's murder was revenge by a relative for the death of one of the Byzantine officials killed at Vitalian's order at the time of his rebellion.

10. Justinian I's Policy with Regard to the Antes and the Bulgars.

The reign of Justinian (527–65) is one of the most significant periods in Byzantine history.[179] In many respects it was a period of

174. Kulakovskii, I, 469. Cf. Vasiliev, *Slaviane*, p. 407.
175. Marcellinus, *s.a.* 517, referring probably to Jeremiah, 6.22.
176. See Sec. 4, above.
177. We may draw such conclusion from Procopius, *Anecdota*, XVIII, 20.
178. Procopius, *Anecdota*, VI, 27-28.
179. On the reign of Justinian I see Bury, II; Ch. Diehl, *Justinien* (Paris, 1901); Kulakovskii, II, 37-334.

full cultural blossoming. The church of St. Sophia and the codification of the Roman law are the two most ambitious monuments of Justinian's age. As to foreign policy, he set as a goal for himself the colossal task of restoring the Roman Empire to its former boundaries—a goal which, as events showed, was unattainable. To approach his objectives Justinian was obliged to wage incessant wars, for the sake of which he not only squandered all the funds left in the treasury by Anastasius, but shattered the imperial finance as a whole and overstrained the capacity of the taxpayers for years to come. Justinian's attention was divided between the west and the east. On the one hand, an exhausting struggle against the Sassanian kings was going on; on the other, Byzantine troops were fighting the Goths and the Vandals to restore Italy, Africa, and Spain to the empire.

In view of this situation, the Danubian frontier attracted little attention from Justinian's diplomats and generals. Their main strategy on the lower Danube was that of defense. However, even such a limited objective presented great difficulty because of the Slavic drive, which had been temporarily stopped under Justin I but now assumed new momentum.

From this juncture, thanks to Procopius our information concerning the Slavs becomes more precise. As we have seen[180] Procopius divides the Danubian Slavs into two groups, the Sclaveni and the Antes. The Sclaveni may be considered the forefathers of the Serbs, and the Antes, of the Russians and the Bulgars. The ancestors of the Croats, at least the so-called "White Croats," were probably nearer to the Antes than to the Sclaveni. In his *Secret History* Procopius says of the Slavic raids: "And Illyricum and Thrace in its entirety, comprising the whole expanse of country from the Ionian Gulf to the outskirts of Byzantium, including Greece and the Thracian Chersonese, was overrun practically every year by Huns, Sclaveni, and Antae, from the time when Justinian took over the Roman Empire, and they wrought frightful havoc among the inhabitants of that region. For in each invasion more than twenty myriads of Romans, I think, were destroyed or enslaved there, so that a veritable 'Scythian wilderness' came to exist everywhere in this land."[181] Likewise in his *History of the Wars*, Procopius, commenting on the events of the fourth year of Justinian's reign (531),

180. See Chap. III, Sec. 7.
181. Procopius, *Anecdota*, XVIII, 20-21.

speaks as follows: "The Huns and Antae and Sclaveni had already made the crossing (of the Danube) many times and done irreparable harm to the Romans."[182]

From the very beginning of Justinian's reign his government took a series of measures, of both diplomatic and military nature, to protect the Danubian frontier. As we have seen, a characteristic method of Byzantine diplomacy consisted in making use of the dissensions among the barbaric peoples and in opposing one to another. Through its agents and spies the imperial government watched political developments carefully, not only on the frontier itself but deep in the steppes as well. In search of peoples who could be opposed to the Slavs the Byzantine diplomats naturally recalled the Bulgars. The Bulgarian hordes controlled both the Pontic steppes and the region of Azov and northern Tauria so that the Taurida (Crimea) was the most convenient place both to watch over their movements and to get in touch with them. The city of Cherson in the Crimea had been firmly in Byzantine hands since Roman times, but Bosporus (Kerch), which was independent, was of even more importance to the empire. In the reign of Justin I an envoy was sent to Bosporus with a commission to hire a band of the Kutriguri Huns (Bulgars) in the service of the empire. The mission was not successful, but it prepared the way for subsequent negotiations.

In the first year of Justinian's reign a barbaric chieftain by the name of Grod came to Constantinople from the Crimea. He was a Hun, according to some sources; a Herul, according to another version.[183] He was baptized and sent back to the Taurida as the emperor's "ally." However, his kinsmen and tribesmen met him with suspicion and before long a revolt against his rule started which was led by a certain Mugel or Muil.[184] The name is known only in Greek transcription. In order to restore the original name we must remember that the consonants "m" and "b" are often interchanged in Turkish dialects. Could not the name of the leader of the revolt be Buil, or Boil, instead of Muil? If so, it must probably be considered a title rather than a personal name, since we know that in

182. *Idem,* VII, 14, 2.

183. Two similar episodes are recorded in Malalas' chronicle, one concerning the Hunnic king Grod or Gord (Γρώδ), and the other the Herul leader, Gretes or Grepes (Γρέπης). See Malalas, pp. 427-428, 431-433. Cf. Bury, II, 311; and Schmidt, p. 554. J. Bromberg considers the two personages identical, see *SR, 20,* 358.

184. Μοῦγελ, Malalas, p. 432.

the later realm of the Danubian Bulgars chieftains or grandees were called *boil*.[185] It is therefore possible that the revolt against Grod was organized by his boyars. In any case, Grod was defeated and killed by his opponents.[186]

Justinian then sent a naval squadron to the Bosporus, and the city of Bosporus (Kerch) was temporarily occupied by Byzantine troops. Justinian, however, did not deem it proper to annex Bosporus outright to his empire, and decided to restore the old Bosporan kingdom instead. A descendant of former Bosporan kings was put on the throne under the name of Tiberius Julius Diuptunus. In a contemporary inscription,[187] along with the new king two of his subordinates are mentioned: Isgudius, the *eparchus*, and Opadinus, the *comes*.[188] The titles are Byzantine but the names sound native. The new Bosporan king was certainly Justinian's vassal, although his official title was: "Friend of Caesar, friend of the Romans."

Having established his control of the Bosporus, Justinian turned his attention to the security of the Danubian frontier. In 531 one of the ablest officers of the imperial army, Khilbud (Chilbudius) was appointed commander-in-chief in Thrace with the instruction not to let the Slavs cross the Danube.[189] Khilbud did not limit his effort to purely defensive operations, but crossed the river himself and undertook several campaigns into the land of the Slavs to the north. In 534 he was killed in battle. Khilbud's name is Antic, and it is possible that he was an Antas by origin. According to Procopius he had been before his appointment to the Danubian army a member of Justinian's private guard unit (οἰκεία), and such units were usually at this time composed of foreign soldiers.

Khilbud's death resulted in the retreat of the Byzantine army, and the Slavs were now able to raid Thrace once more. Further threat was averted by the skillfulness of Byzantine diplomacy, which succeeded in sowing seeds of discord between the Sclaveni and the Antes. These two peoples started quarreling among themselves and for some time left Byzantium alone. It was during this Sclaveno-Antic war that a young Antas whose name was likewise Khilbud

185. See Chap. VI, Sec. 6, below.
186. Bury, II, 311.
187. *IPE*, II, No. 49. See Kulakovskii, *Tavrida*, p. 59; Vasiliev, p. 71 (with chronological adjustment).
188. Cf. Sec. 6, above.
189. Procopius, VII, 14, 1-2; cf. Levchenko, pp. 38-39.

was taken prisoner by the Sclaveni.[190] His Sclavenian master liked him and treated him as a member of his retinue rather than a slave. Khilbud in his turn attached himself to his master and became a loyal follower. We must keep in mind this episode, since it was to have some important repercussions.

Let us now turn to the general development of events. We have seen[191] that in the fourth and the fifth centuries the imperial government hired Goths, Alans, and Huns for the protection of its boundaries. Similarly, Justinian had Bulgar and Slavic detachments in his army and they proved very useful in his war against the Ostrogothic kingdom of Italy. In the spring of 537 the Byzantine commander-in-chief, Belisarius, was besieged by the Goths in Rome. The Byzantine garrison was small, and its position was critical when several cavalry squadrons, numbering altogether sixteen hundred men, came to Belisarius' rescue. According to Procopius these squadrons consisted of Huns (Bulgars), Sclaveni, and Antes.[192] With their help the commander succeeded in beating off enemy attacks, and in March, 538, the Goths retreated from Rome.

While a number of Bulgars entered the imperial service and joined the Byzantine troops in Italy, the main Kutriguri horde took advantage of the Gothic war to attack Byzantine possessions in the Balkan peninsula, which were almost stripped of imperial troops. In 539-540 the Bulgars raided Thrace down to the Aegean litoral and Illyricum down to the Adriatic Sea. Soon after, the Antes followed suit and went about looting Thrace for their own benefit. It appears that the Antes now had the idea of seizing Thrace permanently as Vitalian had attempted to do a quarter of a century before. They needed, however, a leader who could claim the position of governor of Thrace, as Vitalian had, and whose authority would be recognized not only by the Slavs but by Greeks as well. In these circumstances the name of the late general Khilbud was remembered, and a Pseudo-Khilbud coached for leadership. According to Procopius[193] one of the Greek prisoners taken by the Antes in Thrace contrived the scheme. His original motive must have been purely personal—the desire for freedom from captivity. His first move was to suggest to his master that he knew a secret the knowledge of which

190. *Idem,* 14, 8.
191. See Secs. 3 and 4, above.
192. Procopius, V, 27, 1.
193. *Idem,* VII, 14, 12 ff.

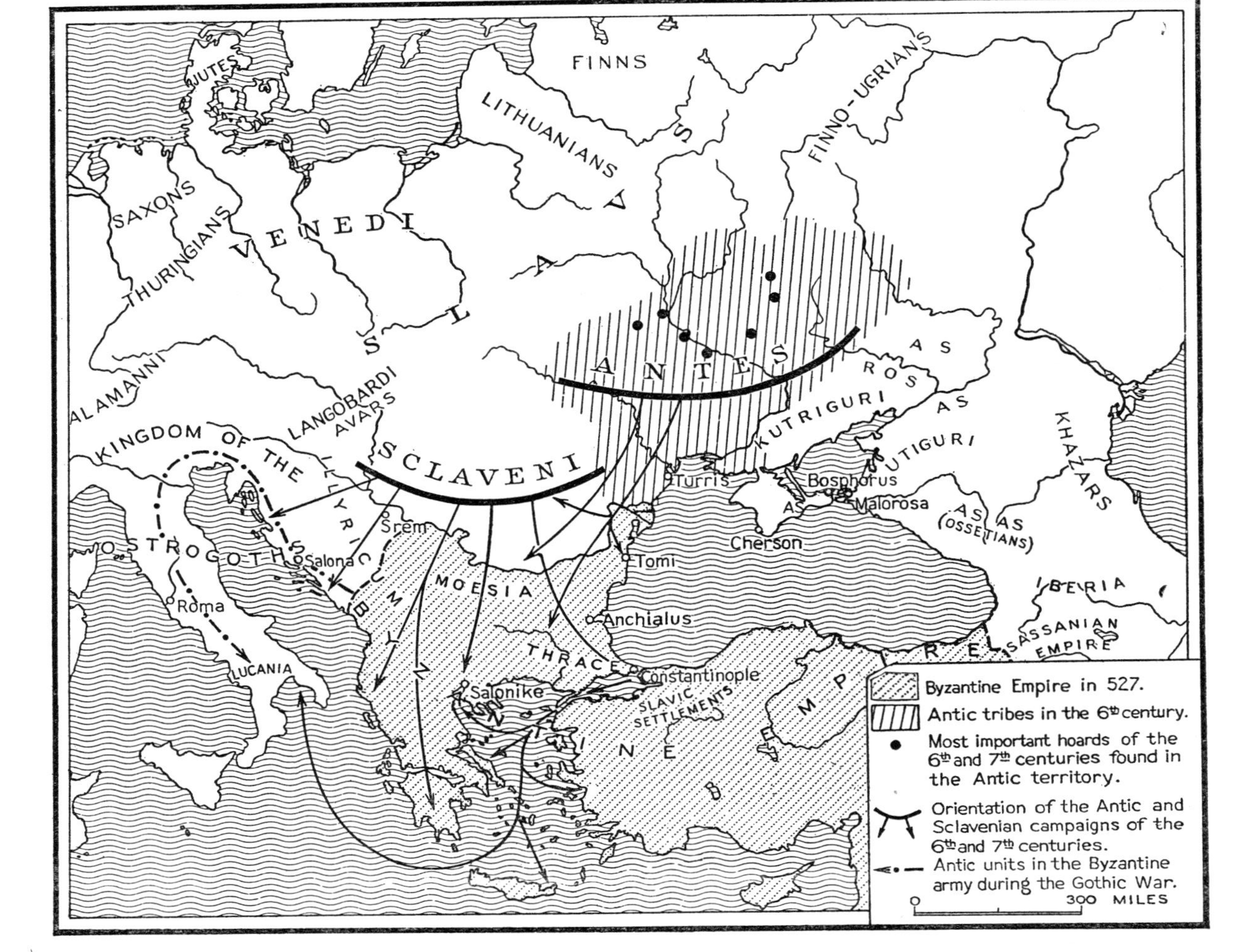

THE EXPANSION OF THE SCLAVENI AND THE ANTES

would enable him (the master) to gain a considerable sum of money. The master proved eager to be informed, and thereupon the Greek told him that General Khilbud although considered dead was actually living in captivity in the land of the Sclaveni. If he were redeemed and brought to Constantinople a large reward would be paid by the imperial government to the man who had helped him. The Greek's master was willing to try, and they went together to the land of the Sclaveni, located Khilbud the Antas, and redeemed him from his Sclavenian master. However, when this Khilbud was brought to the land of the Antes and honored by his redeemer as General Khilbud, he repudiated the identification. The Greek who had originated the scheme now told his master that the man was actually the general but was afraid to confess before being brought back to Constantinople.

The rumor of the arrival of General Khilbud spread rapidly among the Antes, a general assembly was called, and Pseudo-Khilbud was proclaimed leader of the Antic tribe. It was decided to petition the emperor to have him reappointed to the post of commander-in-chief of the Danubian army. Meanwhile the emperor, without any knowledge of the appearance of Pseudo-Khilbud, on his own part sent envoys to the Antes offering his friendship if they would emigrate to Turris, a town "north of the Danube" as Procopius says rather laconically. This must be identified as Tyras at the mouth of the Dnieper River (Akkerman).[194] By urging the Antes to settle there Justinian obviously had in mind to use them as guardians of the northeastern frontier of the empire against the Bulgars. The Antes accepted on condition that Khilbud should be appointed commander of the frontier region. The new Antic leader was sent to Constantinople for personal negotiations with the emperor. However, it so happened that on the way he met the Byzantine general Narses, who was on his way to Italy. Narses had known the former Khilbud personally and was thus able to reveal the fraud. He arrested the pretender and brought him to Constantinople, where he was detained.

In spite of the arrest the Antes agreed to garrison Tyras (around the year 544).[195] In 547 an auxiliary battalion of Antes assisted the Byzantine army in Lucania against the Ostrogoths. Although the unit was rather small—three hundred men only—it proved very

194. Bromberg, pp. 58-59; cf. Brun, I, 243.
195. Bury, II, 297.

valuable because of the skill of the Antes in waging war in hilly localities.[196]

Thus both in Italy and in the Pontic steppes the Antes served the empire. It appears that they now formally recognized the suzerainty of the emperor, and it is characteristic that Justinian presently added the epithet "Anticus" to his title.[197] As to the Sclaveni, no agreement was concluded with them, and beginning in 547 they resumed their raids on Thrace, which continued for five years.[198]

While an Antic garrison was stationed in Tyras to forestall the attacks of the Kutriguri Bulgars, this safeguard did not apparently seem sufficient to Justinian, and he decided to encircle the Kutriguri by making an alliance with the eastern branch of the Bulgars, the Utiguri, who lived southeast of the Sea of Azov. Rich presents and money were sent to the khan of the Utiguri to induce him to attack the Kutriguri from the rear. The offer was accepted and presently the Utiguri moved north accompanied by two thousand Trapezite Goths. After a protracted struggle the united forces of the Utiguri and the Goths defeated the Kutriguri, taking many prisoners and herds of horses. Justinian was not willing, however, to upset entirely the balance of the steppe powers by allowing too much advantage to the Utiguri, so he now made an about-face and offered his protectorship to the Kutriguri.[199] The device did not work, since the treacherous nature of Byzantine policy was becoming only too obvious; instead, the two Bulgarian tribes now united against the empire.

In 551 bands of Kutriguri broke through the Antic barrier and raided Thrace.[200] In the winter of either 558 or 559 a huge horde of both Bulgars and Slavs led by Khan Zabergan crossed the Danube, looted both Thrace and Macedonia, and appeared at the neck of the Thracian Chersonese (Gallipoli).[201] Leaving there a part of his Bulgaro-Slavic troops, Zabergan with the main body of Bulgars approached Constantinople itself. It was only with the utmost effort that the veteran general Belisarius succeeded in organizing the defense of the capital and in pushing Zabergan's forces back beyond

196. Procopius, VII, 22, 3-4.
197. Codex Justinianus, ed. Krueger, p. 3.
198. Kulakovskii, II, 220-221.
199. Procopius, VIII, 18, 18-24; 19, 7-22. Cf. Bury, II, 303.
200. Kulakovskii, II, 225.
201. Agathias, 5, 12-15; Theophanes, pp. 233-234. Cf. Bury, II, 304-308; Kulakovskii, II, 225-227.

the Long Wall. The Slavs in Zabergan's army, however, made an attempt to attack Constantinople by sea. Having no boats, they hastily made a number of rafts on which they ventured forth. This improvised flotilla was easily destroyed by the Byzantine navy, as might be expected.[202]

In spite of these reverses Zabergan's overland army was still in a position to do much harm to Constantinople by cutting the capital's connections with Thrace. His headquarters were temporarily established in Arcadiople (Lule-Burgas). The Byzantines were obliged to send rich "presents" to the invading khan as the price of his return to the steppes. There was, however, another reason for Zabergan's retreat: news had been received of the appearance of a previously unknown warlike horde east of the Don, coming from the Mongolian deserts. The news spelled danger, and the Bulgars hastened home. The new horde was that of the Avars.

202. *Idem,* 5, 12; cf. Kulakovskii, II, 226-227.

CHAPTER V.

THE AVARO-ANTIC PERIOD, 558-650.

1. Preliminary Remarks.

THE invasion of the Avars and the subsequent drive of the Turks into the Azov region upset the balance of power in the northern Black Sea area and thus inaugurated a new period in the life of the peoples of western Eurasia, affecting particularly the vicissitudes of the Antes. Although the Antic state in Bessarabia had been broken up by the Avars, a part of the Antic tribes remained in the region of the lower Danube for a considerable time thereafter. Antic chieftains also controlled some of the Sclavenian communes. At times the Antes joined the Avars in the latter's attack on Byzantium; at other times, on the contrary, they concluded friendly agreements with the Byzantine Empire. In the second half of the sixth and the beginning of the seventh century the Antes started to spread in Thrace, south of the Danube. The drive of the Sclaveni into both Thrace and Illyricum was no less persistent. The Avar period may be thus characterized as the age of the Anto-Slavic colonization of the Balkan peninsula.

Following the imperialistic ventures of Justinian I a reaction was felt in Byzantine diplomacy. The forces of the empire had been well-nigh exhausted by that emperor, so that it was no longer able to protect the vast circle of its Mediterranean dominions. In 568 the Teutonic tribe of Langobardi (Lombards) invaded Italy and succeeded in occupying most of it. In the trans-Pontic areas such as Georgia and the Taurida the imperial troops were on the defensive, and the situation there became before long very tense. It was obvious that the empire lacked sufficient military strength to secure her borders. Diplomacy was called upon to help the army. Maneuvering skillfully to offset the claims of various "barbaric" peoples, such as the Avars, the Hunno-Bulgars, the Turks, the Alans, and the Persians, imperial diplomacy used its favorite method of sowing of seeds of discord between its enemies, thus preventing them from uniting, and instigating quarrels among them. For some time this diplomatic game scored a considerable success; meanwhile the army was being strengthened. The emperor, Heraclius, defeated the Avars and invaded Persia. At this juncture, however, a new danger rose in the east—that of the Arabs.

Mohammad's epochal flight (Hegira) from Mecca, A.D. September 23, 622, opened the new Islamic era (A.H.). Islam—the word literally means "obedience"—was a militant religion, and the object of its early leaders was to carry their banner the world over. The whole world was for them divided into two parts: the House of Islam (*Dar-ul-Islam*) and the House of War (*Dar-ul-harb*). Simultaneously, in the northeast the growth of the Turko-Khazar Empire gathered momentum. The Bulgars were unable to withstand the Khazar pressure and finally one of the Bulgar hordes moved from the Azov region to the lower Danube. The establishment of the Bulgar Khanate on the lower Danube meant a new threat to the Byzantine Empire and, on the other hand, resulted in the dependence of the Antic tribes in Bessarabia on the Bulgars. In this way the Avaro-Antic period came to a close and a new era, which we may call the Bulgaro-Khazar period, was inaugurated. Meanwhile new commercial highways were opened as a consequence of the rapid expansion of the Arabian Empire.

Of the Byzantine historians of the Avaro-Antic period the name of Menander Protector must be mentioned first. Both because of his legal training and because of his high standing in the imperial administration he was well prepared for his task as historian. The period he deals with in his history covers the last years of the reign of Justinian I as well as the reigns of Justinus II and Tiberius I (558-82). Unfortunately only a few fragments of Menander's work have been preserved. But since he was especially interested in the relations of the empire with the nomadic peoples of western Eurasia, these mere fragments contain precious materials on the history of both the Avars and the Antes. The events of the reign of the emperor Mauricius (582-602) are described by Theophylactus Simocatta, an Egyptian Greek who lived in the reign of Heraclius (610-41). Theophylactus was a conscientious scholar, but much less prepared for his task and possessing much less inside information than either Procopius or Menander. More often than not he failed to appreciate the importance of the happenings he described, and at times would get lost in insignificant details.

With regard to events of the seventh and eighth centuries one must turn primarily to the chronicle written by Theophanes Confessor, a Byzantine monk who wrote in 810-15 a brief survey of the years from Diocletianus to Leo V. In 873-75 the librarian of the Pope, Anastasius, translated Theophanes' chronicle into Latin; since he added some information from other sources his translation has a special value. A contemporary of Theophanes, the Patriarch Nicephorus (Patriarch 806-15) left two historical works which became quite popular, to wit: (1) the so-called *Brief History* (Ἱστορία σύντομος) which covers the period 602-769; and (2) *Brief Chronicle* (Χρονογραφικὸν σύντομον) from Adam to A.D. 829.

In the reign of the emperor Michael III (842-67) another chronicle appeared, by the monk George Hamartolos ("The Sinner"). It was meant as an outline of world history from the Creation to the death of the emperor Theophilus (842). George used the works of both Theophanes and Nicephorus, adding information from other sources as well, so that his chronicle supplies some additional material to that collected by the other two. George's chronicle is perhaps more than all others permeated by the spirit of Byzantium. It is not only a pragmatic outline of history but likewise a philosophy of history. The author's main object is to explain the meaning of historical events from the point of view of a Christian monk. Adapted to the interests of its readers, this chronicle was very popular in Byzantine society and later, when a Slavonic translation of it appeared, was much read in Slavonic countries as well, especially in Russia.

It may be not amiss to point out that the Russian translator of George's chronicle in some cases—as for example in the translation of tribal names—used his own judgment, taking into account historical traditions beyond the information supplied by George. Therefore the Russian translation of the chronicle, made at the end of the tenth or in the beginning of the eleventh century, is an evidence of the rise of Russian historical thought at that time. Russian historical writing as such developed in any case under the obvious influence of the works of George Hamartolos and the Patriarch Nicephorus. It was in the eleventh century that the first Russian chronicles were written, in Kiev and Novgorod respectively. In the beginning of the twelfth century these early chronicles were revised and a more ambitious historical outline of the Russian past appeared, known as the *Povest' Vremennykh Let* ("Book of Annals").

Among several variants and recensions the Laurentius version of the end of the fourteenth century, and the Hypatius version, of the beginning of the fifteenth century, are the two most important. One must take into account the possibility that, while the original ("primary") chronicle which forms the foundation of the *Povest* was compiled in the eleventh century, its author may have used some earlier records as well as oral tradition. The *Povest* may therefore contain fragments of authentic information even with regard to the period from the seventh to the tenth century. Old tradition has been better preserved in the Hypatius than in the Laurentius version.

As to the works of the Syriac historians, in addition to those mentioned before,[1] the chronicle of Gregory Ab-ul-Faraj, alias Bar Hebraeus, a Nestorian, may be mentioned. Gregory wrote in the thirteenth century but used a number of earlier sources as well. Arabic historiography will be dealt with in the next chapter.

2. *The Invasion of the Avars and the Appearance of the Turks.*

In order to understand properly the background of the migration of the Avars, it is necessary to turn once more to the development of events in the inner regions of Eurasia. After the Huns moved from Mongolia to the Pontic steppes in the fourth century A.D., their place in Mongolia was occupied by another nomadic people which is mentioned in the chronicles under the name of Zhen-Zhen. While the Huns were attacking the Roman Empire, the Zhen-Zhen struggled with China. They succeeded in building up a vast state stretching along the zone of steppes and deserts from Manchuria to Turkestan. They also succeeded in occupying some border provinces of China.[2]

Among the tribes conquered by the Zhen-Zhen were the Turks who inhabited the Altai mountain region. This region, as we know, was rich in ores, and the natives had long been acquainted with the use of metals.[3] In any case there were skilled blacksmiths among the Turks, as a result of which they were well supplied with arms. At the end of the 540's the Turks revolted against the Zhen-Zhen, and the latter were unable to put the rebellion down. The Turks then started an offensive and in 552 the Turkish khan, Bumyn, adminis-

1. See Chap. IV, Sec. 1.
2. Grousset, pp. 124-125.
3. Cf. Chap. I, Sec. 5, and Chap. II, Sec. 1.

tered a crushing defeat to the Zhen-Zhen army,[4] after which he assumed the title of kagan,[5] *i.e.*, emperor. The Zhen-Zhen horde dissolved. Parts of it submitted to Turkish control; others migrated to China and were used by the Chinese as border guards. Another division of the Zhen-Zhen consisting of mixed clans of Turkish, Mongolian, and possibly Manchu stock rushed westward. It was this branch of the Zhen-Zhen and affiliated clans which became known in the west under the name of the Avars; they are called Obry in Russian chronicles. The Avar army numbered originally around twenty thousand horsemen; it was led by Khan Bayan.[6]

By the beginning of the year 558 the Avar horde reached the confines of the North Caucasian area and came into contact with the Alans. The Alan king, who was in friendly relations with the Byzantine Empire, conveyed news of the approach of the Avars to the commander of the Byzantine army in Transcaucasia, Justinus; who, grasping the importance of the news, immediately sent a messenger to Constantinople.[7] The Byzantine diplomats made a quick decision to enter into negotiations with the newcomers, with the object of using them against the Hunno-Bulgars who at that time were pressing hard on Constantinople.[8] Thus in the midst of the Bulgar war the Avar envoy appeared in Constantinople and was met with honors. He offered, on behalf of the khan, assistance against the Bulgars provided the Avar Horde received a suitable sum in return and lands for settlement. The demands were accepted, the envoy received rich presents, and the emperor's equerry, Valentin, was sent to the khan as the Byzantine envoy.[9] As we have seen,[10] news of the appearance of the Avars was the chief cause of the Bulgar retreat from Constantinople. The Bulgars rushed back to the steppes to forestall attack.

While the Avar army was not numerous it proved stronger than

4. Grousset, p. 126.

5. "Kagan" is the correct transliteration of the old Russian form of the title. There are several ways of spelling the original Turkish title such as "khagan," "khaqan" etc. The spelling "kagan" is preferred since it corresponds to that of the official title of the Russian rulers of Tmutorokan and Kiev, respectively, from the ninth to the eleventh century A.D.

6. Bury, II, 313-316; Grousset, pp. 226-227; Kulakovskii, II, 230-231

7. Menander, frg. 4 (p. 4).

8. See Chap. IV, Sec. 10.

9. Menander, frgs. 4-5 (pp. 4-5).

10. See Chap. IV, Sec. 10.

the Bulgars. One of the reasons for Avar superiority may have been such an apparent triviality as the stirrups used by the Avar horsemen. We have seen[11] that leather straps, performing the function of a kind of stirrup, were known to the Scythians. Iron stirrups are occasionally found in Sarmatian kurgans of a later period as well as among the Hunnic antiquities in Hungary.[12] Generally speaking, however, iron stirrups became prevalent in Central Eurasia long before their popular use was known on the Pontic steppes, and it was only after the coming of the Avars that they were introduced in the cavalry of Europe.

Another cause of superiority was psychological. Fleeing from the Turks, who might be expected to follow closely at their heels, the Avars had no alternative to a break-through into the Pontic steppes, held by the Bulgars. They were in desperate plight, since they had no supplies or source of arms, no cattle and no smithies. They had nothing to lose and everything to gain; otherwise they were doomed to famine and destitution.

The Sabiri in the eastern section of the North Caucasian area were the first Hunnic tribe to be attacked (559).[13] Having crushed the Sabiri, the Avars raided the country of the Utiguri, on the eastern shores of the Sea of Azov (560).[14] The Utiguri were forced to recognize Avar suzerainty over them. Thereupon the Avars crossed the Don River, breaking into the land of the Kutriguri.[15] The latter, as it seems, asked their western neighbors the Antes to help them, but the latter refused to move. The Kutriguri were then defeated and the Kutrigur khan—probably the same Zabergan who threatened Constantinople in 558—became Khan Bayan's vassal. It is probably at this time that Bayan assumed the title of kagan by which he was later known.

Having disposed of the Kutriguri the Avars now approached the Dniester River (561). Bessarabia, home of the Antes, was now their next objective. The Antes at first offered a furious resistance, but later entered into negotiations with the invaders. According to Menander[16] the name of the Antic envoy was Mezamer. He was the son

11. See Chap. II, Sec. 2.

12. N. I. Veselovskii, "Kurgany Kubanskoi oblasti v period Rimskogo vladychestva," *TAS*, XII, *1* (1905), 15; Rostovtzeff, *Skythien*, pp. 557-558.

13. Menander, frg. 5 (p. 5); cf. Bury, II, 315.

14. Menander, frg. 5 (p. 5).

15. Kulakovskii, II, 231.

16. Menander, frg. 6 (pp. 5-6).

of Idarisius and brother to Kelagast. The first of these names is probably Slavic (Bezmer), the other two sound Iranian or Turkish.[17] In the whole course of the negotiations Mezamer's behaviour was haughty and independent. From this we may surmise that the Antes did not consider themselves defeated. At this juncture the Kutrigur khan stepped into the picture. If our surmise is correct (that he had previously asked the Antes for help, but met with a refusal), it will explain his hostile attitude towards them at this moment. He succeeded in convincing Bayan that Mezamer was a dangerous foe, especially since he enjoyed so much authority among his people, and that the best thing to do was to get rid of him at once and then attack in full force. Bayan liked the advice and ordered Mezamer put to death in violation of a cardinal principle of international law even then universally accepted.[18]

Following Mezamer's execution the Avars broke into the land of the Antes, devastating it and taking many prisoners. However, the Antes before long recovered from the first shock and for some time continued a stubborn resistance. Finally the Avars penetrated to the Dobrudja (562), where they decided to stay. Such a turn of affairs was incompatible with the policies of the Byzantine diplomats. In the treaty concluded with the Avars four years before (558) they had arranged to use them against the Bulgars, but did not expect and did not want an overwhelming Avar victory, which might—and in fact did—make the invaders as dangerous to the empire as the Bulgars had been.

It was not long before Avaro-Byzantine relations became very strained indeed. Byzantine garrisons along the southern bank of the Danube were reinforced; the Antes in their turn continued to harass the newcomers from behind. Finally, having no hope of breaking into Thrace, the Avars decided to penetrate to Pannonia.[19] Part of them proceeded up the Danube River, while others went up the course of the rivers Pruth and Dniester to Galicia, whence they could use several mountain passes to emerge upon the Pannonian plains. Before proceeding from Galicia south to Pannonia, they conquered the Khorvats (Croats) and the Dulebians, two Anto-

17. Markwart, p. 147; Markwart, *Chronologie,* pp. 78, 82; Zlatarski, I, 1, pp. 383-387.

18. Menander, frg. 6 (p. 6).

19. See L. Hauptmann, "Les rapports des Byzantins avec les Slaves et les Avars," *Byz., 4* (1929), 137-170; cf. Hauptmann, Kroaten, p. 337.

Slavic tribes who lived in the region of the upper Dniester River.[20] Then descending on Pannonia they defeated the Gepids, a German tribe which had settled there. Pushing the Gepids out, the Avars made the prairies of the region of the middle Danube the center of their khanate.[21] Meanwhile new troubles were in store for Byzantine diplomats, who were watching carefully the development of events in the East. The Avars, as we have seen, rushed westward because of the Turkish menace.[22] By the middle of the 550's the Turks appeared at the confines of Turkestan, the very name of which was coined after their migration thither. At that time the country was controlled by the so-called Ephtalites, or White Huns, who carried on a protracted struggle with the Persian Sassanids.[23] As soon as the Shah Khusraw I received news of the advent of the Turks he hailed them as potential allies in the struggle. Before long the Turks and the Persians concluded an alliance to combat the Ephtalites jointly. The latter were soon crushed between two enemy armies converging upon them from opposite directions. Turkestan was now divided between the Turks and the Persians, with the river Amu-Daria as boundary.[24]

It was not long before the recent allies quarreled over the booty; as a result, the Turks began seriously to consider the possibilities of a diplomatic encirclement of Persia. Since relations between the Sassanids and the Byzantine Empire were strained at the time, it was only natural that the Turks should try to establish contact with the empire. In 563 a Turkish envoy came to Constantinople.[25] The details of the negotiations are unknown. It should be mentioned in this connection that the relations of the Turks with both Persia and Byzantium were motivated not only by political but by commercial considerations. Their major object, as in the case of the Huns before them, was to seize control of the great overland highway from China to the Mediterranean, in order to monopolize the export of Chinese silk. On the other hand, Shah Khusraw in his turn was

20. Hauptmann, *Kroaten*, p. 337; Markwart, pp. 146 f., 325 f.; Niederle, IV, 172 ff.

21. Bury, pp. 115-116; Kulakovskii, II, p. 344-345.

22. On the Turks see W. Barthold, "Turks: Historical and Ethnografical Survey," *EI*, IV, 900-908; E. Chavannes, "Documents sur les T'ou-kiu occidentaux," *STO*, VI (1903); Grousset, pp. 124-126; V. Radlov, *Die alttürkische Inschriften* (see Sources, I, 1); V. Thomsen, "Alttürkische Inschriften," (see Sources, I, 1).

23. On the Ephtalites see Chap. IV, Sec. 2.

24. Grousset, p. 127.

25. Theophanes, p. 239; cf. Kulakovskii, II, 230.

interested in controlling the silk trade. When Turkish envoys, therefore, on one occasion brought with them a load of silk, Khusraw ordered it burnt. The envoys themselves were then imprisoned, which resulted in a final break between the Turks and Persia. The Turks subsequently sent new envoys to Constantinople (568).[26] These carried in their train loads of silk which they hoped to sell in the metropolis at great profit. In these hopes they were disappointed, since by this time Byzantium had already started its own silk industries. It is said that two Syriac monks, traveling as far as China, secretly brought with them on their way back several cocoons of the silk worm, which they concealed in the hollows of their walking staffs (552).[27]

While commercially the Turkish embassy of 568 was a failure, it brought about important political results. An alliance was concluded between the kaganate and the empire. Emperor Justinus II then sent to the kagan his own envoy, Zemarch. Menander has preserved in his history an interesting description of Zemarch's journey to the kagan's headquarters in the Altai mountains.[28] The Persians naturally resented the *rapprochement* between Byzantium and the Turks, and in 572 a war started between Persia and the empire, which lasted for three years with varying success.[29]

Meanwhile the Turks crossed the Volga River and invaded the North Caucasian area. Already at the time of Zemarch's mission the Utigurs had recognized the suzerainty of the Turkish kagan. Soon after, the vanguard detachments of Turks reached the Black Sea shores at the mouth of the Kuban River.[30] In this way they were in a position to threaten Byzantine possessions in the Crimea, a situation which could not but worry the Byzantines. Thus the usual course of events repeated itself: while a nomadic horde was separated from the empire by other peoples, inimical to it, Byzantine diplomacy tried to make an alliance with the enemy of its enemies and for some time such an alliance was useful. But when the horde in question itself moved to the very confines of the empire, friendship gave way to animosity. Such had been the case with the Avars; such now became the case with the Turks.

26. Menander, frg. 18 (pp. 47-49).
27. Kulakovskii, II, 290, 356.
28. Menander, frg. 19-22 (pp. 49-56).
29. Kulakovskii, II, 361-369.
30. By inference from Menander, frg. 43 (p. 89).

In 576 a Turkish brigade, reinforced with Utigur detachments, crossed Kerch Strait and seized the fortress of Bosporus (the old Panticapaeum); this gave the Turks a foothold in the Crimea.[31] In 581 they appeared before the walls of Cherson.[32] Though the Byzantine garrison had no hope of withstanding the onslaught, the Turks unexpectedly left the siege and retreated inland. The reason for their withdrawal was the news received by their commanding officers of internal strife at the headquarters of the kagan in Turkestan.[33] A protracted civil war now weakened the Turkish state for about two decades, during which period the Turks abandoned any offensive plans in the Pontic area.

3. Byzantium, the Avars, and the Antes in the Reign of Mauricius.

The migration of the main Avar horde to Pannonia brought to the tribes of the lower Danube no release from Avar authority. While his headquarters were established in Pannonia, Bayan, like Attila before him, understood well the importance of controlling the lower Danube area as a bridge to the steppe zone commercial highways. Both the Kutriguri horde and part of the Anto-Slavic tribes still recognized the suzerainty of the Avar kagan for more than half a century to come. With the help of Kutrigurian and Anto-Slavic auxiliary brigades the Avar kagan remained for years a redoutable foe to the Byzantines.

Hardly a decade had passed since the establishment of the Avars in Pannonia when Bayan, repeating Attila's strategic plan, began to press upon Byzantine possessions in northern Illyricum; that is, in the basin of the lower Sava River. In 581 the Avars seized Sirmium[34] on the lower Sava, an important Byzantine fortress which in fact was the key to the whole Byzantine defensive line in northern Illyricum. The emperor Tiberius, to forestall their further expansion southward, hastened to conclude peace with the Avars, promising to pay them a yearly present of 80,000 gold coins.[35]

Soon after the conclusion of this treaty Tiberius died. His suc-

31. Menander, frg. 43 (p. 89). The name of the Turkish general who captured Bosporus was, according to Menander, Bokhan (Βώχανος); it is probably to be read "Bogha-Khan," for which name see *EI*, I, 736-737.

32. Menander, frg. 64 (p. 125).

33. Grousset, pp. 133-138.

34. Now Sremska Mitrovica.

35. Kulakovskii, II, 395; Stein, p. 113.

cessor was Mauricius (582–602),[36] an Armenian by birth and a miser by disposition. In the first year of his reign he reluctantly agreed, however, not only to pay the stipulated amount but even to add 20,000 to the original sum. A few months later the kagan demanded still more money. This was too much for Mauricius and he bluntly refused to comply, whereupon the Avars invaded Illyricum ravaging every town and village on the way (583). Meeting no serious resistance, Bayan crossed the Balkan mountain range and reached the Black Sea shore near Burgas. For some time the kagan's headquarters were at Anchialus, a renowned Byzantine spa. According to the historian Theophylactus, the kagan's wives enjoyed the warm baths there very much.[37] Bayan's invasion was only the prelude to a protracted and exhausting war between Byzantium and the Avars, which lasted with brief intermissions throughout the whole period of Mauricius' reign. Avar inroads alternated with Slavic expeditions, the Slavs acting apparently on the instigation of the kagan. During the first decade of the war the initiative lay with the Avars and the Slavs, while the Byzantine troops were on the defensive. In 590 Mauricius was obliged to agree to a humiliating armistice. His position was the more difficult since he had simultaneously to wage war against Persia. As soon as the Persian war was over, however, and a peace treaty signed with the shah (591), Mauricius had a better opportunity to settle the Balkan affair.

Not willing to break the armistice with the Avars at once, he decided first to teach a lesson to the Slavs. Before long all the Slav raiding parties were pushed back over the Danube, and a campaign against the Slavs across the Danube was considered. In 592 an able general, Priscus, was sent to Dorostol (Silistria) with a strong division. The Avars lodged a lively protest against what they considered a breach of the peace, since the Slavs were their vassals. Priscus' answer was that his object was only to punish the Slavs for their raids and that he had no inimical intentions against the Avars. The latter were momentarily silent.

The Slavs against whom Priscus waged war are called Sclaveni in the sources. It is possible, however, that actually they belonged to the Antic group, since the Byzantine historians of the seventh and eighth centuries had no such precise knowledge of the Slavic tribes

36. On Mauricius see Bury, 1889, pp. 83-94; Kulakovskii, II, 419-495. On Byzantino-Slavic relations at the time of Mauricius see Levchenko, pp. 41-46.

37. Theophylactus, I, 4, 5.

as Procopius had had before them. The name of the Slavic prince who was Priscus' chief opponent, as mentioned in the sources, was Ardagast[38]—an Iranian name; that is, rather Antic than Slavic. Of course it is conceivable that an Antic prince was the head of a Sclavenian tribe.

Priscus started his campaign by crossing the Danube. He attacked the Slavic encampment in the dead of night, caught the Slavs unawares and put them to flight. Ardagast himself barely escaped captivity by plunging into the water. Possibly he saved himself by a device described in Mauricius' *Strategicon.*[39] According to this treatise the Slavs could spend hours in the water, keeping reeds in their mouths through which they breathed. Later the Zaporozhie Kozaks were known to do the same. Soon after his victory over Ardagast Priscus received information through his spies that a new Slavic division was approaching from the northeast. Priscus sent part of his troops to occupy vanguard positions on the banks of the river Helibacius (probably the modern Yalomnitsa).[40] The head spy with this Byzantine division was a Gepid converted to Christianity and thoroughly familiar with the Slavic tongue. With his help the Byzantines were able to seize a number of Slavic warriors across the river. The captives disclosed that they were among vanguard detachments of the approaching army and that the name of their king, or prince, was Musokius.[41]

According to Harkavy, Musokius should be identified as Majak, prince of the Slavic tribe of Valinana, who is mentioned by the Arabic geographer Mas'udi.[42] I consider such an identification hardly possible since Mas'udi wrote more than three centuries after the events now described, and must therefore have had in mind some other prince. Moreover, the Arabic *j* (in Majak) should represent the Greek γ rather than the Greek σ (in Mu*s*okius). In my opinion, it is the first letter in the name Musokius which gives the key to its origin. We have already mentioned[43] that the sounds of *m* and *b* are frequently interchanged in Turkish dialects. This is also true, under certain conditions, in Ossetian.[44] Thus, the original name may

38. *Idem,* 7, 5.
39. Mauricius, XI, 5.
40. See Bromberg, p. 458.
41. Theophilactus, VI, 9, 1.
42. See Markwart, p. 146.
43. See Chap. IV, Sec. 10.
44. Miller, *Sprache,* p. 34.

have been Busokios and not Musokius. And the name Busokius (Busok) makes interesting comparison with the name of the Antic chief, Bus (Boz), mentioned by Jordanis.[45] Whatever his name, the Slavic prince in question was probably the ruler of the north Dniester area, that is, of the region later known as Podolia.

Busok's campaign ended in catastrophe. With information from prisoners and spies concerning his approach, Byzantine troops first seized the Slavic fleet on the Danube, consisting of around one hundred fifty boats (*monoxyla*), and then by a surprise night attack smashed Busok's camp. He himself was taken prisoner.[46] Upon receiving news of the defeat of Busok's army the Avar kagan voiced his protest against the Byzantine invasion of the Slav country, which he considered his dominion. Fearing a new war with the Avars, Priscus offered to split the booty, and the kagan accepted. Accordingly, five thousand Slav prisoners were turned over to the Avars despite the indignation of the Byzantine soldiery, thus deprived of part of their spoils.[47]

The emperor Mauricius was displeased with Priscus' action and removed this experienced general from the command. The emperor's brother Peter was appointed instead. Meanwhile the Slavs gathered new forces, crossed the Danube, and raided lower Moesia. Several years passed before Peter succeeded in pushing them back. Only after clearing the southern banks of the Danube of Slavs did Peter venture to cross the river to attack them, in their own country (597). Prince Peiragast was now the leader of the Slavs.[48] Since the name is Iranian, we may suppose that he was, like the former leader Ardagast, an Antas and not a Sclavenus. The first battle, in which Peiragast was mortally wounded, ended in favor of the Byzantines. However, as Peter went deeper into enemy country his army was defeated by the Slavs north of the river Helibacius. The Byzantines suffered great losses and had no alternative but to retreat. As a result of this setback, Mauricius dismissed Peter and reappointed Priscus in his stead.

By this time the general situation had deteriorated from the Byzantine point of view, because of the intervention of the Avars. In 597 one Avar horde besieged Singidun (modern Beograd), while

45. Jordanis, Sec. 247.
46. Theophylactus, VI, 9, 5-13.
47. Kulakovskii, II, 459.
48. Theophylactus, VII, 4, 13.

another invaded Thrace and Macedonia down as far as Salonika. In the next year (598) the first Avar horde plundered Dalmatia while still another rushed along the southern bank of the Danube to lower Moesia and Scythia (Dobrudja). Priscus concentrated his troops at Tomi (Constanta) on the Black Sea where he was besieged by the Avars. In the spring of 599 the emperor Mauricius sent another Byzantine corps under the command of Comentiolus to rescue Priscus at Tomi. Before reaching the city Comentiolus was himself attacked by the Avars and had to retreat hastily back toward Constantinople. Pursuing Comentiolus' troops the Avars reached the Long Wall, which was defended by Mauricius personally. Failing in their effort to break through the wall, the Avars agreed to negotiate a peace treaty (600). According to the provisions of this treaty the Danube River bed was recognized as the boundary line between the Avars and the Byzantines, but the Byzantines reserved for themselves the right to cross the lower Danube whenever it became necessary to forestall Slavic inroads. Payment by the emperor to the Avars of annual "presents" to the amount of 20,000 gold coins was stipulated.[49]

Mauricius needed a truce for the rebuilding of his shattered army. He did not intend, however, to keep the provisions of the treaty, and as soon as the reorganization of the Byzantine army was complete he sent a strong corps under Priscus' command to upper Moesia to attack the Avars without warning. Priscus succeeded in defeating the Avars near Viminacium (modern Kostolac), after which he crossed the Danube and drove them upstream to the mouth of the Tisa River. There he overtook them and administered another defeat to the now disordered people. Three thousand Avars and thousands of Slavs were taken prisoners.[50] Meanwhile another Byzantine corps under the command of Gudwin was sent across the lower Danube to combat the Slavs. Gudwin was of German extraction, probably a Gepid. By this time the imperial diplomacy had succeeded once more in separating the Antes from the Sclaveni. It was against the Sclaveni that Gudwin waged war, while the Antes concluded an alliance with the empire.[51] Gudwin's campaign appears to have been a success, but when he returned to Thrace the Avar kagan

49. Kulakovskii, II, 467.
50. *Idem*, pp. 469-470.
51. Theophylactus, VIII, 5, 12.

sent his troops into the lower Danube area to punish the Antes for their pro-Byzantine inclinations.[52]

4. *Avaro-Slavic Relations.*

In the preceding section we have offered a brief outline of Byzantine relations with the Avars and the Slavs in the second half of the sixth century. Such an outline cannot give an adequate idea of either Avar or Slavic history because of the fragmentary nature of the evidence. The Byzantine chronicles mention both the Avars and the Slavs only so far as these two people affected the course of Byzantine policy. But the history of the Slavs and their relations with the Avars is what matters primarily from our point of view.

In order to understand the nature of the Avar domination over the Slavs we must first acquaint ourselves, if only briefly, with the organization of the Avar horde itself.[53] Being nomads, the Avars found the country in the basin of the lower Danube well suited to their needs. They were not obliged to change their habits and could raise horses and cattle on the Pannonian plain just as they had before in the Pontic or Transcaspian steppes. On the other hand, they were now in closer contact with native agricultural peoples and meant to take full advantage of this. To insure the complete subjugation of Slavic tribes in Pannonia, Avar troops were placed in nine fortified camps strategically located to command the whole area of present Hungary.[54] Each such camp (*hring*) was protected by a ring of earthen ramparts. Stores of grain and other foodstuffs supplied by the Slavic peasants, as well as military booty and treasures, were kept by the Avars in these camps.

The life of the Pannonian Slavs controlled by the Avars was precarious. Russian chroniclers record a characteristic story of Avar domination over the Slavic tribe of Dulebians.[55]

52. *Idem*, 5, 13.

53. H. Howorth, "The Avars," *JRAS*, XXI (1889), 721-810; Uspenskii, I, 468-469; Uspenskii, *Monarkhii*, pp. 7-18. For the archaeological evidence see A. Alföldi, "Zur Historischen Bestimmung der Avarenfunde," *ESA*, *9* (1934), 285-307; D. Bartha, "Die Avarische Doppelschalmei von Janoshida," *AH*, *14* (1934); N. Fettich, "Das Kunstgewerbe der Avarenzeit in Ungarn," *AH*, *1* (1926); *idem*, "Die Tierkampfscene in der Nomadenkunst," *RK*, pp. 83 ff.; T. Horwath, "Die Avarischen Gräberfelder von Ulbo und Kiskoros," *AH*, *19* (1935); A. Marosi and N. Fettich, "Trouvailles Avares de Dunapentele," *AH*, *18* (1936).

54. Feher, p. 34.

55. Hyp., col. 9.

And the Avars [Obry] made war upon the Slavs, and harassed the Dulebians who were Slavs. They [the Avars] did violence to the Dulebian women: when an Avar made a journey he did not cause either a horse or a steer to be harnessed, but gave command instead that three or four or five [Dulebian] women should be yoked to his cart and be made to draw him. Even thus they harassed the Dulebians.

The Dulebians lived originally in western Volynia. The Avars first conquered them on their roundabout march from Dacia to Pannonia along the eastern slopes of the Carpathian Mountains.[56] The Avars then compelled a part of the Dulebian tribe to join them in their further march. This section of the Dulebians were presently settled on the upper Tisa.[57] It is probably to these Dulebians that the narrative of the Russian annals refers.

The Slavs were bound to supply auxiliary detachments whenever the Avars waged war. The Frankish chronicler Fredegarius, who wrote in the middle of the seventh century, informs us that during battle the Slavs were placed in the front lines to bear the brunt of the fighting and save their masters, the Avars, from excessive losses.[58]

It was the Pannonian Slavs who suffered most under the Avar yoke. The position of other Slavic tribes was not so pitiful as that of their Pannonian kin. While, for example, the Illyrian Slavs likewise recognized the authority of the kagan, paid tribute to him, and supplied auxiliary troops, their communities retained a considerable autonomy. Moreover, they soon proved especially valuable to the Avars because of their skill on the water. At the end of the sixth century the Slavs reached the Adriatic coast in Dalmatia and were eager to put to sea. Anxious to assist them, the kagan hired experienced shipbuilders from Italy to be their instructors.[59]

Like the Illyrian Slavs, the Anto-Slavic tribes of the region of the lower Danube were in much better position than Pannonian Slavs. We have now to remark the interesting fact, already mentioned,[60] that from the time of the Avar invasion and down to 602 Byzantine chroniclers do not differentiate between the Sclaveni and the Antes, while on the other hand, Slavic chiefs mentioned in the sources bear Antic names. The possible explanation is that when the Avars

56. See Sec. 2, above.

57. Markwart, p. 129; Niederle, III, 196.

58. Fredegar, IV, 48.

59. Kulakovskii, II, 482; III, 52.

60. See Sec. 3, above.

succeeded in subordinating a part of the Antic tribes (561), some Antic princes became vassals of the kagan. The latter apparently placed some of them at the head of the Sclavenian communities in order to keep the Sclaveni in check. The Byzantine drive at the time of Mauricius broke up the Anto-Slavic unity, and therefore at the beginning of the seventh century these two groups once more act independently of each other.

With regard to the Antes we must take into consideration that it was certainly more difficult for the Avars to control them than to control the western Slavs, since only one section of them—the Antes of Bessarabia—recognized Avar authority. Antic tribes east of the Dnieper River, in the area of Poltava and Kharkov provinces, were independent in spite of the fact that some of the East Antic leaders occasionally joined the Avar horde at the time of the Avar inroads into Byzantine possessions on the Balkan peninsula. It is to one of these Antic expeditions to the Balkans that the origins of the so-called Pereshchepino treasure hoard[61] should be referred. The Pereshchepino treasure was buried in or after 668, since one of the Byzantine coins of the treasure is dated in this year. Other items in the treasure are of much earlier date, as for example a gold-plated silver dish made in the reign of Anastasius (491-518). The dish, according to the inscription on it, originally belonged to Bishop Patern, a contemporary of Anastasius. He was Bishop of Tomi, therefore the dish was probably obtained by an ancestor of the owner of the Pereshchepino treasure during one of the sieges of Tomi. Tomi was besieged by the Avars, the Bulgars, and the Anto-Slavs several times in the course of the sixth and the seventh centuries, and its citizens were forced every time to pay an idemnity to the besiegers for calling off the siege. In this way the dish may have been obtained by some Antic prince as his share of the booty. This may have happened in 599,[62] or perhaps at some later time.

5. *The Taurida and the Northern Caucasus in the Sixth Century.*

In the course of the preceding narrative we have had opportunity to deal, on several occasions, with the attitude of the Byzantine Government toward the nomadic tribes in the northeastern part of the Pontic area. We have now to dwell on the development of events

61. See Chap. IV, Sec. 8.
62. See Sec. 3, above.

in the Taurida and the North Caucasian area in more detail.

With regard to the political life of these regions two facts deserve special attention, to wit: the restoration of the Bosporan kingdom under the protection of the Byzantine Empire, and the growth of the Alanic kingdom in the Northern Caucasus. As we have already seen,[63] the new Bosporan kingdom was formally an ally of the Byzantine Empire. Actually, to be sure, the king of Bosporus was the emperor's vassal and his kingdom controlled by the imperial government. An imperial commissioner acted in the capacity of royal adviser. His title was that of *comes* during the reign of Justinian, and *dux* in the later period.[64] It may be noted that the Byzantine government tried to establish its protectorate over both sides of Kerch Strait. A Byzantine inscription of 533 has been found in Taman.[65]

In view of the importance of the Taurida as a whole for the control of Bosporus, Justinian paid great attention to the maintenance of fortifications along the southern coast of Crimea. As we have seen[66] the fortifications of Cherson were improved in the reign of Zeno (488). Later on, they were apparently in a state of decay, since Justinian had to order the restoration of the city walls and the building of new ramparts.[67] Two new forts were built on the south shore, namely, Aluston (modern Alushta) and Gorzuvitae (Gurzuf). The Bosporan king, on his part, erected a new tower in Panticapaeum (Kerch). In the reign of Justin II, more fortifications were added.[68]

However, Byzantine statesmen understood very well that for the defense of the Taurida as a whole it was not enough to build forts on the shore, but the Crimean mountain range must be sufficiently protected also. The mountainous region of the Taurida was inhabited by the Goths. Common danger from the Hunno-Bulgar tribes compelled the Goths and the Byzantines to join forces, and in the reign of Justinian the Goths recognized the authority of the emperor and bound themselves to supply three thousand soldiers upon request.[69] On his part, Justinian sent engineers and architects to Gothia to build fortifications. Walls were erected to protect the

63. See Chap. IV, Sec. 10.
64. Kulakovskii, *Tavrida,* p. 62.
65. Vasiliev, p. 71.
66. See Chap. IV, Sec. 7.
67. Procopius, *Buildings,* III, 7, 10-11.
68. *AK, 18,* 121-123.
69. Procopius, *Buildings,* III, 7, 13-14.

city of Doras, and on the northern slopes of the Crimean mountains a chain of forts was built. While the Goths had to supply troops the shore cities such as Cherson and Panticapaeum, assumed the duty of building ships for the imperial navy as decreed by Tiberius, in 575.[70]

Our information concerning the life of the people is almost as scant as for the preceding period. Procopius, in his *Buildings* says that the land of the Goths is fertile enough for agriculture and the raising of grapes. The Goths, according to this source, liked village life and did not care for cities.[71] There was, however, at least one city in Gothia even at this time, Doras, mentioned above. It has been accepted that Doras was located at the site of Mankup, but on the evidence of recent excavations it appears that it must have been originally situated at the site of Eski-Kerman.[72] In this case it is necessary to admit that another Gothic city existed at Mankup, since the foundation of a Christian basilica of the period of Justinian has been found there.[73] Incidentally, the existence of this church shows that by Justinian's time Christianity was firmly established among the Crimean Goths. In the twenty-first year of Justinian's reign (547-48) the Taman Goths asked the emperor to send them a bishop,[74] and their desire was fulfilled.

The Taman Goths must have been under the authority of the Utigurs, whom they joined in the war against the Kutriguri in A.D. 540.[75] In the Taman region, besides the Goths there lived also some As clans. Their chief settlement in this area must have been Malorosa.[76] Among these As there were probably Aso-Slavs (Antes). South of the mouth of the Kuban lived the Kasogi (Circassians), and east of them, between the middle course of the Kuban River and the Caucasian mountain range, the main body of the North Caucasian As or Alans (Ossetians) was concentrated. The Alans were organized by clans and tribes. In the sixth century one of the Alanic tribal chiefs assumed supreme authority over the whole people. His name, as given in Byzantine sources, was Sarosius.[77]

70. Novella *163*, 2.
71. Procopius, *Buildings*, III, 7, 15-16.
72. Vasiliev, p. 51.
73. *Idem*, pp. 71-72.
74. Kulakovskii, *Tavrida*, p. 62.
75. See Chap. IV, Sec. 10.
76. *Idem*, Sec. 6.
77. Σαρώσιος, Menander, frg. 4 (p. 4); Σαρώδιος, Menander, frg. 22 (p. 55).

It is possible that in this case his title was understood as a proper name. Menander calls him "Leader (*hegumenus*) of the Alans," which is apparently a translation of the Iranian *Sar-i-Os,* that is "Head of the As."

According to Procopius, the land of the Alans stretched along the Caucasian mountain range eastward to the "Caspian Gate." [78] By this name Procopius meant the Daryal Gorge (*Dar-i-Alan,* "the Gate of the Alans"). To the south the neighbors of the Alans were the Svans,[79] and to the west, the Abasgians; however, between the Alans and the Abasgians Procopius mentions still another tribe, the Brukhians.[80] Since the Abasgians were converted to Christianity around 540, the faith must have begun to spread among the Alans as well, soon after.

East of the Alans, in Daghestan, were the abodes of the Sabiri Huns.[81] While Procopius does not define the northern boundary of the Alanic state, we may assume that single As settlements extended both down the Kuban River and to the north of the Kuban. There were also As settlements in the region of the lower Don River.[82] Controlling as they did most of the mountain passes in the western and central part of the Caucasian range, the Alans commanded strategic positions on the routes from the North Caucasus to Transcaucasia. The latter was at this time divided between the Byzantine Empire and Persia. Both these countries naturally attempted to use the Alans as allies. In 541 the Alans assisted the Persians in their campaign against Lazica (Georgia).[83] In 549 they (the Alans) sided with the Byzantine Empire, from which they received—jointly with the Sabiri—reward to the amount of 300 pounds of gold.[84] However, in 551 Alan warriors are again mentioned as serving with the Persian troops.[85] In 558 the Alan chief, Sarosius, performed a great service to Byzantium by sending timely word of the appearance of the Avars.[86] Later on, he protected the Byzantine envoys during their trip to the Turkish kagan, when the Persians

78. Procopius, VIII, 3, 4.
79. *Idem,* I, 15, 1.
80. *Idem,* VIII, 4, 1.
81. On the Sabiri see Artamonov, pp. 115-118.
82. Miller, pp. 66-68.
83. Procopius, VIII, 1, 4.
84. *Idem,* II, 29, 29.
85. *Idem,* VII, 8, 37.
86. See Sec. 2, above.

tried to bribe the Alans to kill them.[87] In 571-72 Sarosius, in accordance with Byzantine policy, supported the Armenians in their revolt against Persia.[88] Four years later the Alanic state was badly shaken by the Turks (576).[89] Before long, however, trouble started in the Turkish Kaganate,[90] and it is possible that the Alans succeeded, at least temporarily, in regaining their independence.

6. The Avars, the Slavs, and Byzantium in the First Quarter of the Seventh Century.

In the year 602 riots broke out in the Byzantine army quartered on the banks of the Danube. The soldiers were already aroused at not having received their pay for several months, when word came from the capital that in the future their allowance was to be cut. This precipitated the revolt. General Phocas was proclaimed emperor in order to lead the army back to Constantinople. At the approach of Phocas' army the population in its turn rose up against the lawful emperor, Mauricius. Mauricius was arrested, five of his sons killed before his eyes, and then he himself executed.[91]

Phocas, whom the revolt brought to the throne, was a commoner by birth.[92] The Byzantine aristocrats intended to use him as their tool against Mauricius and then get rid of him. An uneducated, spiteful, and cruel soldier, Phocas was also a man of strong will and did not shrink from embarking upon a regime of wholesale terror against the aristocrats. While Phocas' government concentrated its attention on domestic affairs it was unable to maintain a firm foreign policy. The Persians took full advantage of this by invading the eastern provinces of the empire. In order to have his hands free against the Persians, Phocas had to increase the tribute to the Avars as the only way to prevent an Avar attack on Constantinople.

Nevertheless, the Byzantines were not able to push the Persians back. After a series of defeats the situation became critical, and the empire was saved only by Phocas' overthrow. His successor Heraclius, an able military leader, could not however stop the Persians at once, since a thorough reorganization of the Byzantine army was essential before effective action could be taken. For a number of

87. Kulakovskii, *Alany,* p. 48.
88. *Ibid.*
89. Menander, frg. 43 (p. 87).
90. See Sec. 2, above.
91. Kulakovskii, II, 484-496.
92. On Phocas and his reign see Bury, *1889,* pp. 197-206; Kulakovskii, III, 1-27.

years, therefore, the Persian offensive continued. Syria, Palestine, and finally Egypt, the granary of the empire, were occupied by Persian troops. It was only by a supreme effort that Heraclius gradually succeeded, first in stopping the Persians, then in a counterattack.[93]

One of the concomitant results of the weakness of the Byzantine Empire in the first quarter of the seventh century was the spread of Slavic colonization over the greater part of the Balkan peninsula.[94] As we have seen, the inroads of the Antes and the Sclaveni on Thrace and Illyricum started in the reign of Anastasius[95] and continued in the era of Justinian and his successors.[96] Originally the Slavs were interested in plunder only, but from the end of the sixth century bands of them began to settle in the lands they raided. The Slavic expansion went on in two main directions: towards Solun (Salonika) and the Aegean Sea, and toward the Adriatic (Istria and Dalmatia). By the middle of the seventh century the Slavs constituted a majority of the population in Thrace and Illyricum and had also penetrated into some provinces of Greece proper. Since the Slavs were under the authority of the Avar kagan, the latter, under the provisions of his agreement with the emperor Phocas, should have stopped the Slavic raids. Even had the kagan disposed of sufficient forces to control the Slavic expansion, however, he would hardly have done so, since he received from the Slavs his share of the booty and the whole business was quite profitable to him. Moreover, the kagan was interested in developing the Slavic navy both in the Aegean and in the Adriatic, as it increased the odds in his favor in case of a war with the Byzantines. In 602 he concluded an alliance with the Langobard king Agilulfus, and the latter sent, at his request, experienced Italian shipwrights to Dalmatia.[97] Thus the Slavic marine was founded which was to blossom later on with Dubrovnik (Raguza) as its center.

In 617 the Avar kagan—either Bayan, or Bayan's son—died, and, according to the then prevailing customs of international law, the Avaro-Byzantine treaty required new ratification. The succeeding kagan took this opportunity to deal a blow at Byzantium. His

93. On Heraclius and his reign see Bury, *1889*, pp. 207-257; Kulakovskii, III, 28-170; Ostrogorsky, pp. 54-66.

94. See Levchenko, pp. 47-48; Vasiliev, *Slaviane*, pp. 413 ff.

95. See Chap. IV, Sec. 9.

96. See above, Secs. 2 and 3; Chap. IV, Sec. 10.

97. See Sec. 4, above.

scheme was to seize the emperor Heraclius during the parleys. The kagan, therefore, suggested that they be held in the town of Heracleia (present-day Eregli) on the shore of the Sea of Marmora, and insisted that the emperor appear in person. Heraclius, who at first had no suspicions, readily agreed and set out for the appointed place. Hardly had he reached Heracleia when he was warned by his spies of the treacherous plot and immediately galloped back to Constantinople. The enraged kagan ordered his horde to attack the capital, but Heraclius' guard regiments with the help of the regular garrison were able to beat off the Avar onslaught. The horde plundered the outskirts of Constantinople and went north, leading thousands of captives.[98]

Heraclius could not send troops to avenge the Avar treachery since his whole attention was concentrated on the struggle with Persia. However, in order to curb the Avars somehow he had recourse to the traditional maneuver of Byzantine diplomacy, instigating one "barbaric" horde against another. Justinian I, as we know,[99] tried to avert the Kutrigurian menace by an alliance with the Utiguri. Now Heraclius attempted to establish friendly relations with the Kutriguri, having in mind to use them later against the Avars. We have seen[100] that soon after the first onslaught of the Avars the Kutrigur Khan acknowledged himself a vassal of the Avar kagan. In 582 the kagan appointed Gostun as khan of the Kutriguri. Judging from his name Gostun may have been an Antas rather than a Kutrigur.[101] Gostun's successor was Kurt, who was to found Great Bulgaria.[102] According to Zlatarski Kurt reigned during fifty-eight years, from 584 to 642.[103] If so, he must have been a mere boy at the time of his accession to the throne, and there is some evidence that his uncle Organa was regent during the first decade of his reign.[104] At the beginning of the seventh century, however, Kurt must have already assumed full authority over the Kutrigur horde. Since the Kutriguri resented the suzerainty of the Avar kagan, they

98. N. H. Baynes, "The Date of the Avar Surprise," *BZ, 21* (1912), 110-128; Kulakovskii, III, 53-55.

99. See Chap. IV, Sec. 10.

100. See Sec. 2, above.

101. Gost-un; the -un, according to Markwart, 147, is a "hypocoristicon." See, however, Zlatarski, I, 1, pp. 383-387.

102. Kurt or Kubrat. On him and his reign see Runciman, pp. 11-16; Zlatarski, I, 1, pp. 84-122.

103. Zlatarski, I, 1, p. 84.

104. Runciman, p. 14; Zlatarski, I, 1, pp. 84-86.

proved willing to negotiate with Byzantium. In 619 Kurt appeared in Constantinople with his chief wife and his *archonts* ("boyars"), each of whom likewise brought his chief wife. They were all baptized and Kurt was granted the rank of *patricius*.[105] According to the Byzantine concept, Kurt now became not only an ally of the emperor but placed himself under the authority of both the empire and the Church.

In view of the danger of a full-fledged alliance between Byzantium and the Bulgars, the Avar kagan hastened to conclude peace with the empire (620).[106] It proved to be a temporary truce only, which the Avars needed for the preparation of another attack on Constantinople. In order to assure their success they entered into negotiations with the Persians concerning a simultaneous offensive against Byzantium. Owing to the distances and the necessity of using roundabout routes for the envoys of each side, the negotiations lasted several years, and it was only in the spring of 626 that the Persian army reached the Asiatic shores of the Bosporus. In June of the same year the vanguard bands of the Avars reached the Long Wall. Constantinople was thus under threat of siege from two sides. The Avars succeeded before long in breaking through the fortifications of the wall and on July 29 their horde appeared before the walls of Constantinople itself. The Avar line, having the form of an arc, stretched from the Golden Horn to the Sea of Marmora. In addition to his own horde the Avar kagan had under his command bands of Bulgars, Gepids, and Slavs.[107] The participation of the Bulgars seems rather unexpected in view of the previous agreement between Heraclius and the khan Kurt. However, it is possible that the Bulgars who joined the Avar kagan belonged not to the Kutriguri but to some other Bulgar horde not subject to Kurt.

The participation of the Slavs was significant in view of their navy. It is probable that the light boats of the Slavs cruised the western shore of the Black Sea from the mouth of Danube south to Derkos, whence they were hauled overland to the Golden Horn. On August 7, 626, the Avar kagan ordered Constantinople stormed from land and sea. However, as in the time of Vitalian's attack a century before, Byzantine battleships easily defeated the light Slavic boats. No use of the Greek fire is mentioned this time. Simul-

105. Runciman, pp. 13-14.
106. Kulakovskii, III, 56.
107. *Idem*, p. 80.

taneously with the naval battle the garrison of Constantinople undertook a successful sortie, smashing at the besiegers. The kagan was greatly perturbed and ordered a general retreat to the Long Wall, from which he hoped to keep Constantinople under constant threat of a new attack. However, lack of food and the spread of epidemics compelled the Avars to lift the siege completely and return to their haunts in Pannonia.[108] When the Persians who camped on the Asiatic shore of the Bosporus became aware of the kagan's failure, they had no alternative but to retreat as well.[109] The whole situation changed so drastically and unexpectedly in favor of the empire that the people of Constantinople ascribed the miracle to the intercession of the Virgin Mary.[110]

7. Great Bulgaria, the Avars, and the Slavs in the Second Quarter of the Seventh Century.

The campaign of 626 was the last attempt of the Avars to conquer Constantinople. Both the kagan's prestige and the strength of his army were greatly undermined by the failure, and it is from this date that the downfall of the Avar Kaganate begins. Shortly after, the Czechs revolted against the Avars. Tradition has it that the leader of the uprising was a Frankish merchant by the name of Samo. Having united the Czech and Moravian tribes and freed them from the Avar yoke, Samo turned against the Franks and defeated a Frankish army sent by King Dagobert (630). Information concerning the first Czech state is very scarce.[111] It apparently disintegrated some thirty-five years after its foundation.

Another, and no less important, result of the campaign of 626 was the final emancipation of the Kutriguri horde from Avar control. We have seen that the Kutrigur khan Kurt was converted to Christianity at the time of his visit to Constantinople in 619.[112] Thereafter he kept quiet for several years, and offered no help to Byzantium in 626. However, on the retreat of the Avar kagan from Constantinople Kurt proclaimed his independence. It is even possible that he now accepted the title of kagan.[113] By this time the former enmity between the two leading Bulgar tribes, the Kutriguri and the Utiguri,

108. *Idem,* pp. 84-85.
109. *Idem,* p. 85.
110. *Idem,* pp. 85-86.
111. Fredegar, IV, 48; IV, 68. Uspenskii, Monarkhii, p. 17.
112. See Sec. 6, above.
113. Runciman, pp. 14-15; cf. Kulakovskii, III, 246.

had subsided and a coöperation between the two was established instead. Its basis may be easily understood. The Kutriguri were oppressed by the Avars, and the Utiguri by the Turks. Each tribe was too weak to fight its respective oppressors single handed. United, they became considerably stronger. It must also be noted that the Utiguri might count on the support of the Onoguri, an Ugrian (Magyar) tribe which had been in friendly relations with them since the sixth century.[114]

Such was the background for the unification of the Bulgar and Ugrian tribes in the Pontic and Azov steppes. The centripetal tendencies at work among these tribes were skillfully directed by Kurt. Although he was originally khan of the Kutriguri only, gradually both the Utiguri and the Onoguri recognized his authority. Thus the so-called Great Bulgaria came into being, of which Kurt was the kagan.[115] While Kurt was baptized in 619 together with his boyars, we have no evidence of the spread of Christianity in his realm on any large scale. It is therefore doubtful that he kept his Christian faith for long. Very likely he abandoned it because of opposition on the part of his people and returned to his original faith, which must have been of Altaic brand.

As to the Balkan Slavs, they likewise attempted to emancipate themselves from the Avar authority. According to information given by the emperor Constantine Porphyrogenitus in his book *De Administrando Imperio* it may be seen that some time in the seventh century the Croats expelled the Avars from Dalmatia.[116] It is probably to this event that the following words in George Pisidas' poem refer: "The Scythian [i.e., the Avar] kills the Slav and perishes himself; so they fight all in blood for their mutual destruction."[117] The poem was written in 630 on the occasion of the restoration of the Holy Cross to Golgotha by the emperor Heraclius after his victory over the Persians.

A little later than the Illyrian, the Macedonian Slavs must have revolted against the Avars in their turn. In any case, by the middle of the seventh century the Macedonian Slavs had ceased to recognize the authority of the kagan.[118] Neither did they submit

114. See Moravcsik; also, J. Schnetz, "Onoguria," *ASP, 40* (1926), 157-160. Cf. Vasiliev, p. 100.

115. Moravcsik; Runciman, pp. 15-16; Zlatarski, I, 1, pp. 99-100.

116. *De Adm.,* 30.

117. Kulakovskii, III, 89.

118. *Idem,* pp. 88-89.

to that of the emperor. Both in the 630's and the 640's the whole attention of the Byzantine Government was focused on the eastern wars, first against the Persians and then against the Arabs. The empire had neither time nor strength to keep either the Thracian or the Macedonian Slavs in check.

8. The Origins of the Khazar State and the Downfall of Great Bulgaria.

Great Bulgaria, founded by Kurt, was in the last years of his reign independent of both the Avars and the Turks. After the failure of the Avar raid on Constantinople (626), danger from the west seemed to be definitely over. The situation in the east was not so favorable to the Bulgars.

During their first onslaught on the North Caucasian area the Turks succeeded in establishing their control over the Utiguri, after which they penetrated into the Taurida.[119] In 581 a Turkish division had besieged Cherson but lifted the siege without taking the city and went back to Turkestan to take part in the civil war there. For about twenty years the Turkish state was weakened by internal dissension among the khans. The Utiguri took advantage of this situation and succeeded in emancipating themselves from Turkish control. However, the Turks kept their hold on the eastern part of the North Caucasian area, as well as over the lower Volga region. As a result of the internal strife in Turkestan the western group of Turks seceded from the main khanate in Turkestan.[120]

The western horde of the Turks cannot have been very numerous, and the local tribes conquered by them retained a certain amount of self-government. The ethnic composition of the tribes of the North Caucasian area was mixed. To the original Japhetide background various racial strains were added through the new tribes coming into the area, such as the Sarmatians, the Hunno-Bulgars, and the Ugrians. In the course of the fifth and sixth centuries one of these mixed tribes became known as the Khazars. Together with other local tribes the Khazars recognized Turkish authority around the year 570. Before long they became loyal supporters of the Turkish state and gradually mixed with the Turks. By the time the western Turkish horde in the North Caucasian area emancipated itself from the main horde in Turkestan the Khazars already constituted

119. Cf. Secs. 2, and 5, above.
120. Grousset, pp. 133-138.

the backbone of the North Caucasian state, which soon became known as the Khazar Kaganate.[121]

Due to their geographical position the Khazars, like the Alans before them, were destined to play an important role in the international politics of Hither Asia. As we have seen,[122] the Byzantine Empire was in 626 attacked simultaneously by the Avars and the Persians. Emperor Heraclius needed allies and was quick to grasp the possibility of using the Khazars against the Persians. Consequently a Byzantine envoy was sent to the Khazar kagan with the offer of an alliance against Persia.[123] Byzantine interests coincided with the Khazar in this matter, and the kagan was eager to accept. In 627 he led his army personally into Iberia and besieged the city of Tiflis. Heraclius on his part set forth for Tiflis from Lazica, as the western portion of Georgia was then known. The allies met in the vicinity of Tiflis, and Heraclius entertained the kagan at a sumptious banquet after which he presented the kagan with his golden dinner service.[124]

The siege of Tiflis continued for two months without result, however. Tired of inactivity, the kagan returned home leaving with Heraclius a corps of his troops—forty thousand men if we are to believe the sources.[125] It is probable that this corps consisted chiefly of White Ugrians (Saraguri), who were Khazar vassals. In any case it is stated in the Slavic translation of George Hamartolos' chronicle that the White Ugrians assisted Heraclius in the latter's war against the Persians.[126] Another Ugrian horde, that of the Onoguri, was at the time a part of Great Bulgaria under Khan Kurt, as has already been mentioned.[127] Thus the Ugrian tribes of the North Caucasian area in this period divided their loyalties between the Khazars and the Bulgars.

While Kurt lived, he was strong enough to resist the pressure of the Turko-Khazars. After his death, however, Great Bulgaria was dismembered between his sons just as the Hunnic Empire had been

121. Artamonov, pp. 88-134; Vernadsky, *Conversion,* pp. 76-77.

122. See Sec. 6, above.

123. Kulakovskii, III, 93.

124. *Idem,* pp. 93-94.

125. *Idem,* p. 94.

126. Hyp., cols. 9-10; Istrin, *Khronika,* II, 306 ff. Cf. Vernadsky, *Lebedia,* pp. 182-185.

127. See Sec. 7, above.

partitioned after Attila's death. Each of Kurt's sons now was at the head of his own horde, and none of them had forces large enough to cope with the Khazars. Under Khazar pressure the Bulgar hordes were compelled to leave their former abodes and look for safer regions.[128]

One of the hordes, which consisted chiefly of the Kutriguri clans, went north and finally settled in the area of the middle Volga and Kama rivers. These were the ancestors of the so-called Black, or Silver, Bulgars,[129] whose state was destined to play for some time an important role in the history of Western Eurasia.[130]

Two other Bulgar hordes, likewise for the most part Kutriguri, went west. One of them eventually reached Pannonia and joined the Avars.[131] The other penetrated as far as Italy. The Langobardi who controlled most of Italy at the time let the Bulgars in as their vassals and allowed them to settle around the province of Benevento.[132]

The fourth Bulgar horde, under Khan Asparukh, likewise went west but stopped in the region of the lower Danube (around 650). It consisted chiefly of Utiguri clans.[133]

The fifth horde, predominantly Ugrian, recognized the suzerainty of the Khazars and remained in the Azov region. This horde later merged with the "White Ugrians," who had been controlled even earlier by the Khazars. Gradually the Ugrians moved into the South Russian steppes and for some time occupied both the upper Donets region and the lower Dnieper and Bug area.[134] The Russian *Book of Annals* mentions them as the White Ugrians.[135] The country controlled by the Ugrians (Magyars) was known as Lebedia.[136] Before the coming of the Magyars the Lebedia area was populated chiefly by the Antes.[137] Some Antic tribes were now probably pushed out of the country, while others had to accept Magyar domination.

It should be noted that at about the same time as the Khazars

128. Theophanes, pp. 356-358; cf. Runciman, chap. i.

129. On the term "Black Bulgars" see Chap. VI, Sec. 3; for the term "Silver Bulgars" see Niederle, IV, 49.

130. See below, Chap. VI, Sec. 3.

131. Runciman, p. 19.

132. *Idem,* p. 21.

133. *Idem,* pp. 25 ff.

134. See below, Chap. VI, Sec. 5.

135. Vernadsky, *Lebedia,* pp. 182-185.

136. *De Adm.,* 38.

137. See above, Chap. IV, Sec. 8.

broke up Great Bulgaria they must also have conquered (around 650) the North Caucasian Alans, or As; [138] the Alan rulers thus becoming vassals of the Khazar kagan.

Simultaneously with the loss of their independence by the North Caucasian As, a period of troubles set in for the Danubian Antes who were much affected by the invasion of Asparukh's horde. The region first occupied by Asparukh is called Onglos (Ὄγγλος) by some Byzantine historians.[139] From Onglos the Bulgars soon penetrated among the islands of the Danubian delta as well as into the Dobrudja. Asparukh's headquarters were apparently on the island of Peuce, the old abode of the Bastarnai.[140] As a result of the Bulgar invasion a part of the Antic tribes moved north; most of them, however, recognized Asparukh as their suzerain. In the course of time the Bulgars merged with the Anto-Slavs, and from this mixture of conquerors and conquered a new nation arose, the modern Bulgars, or Bulgarians. The name reflects the Turkish origin of the former ruling clan; but the new nation as a whole is Slavic in language and civilization.

138. By inference, from the lack of source evidence on any independent Alanic state since that time. Cf. Kulakovskii, *Alany,* p. 49.

139. The spelling is not quite certain. Nicephorus (p. 34) has Ὄγλος; Theophanes, Ὄγγλος or (in other codices) Ὄγκλος; Anastasius in his Latin trans. of Theophanes' *Chronicle* has both Hoglos and Onglos; cf. Zlatarski, I, 1, pp. 96, 126. Feher, p. 24, accepts the reading Ὄγλος which he interprets as *aγul,* to be compared with the Magyar *ól* ("stable") and the Tatar *aul* ("village"). From this point of view the name Ὄγλος should be referred not to the country at large but to Asparukh's camp specifically. See also above, n. 34 to Chap. III.

140. See Chap. III, Sec. 6.

Chapter VI.

THE KHAZARO-BULGAR PERIOD, 650-737.

1. *Preliminary Remarks.*

As we have already mentioned,[1] a political and cultural upheaval of tremendous importance took place in the Near East in the middle of the seventh century: the Arabian Empire, known as the Caliphate, was born. In a brief span of time the Arabs conquered Egypt, Palestine, Syria, Persia, Transcaucasia, and then penetrated into Turkestan. At the end of the seventh century Arabic troops pushed westward along the Lybian littoral of the Mediterranean Sea, moving victoriously on and destroying the last vestiges of Byzantine administration and culture in Lybia; at the beginning of the eighth century they crossed the Strait of Gibraltar into Spain. The very name "Gibraltar" is a memorial of the event: Djabal-Tarik, the Mountain of Tarik.[2]

As a result of Arab victories and the loss of its eastern provinces, the Byzantine Empire ceased to be a world power and became a national Greek state confined to the Balkan peninsula and Asia Minor. The latter could now be defended from the assault of the Arabs only with the utmost effort, while in the Balkans the Bulgaro-Slav state was before long to be established.

The wide range of Arabic commercial interests influenced the economic history of both the Mediterranean and the Caspian area, including the Volga region. Even before the Arabs, the turnover of goods between the Russian north on the one hand and Persia and Byzantium on the other had been a considerable factor of economic progress. Trade between north and south now assumed a new impetus. The Khazar state which established itself in the North Caucasian area and in the lower Volga region took full advantage of its geographical position, and became a bridge through which lively commercial intercourse became possible between the Arabs

1. See Chap. V. Sec. 1.

2. Tarik was the commander of the Arab troops that crossed to Spain and occupied the rock now known as Gibraltar (*EI*, IV, 666).

and the north. It was through Khazaria that Arabian merchants obtained precious furs. The Bulgar horde which had been pushed by the Khazars from the Azov region and had settled in that of the middle Volga[3] became another link on the great commercial route. The Volga Bulgars were, like the Khazars, quick to grasp the advantages of their position. As to the Ugrians (Magyars), who were to a certain degree dependent upon the Khazars, they succeeded eventually in seizing control over the Donets way.

As we know,[4] some kind of commercial relations must have been established between the tribes of the upper Volga region and those of the Baltic littoral as early as in the New Stone and the Bronze Ages. The new rise of Volga commerce in the Khazar period could not but influence Baltic trade as well. It was Scandinavian merchants, known as the Varangians, who gradually succeeded in controlling the Baltic approaches to the upper Volga. To be sure, the Scandinavian *Drang nach Osten,* first of all to the eastern shores of the Baltic, was partly the result of local Scandinavian developments, such as an increase of the population beyond the density at which it could maintain itself, given the prevailing primitive conditions of husbandry. But in addition to these local causes there were also more general ones which pushed the Varangians to the Eastern Way (*Osterweg*). The Arab seizure of both the southern Mediterranean and Spain broke, or at least undermined, for some time the commercial intercourse between western Europe and the Orient.[5] Roundabout routes had to be established, and it was in search of such routes that the Varangians began their exploration of the Russian riverways. They finally succeeded in opening a new way from the Baltic to the Black Sea and Caspian region.

Let us now turn to the survey of sources. As to the Byzantine writers, the works of the emperor Constantine Porphyrogenitus (912-957) deserve special attention. As a ruler Constantine did not show any particular abilities, but his contributions to the field of history are invaluable. Attributing great importance to historical research, Constantine organized a circle of learned historians whom he commissioned to write biographies of some of his predecessors on

3. Cf. Chap. V, Sec. 7.
4. See Chap. I, Sec. 4; and Chap. II, Sec. 1.
5. H. Pirenne, *Mediaeval Cities* (Princeton, 1925), pp. 25-55. See, however, Dopsch, II, 433 ff. (English ed. pp. 388-389).

the Byzantine throne; to continue the work of the former chroniclers and annalists; and to gather every kind of historical material. Thus upon his initiative a collection of excerpts from the most important historical books was made, which was arranged according to topics, such as: materials on diplomatic activities; materials on political unrest; materials on military campaigns of the Byzantine emperors, etc. In this way Constantine preserved valuable information for the use of the future historians, and it is in his *Excerpta* that the existing sections of Menander's *History* have been preserved. In addition to his activities as a sponsor of historical studies. Constantine was himself the author of several important works. To be sure, his books are of the nature of a compilation of materials of which he was only the editor, but he deserves the warm gratitude of modern historians none the less. The treatise *De Ceremoniis Aulae Byzantinae* is of paramount importance for the study of Byzantine life. For the student of Russian history the minutes of the reception of Princess Olga (957) are especially significant. For the earlier period with which we are now dealing, two other books by Constantine are even more valuable, to wit: his description of the military districts of the Byzantine Empire (*De Thematibus*), and his treatise *De Administrando Imperii*—these works are closely connected. In both of them the writer conveys much information concerning the neighbors of the empire, the Khazars, the Magyars, and the Rus among others. While Constantine wrote in the middle of the tenth century, he used some earlier sources as well. Sometimes, however, his knowledge of certain events of the past is rather vague and nebulous, a fact which he himself, incidentally, at times admits.

Following the rise of the Caliphate the Arabic language became an important vehicle of cultural progress, and among other branches of Arabic science, historiography assumed special significance. To be sure, not all the historians and geographers who wrote in Arabic were Arabs; on the contrary, some of the most outstanding were not Arabs by birth, but either Persians, Syrians, or Greeks—however, since they all used the Arabic language, they contributed by their work to the general flowering of that culture. Altogether, the rise of Arabic historiography is a remarkable phenomenon in the development of historical science. It is no less rich, and is more diverse, than the Byzantine. Among the geographers and historians of the Arabic tongue were men of eminent ability, and the very expansion of the culture, from Spain to Turkestan, resulted in widening the range of interests of the Arabic scholars. In most cases they were interested in the history and geography not only of the Arabic Empire proper, but of neighboring countries and peoples as well. This explains the fact that we find in the Arabic works so much information concerning the Khazars, the Bulgars (both the Volga and the Danubian groups), the Magyars, the Slavs, and the Rus. On the whole the information they convey is reliable, but in order to use it properly one must take into account some peculiarities of method of the Arabic authors: first of all, their system of arranging materials. The correlation of the peoples and countries described in most Arabic works must be explained by the orientation of each author, and it is only when his bearings are established that the geographical background of the various tribes mentioned can be elucidated and the tribes themselves properly identified. Moreover, it is not always clear to what period the information conveyed should be referred. An Arabic author of the tenth or the eleventh century may have used earlier sources not accessible to us. To the information he has drawn from these sources he may add more recent data without properly differentiating between the two items. It would be dangerous, therefore, to rely on the work of a tenth century Arabic author for the study of tenth century events. His data, or some of them, may actually reflect things which have happened much earlier. It is essential in each case to analyze carefully the sources of information of the author quoted. All the above suggestions are of course applicable to any literary sources of any period, but the point is here emphasized with regard to the Arabic historians because of the fact that until recently students of Russian history have not adequately sifted the information conveyed by these chroniclers.

Of the Arabic writers only those whose work is most important for the study of Russian history will be mentioned here. The first in any such list would be Ubaidallah Ibn-Khurdadhbih, who occupied the office of postmaster general of the Caliphate. His book on *The Routes and Kingdoms,* which was written around A.D. 846, is of the nature of a brief manual; its information is terse but precise and it is very useful. His other work, the *Book of Genealogies of the Persians and their Colonies,* which was known to the Persian historian Gardizi in the eleventh century, has not been preserved. Another important historical source is Ahmad al-Baladhuri's *Book of the Conquest of Countries.* For our purpose the section on the North Caucasian campaign of the Arabic general Marvan (737) is especially valuable. Baladhuri was of Persian ancestry, but his father had settled in Egypt. Ahmad wrote the book not long before his death, which occurred in A.D. 892. At the beginning of the tenth century Mohammad Ibn-Rusta, a resident of Ispahan, wrote a comprehensive encyclopedia of history and geography, of which we have only the geographical part. In 921 Abu Zaid al-Balkhi compiled a similar geographic manual under the title *The Pictures of the Climates*. This work was revised and enlarged by Ibrahim al-Istakhri in 953. Ibrahim's work was in its turn revised and supplemented by Ibn-Hauqal, in 977. All the above manuals of encyclopedic character contain valuable information on the Pontic and Caspian countries and peoples.

Of a different nature but of paramount importance is the book written by Ahmad Ibn-Fadhlan, who took part in the diplomatic mission sent by the caliph to the Volga Bulgars in 921-22. This is not a scientific treatise but a traveler's report. Chronologically Ibn-Fadhlan's report falls beyond the time limit set for the present volume, but Ibn-Fadhlan's comment on the life and customs of the Volga tribes are nevertheless valuable for our purpose, since so many habits and traditions of his time were survivals from an older period. Until recently Ibn-Fadhlan's work was known only in an abridged version from Yakut's geographical dictionary, but in 1923 a fuller manuscript copy was found in Meshed, photostats of which were sent by the Iranian Government to the Soviet Academy of Sciences in 1935. They were used for a new Russian translation of the work, under I. Yu. Krachkovskii's editorship (1939).

Mohammad Ibn-Jarir at Tabari (838-923) is traditionally considered the "father of Arabic historiography." A. E. Krymskyi calls him the Arabic "Nestor," referring to the Kiev monk of the eleventh century, Nestor the Chronicler, allegedly the author of the *Russian Primary Chronicle*. Tabari, a Persian by birth, set out to write a comprehensive history of the world. After devoting much attention to the ancient periods he apparently became afraid that he would not have time to complete his work on the same scale, and therefore tried to make the narrative more concise. The last part of his work consists only of brief annual notes. For this reason Tabari's book is less important for the student of Russian history than would otherwise have been the case. Of much more account is the work of Ali al-Mas'udi (d. A.D. 956). Mas'udi belonged to a distinguished Arab family; he was born in Bagdad, traveled a great deal, and died in Cairo. He wrote a comprehensive treatise on history and geography, now lost; only an abridgment made by the author himself has reached us.[6] Another prominent chronicler was Abdallah al-Bakri. His father lived in Cordova, Spain, and Abdallah himself was for some time connected with the court of Seville. He died in A.D. 1094. His book entitled *On Routes and Countries*—a kind of geographical guide—was very popular in his time. It contains a valuable section on the Pontic peoples, including the Slavs and the Rus. Al-Bakri used in part the same sources as Ibn-Rusta and al-Mas'udi, but also introduced additional evidence. Of the Arabic authors of later generations the great geographers Mohammad al-Idrisi (born A.D. 1099; completed his work by 1154) and Yakut (1178-1229) may be mentioned here. The latter's *Geographical Dictionary* contains much valuable information which partly refers to earlier periods. A contemporary of Yakut was Ibn-al-Athir (d. 1234), author of a world history meant to supplement Tabari's chronicle.

Persian historiography is likewise of great value for our purpose. Following the Arab conquest (second half of the seventh century) Persia was under Arabic control not only politically but culturally as well. Persia accepted Islam, and Arabic became for some time the language of the Persian upper class. The vitality of the Iranian people was not exhausted, however, and Iranian culture began gradually to gain ground within the frame of the Arabic superstructure. A new Persian language emerged from the mixture of old Persian and Arabic. Nor was political emancipation long in coming. An Iranian dynasty, known as the Samanids, established itself in the ninth century in southern Turkestan with Bokhara as its capital. That city became the center of the Iranian revival. Interest in Iranian history and geography increased, and at the beginning of the tenth century the vizier of the Samanid state, Abu-Abdallah Mohammad al-Jaikhani, compiled a geographical treatise known as the *Book of Routes and Kingdoms*. The manuscript was lost, but we know of its contents from quotations in later works. It appears that Jaikhani used the same sources as Ibn-Rusta; as for al-Bakri, he probably had Jaikhani's book at his disposal. In A.H. 372 (A.D. 982-83) another outstanding Persian geographic treatise was set down. Its title is *Hudud-al-Alam* ("The

6. Mas'udi's work is usually referred to as "Meadows of Gold" (*Prairies d'or* in Barbier de Meynard's French trans.), although this is not a correct trans. of the Arabic title.

Boundaries of the World"). The name of the author is unknown. The only extant manuscript copy of this work was discovered in Askhabad in 1890 by the Russian scholar Tumanskii. In 1930 the manuscript was reproduced phototypically in Leningrad, with a preface by V. V. Bartold who also translated into Russian some excerpts bearing on the Slavs and the Rus. In 1937 an English translation of the whole work was published in London by V. F. Minorsky, who supplied a valuable commentary as well. The author of the *Hudud al-Alam* appears to have used the books of both Ibn-Khurdadhbih and al-Jaikhani. The same sources were used later on by Abu Said Gardizi, of whom little is known besides his name. His work, entitled *Zayn al-Akhbar* ("Adornment of Narratives"), contains a history of Persia down to A.D. 1032 and, as a supplement, a history of Khorasan (one of Persia's provinces) down to 1041. Gardizi completed his work in the reign of Abd-ar-Rashid (1049-1053), of the house of Gaznevids. Reference may also be made here to a Persian version of Tabari's chronicle, by the Khorasan vizier Bal'ami, who added some information from Persian traditions (around A.D. 970).

Another important Persian compilation is *Tabai al-hayawan* by Marvazi, of the eleventh century, of which V. F. Minorsky has prepared an edition and which he characterizes as "a kind of super-Hudud al-Alam."[7] The works of some of the Persian historians of the later Middle Ages should likewise not be overlooked, since we occasionally find that these writers made use of sources and traditions now lost. Mirkhwand's *Rawdatu's Safa,* written in the fifteenth century, may be mentioned in this connection.

In addition to Arabic and Persian sources there exist also a number of Hebrew texts allegedly of the Khazar period. Part of them were first published in the sixteenth century, and in 1932 a new edition appeared, edited by P. K. Kokovtsov under the title *The Hebrew-Khazar Correspondence of the Tenth Century.* It includes, among other texts, (1) a letter from a Spanish Jew to the Khazar king, Joseph; (2) an answer by the latter, known in two different versions; (3) a fragment of a letter from an unknown Khazar Jew. These documents contain much interesting, although somewhat nebulous, information concerning the history of both the Khazars and their neighbors, including the Rus. The authenticity of the

7. Professor Minorsky's letter to me of December 24, 1940.

sources was questioned by the late Joseph Markwart, and recently Henri Grégoire has likewise expressed his doubts concerning the origin of the documents (1937).[8] On the other hand, Maximilian Landau, after a detailed analysis of the text of the letter of Hasai ibn Shaprut to King Joseph as well as of the Cambridge fragment, has come to the conclusion that both these documents must be held authentic (1938).[9] Altogether, until a thorough reconsideration of the entire problem has been made, caution is advisable in using the evidence of the "Correspondence" as a whole.

We now turn to modern historiography. In a preceding chapter both Markwart's *Streifzüge* and the leading outlines of Byzantine history have already been mentioned.[10] It should be noted here that Kulakovskii's *History of Byzantium* stops at A.D. 717. A very useful work is V. N. Zlatarski's *History of the Bulgarian State,* Volume I of which deals with the oldest period of Bulgarian history, down to 867. There is also a more recent outline of Bulgarian history in English by S. Runciman (1930). On the Magyars, J. Nemeth's book may be mentioned, of which I know only the resumé in the *Nouvelle Revue de Hongrie,* 1932. Another Magyar scholar, G. Moravcsik, has published a valuable study on the history of the Onoguri (1930). C. A. Macartney's *The Magyars in the Ninth Century* should also be referred to in this connection (1930). An excellent bibliography of the Khazars appeared in the *Bulletin of the New York Public Library* in 1938. V. V. Grigoriev's articles on the Khazars published in 1834-35 still deserve attention although they are out of date. Among recent literature, M. I. Artamonov's *Studies in Khazar History* may be mentioned here (1934). As to the history of the Arabs there is a wealth of works in various languages. I shall limit myself here by referring to A. E. Krymskyi's *History of the Arabs and their Literature* (in Russian, 1912), as well as to the recent outline of the history of Islamic peoples by K. Brockelman (in German, 1939). Brockelman is also the author of the standard history of Arabic literature (in German, 1898-1902). For the history of Persia see, among other publications, Krymskyi's *History of Persia and its Literature* (in Russian, 1909; revised edition in

8. H. Grégoire, "Le Glosel Khazar," *Byz., 12,* 225-266.

9. M. Landau, "Beitraege zum Chazarenproblem," *Schriften der Gesellschaft zur Foerderung der Wissenschaft des Judentums,* No. 43 (1938). I am indebted to Dr. A. S. Yahuda for this reference. See also Yu. D. Brutskus, *Pismo Khazarskogo Evreia* (Berlin, 1924).

10. See Chap. IV, Sec. 1.

Ukrainian, 1923), and E. G. Browne's *Literary History of Persia from Ancient Times to Firdowsi* (1902).

2. *The Khazar Kaganate.*[11]

The structure of the Khazar state followed the traditional pattern of the nomadic empires of Eurasia. The Khazars were originally a horde of horsemen which succeeded in controlling politically the neighboring agricultural tribes. Their domination was, however, much milder for the subject peoples than that of the Avars or even of the Bulgars.

The Khazars' interest in trade added a peculiar feature to the character of their power. Occupying as it did the North Caucasian area, the Azov region, and the basin of the lower Volga, the Khazar state was strategically located to control the junction of the most important commercial highways of western Eurasia. It was the protection of these highways that constituted the main objective of the kagan's policy, and he was rewarded by collecting customs duties from the caravans and ships plying north and south, west and east. We have just called the Khazars originally a nomadic people, but such statement must now be somewhat qualified. They were a mixture of Turks, North Caucasian "Huns," and some native "Japhetic" tribes of the North Caucasian area.[12] Long before the coming of the Turks, trade and handicrafts played an important role in this area, and settlements of an urban type had been established there from time immemorial.[13] To be sure, the Turkish horde which invaded the northern Caucasus in the second half of sixth century consisted of nomads, but at the time of the rise of the Khazar state a century later some of these nomads were already familiar with the ways and habits of a more settled life. While generally speaking the Khazars spent most of their time in the steppes, many a Khazar grandee had also gardens, vineyards, and fields, in which his serfs labored and which he was fond of visiting.

It is not easy to delineate the precise boundaries of the Khazar state, especially since a distinction must be made between Khazar

11. On the Khazars see Artamonov; V. Bartold, "Khazar," *EI, II,* 935-937; Gotie, pp. 70-90; Grigoriev, pp. 45-78; Markwart, pp. 1-27, 270-305, 474-477, Vernadsky, *Conversion.* For a comprehensive bibliography of the Khazars see *NYPL* (September, 1938), pp. 695-710.

12. On the ethnic background of the Khazars see Artamonov, pp. 88 ff.; Vernadsky, *Conversion,* pp. 76-77.

13. See Chap. I, Sec. 5.

lands proper and those of the tribes subjected to Khazar domination but enjoying a modicum of autonomy. The main nucleus of the Khazar state comprised the North Caucasian area and a triangular bulge to the north, between the lower Don and the lower Volga. For some time the Khazars also controlled the steppes and deserts east of the Volga to the Yaik River.[14] Thus the eastern frontier of the Khazar state followed the Caspian littoral from the mouth of the Yaik to the pass of Derbend or the so-called Derbend Gate, which was protected by a strong Khazar garrison. The southern boundary of the state followed approximately the main mountain range of the Caucasus. The Daryal Gorge in the middle of the Caucasian range was guarded by the As (Alans), who were the Khazars' subjects. The Pontic littoral from the mouth of the Kuban to Kerch Strait may be considered part of the western boundary of the Khazar state. The city of Bosporus (Panticapaeum, Kerch) was occupied by a Khazar garrison. The Sea of Azov formed a natural boundary to the northwest.

We may thus see that the areas populated by both the north Caucasian As and the Azov Aso-Slavs (Antes) were included in the Khazar state. It follows that the Iranian and Slav As (Antes) must have played an important role, since the As were probably the most advanced people within the boundaries of this political sphere. Some light may be thrown on the culture of the As of this period by examining archaeological materials; such, for example, as the finds in the North Caucasian area on the one hand, and in the Don and Donets region on the other.[15] From literary sources it is known that there were Aso-Slav contingents in the Khazar army. The North Caucasian As guarded the Daryal Pass for the Khazars. As and Aso-Slav troops were, however, used elsewhere as well. The name of the city of Astrakhan in the Volga delta is characteristic in this connection since it must be derived from As-Tarkhan ("commander of the As division").[16] An interesting evidence of Slavic influence on Khazar life is the use of the Slavic word *zakon* ("law") by the Khazars.[17]

In addition to peoples and tribes directly subject to the Khazars there were others who, while recognizing the authority of the kagan,

14. The Yaik River is now known as the Ural River.
15. See Secs. 5 and 8, below.
16. See Minorsky, p. 451.
17. *De Adm.*, 38.

retained their autonomy. Such was the case of the Magyars—allies of the Khazars, according to Constantine Porphyrogenitus, for three hundred years.[18] Some of the Finnish tribes in the Oka and middle Volga region were also at one time or another connected with the Khazar state. Ibn-Rusta mentions for example that the Burtas (Mordva) were under the suzerainty of the kagan.[19] Later on the Burtas became subject to the Volga Bulgars. These latter, however, must have been themselves for some time under Khazar rule. The question is not clear, and the only evidence is the purported "Letter of the Khazar King Joseph."[20]

Among the cities of the Khazar Empire the following four may be mentioned here: Khamlij (or Khamlikh), and Itil, both on the lower Volga; Samandar, near the Caspian shore of the North Caucasian area (identified as either Makhach-kale or Kizliar); and Balanjar, in Daghestan, half-way between Samandar and the Daryal Gorge.[21] With regard to Khamlij, its exact location has not been established. In my opinion it must have been located at the Volga end of the Don-Volga portage, near present Stalingrad (Tsaritsyn). Itil was somewhere on the Volga delta, near Astrakhan. As to this latter, we may suppose that it was at this time a military fort protecting Itil. Judging from its name, it must have been garrisoned by an As detachment. It should be noted, however, that Astrakhan is not mentioned among the Khazar cities listed by Arabic authors.

Another important Khazar fort was that of Tmutorokan on the Black Sea at the Kuban delta. It was situated somewhere near Malorosa; [22] perhaps it was another name for Malorosa. The name Tmutorokan is to be derived from the Altaic words *tma* (cf. Persian *tuman*), a division of troops ten thousand strong, and *tarkhan* ("chief"). Presumably at the time of the Turkish invasion of North Caucasian area in the sixth century,[23] the commander of a Turkish division (*Tma-Tarkhan*[24]) established his headquarters at the Taman delta, hence the name of the city. The Greeks Hellenized the name, changing it to Τυμάταρχα or Tamatarcha, the latter probably

18. Grégoire, *Habitat,* p. 267.
19. Macartney, p. 194.
20. Kokovtsov, pp. 98-99; cf. sec. 1, above.
21. Minorsky, pp. 451-454.
22. See Chap. IV, Sec. 10; and Chap. V, Sec. 5.
23. See Chap. V, Sec. 2.
24. The name of the Turkish commander was Bokhan (Bogha-Khan?). See n. 31 to Chap. V.

from "Tagmatarcha." [25] Since in Greek *tagmatarches* means "commander of a regiment," [26] the name kept its original meaning even in the Hellenized form. Tamatarcha is mentioned in the Byzantine sources beginning with the eighth century. The city itself was certainly founded earlier, and as we have just seen its name may be connected with the appearance of the Turks in the sixth century. Incidentally, the Russian Turkologist V. D. Smirnov likewise connects with the Turkish drive the name of the city of Kerch (Panticapaeum) on the opposite side of the Cimmerian Bosporus. According to Smirnov the name Kerch is to be derived from the Turkish word *Karshi* ("beyond," "on the other side"), since for the Turks approaching from the North Caucasian hinterland that city lay beyond the strait.[27]

Some of the commercial cities in the Khazar state achieved considerable prosperity. Of Samandar Ibn-Hauqal says that it had many orchards, and in and around it were about forty thousand vineyards. "Its population consisted of Moslems and others; the Moslems had their mosques, the Christians their churches, and the Jews their synagogues." [28] With regard to Itil Ibn-Fadhlan reports that "this is a large city. It is composed of two sections; one is inhabited by the Moslems; in the other the king (kagan) and his courtiers live." [29] According to Mas'udi there were seven judges in Itil: "two for the Moslems; two for the Khazars in accordance with the Law of the Tora; two for the Christians in accordance with the Gospel; and one for the Slavs, the Rus, and other heathen: he tries them in accordance with the Natural Law, that is with reason." [30] The expansion of several major religions in the Khazar state was partly the result of the international scope of its commercial relations, due to which there were so many foreign merchants settled in the Khazar cities. The original religion of the Khazars

25. See Smirnov, *Tmutorokan,* p. 34. As to the form Τυμάταρχα, it was obviously derived directly from the Turkish *Tma* (*Tuma*)-*Tarkhan.* For the mixture and close interrelation of the Greek and Turkish terms it is interesting to note that on one occasion Menander mistakes the first part of the title, *Tma* (which he quotes, curiously enough, in its Hellenized form) for a personal name: "The name of the (Turkish) envoy was Tagma (Τάγμα), and his rank, *Tarkhan* (Ταρχάν)," see Menander, frg. 20 (p. 53).

26. Ταγματάρχης, "the leader of tagma" (Liddell-Scott); in modern Greek, "major."

27. Smirnov, *Tmutorokan,* pp. 68-71.

28. Harkavy, p. 220; Karaulov, p. 114.

29. Ibn-Fadhlan, p. 85.

30. Mas'udi, II, 11.

themselves was of the Altaic Shamanistic type, but later the upper strata of the Khazars were converted to either Islam or Judaism. The kagan himself was finally converted to Judaism as we shall see in the proper place.[31]

As to the organization of the Khazar government, its peculiarity consisted in the dual nature of the supreme power, represented by two rulers usually called the kagan and the beg.[32] This feature is mentioned by Constantine Porphyrogenitus (tenth century) as well as by a number of Oriental writers of the tenth and eleventh centuries. It is possible, however, that the dual aspect of the supreme power was not an original arrangement with the Khazars. For example, both the Patriarch Nicephorus and Georgios Hamartolus, speaking of the negotiations between the emperor Heraclius and the Khazars in 621, mention only one ruler of the Khazars.[33] So also does the Armenian historian Moses Kalankatvaci.[34] In my opinion the duality of the supreme power in the Khazar state may have been the result of the heterogeneous ethnic composition of the nation. The original type of Khazar chief, the kagan, from time to time accepted the assistance of another ruler, who represented some other ethnic group influential at some specific period. Gradually this arrangement became permanent.

With such possibilities in mind, let us now analyze the respective titles of the two rulers as given by various authors.[35]

Authority	*1st Ruler*	*2d Ruler*
Constantine[36]	*Khaqan*	*Pekh*
Ibn-Rusta[37]	*Khazar-Khaqan*	*Aysha*
Ibn-Fadhlan[38]	*Khaqan*	*Khaqan-Bekh*
Mas'udi[39]	*Khaqan*	*Malik*
Ibn-Hauqal[40]	*Khaqan-Khazar*	*Malik-Khazar*
Gardizi[41]	*Khazar-Khaqan*	*Abshad (Anshad)*

31. See Chap. VIII, Sec. 6.
32. Gotie, p. 82; Grigoriev, pp. 66-78.
33. Nicephorus Patriarcha, *Brief History,* p. 15; Georgios Monachus, II, 671.
34. Moses Kalankatvaci, chap. x (Patkanov's trans., p. 15), as quoted by Kulakovskii, III, 93.
35. Cf. Minorsky, p. 451.
36. *De Adm.,* 42.
37. Macartney, p. 197.
38. Ibn-Fadhlan, p. 84.
39. Minorsky, p. 451.
40. *Idem,* p. 451.
41. Macartney, pp. 197-198.

It is characteristic that the first ruler is always known as kagan or Khazar-kagan. We may understand this title either in the sense that this ruler was the chief of the Khazar state as a whole, or in the sense that he was the chief of the Khazars proper, of the specific Khazar group. As to the titles of the second ruler, *Bekh* or *Pekh* is certainly a transcription of the Turkish title "beg" ("bey"), "prince." Judging from the title it seems almost certain that at such time as the second ruler was known as beg he represented the Turkish group within the Khazar state. Malik is an Arabic translation of the same title. More intriguing are the titles *Aysha* or *Abshad* (*Anshad*). The two names are probably different transcriptions of the same original term. In this connection we may also mention the name Ansa mentioned in the Persian treatise *Hudud al-Alam:* "Atil . . . is the capital of the Khazars and the seat of the king, who is called *Tarkhan Khagan* and is one of the descendants of Ansa." [42]

We thus have three variants of the name: *Ansa, Anshad, Aysha.* If we surmise that in this case, as in the case of "beg," the second ruler represented a specific ethnic group, the closest ethnic name to which we can refer it is that of the As, or Antes. The nasal sound in *Ansa* may well correspond to the old Russian name for the As—Ias. It is significant that the title "descendant of Ansa" is, according to *Hudud al-Alam, Tarkhan Khaqan.*[43] He was probably the *Tarkhan* ("chief") of the As (Ansa). We may imagine that eventually the *As-Tarkhan* became powerful enough to be a deputy kagan, like the Turkish beg at other times. From Constantine's treatise we know that already in the ninth century the deputy kagan was known as beg. It is quite possible that in the eighth century it was the *As-Tarkhan* who enjoyed the position of deputy. Since it is the city of Atil, at the mouth of the Volga near the present Astrakhan, that is mentioned in *Hudad al-Alam* as the seat of the *Tarkhan,* "one of the descendants of Ansa," we may recall in this connection that the name of Astrakhan is derived from *As-Tarkhan.*[44]

Let us now turn to the fourth important ethnic group within the Khazar State: the Ugrians (Magyars). According to Ibn-Fadhlan, aside from the beg there was a deputy beg known as *Kender-*

42. Minorsky, pp. 161-162.

43. *Idem,* p. 161.

44. See n. 16, above.

Kagan.[45] In this connection we must recall that according to both Ibn-Rusta and Gardizi the chief of the Magyars was known as *Kende.*[46] This is probably another transcription of the title, *Kender.* Incidentally, *kender* means "hemp" in Magyar.[47] It may have been originally a totem name of a Magyar clan. We know of another Magyar clan name, Lebedias, which is to be derived either from *lebed'* ("swan"), or from *lebeda* ("orach").[48] Apparently Magyar clan totem names represented for the most part animals or plants. Altogether, it seems probable that the *Kender-Kagan* represented the Magyar ethnic group in the Khazar Government.

We have thus an interesting parallel in the organization of the administration and the judiciary in the Khazar state. Both branches were adjusted to separate groups or communities: religious in the case of the judiciary, and ethnic in the case of the administration.

By the tenth century the actual power in the Khazar state was concentrated in the hands of the beg. According to Ibn-Fadhlan, it is the beg "who leads the army and rules over the affairs of the state . . . it is to him that the neighboring kings express their obedience." [49] The kagan retained by that time only the official prestige. The beg himself had to enter the kagan's tent barefoot. When the kagan rode outside the premises of his palace, all the people in the street were obliged to prostrate themselves before him. The term of the kagan's rule was, according to Ibn-Fadhlan, forty years; if he reached this term, he was to be executed.[50]

The beg's closest assistant was, as we have already seen, the *Kender.* Next in the rank were the *tarkhans,* commanders of single regiments of the Khazar army or of the native auxiliary troops. The border fortresses were headed by governors (*tudun*). The main body of the Khazar army consisted of ten thousand men.[51] The spear was the principal weapon of a Khazar warrior. His body was well protected by a coat of mail.

There were two main sources of revenue for the Khazar state

45. Ibn-Fadhlan, p. 84.
46. Or, *Kanda.* See Macartney, p. 206.
47. Ballagi, *s.v.*
48. See Sec. 5, below.
49. Ibn-Fadhlan, p. 84.
50. *Idem,* p. 85; cf. J. G. Frazer, "The Killing of the Khazar Kings," *Folk-lore,* XXVIII (1917), 382-407.
51. Macartney, p. 199.

treasury: customs duties[52] and taxes. Only natives conquered by the Khazars paid taxes. They were collected from each hearth (*dym*). Thus we know from the Russian *Primary Chronicle* that on one occasion "the Polianians paid tribute of a sword from each hearth (*dym*)." On the other hand, the Viatichians paid per plowshare.[53]

We have seen that security of the commercial highways was the main objective of Khazar policy. Of the most important riverways, the Donets-Don way was controlled by the Magyars, but these recognized the authority of the Khazar kagan. The middle Volga was held by the Bulgars, but it appears that they were likewise at first subordinate to the kagan; later on, though they gained their independence, they remained on friendly terms with the Khazars —which was especially important as it affected the fur trade with the north.

In the east Turkestan was occupied by the Turks, closely related to the Khazars; thus the relations between the Khazar state and Turkestan were likewise on a friendly footing. The situation changed after the Arabic invasion of Turkestan, beginning in the early part of the eighth century. In 737 the Arabs administered a crushing defeat to the Turks.[54]

As to the Khazars themselves, they were attacked by the Arabs much earlier, in the middle of the seventh century. Following the Arab victory over the Sassanian kings, the Arabs claimed all possessions of the Sassanians for themselves, and in 650 or thereabouts Arab troops appeared in Transcaucasia.[55] The defense of the Caucasian mountain passes from Arab onslaught became now the chief task of the Khazar and As troops for decades to come. Since the Arabs threatened the security of the Byzantine Empire as well, some coöperation between the Khazars and the Byzantines became essential. We have seen[56] that in 626 the Khazars concluded an alliance with Emperor Heraclius against Persia. Later, when the Arabs had overthrown Sassanian power in Persia, the Khazars were ready to continue their assistance to the Byzantine troops, now against the Arabs. We must, however, remember that if the interests

52. Gotie, p. 78.
53. Cross, pp. 143-171.
54. Bartold, p. 191.
55. Grigoriev, p. 53.
56. See Chap. V, Sec. 8.

of the Khazars coincided with the Byzantine interests in Transcaucasia, there was a divergence of interests between the two powers in the Taurida. The Khazar control of both sides of Kerch Strait endangered the Byzantine possessions in southern Crimea.[57] The Khazars, however, proved ready to negotiate with Byzantine authorities. Subsequently, nuptial ties between the two reigning houses improved the situation even more. Emperor Justinian II was the first among Byzantine rulers to marry a Khazar princess.[58] The wife of Constantine V (731) was also a Khazar girl.[59] Their son Leo IV (775-780) was known as Leo the Khazar.[60]

Let us now examine the course of the struggle between the Khazars and the Arabs. In 31 A.H. (A.D. 651-52) Arab troops broke through the pass of Derbend to the north and invaded the north Caucasian area. The Khazars attacked them near Balanjar and administered a serious defeat to the invaders.[61] Since the main Arab forces were at the time involved in the Byzantine War, the Arabs were not able to send adequate reinforcements to the Caucasus and the Khazars succeeded in retaking the Caucasian mountain passes, which was important for watching events in Transcaucasia.[62] It is significant that in 681-82 a Christian mission arrived at Balanjar from Transcaucasia, at the head of which was an Albanian bishop.[63]

In 683 a strong Khazar army invaded Armenia and defeated the Arab troops stationed there.[64] Because of internal troubles in the Caliphate the Arabs were not immediately able to restore their control over Armenia, and it was only at the end of the seventh century that the caliph Abd-al-Malik was able to resume the conflict with the Khazars. The war proved to be a protracted one, and progressed with intermittent success for either side. In 714 the Arab general Muslima seized Derbend.[65] Three years later, in 717, the Khazars struck back once more by invading Azarbaidjan.[66] Since at

57. Vasiliev, pp. 85-87.
58. See Sec. 7, below.
59. Bury, *1889*, p. 458.
60. Bury, *loc. cit.;* cf. Ostrogorsky, p. 119.
61. Grigoriev, p. 53.
62. *Idem,* p. 54.
63. Markwart, pp. 16 ff. and 302.
64. Grigoriev, p. 54.
65. *Ibid.*
66. Grigoriev, *loc. cit.*

that time Constantinople was in a critical position under Arab attack,[67] the Khazar campaign to Azarbaidjan may have been arranged by Byzantine diplomacy to divert attention from Byzantium. The diversion was a failure, however, since the Arab troops stationed in Azarbaidjan repulsed the invaders.[68] Five years later the Arab governor of Armenia, Abu Ubeid Jarrakh, raided Khazar possessions in the North Caucasian area and returned with rich booty, which induced him to repeat the raid in the next year.[69]

In 726 the Khazar kagan decided to take revenge, and raided Azarbaidjan. The result of this campaign is not clear. According to Theophanes Confessor the Khazars defeated the Arabs, but in Arabic sources it is the Arabs who are victorious.[70] In any case it is known that in 728 the Arabs penetrated to Khazar possessions in the northern Caucasus once more, after which the war became especially embittered. At first the advantage was with the Khazars, but in 732 the Arabs succeeded in retaking Derbend, this time permanently. Fourteen thousand Syrian Arabs were settled in Derbend to garrison it.[71] In 733 the energetic Arab general Marvan was appointed governor of Armenia and Azarbaidjan. He was to start before long a far-reaching offensive against Khazar possessions in the North Caucasian area.

3. The Volga Bulgars.

The Volga Bulgars are considered the forefathers of the Chuvashians.[72] As we have seen,[73] this branch of the Bulgars separated from their kinsmen at the time of the breaking up of Great Bulgaria following the death of Khan Kurt. Under the pressure of the Khazars they moved north to the watershed between the Don and the Volga and finally settled in the region of the middle Volga and Kama rivers. In the Russian chronicle the Volga Bulgars are sometimes called the Silver Bulgars,[74] possibly because of the abundance of silver among them, which was imported from beyond the Urals.

67. See Sec. 7, below.
68. Grigoriev, p. 54.
69. Grigoriev, *loc. cit.*
70. *Idem,* pp. 54-55; Theophanes, p. 407.
71. Grigoriev, p. 55.
72. Gotie, p. 178; Marr, V, 387-388. Cf. N. I. Ashmarin, "Bolgary i Chuvashi," *KUO, 18* (1912).
73. See Chap. V, Sec. 8.
74. Cf. Niederle, IV, 49.

They were also known as the Black Bulgars.[75] This name may be explained in the light of the Chinese tradition by which each of the four directions of the horizon had its specific color.[76] Black was the color of the north. The term Black Bulgars meant, apparently, the northern Bulgars.

The state of the Volga Bulgars,[77] like the Khazar state, thrived on foreign trade and therefore depended upon its control over a network of commercial highways. The upper Volga offered the Bulgars a line of communication with the Baltic area, and the Kama River with the Ural region and Siberia. Down the Volga goods could be shipped from the Bulgar state either to the Caspian Sea or, using the portage between the Volga and the Don, to the Azov Sea. Since the region of the lower Volga and the lower Don formed part of the Khazar state, Bulgar commerce there depended upon the good will of the Khazar kagan, and of course Bulgar goods were subject to tithe in accordance with the general regulations in Khazaria. It appears that originally the dependence of the Bulgars on the Khazars was not only of an economic but also of a political nature. More likely than not, the Volga Bulgars recognized the suzerainty of the Khazar kagan until at least the middle of the eighth century.

In order to become independent of the Khazars economically, the Bulgars needed new routes of commerce with the south to avoid those under Khazar control. Eventually they succeeded in establishing a direct connection with Turkestan by using the Yaik riverway. The Arab mission which was sent from Khoresm to the Bulgars in 921 used the Yaik way.[78] As to the Azov and the Black Sea regions, the Bulgars were likewise interested in establishing a direct way thither. It appears that they were able from time to time to raid the Taurida; at least in his treaty with Byzantium of 944 the Russian prince Igor promises not to let the Black Bulgars attack the Taurida.[79]

75. In applying the name "Black Bulgars" to the Volga Bulgars I admit the controversial nature of the problem. See D. I. Ilovaiskii, "Bolgare i Rus na Azovskom pomor'e," *ZMNP, 177* (1875), 368-378; C. A. Macartney, "On the Black Bulgars," *BNJ,* VIII (1931), 156-158; Markwart, p. 503; Minorsky, p. 439; Westberg, pp. 386-388.

76. Groot, Hunnen, I, 20.

77. On the state of the Volga Bulgars see W. Barthold, "Bulghar," *EI,* I, 786-791; Gotie, pp. 156-185; Grigoriev, pp. 79-106; I. N. Smirnov, "Volzhskie Bolgary," Dovnar-Zapolskii, I.

78. Ibn-Fadhlan, p. 66.

79. Cross, p. 162; *Khristomatiia,* I, 13. Here again, while identifying the Black Bulgars of the treaty as the Volga Bulgars, I realize the controversial nature of the topic.

The Bulgar horde of the middle Volga region was hardly numerous. According to Al-Bakri there were only five hundred Bulgar householders; the figure probably refers to the number of clans of families, however.[80] Gardizi mentions five hundred thousand families, which must be a slip or a poetic amplification.[81] In *Hudud al-Alam* the figure of twenty thousand Bulgar horsemen is mentioned.[82]

This horde consisted of three tribes or divisions (*ulus*), to wit: Barzula, Ishkil (Ashgil), and Balkar.[83] All three of these names may be connected with names of tribes or localities in the North Caucasian area. A tribe of Turkish extraction known as the Balkars still exists in the North Caucasus.[84] The name Berzylia (or Barsilt) is mentioned in some Byzantine sources.[85] As to Ishkil, there is a village (*aul*) Iskilty in the Kabarda region.[86] We may suppose that when the bulk of the Bulgars went north (in the seventh century), part of the people remained in the North Caucasus, so that from each tribe or *ulus* some migrated and some stayed in their original abodes.

The boundaries of the state of the Volga Bulgars can be only approximately defined. As with the Khazar state, we must distinguish between the original nucleus of the Bulgar state and later annexations. The core of the state was in the middle Volga and Kama area. Here the two principal cities, Bulgar and Suvar, were situated.[87] They served as entrepôts and exchange centers for the Volga region as well as for the Ural area. The city of Bulgar, or "the Great Bulgars," still existed in the thirteenth century. Its ruins are near the village Uspenskoe, Spassk district, Kazan province, on the eastern side of the Volga 30 kilometers below the mouth of the Kama.[88] At present the ruins are at a distance of 6 kilometers from the bank of the Volga, but the river has changed its course since

An entirely different interpretation of this clause of the treaty has been recently suggested by Bromberg, pp. 33-42.

80. Macartney, p. 192.
81. Macartney, *loc. cit.*
82. Minorsky, p. 163.
83. *Idem*, p. 461.
84. *MSE*, I, 565.
85. Minorsky, 461.
86. Semenov, *Slovar*, II, 365.
87. Gotie, pp. 162-164; Minorsky, p. 461.
88. See V. F. Smolin, *Po razvalinam drevnego Bulgara* (Kazan, 1926).

then; at the time of the city's flourishing it was probably located directly on the river bank. Judging from what is left of the city it must have been a big one.[89] It was situated on a hill and protected by a moat and ramparts. Remnants of its wooden wall may still be seen. At the south end of the site was an inner castle in which the khan's palace was probably located. The extant ruins of mosques and other stone buildings are of comparatively late architectural style and may be referred to the twelfth and thirteenth centuries. Since no older ruins have been found, it is considered possible that this is not the site of the original city. It has even been suggested that the original site may have been in a quite different place, about 70 kilometers from "the Great Bulgars," near the modern town of Biliarsk.[90]

The city of Biliar is mentioned in some Arabic sources and it has been supposed that the name may be a corruption of Bulgar.[91] On the other hand one must remark that the Biliarsk site is located not on the Volga but on the Cheremshan, a tributary of the Volga, and the author of *Hudud al-Alam* says expressly that the city of Bulgar is situated on the bank of the Atil (Volga).[92] Therefore Biliar cannot be identical with Bulgar.

As to Suvar, its site is near the village of Kuznechikha on the banks of the Utka, a tributary of the Volga in the Spassk canton of the Autonomous Tatar Republic, that is, below "the Great Bulgars."[93]

The Bulgars gradually succeeded in extending their control over neighboring Finnish tribes such as the Burtas (Mordva), Mari (Cheremissians), etc.[94] The Burtas were at the time a strong tribe, capable of mustering ten thousand horsemen. As we have seen,[95] they were subordinated first to the Khazars and then to the Bulgars. According to Ibn-Rusta, "they have no chief to rule over them. . . . In every one of their districts there is an elder or two to whom they bring their cases for judgment."[96] Because of the lack of central

89. Gotie, p. 162.
90. *Idem,* p. 163.
91. *Idem,* pp. 163-164.
92. Minorsky, p. 163.
93. Gotie, p. 164; Minorsky, p. 163.
94. On the Finnish tribes see Sec. 4, below.
95. See Sec. 2, above.
96. Macartney, p. 194

authority among the Burtas, the Bulgars had to deal with each elder separately and force their authority by sending troops to collect taxes.

Honey and furs constituted the main wealth of the Burtas, according to Ibn-Rusta. In this connection we may also recall Ibn-Hauqal's information concerning the Erzia, which was another name of the Mordva tribe.[97]

He says: "the Erzia arrive [at Bulgar] coming down the Itil River and bring their goods but they tell nothing about their commercial affairs or about their land and allow nobody to accompany them when they return home. It is from the Erzia that sable and marten furs as well as lead are obtained." [98]

It may be seen from this statement that some kind of control over the Finnish tribes was essential for the Bulgars, especially because of the trade in furs. It is significant that until the tenth century the Bulgars had no coinage, and pieces of fur were used as currency.[99]

It may be suggested that in addition to their intercourse with the Finns the Bulgars were also in touch with some of the As or Aso-Slav tribes. Ibn-Fadhlan says that the king of the Bulgars had a vassal who was known as King Askal, that is, king of the Askal tribe.[100] The Askal may be most plausibly located in the region of the Oskol River and identified as the Spali-As.[101] We shall see below[102] that the As of the upper Donets region were by the beginning of the eighth century controlled by the Magyars. The Bulgar control over that region may have preceded the Magyar domination, and the Oskol country may have become later on a disputed area between the two peoples. In any case, there must have been some intercourse between the Magyars and the Bulgars, and it is significant that the name of the Bulgar khan Almush,[103] who received Ibn-Fadhlan in 922, sounds Magyar. It is identical with the name of a prominent Magyar chief (*voevoda*) of the ninth century.[104] By the tenth century the main Magyar horde had moved to the region of the

97. The name of the Russian city Riazan is said to be derived from the name Erzia.
98. Gotie, p. 167.
99. *Idem*, pp. 177-178.
100. Ibn-Fadhlan, p. 76.
101. See Chap. III, Sec. 7.
102. See Sec. 5, below.
103. Ibn-Fadhlan, p. 65.
104. See Chap. VIII, Sec. 4.

middle Danube, and at this time there was no longer any direct contact between the two nations. We may therefore consider the appearance of a Magyar name for a Bulgar khan of the tenth century as the survival of an older tradition.

With regard to the economic organization of the Bulgars: foreign trade having a paramount importance, the bulk of the treasury revenue was derived from customs duties. As in the Khazar state, foreign merchants paid 10 per cent duty *ad valorem*.[105] Another important branch of Bulgar economy was horse breeding. According to Ibn-Rusta, "when any man among them marries, the king takes from him a horse or two."[106] In addition, they engaged in agriculture as well. Wheat, barley, and millet were grown.[107]

Due to the high level of their economic development the Bulgars had among their neighbors the reputation of wealthy people. There is a characteristic story in the Russian *Book of Annals* of Prince Vladimir's campaign against the Bulgars in 985. In spite of the victory in the first battle, Vladimir's general, Dobrynia, advised him to negotiate a peace. "Said Dobrynia: 'I have seen the prisoners, who all wear boots. They will not pay us tribute. Let us rather look for foes with bast shoes.' So Vladimir made peace with the Bulgars."[108]

Information concerning Bulgarian government and administration is rather scarce. The title of the ruler was, according to the Arabic sources, *malik* ("king"), which is probably a rendering of the Turkish title khan.[109] According to Ibn-Fadhlan the name of the khan who reigned in 921-22 was Almush, son of Shilka.[110] In another passage of Ibn-Fadhlan's report the name, according to the Yakut's version, is as follows: "Almush, son of Shilka, Bltvar."[111] In the Meshed manuscript the name in this passage is given as "Hasan, son of Bltvar."[112] Both O. I. Senkovskii and Ch. M. Fraehn understood the word *Bltvar* not as a personal name but as the title of the Bulgarian ruler, and interpreted it as a mutilation of the

105. Macartney, p. 193.
106. Macartney, *loc. cit.*
107. Gotie, p. 171.
108. Cross, p. 183.
109. Ibn-Rusta, p. 141 (of the Arabic text).
110. Ibn-Fadhlan, p. 65.
111. *Idem,* n. 8, p. 88.
112. *Idem,* p. 55.

Slavonic term *vladavats* ("ruler").[113] Such a word still exists in Serbian, but is not known in Russian, which makes the interpretation somewhat dubious. Some other explanation must be offered. In my opinion *Bltvar* is a compound word consisting of two words, *bl,* and *tvar.* The first word, *bl,* may be read *byl.* This word occurs in the form *byl'* in the famous *Lay of Igor's Campaign* (1185).[114] Its meaning is identical with the word *boil* used by the Danubian Bulgars, from which the Russian term "boyar" was derived.[115]

For the elucidation of the second part of the compound, *tvar,* we must likewise look to the terminology of the Danubian Bulgars. According to Anastasius the Librarian, one of the Bulgar envoys who came to Constantinople in 869 to take part in the church council of that year bore the title of *tabar.*[116] We have here obviously the same term as *tvar* in slightly different transcription. Thus *Bltvar* of the Volga Bulgars is a compound title, to be read as *Byl Tavar.*

4. *The Lithuanians and Finns in Northern Russia.*

In the preceding narrative we have given our chief attention to the fortunes of South Russia. We have been partly compelled to this approach by the fact that there is very little information concerning North Russia in either the Byzantine or the Oriental sources. However, even irrespective of the difference in information available as to the south and the north, the political importance of developments in the Pontic steppes inclines the student of Russian history to give preference to the south, to a certain extent, and down to a certain period. It is obvious that the Antes were the strongest of the proto-Russian tribes, and it is equally obvious that they were closely connected with the Pontic area, both economically and politically. On the other hand, however, we must not forget that some of the Slavic tribes started to move northward in an early epoch; for example the migration of the Sclaveni (*Slovene*) to the Lake Ilmen area may be dated at the end of the fourth century.[117] With the increase in turnover of trade in the Baltic region in the seventh and the eighth centuries—which was exploited by the Norse-

113. *Idem,* p. 88, n. 8.
114. Slovo, p. 27; cf. Melioranskii, I, 285-286.
115. See Sec. 6, below.
116. Zlatarski, I, 2, 795 ff.
117. See Chap. III, Sec. 6.

men—and with the ascendency of the commercial empire of the Volga Bulgars,[118] the North Russian tribes found themselves strategically located at the junction of important commercial highways.

In their forward march to the Lake Ilmen area the Slavs wedged themselves in between some of the Lithuanian and Finnish tribes.[119] Having reached the sources of the Volga and subsequently continued their expansion down the upper Volga in a general eastward direction, the Slavs entered into even closer relations with various Finnish tribes. In order to obtain some idea of the conditions of this early Slavic expansion in North Russia we have now to examine its general historical and ethnic background, and consequently to say a few words concerning the Lithuanians and the Finns as the aborigines of the northern country. There is very little information on the subject in the written sources, and the student is obliged to depend chiefly on linguistic and archaeological data as well as those of comparative ethnography.

The Lithuanian language belongs to the Baltic group of the Indo-European family, which is nearer to the Slavic group than to any other from the linguistic point of view.[120] This circumstance made easier the contact between the Slavic and the Lithuanian languages in the early periods but at the same time has made it more difficult for philologians and historians to determine which language influenced which. While there are in the Lithuanian many words similar to the Slavic and vice versa, the likeness may be on many occasions caused by the community of Balto-Slavic roots rather than any influence of one language upon the other. Granting that one must approach the problem with great caution, an examination of the vocabulary of both languages reveals a number of words undoubtedly conveyed from one to the other.[121]

Among Lithuanian words borrowed by the Russians, the word *iantar* ("amber") may be mentioned first. Amber was the main

118. See Sec. 3, above.

119. See Chap. III, Sec. 6.

120. On the ancient Lithuanians see Brueckner, I, 405-413; Brueckner, *Litwa;* G. Gerullis, "Baltische Völker," *RL, 3,* 354-383; Gotie, pp. 186-207; Muellenhoff, pp. 11-34; Niederle, IV, 38-47; Vasmer, *Beitraege,* I; E. Volter, "Litovskii Yazyk" and "Litovtsy" *ES, 34,* 815-830; Zeuss, pp. 667-683.

121. A. Brueckner, *Litu-Slavische Studien* (Weimar, 1877); H. Petersson, "Baltisches und Slavisches" *LUA, 12* (1916); *idem,* "Baltische und Slavische Wortstudien," *LUA, 14,* 2 (1918); Wanstrat, pp. 87-89.

item of the Baltic trade in ancient times, and it was exported from the region controlled by the forefathers of the Lithuanians. Linguistic borrowing merely reflects in this case the direction of the commercial transaction. The following Russian words are likewise supposed to be derived from the Lithuanian: *kovsh* ("dipper"), *kuvshin* ("pitcher"), *punia* ("store-room," "hay-loft"), *iandova* ("copper bowl"). As to Slavic words in the Lithuanian, a number were probably borrowed in the period of the thirteenth to sixteenth centuries when West Russia was part of the Grand Duchy of Lithuania. However, some of these words may represent borrowings of a much earlier age.

We note a few words bearing on food and husbandry, such as the Lithuanian *asetras,* Russian *osetr* ("sturgeon"); *ikrai,* Russian *ikra* ("caviar"); *bartys,* Russian *bort'* ("beehive in a trunk hollow"); *kasa,* Russian *kosa* ("scythe"). Some words referring to city life and trade are also characteristic, for example the Lithuanian *miestas,* West Russian *miesto* ("town," "city"); *svetlycia,* Russian *svetlitsa* ("room"); *miera,* (identical in Russian and Lithuanian for "measure").

Since the Lithuanians in their expansion to the north came into contact with the Finns (from whom later on they were partly cut off by Slavic infiltration), it is but natural that the Finnish language became subject to considerable influence by the Lithuanian.[122] As a result, a number of Finnish words are derived from Lithuanian roots: such, for example, as *tutar* ("daughter"), from the Lithuanian *dukter; silta* ("bridge"), from the Lithuanian *tilta; tuohi* ("birch-bark"), from Lithuanian *toszis,* etc.

The mutual interrelations between the Lithuanians and Slavs and the Lithuanians and Finns may also be illustrated by archaeological data. In this connection we have first to examine the archaeological evidence for the study of ancient Lithuanian civilization as such.[123] During the last few decades a considerable number of barrows and sites dated from the seventh to the tenth century have been excavated by Russian and Lithuanian archaeologists in the area of early Lithuanian expansion; that is to say, the regions of Vilno, Kovno,

122. Setälä, p. 25.

123. On Lithuanian archaeology see Gotie, pp. 186-191; F. Jakobson, "Südostbaltikum: Litauen," *RL, 13,* 29-32; Niederle, *Rukovet,* pp. 122-125, 260; F. V. Pokrovskii, "Kurgany na granitse sovremennoi Litvy i Belorussii" *TAS,* IX, *1* (1895); A. A. Spitsyn, "Predpolagaemye Litovskie kurgany," *RAO, 8,* 1-2 (1896).

Suvalki, and in Kurland. Ancient Lithuanian sites (*gorodishcha*) are usually located on the steep bank of a river or lake, so as to make the settlement inaccessible to surprise attack. The approaches were, whenever necessary, reinforced by an earthen rampart and a moat. As to the Lithuanian kurgans, they are usually very low. In certain regions, as in western Kurland, there is no tumulus whatever. Since it is known that in the pre-Slavic period Lithuanian tribes spread to the east beyond Smolensk, even reaching the Oka River,[124] some of the ancient kurgans of the Smolensk and Kaluga provinces may be considered Lithuanian as well.

With the coming of the Slavs, these people settled in many cases in towns which had previously been held by the Lithuanians, and so in some sites the antiquities of the older layer are Lithuanian and those of the top layer Slavic. One of the most important sites of this kind is the famous Gnezdovo mound area near Smolensk.[125] Over thirty-eight hundred kurgans have been counted in this area; most of them are low, but some as high as 7 meters. Situated as it was at the junction of several important commercial highways, Gnezdovo must have played an important role in the development of the northwestern area even as early as the Sarmatian period, but the majority of the grave goods so far excavated are referred to the ninth and tenth centuries A.D. The Gnezdovo antiquities of this period are Slavic, Norse, or Oriental—evidence of the wide range of commercial transactions of the Gnezdovo merchants.

The group of graves attributed to the seventh and eighth centuries found in various kurgans of the Gnezdovo area is also important, since some of the objects they contain are of the type found in the Azov and North Caucasian area, which points to the probability of commercial relations between Gnezdovo and the southeast even at that early period. The market at Verkhni Saltov on the upper Donets may have provided a meeting place for Gnezdovo merchants on one hand and the Alanic (As) merchants on the other hand. As to Lithuanian antiquities proper, they are found in the oldest kurgans of the Gnezdovo area, especially in those on the bank of the Olsha River near the village of Bateki, which were explored in 1922.[126]

124. See Chap. III, Sec. 6.

125. Gotie, pp. 107-108, 209-210, 234-236, 253-255; E. Kletnova, pp. 309-322; V. I. Sizov, "Gnezdovskii Mogilnik," *MAR, 28* (1902).

126. Kletnova, pp. 311-312.

Among the objects found in the Lithuanian kurgans at Gnezdovo and elsewhere, curved iron sickles of a characteristic type with curved blade and a long handle may be mentioned first. Iron bits, stirrups, copper bells and other items of harness trappings are likewise interesting; as to the copper bells, they are similar to those found in the North Caucasian area. Of weapons there are iron halberds, spears, and swords; of ornaments, heavy bronze bracelets, torques, and rings may be mentioned here.[127]

Judging from the inventory of Lithuanian graves and sites, it may be surmised that the Lithuanians were a warlike people and horsemen. However, since most of the Lithuanian kurgans belong to a later period and others cannot be dated with precision, it is difficult to say at what time the Lithuanian cavalry originated. With regard to economic life, the sickle points to a considerable development of agriculture. However, since most of the area of Lithuanian expansion was in the forest zone and only a small part of the forest could have been cleared at that remote time, only part of the population can have been occupied in agriculture, leaving hunting and fishing as the major branches of economy. Dwellings were probably log cabins in most cases, and precisely because the houses were made of wood no traces of the old dwellings remain in that area. According to a seventeenth century description the typical Lithuanian house was built of fir tree logs; a large stove made of stones occupied the middle of the room; there was no chimney; in winter, cattle were kept in the house.[128]

Presumably the forefathers of the Lithuanians lived not in village communities but on isolated farms, just as in the sixteenth and seventeenth centuries. Each farm housed a large family with two or three generations living together, thus forming a miniature clan the head of which yielded an absolute authority over all other members.[129] In case of danger from outside several clans united, and it is from such clan unions—at first provisional only—that the early Lithuanian tribes originated.

The Russian *Book of Annals* lists the following Lithuanian tribes: [130] the Litva (i.e., the Lithuanians proper); the Prussians; the Kors, or Kur (hence, Kurland); the Zimigola; and the Letgola

127. Gotie, pp. 189-190.
128. *Idem*, p. 197.
129. *Idem*, p. 199.
130. Barsov, pp. 38-44; Cross, p. 140.

(the Latgalians). The abodes of the latter two were in the region of the Western Dvina River, on the northern border of Lithuanian expansion. The origin of the names of these two tribes has been explained accordingly: *zemegola* means in Lithuanian the "end (border) of the land"; *latvingola* (Letgola), the "end (border) of Litva" (Lithuania).[131] To the above list the following tribal names may be added: Zhmud, at the mouth of the Nieman; Yatviagians (Yatvingi) in the upper parts of the Nieman and the Narev; and the Goliad (Galindi) on the banks of the middle Oka River.[132]

The religion of the ancient Lithuanians[133] was apparently very close to that of the ancient Slavs. Thunder and lightning, sun and fire were worshipped. It appears that Perkunas, God of Thunder, was the main Lithuanian deity (to be compared with the Slavic Perun). However, the names of several other gods are known, some of them connected with animals and plants. Thus according to the later Kievan chronicle, Prince Mendovg of Lithuania (of the thirteenth century) even after he was baptized "worshiped his [pagan] gods in secrecy: [he worshiped] Nonadey, and Telyavel, and Diverkiz, the god of the hare and of the snake." [134] The veneration of both snakes and ants was apparently widespread among the Lithuanians. Witchcraft, divination, and sorcery seem to have been popular, partly perhaps, under the Finnish influence. As to Lithuanian funeral customs, cremation was the prevailing habit; the ashes were buried, and various vessels usually put into the graves.

Let us now turn to the Finns.[135] The Finno-Ugrian peoples (that

131. Barsov, p. 43.

132. *Idem,* pp. 41, 43-44; Gotie, pp. 201-202.

133. Brueckner, *Litwa;* A. Mirzynski, *Zrodla do mytologii Litewskiej,* 2 vols. (War saw, 1892-96) (neither of the above is accessible to me). Cf. Gotie, pp. 201-203.

134. *PSRL,* II, 188.

135. Barsov, pp. 44-67; Gotie, pp. 122-155; J. Kalma, *Die Ostseefinnischen Lehnwörter in Russischen* (Helsinki, 1915); H. Jacobsohn, *Arier und Ugrofinnen* (Gottingen, 1922); R. Meckelein, *Die Finnisch-Ugrischen Elemente in Russischen* (Diss. Berlin, 1913); J. Mikkola, *Berührungen zwischen den Westfinnischen und Slavischen Sprachen* (Helsinki, 1894); *idem,* "Die älteren Berührungen zwischen Ostseefinnisch und Russisch," *SFO, 75* (1938) (Cf. M. Vasmer's review of this study, *ZSP, 15* [1938], 448-455). Muellenhoff, pp. 39-77; Niederle, IV, 28-38; U. T. Sirelius, *The Genealogy of the Finns* (Helsinki, 1925); Smirnov, *Populations;* Tallgren, *Orient;* Tallgren, *Provinces;* Vasmer, *Beitraege,* II-III; M. P. Veske, "Slaviano-finskie kulturnye otnosheniia," *KUO,* VIII (1890) (inaccessible to me); K. W. Wiklund, "Finno-Ugrier," *RL, 3,* 354-383; Zeuss, pp. 683-691.

is, more precisely, peoples speaking Finno-Ugrian languages) may be divided into two main branches: the Ugrian, and the Finno-Permian. The Magyar, Vogul, and Ostiak languages belong to the Ugrian branch. The Finno-Permian branch comprises the following three groups of languages: (1) the Permian group, to which the Udmurt (Votiak) and the Komi (Zyrianian and Permian) languages belong; (2) the East Finnish group, that is, the Mari (Cheremissians) and the Mordva (Erzia and Moksha) languages; and (3) the West Finnish group which consists of the following languages: the Karelian, the Estonian, and the Suomi (that is, Finnish proper).

As we have seen,[136] the forefathers of the Finno-Ugrian tribes occupied in the Sarmatian period the whole northern part of Russia. The southern boundary of their expansion may be tentatively determined as following a line from the Gulf of Finland to the middle Volga. East of the Volga the Permian and Ugrian tribes spread far beyond the Ural Mountains. It is to be noted that in the fifth century A.D. some Ugrian tribes migrated from the Ural and trans-Ural regions to the North Caucasian area, where they were controlled first by the Huns and then by the Khazars.[137] It was this branch of the Ugrians that later on, after the dismemberment of Great Bulgaria, moved to the South Russian steppes. The Russian *Book of Annals* mentions these as the White Ugrians.[138] They were the ancestors of the Magyars. Another section of the Ugrians migrated from the Ural area to Hungary at the end of the ninth century A.D. They were known to the Russians as the Black Ugrians.[139] On reaching Hungary they merged with the White Ugrians. The section of them which remained in the Ural area later mixed with the Tatars, and became known as the Bashkirs.

The Vogulians and the Ostiaks, both of whom likewise belong to the Ugrian branch of the Finnish peoples, are now living in the northern part of the Ob River basin, beyond the Ural. To the Russian chronicles the Voguls were known as the Iugra.[140] In old times part of them spread west of the Urals into the region where the Zyrianians (Komi) are now settled.

136. See Chap. III, Sec. 6.
137. See Chap. IV, Sec. 7; and Chap. V, Secs. 7 and 8
138. Vernadsky, *Lebedia*, pp. 182-185.
139. *Idem*, pp. 184-185.
140. Barsov, pp. 60-64.

As to the East Finnish tribes, the Mordva and the Cheremissians (Mari) some time after the seventh century recognized the authority of the Volga Bulgars.[141] It is to the East Finnish group that the old tribes Meria and Muroma, now extinct, must have belonged.[142] These tribes originally occupied the Rostov and Murom regions, but were later subdued by the Slavs and completely Russianized. Of the West Finnish tribes the Russian *Primary Chronicle* knows the Chud, the Ves, and the Yem,[143] of which the first belonged probably to the Estonian group.

Since the Finns were the aborigines and the Slavs the newcomers in Northern Russia the latter were subject to considerable influence from the people whose country they had entered. Through mixed marriages, there are some Finnish features in the anthropological type of the North Russian. It is only natural that a number of names of localities and rivers in North Russia should be of Finnish origin. However, the question is very involved since in many cases alleged Finnish influence in the toponymics may be reflected rather than direct. As M. Vasmer[144] rightly points out, some words of Finnish origin, such as *selga* (a "clearing in the woods"), *mandera* ("subsoil"), *lakhta* ("bay"), etc., had entered the North Russian vocabulary and become naturalized, so to speak, at a very early period; therefore the presence of such a word in the name of a village or town does not prove that it was founded by Finns. It may have been founded by Russians in whose dialect the word (originally Finnish) already existed.

Furthermore, we have to take into consideration the geographic distribution of the Finnish dialects themselves. The vocabulary of the Permian or Ugrian dialects can hardly help us in analyzing the toponymics of the upper Volga—Oka region, since this was settled by other Finnish tribes who spoke other dialects. In view of this, we cannot accept V. O. Kliuchevskii's suggestion[145] that the name of the river (and of the city) Moskva (Moscow) is to be derived from the alleged Finnish word *va* ("water"). *Va* occurs in the Zyrian dialect only, while in the Finnish dialects proper the word for "water" is *vesi*.[146]

141. See Sec. 3, above.
142. Barsov, pp. 51-56; Vasmer, *Beitraege,* III, 510 ff.
143. Barsov, pp. 44-67, 49-51, 57-60; cf. Vasmer, *Beitraege,* II, *passim.*
144. Vasmer, *Beitraege,* II, p. 365.
145. Kliuchevskii, I, 363.
146. Vasmer, *Beitraege,* II, 357

None the less, we may still remark that Finnish survivals in the toponymics of northern and central Russia are numerous indeed. M. Vasmer has been able to compile an impressive list of names of localities of West Finnish origin for the area comprising the territory of the former Pskov, Tver, Novgorod, St. Petersburg, Olonets, Arkhangelsk, and Vologda provinces.[147] It is characteristic that even the name of Lake Ilmen (in Old Russian, Ilmer) on the bank of which the chief northern city of mediaeval Russia, Novgorod, was built, is of Finnish extraction—cf. the Estonian *Ilmjarv* (*ilm*—"wind," "weather"; *jarv*—"lake").[148] In analyzing local names in the territory of the former provinces of Kostroma, Yaroslavl, Vladimir, Moscow, Riazan, and Nizhni-Novgorod, M. Vasmer came to the conclusion that many of these names may be explained by the East Finnish dialects, thus giving evidence of the expansion over this territory in olden times of the East Finnish tribe of Meria (now extinct), which was related to the Cheremissians.[149]

While the Slavs underwent a considerable Finnish influence, the Finns themselves were subject to the influence, first of the Iranians, and then the incoming Slavs. A number of words in the Finno-Ugrian languages denoting metals—such, for example, as for copper, silver, gold, and tin—are of Iranian origin.[150] Likewise, many Finnish words denoting weapons and tools (for example, the words for "knife," "ax," "sword," "arrow," "hammer," "plowshare") were derived from the Iranian. Of Finnish words borrowed from the Russian[151] the following may be mentioned here: *turku* ("market," in Russian *torg*); *luokka* (duga, "shaft-bow"; derived from the Russian word *luk* which means, "bow"); *tappara* ("halberd"; from the Russian *topor,* "ax"); *kloptalo* ("flax or hemp ready for spinning"; *kudel* in Russian); *suntio* ("church watchman"; derived from the Russian *sudia* which means "judge").

From the archaeological point of view the area of expansion of East Finnish and Ugrian tribes may be identified as that of the former cultural spheres of Fatianovo, Seima, and Ananyino.[152] The countless settlements and grave sites of the subsequent era—that is,

147. *Idem,* pp. 365 ff.
148. *Idem,* p. 373.
149. *Idem,* III, especially, p. 579.
150. Gotie, p. 133.
151. Setälä, p. 25.
152. See Chap. I, Secs. 4 and 5; and Chap. II, Sec. 1.

of early Finno-Ugrian type—are hard to date; generally speaking they may be referred to the period from the sixth to the ninth century.[153] The Finno-Ugrian *gorodishcha* were built either as sanctuaries or as forts; whatever their original purpose, most of them also served as trade centers. They were located mostly on hills or steep river banks and protected by earthen ramparts and moats.

The Finno-Ugrian graves of this period are usually without tumuli, or with only a low mound. The objects found in the sites of the Kama and Ural region bear witness to an uninterrupted cultural development from the Ananyino period, but bronze is now replaced by iron. A link between the Ananyino culture and the culture of the grave sites of the period we are now discussing is presented by the Pianoborsk culture,[154] so named from the typical grave site at Piany Bor on the Kama River (in the former Sarapul district of Viatka province). A grave site of the seventh and eighth centuries, the so-called Atamanovy Kosti ("the Ataman's Bones"), was excavated by A. A. Spitsyn near the town of Malmyzh in the former Viatka province.[155] Similar grave sites have been examined in the middle Volga area in the territory of the former provinces of Penza, Tambov, Riazan, and Vladimir.[156] Ornaments found in these graves indicate the continuity of the tradition of animal style as well as of trade relations with the Caspian Sea area. The grave sites in question are in the area of expansion of East Finnish, Permian, and Ugrian tribes. Among the sites of the area of West Finnish tribes, that found near the town of Liutsin (in the former Vitebsk province, now in Latvia) is worthy of attention.[157] It is located on the bank of a lake. The funeral ritual of the Liutsin people seems to have been similar to that of the people of the middle Volga, but the inventory and style of the objects in the grave are closer to the Lithuanian antiquities.

With regard to the Finno-Ugrian *gorodishcha,*[158] their remnants

153. Gotie, pp. 113-114, 137 ff.; Tallgren, *Orient;* Tallgren, *Provinces.*

154. Spitsyn, *Drevnosti Kamy,* pp. 1-7 and Plates I-IV; Tallgren, *Col. Zaus.,* II, 11-13; cf. Tallgren, "Neues über russische Archaeologie," *FUF,* XVII (1925), 33-34.

155. Spitsyn, *Drevnosti Kamy,* pp. 8-9 and Plate V.

156. P. P. Efimenko, "Riazanskie mogilniki," *ME,* III (1926); Gotie, pp. 111; N. V. Yastrebov, "Liadinskii i Tomnikovskii mogilniki," *MAR, 10* (1893); cf. Fettich, pp. 190 ff.; Tallgren, *Provinces,* pp. 6 ff.

157. A. A. Spitsyn, "Liutsinskii mogilnik," *MAR, 14* (1893).

158. Gotie, pp. 95-99; A. A. Spitsyn, "Gorodishcha Dyakova tipa," *ORSA,* V (1903).

have been discovered in the upper Volga and Oka region as well as in that of the middle Volga, and east of the Volga in the Ural area. One of the best known is the Dyakovo *gorodishche* on the bank of the Moskva River, 8 kilometers below Moscow.[159] The *gorodishcha* of the Dyakovo type are usually small. In spite of their protection by earthen ramparts, they were probably sanctuaries rather than forts, and of course there must have been a settlement around each of them. Pottery, hewn stones, spindles, knives, sickles, fishhooks, and arrowheads have been found in abundancy in these *gorodishcha.*

The finds show that the people in this area practiced agriculture as well as fishing and hunting. However, agriculture must have been of but secondary importance. Fishing provided food for the native population, while trapping supplied the merchants with the furs which had such value in the international commerce of those times; trade in which made the Finns indispensable to the prosperity of both the Volga Bulgars and the Khazars. Thus hunting and trapping may be considered, from the point of view of general history, the most important branches of economy of the Finnish tribes of this area. In exchange for their furs the Finns received from the Volga Bulgars and the Khazars metal tools, weapons, and ornaments.

The dwelling of a Finno-Ugrian of that age was probably a low wooden shack built over a dugout. The roof had only one slope, and was in winter covered with earth to keep the inside of the building warm. There was a rough stone oven, and no chimney. Remnants of such buildings have been found in some *gorodishcha* of the Dyakovo type. The Votiaks lived in similar primitive houses even in the eighteenth and nineteenth centuries.[160] The Mordovian barn for drying crops is of the same type.[161] Judging from pieces of cloth found in the graves, the garment of a Finno-Ugrian was made of burlap or rough wool. A kind of caftan was worn over the shirt and loose trousers. Men wore metal neck rings as ornaments. The women's headdress was very elaborate, consisting of several bands with decorative metal plaques sewed on them. Women also wore bronze and silver pendants, earrings, and buckles.[162]

The funeral was by inhumation, and only in a few cases have

159. V. I. Sizov, "Dyakovo Gorodishche," *TAS,* IX, *2.*
160. I. N. Smirnov, "Votiaki," *KUO, 8,* 2 (1890), 88.
161. *Idem,* pp. 137-324.
162. Gotie, pp. 137-141.

traces of cremation been observed. The corpse was wound in birch-bark. Pots with food were placed in the grave, indicating a belief that life continued after death and was similar to the one before death. The existence of sanctuaries is evidence of a special order of priests or magicians. In Russian chronicles, Finnish magicians or sorcerers (*volkhvy*) are mentioned frequently.[163] The Norsemen considered them very dangerous, and their art was also praised by Saxo Grammaticus.[164] It is probable that in the main Finnish sanctuaries human sacrifices were practiced, and symbolic survivals of such practices may be detected in the folklore of some East Finnish tribes even in modern times.[165]

The religion preached by the magicians was probably close to Siberian Shamanism.[166] There must have been some hazy idea of a Supreme Being, which the Permians called Yen; the Cheremissians, Yuma; and the Western Finns, Yumala. The simultaneous existence of hosts of spirits of somewhat lower grade, mostly evil and malevolent, was recognized. Such spirits were believed to be able to assume the shape of animals and birds. Presumably therefore numerous bronze effigies of both animals and birds found in the Finnish graves have a magic significance.

5. The Ugrians and the As in South Russia.

As we have seen,[167] the Ugrian tribes who migrated in the fifth and sixth centuries from the Ural and trans-Ural region to the North Caucasian area submitted to the Hunno-Bulgars and in part to the Khazars. After the dismemberment of Great Bulgaria the North Caucasian Ugrians, in any case the tribe of the Saraguri (the White Ugrians of the Russian chronicles), moved northwest to the Pontic steppes. This second migration of the Ugrians took place, we believe, at the end of the seventh century. It has long been supposed that the Ugrians, alias the Magyars, stayed in the South Russian steppes only a short while. This assumption was based on the wrong understanding of a passage in Chapter 38 of Constantine Porphyrogenitus' work, *De Administrando Imperii.* In all printed editions of this work

163. See, for example, Cross, p. 240.
164. Saxo Grammaticus, p. 138.
165. Gotie, p. 153.
166. *Idem,* 154-155.
167. See Chap. V, Sec. 8.

it appears that the Turks (as Constantine calls the Magyars) stayed with the Khazars, assisting the latter in all their wars, for *three years*.[168] Therefore it has been suggested that the Magyars spent in the South Russian steppes, if not literally three years, in any case a brief period of time only. However, Henri Grégoire has recently proved that the editions of Constantine's book are faulty and that we are to read *three hundred* years instead of three.[169]

Since the Magyars came to Hungary at the end of the ninth century, it may be assumed, on the basis of Constantine's statement, that they had left their North Caucasian abodes to move into the South Russian steppes by the end of the sixth or at the beginning of the seventh century. But the figure "three hundred years" is, of course, approximate only, and if we try to discern what event could compel the Ugrians to leave the North Caucasian area, we naturally think of the downfall of Great Bulgaria and the subsequent wholesale migration of both the Bulgar and the Ugrian tribes. It seems safe therefore to date the first Ugrian *Landnahme* in the second half of the seventh century.

Both toponymical and archaeological evidence likewise indicates that the Magyars stayed in South Russia for a protracted period which could be measured by decades or even centuries rather than by years.[170] Had they merely paraded through the Pontic steppes without staying there for a number of decades, they would hardly have left so many traces in local names and in the kurgan graves.

Let us deal first with the toponymics. Constantine Porphyrogenitus calls the country occupied by the Magyars "Lebedia."[171] The following names of South Russian localities and rivers may be mentioned in this connection, since some of them may have kept the tradition of the old Lebedia: Lebedin, village in the Chigirin district of Kiev province; Lebedin in Braslav province (recorded in the sixteenth century);[172] Lebedin in Kharkov province; Lebedian in Tambov province; Lybed River discharging into the Dnieper at Kiev; two rivers of the same name in Chernigov and Riazan provinces respectively. It is noteworthy that the first Lebedin of the list is near the source of the Ingul River, and Constantine

168. *De Adm.*, 38 (*PG, 113*, col. 317).
169. Grégoire, *Habitat*, p. 267.
170. Vernadsky, *Lebedia*, pp. 190-193.
171. *De Adm.*, 38.
172. Hrushevskyi, VII, 15.

mentions a river Chingilus in Lebedia, which may stand for either Ingul or Ingulets.[173] In addition to the name Lebedia, traces of the tribal name of the Magyars (Ugrians) may be seen in the toponymics. Thus, near ancient Kiev there was a locality known as Ugorskoe.[174] In the *Book of the Great Delineation* a River Ugrin is mentioned, tributary to the Uda which in its turn is a tributary to the Donets.[175] One of the Oka's tributaries is likewise called Ugra. It is possible that such names of towns as "Kut" or compounds with "Kut" are of Magyar origin; *kut* means "well" in Magyar (it has the meaning of "corner" in Ukrainian). We may note here Kut Snezhkov of the Valki district, and Krasny Kut of the Bogodukhov district, both in Kharkov province.

Examining the above toponymic data we see that a number of names which may point to Magyar background refer to the upper Donets region (former Kharkov province); another group is connected with Kiev province and the basin of the rivers Ingul and Ingulets. It may be suggested that the Magyars centered first in the upper Donets and then in the Ingul region. As to the river Ugra, it is situated north of the upper Donets area and it seems probable, if there was a Magyar settlement on the Ugra River, that it was of the nature of a garrison to protect the northern frontier.

It must be noted that N. Fettich and V. V. Arendt have recently defined some of the antiquities found in certain settlements and grave sites of Kharkov, Tambov, and Voronezh provinces as Magyar.[176] To this group belong the sites of Verkhni Saltov, Liada, Vorobievo, and Gaevka. The famous Chernigov horn likewise, according to Dr. Fettich, is to be referred to the Magyar archaeological sphere. Consequently the archaeological evidence fits well with the toponymics, if only partially. Both archaeology and the toponymic data confirm, to a certain extent, our surmise that the period of Magyar control over South Russia was a protracted one.

Special attention should be paid to the upper Donets region, including the basin of the Oskol River, the abodes of the Spali-As.[177] It is in this region that we may tentatively locate the people of Askal, who had been once upon a time, according to Ibn-Fadhlan,

173. *De Adm.*, 38.
174. Hyp., col. 18.
175. *Kniga*, p. 9.
176. Fettich, pp. 162-172; Zakharov, pp. 78-79.
177. See Chap. III, Sec. 7.

controlled by the Volga Bulgars.[178] This people of Askal may be connected with the clan of Ashkal mentioned by both Ibn-Rusta and Gardizi.[179] These writers say that this country was on the border of Magyar possessions but belonged to the Volga Bulgars. We may suppose that the country of Askal, or Ashkal (that is, in our interpretation, the upper Donets region) may have been for some time controlled by the Volga Bulgars, but that the Magyars later seized it. By the beginning of the eighth century it probably belonged to the Magyars, as is evidenced by the findings of Magyar antiquities at Verkhni Saltov. The Magyars, after the migration from the North Caucasian area, appear to have centered first in the Donets region and to have moved into the Ingul area only later on.

The Magyar horde, according to Constantine Porphyrogenitus,[180] consisted of seven clans, or *ogus*. The chieftains had the title of *voevoda,* which is a word borrowed from the Slavic. The first *voevoda* was called Lebedias. It may be suggested that this was not a personal but a clan name.[181] *Lebed* means "swan" in Russian; *liba* is the Magyar word for "goose." A parallel with the customs of another Finno-Ugrian tribe, the Votiaks, may not be amiss here. Even in recent times each Votiak clan worshiped its own *vorshud* ("totem").[182] We have seen that birds played a considerable role in the mythology of the ancient Finno-Ugrian tribes.[183] It is significant that some of the Votiak *vorshud* ("clan") names[184] are derived from the names of birds (also of plants). Thus *varzia,* which means "crow" (in Mordovian); *chola* (or tsola), "hazel grouse" (*riabchik* in Russian); *iubera,* "thrush"; *chabia* (cf. *chabei*), "wheat." Since the customs of various Finno-Ugrian tribes had much similarity among themselves, we may be allowed to draw certain analogies between the Votiaks and the Magyars. Incidentally, there is the effigy of a swan among the Votiak religious antiquities of the Kazan Museum.[185] Moreover, attention may be drawn to the fact that the leaf of the goosefoot plant (*lebeda*) has the pattern and shape of a

178. Ibn-Fadhlan, pp. 76-78.
179. Macartney, p. 192.
180. *De Adm.,* 38.
181. Vernadsky, *Lebedia,* pp. 188-190.
182. Bogaevskii, I, 130 ff.; II, 95 ff.; Khudiakov, p. 348.
183. See Sec. 4, above.
184. Khudiakov, pp. 352-354.
185. Bogaevskii, I, 131.

goose's (or swan's) foot, and the goose's foot was a favorite motif in the ornamentation of Finno-Ugrian antiquities of the Pianoborsk and similar types. There are for example several pendants having the goosefoot shape in the Zausailov Collection at Helsinki. Similar pendants have been found in the site known as "Atamanovy Kosti" in the Kama basin.[186]

Besides the *voevoda,* of the clan of Lebedias, two other names or titles of Magyar dignitaries are mentioned in the sources. Constantine Porphyrogenitus refers to them as to *gyla* (Γυλᾶς) and *karkhan* (Καρχάν).[187] In Oriental sources the names are rendered as *gila* (or *jila*) and *kende* (*kender*).[188] Is it not possible to consider Constantine's *karkhan* as a contraction of *kender-kagan* (*kender-khan*)? In any case, I am inclined to interpret these as clan names also. Now, having in mind the derivation of the name Lebedias from either *lebed'* or *lebeda,* can we not explain the clan names *gila* and *kende* in a similar way, and assume that each was derived from the name of the respective clan totem? As to the first, the totem may have been a bird; *gila* means "turtle-dove" in Magyar, to be compared with the above Votiak *chola* (*riabchik*). With regard to the *kende* clan, it seems possible that this was a vegetable totem. *Kender* means "hemp" in Magyar. We have seen[189] that one of the Khazar officials was known as *Kender-Kagan,* which title we may liken to the Magyar *Kender* or *Karkhan.* I consider it probable that in the Khazar state the title *Kender-Kagan* was applied originally to the chief of the Magyar auxiliary brigade, and that it was later preserved in Khazaria by tradition.

The Magyar horde was not numerous. According to Ibn-Rusta the army consisted of ten thousand horsemen; [190] Gardizi doubles this figure.[191] Even if we accept Gardizi's figure, the whole Magyar people can have numbered at the time no more than one hundred thousand men and women. In view of this it seems hardly likely that at the coming of the Magyars the natives were completely driven out of the Pontic steppes. Most of them must have remained, only

186. Spitsyn, *Drevnosti Kamy,* Plate V, Figs. 2 and 7; Tallgren, *Col. Zaus.,* II, Plate II, Figs. 25, 27-30, 35. See also Kondakov, *Drevnosti,* V, pp. 76 and 89.
187. *De Adm.,* 40.
188. Macartney, p. 206.
189. See Sec. 2, above.
190. Macartney, p. 206.
191. Macartney, *loc. cit.*

submitting to Magyar authority. Such must have been the case with both the Aso-Iranians and the Aso-Slavs (Antes) in the Don-Donets region. Incidentally, the Magyars must have been in close contact with the North Caucasian As (forefathers of the Ossetians) even before their migration to South Russia.

There is some linguistic evidence pointing to the mutual interrelation of the Magyars and the As (both Iranian and Slavic).

Of the Ossetian (As) words borrowed by the Magyars the following may be mentioned here:[192]

Magyar	*Ossetian*
aladar ("centurion")	*aeldar* ("prince," "ruler")
legeny ("youth," "warrior")	*laeg* ("man")
kard ("sword")	*kard* ("sword")
vert ("shield")	*vart* ("shield")

The above words refer to military organization. Another group of parallel words bear on commerce and ways of communication, as follows:

Magyar	*Ossetian*
vendeg ("stranger," "visitor")	*faendag* ("road")
hid ("bridge")	*khid* ("bridge")
gazdag ("rich")	*haezdug* ("rich")
fizet ("to pay")	*fid* ("to pay")
uveg ("glass")	*avg* ("glass")

In addition let us note the Magyar word *asszony* ("woman") which should be compared with Ossetian *aekhsin, khsin* ("lady"); this is identical with the Alanic word *khsina,* which we know in Greek transcription (χσῖνα).[193]

As to the Slavic words borrowed by the Magyars,[194] their number is very large, but part of them were probably picked up at a later period, when the Magyars had settled in Hungary. On the other hand, some Slavic words must have entered the language during the stay of the Magyars in South Russia, and at least one of them, *voevoda* ("duke," "general"), is mentioned by Constantine.[195] The

192. H. Sköld, "Die ossetischen Lehnwörter im Ungarischen," *LUA,* XX, 4 (1925); cf. Abaev, pp. 884-887.

193. Abaev, p. 892. Cf. D. Gerhardt, "Alanen und Osseten," *ZDMG, 93* (1939), 42.

194. F. Miklosich, II.

195. *De Adm.,* 38.

word *Zakon* (τὸ Ζάκανον) is referred by him to the Khazars, but it seems probable that it was used by the Magyars as well.[196] To this group of ancient borrowings from the Slavic belong probably likewise the following two Magyar words: *rab* ("slave"); and *jarom* ("yoke"). A number of Magyar words borrowed from the Slavic refer to agriculture, as for example: *borona, kosa, lopata, proso, rozs, len, kapusta, repa,* etc.[197]

The pattern of Magyar domination over the Anto-Slav tribes in South Russia probably differed in different cases. Some of the Antic units may have gone over to the Magyar side voluntarily, and so may have been allowed to keep their own organization and their chieftains (*voevoda*); in this way the title *voevoda* may have passed from the Slavs to the Magyars. As a general rule, however, the submission of the Slavs must have been complete, and Magyar control must have been heavy indeed for them. Ibn-Rusta says that the Magyars dominate the Slavs, their neighbors, and impose on them heavy tribute, so that the Slavs are in the position of prisoners of war.[198] According to Gardizi, the Magyars completely subjugated the Slavs, whom they considered slaves and from whom they obtained their foodstuffs.[199]

Having this statement in mind we may perhaps better understand the correlation of the Magyar word *dolog* and the Russian word *dolg*. The first means "work," "labor"; the second, "duty," "debt." The Magyars conscripted the Slavic "labor," to offer which was the Slavs' "duty." The correlation of the Magyar *dolog* and the Russian *dolg* may also be interpreted to mean that at least in some cases the "work" had to be supplied by the Slav peasant in return for the capital (e.g., a horse) he received from his Magyar lord. If so, we have here an early form of the institution of indentured labor, a prototype of the *zakup* status of the Kievan period, or of the *kabala* serfdom of the Mongol age.[200]

196. *De Adm. loc. cit.*

197. Vernadsky, *Lebedia,* pp. 193-195.

198. Macartney, p. 208.

199. Macartney, *loc. cit.*

200. On the *zakup* see Eck, pp. 391-394; Grekov, pp. 117-123; on the *kabala* serfdom, Eck, pp. 395-397; G. Vernadsky, "À propos des origines du servage de "Kabala," *RHD* (1935), pp. 360-367.

6. The Danubian Bulgars, the Anto-Slavs, and Byzantium, 670-701.

From the fortunes of the eastern Antes we turn to the story of the western Antes in the Balkan peninsula. As we already know,[201] the western Antes had to submit themselves to Asparukh's Bulgarian horde. Asparukh moved to the lower Danube around the year 650. It appears that at first only part of the Bulgarian clans (*ogus*) under his authority came with him, but gradually other clans followed, fighting rear-guard battles against the Khazars and the Ugrians, so that it required about a score of years for all the horde to concentrate on the lower Danube. Even thereafter, the Asparukh horde was hardly numerous and could keep its control over the natives only if some of them proved ready to coöperate, as was probably the case. Part of the Danubian Antes must have retreated north at the approach of the Bulgars, but the bulk of the Antic tribes in the Balkan peninsula had to accept Bulgar domination, which in any case was less heavy than that of the Avars. While we have no precise information as to the organization of the Bulgar control over the Antes, judging by analogy from other similar cases (those of the Avars and the Magyars) we may suppose that the Antes were to muster auxiliary troops for the Bulgars and also to supply agricultural products as tribute.[202] The Antes seem not to have been overburdened by taxes, and their position under the Bulgars was apparently better than that of their kinsmen under the Byzantine Empire, since later the Antic population of Thrace showed itself ready to support the Bulgars against the Greeks.

At the time of the occupation of the lower Danube region by Asparukh the Byzantine Empire was in a state of decay, both because of internal riots following the death of Heraclius (641) and by reason of the constant Arab raids on the eastern provinces of the empire. Therefore the Constantinople government was not in a position to defend the Danubian frontier and could at best only keep the Slavic tribes settled in Thrace and Macedonia somewhat in check.

In 658 the emperor Constans, grandson of Heraclius, sent troops to the area of Slav settlements in Macedonia known as Sclavenia.[203]

201. See Chap. V, Sec. 7.
202. Cf. I. Dujčev, "Protobulgares et Slaves," *AIK, 10* (1938), 145-154.
203. Kulakovskii, III, 210.

By this time the Slavs whose abodes were on the banks of the Strimon (Vardar) River had succeeded in gaining control of part of the Aegean coast, and constantly intercepted Byzantine boats plying between Salonika and Constantinople, which did much harm to the grain supplies of the capital. They were even bold enough to attack Salonika itself. It is these Slavic pirates that Constans wanted to punish. According to Theophanes Confessor the Slavs were subdued, by which Theophanes probably meant that they agreed to cease their raids, to pay tribute, and to offer auxiliary units to the army. Such Slavic auxiliaries were not always reliable. Thus in 665, during a war against the Arabs, the whole Slavic brigade which formed part of the Byzantine army deserted and went over to the Arab side. About five thousand of these Slavs were settled in Syria by the order of the Arabian commander-in-chief.[204]

In 672 the caliph Muavia sent a huge fleet against Constantinople itself. During the whole summer of 673 the city was blockaded by the Arabs, but by September of this year the Greeks succeeded in defeating the enemy fleet again, with the help of the device known as "Greek fire." [205] As we have seen, the first case of the use of the flame throwers by Byzantine men-of-war took place in 516,[206] but apparently the formula of the compound was later lost. It was now rediscovered and improved by the Syrian engineer Kalinikos.[207] While as the result of the Byzantine naval victory imminent danger to the capital was removed, the war continued for several years and it was not until 678 that a peace treaty was concluded between the empire and the Caliphate for the term of thirty years.[208] Only then could the emperor Constantine IV, son of Constans, pay some attention to Balkan affairs.

In 679 he organized a well-planned expedition to the mouth of the Danube, hoping to defeat the Bulgars by a combined blow from land and sea. The expedition proved a failure, however.[209] The Bulgars retired, part to the island of Peuce and a part of them to the swamps in the region of the lower Danube, and there waited for the

204. Theophanes, p. 348.
205. Bury, *1889*, pp. 310-311; Kulakovskii, III, 236-237.
206. Chap. IV, Sec. 9.
207. Bury, *1889*, p. 319; Ostrogorsky, pp. 80-81; C. Zenghelis," Le feu grégeois," *Byz.*, 7 (1932), 265 ff.
208. Kulakovskii, III, 238.
209. *Idem*, pp. 247-248.

Byzantine attack. Hampered by the difficult terrain, the Byzantine army prepared for a systematic siege of the Bulgarian hide-outs. The emperor grew impatient, and moreover had a bad case of gout. He therefore left for the Mesembria spa for medical treatment. His departure demoralized the army, which before long began a retreat. The Bulgars were quick to grasp the opportunity; they at once crossed the Danube and, meeting no resistance, occupied two Byzantine provinces: Scythia (Dobrudja) and Lower Moesia. The population of these provinces was by this time mostly Slavic. In this connection Theophanes Confessor mentions a tribe known as the "Seven Clans," and another called the Severians (Σέβερεις).[210] These tribes must be considered Antic;[211] they surrendered to Asparukh without fighting. Thus the foundation was laid for a new Bulgaro-Slav state in the Balkan peninsula, the modern Bulgaria. Asparukh moved his headquarters from Peuce Island to Aboba-Pliska, halfway between modern Varna and Tutrakan. Eventually a palace was built there, and a city grew up around it, the first capital of the Bulgar khans on Balkan ground.

The Bulgar horde was composed of several clans (*ogus*) and sub-clans, for the most part of Turkish, but partly also of Ugrian descent. The elder of the ruling clan had the title of khan, or "glorious khan," as we may translate the Bulgar epithet *uvigi* (ὐβιγή) by analogy with the Cuman *evegü,* which means "high," "glorious."[212] At the formal receptions in his palace the khan appeared in a garment embroidered with beads; he wore a precious necklace (*grivna*) and bracelets; he was girded with a purple belt, from which hung a golden sword; on each side stood the chief boyars, likewise adorned with necklaces, bracelets, and belts.[213]

The titles of the highest Bulgar dignitaries as mentioned in the sources are *kavkhan, tarkhan, tabar.*[214] They may be likened to those in other Turkish states of the period.[215] Clan elders were known as *boils.* The Turkish plural from the word *boil* would be *boilar* or *boiliar* (in Greek, *boliades,* βολιάδες).[216] It is from this term

210. Theophanes, p. 359.
211. See Chap. VIII, Sec. 1.
212. Runciman, p. 284.
213. Kalaidovich, p. 64.
214. Runciman, pp. 286-287.
215. See, for example, Sec. 3, above.
216. Markwart, *Chronologie,* pp. 40-41; cf. Melioranskii, I, 283-287; II, 82-86.

that the Old Russian *boliarin,* plural *boliare* (boyars), was derived.[217] Bulgar knights were known as the "bagain," or "bagatur."[218]

After his defeat by the Bulgars, Emperor Constantine IV accepted the inevitable and did not interfere further with the establishment of Bulgar control over northern Thrace. In 685 Constantine died, and his sixteen-year-old son Justinian II took the throne.[219] The new emperor was a gifted youth of great energy and might have become a great ruler but for his cruelty and perversity. In the third year of his reign Justinian decided to follow the example of his grandfather Constans in strengthening imperial rule over the Macedonian Slavs. Summoning several cavalry squadrons from Asia Minor, he led them personally to Salonika. Some of the Slavic tribes on his way renewed their pledge of allegiance to the empire; others were subdued by force. To weaken the Slavic element in Macedonia, and also in order to use the Slavs in the Arabic war, Justinian moved around thirty thousand Macedonian Slav families to Bithynia.[220] This province was at the time included in the *theme* ("military district") of Opsikion in Asia Minor.

The Slavs ordered to emigrate moved to their new abodes wholesale, by tribes and clans; funds were appropriated from the imperial treasury for their settlement. Out of these Bithynian Slavs a cavalry auxiliary division (λαὸς περιούσιος, that is "supernumerary host") was organized, forming part of the troops assigned to the *theme* of Opsikion. A Slavic prince, Neboulos (Νεβοῦλος), was in charge of the Slavic host.[221] The experiment proved rather a failure, since at the time of the Arab invasion Neboulos with part of his division deserted and went over to the Arab side, as a result of which the Byzantine army was badly beaten by the Arabs.[222] It seems probable that Neboulos' Slavs were induced to desert by some of their kinsmen belonging to the group which had been settled

217. In modern Russian, *boiarin,* instead of *boliarin.* I cannot accept Melioranskii's opinion that the original Russian word was *boiarin* and not *boliarin* (Melioranskii, I. 283). The form *boliare* is used in the text of Igor's treaty with Byzantium, A.D. 945 (Laur., col. 47). See also Sreznevskii, I, *s.v.*

218. Runciman, p. 285; cf. the Russian word *bogatyr'* ("valiant knight").

219. On Justinian II and his reign see Bury, *1889,* pp. 320-330; Kulakovskii, III, 253-276; Ostrogorsky, pp. 84-91.

220. Kulakovskii, III, 258-259; Theophanes, p. 364.

221. Kulakovskii, III, 259-261.

222. *Idem,* pp. 264-265; Theophanes, p. 366.

in Syria in 665.[223] About seven thousand Slavs followed Neboulos, that is about one-fourth of the whole Slavic division. They were settled near Antiochia and Kyrrhos.[224]

Justinian instantly retaliated by having the families of the deserters slain wholesale. The autonomy of that part of the Slavic host which remained loyal was curtailed, and a Byzantine officer was now appointed to command it. His title was that of proconsul (ἀπὸ ὑπάτων).[225] The Slavic host existed in Bithynia as late as in the tenth century. According to Constantine Prophyrogenitus it was then under the charge of three elders ("heads," κεφαλαί).[226]

7. *The Bulgars, the Khazars, and Byzantium, 701-739.*

The old khan Asparukh died in 701, and his son (or perhaps grandson) Tervel succeeded him. This first Bulgar dynasty is known as the House of Dulo, the alleged ancestor of Asparukh, and it appears that Attila's son Ernak was likewise one of Asparukh's forefathers.[227]

Asparukh laid a solid foundation for Bulgaria, and his successor Tervel was able to play an important political role in the Balkans and to intervene in the affairs of the Byzantine Empire, which were in sad estate because of the growing opposition to Justinian on the part of many influential Byzantine statesmen for both personal and political reasons. The constant defeat of Byzantine troops in the Arab War undermined the prestige of the empire in the east, and as a result Armenia severed her ties with Constantinople and recognized the authority of the caliph.[228] This was a severe blow to Byzantine interests since it endangered the security of all the imperial possessions in the Caucasus. Simultaneously, Byzantine relations with the west came to a crisis because of Justinian's conflict with the Pope. As the latter refused to approve the decisions of the so-called Quinisexta Church Council of 692, the emperor sent his emissaries to arrest the Bishop of Port and summon the Pope to Constantinople. The attempt failed.[229]

223. See above in this same section.
224. Kulakovskii, III, 265.
225. *Idem,* pp. 265, 360-362; Panchenko, "Pamiatnik Slavian v Vifinii," *RAIC, 8* (1902), 15 ff.; Ostrogorsky, p. 85, n. 3; G. Schlumberger, "Sceau des esclaves de l'éparchie de Bithynie" *BZ, 12* (1903), 277.
226. *De Cer.,* II, 44 (*PG, 112,* col. 1229).
227. Runciman, pp. 279-280.
228. Kulakovskii, III, 265-266.
229. *Idem,* pp. 274-275.

Widespread popular discontent with Justinian's policies led to an open revolt headed by the *strategos* Leontius. Justinian was arrested and his nose cut off (hence the nickname, *Rhinotmete*), after which he was deported to Cherson.[230] The story of Justinian's subsequent adventures must interest us, since it throws some light on the situation in the Taurida and on the role of the Khazars in northeast Pontic area. Justinian did not stay long in Cherson, but succeeded in escaping to the Gothic city of Dory (Doras) in the Crimean mountains. From there he sent a message to the Khazar kagan, receiving in return an invitation to betake himself to the latter's headquarters in Khazaria.[231] The name of the kagan, as given in the Greek sources and in Greek transcription, was Ibuzir Glavanos (Ἰβούζιρος Γλιάβανος).[232] The second of these two words seems to be a title rather than a name, and may have been derived from the Slavic word *glava,* "head," elder.[233]

Whatever his name, the kagan received the exiled emperor with due honors and even agreed to Justinian's marriage with his sister.[234] This young lady was baptized and given the name of Theodora, probably in memory of the wife of Justinian I. The refugee emperor was then allowed to make his residence at Phanagoria, on the eastern side of Kerch Strait. It is probable that he selected this town because it was easy from there to communicate with the Greeks in Cherson, and through them to watch the development of events in Constantinople. The Constantinople government at once realized the dangerous implications of Justinian's choice of refuge, if he were to start plotting for a return to power. By this time the usurper Leontius was in his turn pushed from the throne by a new pretender, Apsimar, who took the name of Tiberius.[235] The new emperor sent his envoys to the Khazar kagan promising him rich reward for the extradition of Justinian. Thereupon the kagan sent a guard regiment to Phanagoria to protect Justinian from Byzantine agents. Justinian, however, suspected treachery and was afraid that the guards might

230. *Idem,* pp. 275-276.

231. *Idem,* p. 286.

232. *Idem,* pp. 286-287. Kulakovskii does not mention his authority for the name of the Khazar khan. Stritter, IV, 116, gives the name as *Βουσηρης Γλιαβαρος* and refers, in a general way, to Banduri. A. Banduri, *Imperium Orientale,* II (Venice, 1729), 493, mentions Justinian II's wife Theodora and comments as follows: *Busiri Chazarorum Chagani seu Ducis filia fuit.*

233. Cf. *Κεφαλαί,* the elders of the Slavic host in Bithynia, sec. 6, above.

234. Kulakovskii, III, 287.

235. *Idem,* pp. 279-284.

arrest instead of protecting him. He therefore killed the captain, sent his wife back to her brother the kagan, and himself, with a few supporters, boarded a boat and put to sea.[236]

Sailing along the southern littoral of the Taurida, Justinian stopped at Symbolon (Balaklava) where more of his partisans joined him, after which he sailed farther west. As the boat was passing the mouth of the Dniester, it was caught in a gale. According to the chronicle of Theophanes Confessor, one of Justinian's followers addressed him as follows: "We are threatened by death. Do thou promise God that if He restore thee thy kingdom, there will be no revenge on thy part." Justinian's answer was typical of him: "Let God punish me if I show pity to any of my enemies." [237] The boat made safely for the mouth of the Danube, which was by this time controlled by the Bulgars.

As soon as Justinian landed he sent one of his men to the khan, Tervel, asking his help in the impending struggle for the Byzantine throne. As reward, Justinian offered to marry his own daughter (by his first marriage) to the khan. Tervel accepted, since he hoped to take advantage of the prospective troubles in the empire. Justinian was received in the khan's headquarters with great honors. The allies had to act quickly in order to reach Constantinople before the Byzantine government received news of Justinian's arrival. Hastily summoning his Bulgar warriors and Slavic auxiliaries, Tervel set forth accompanied by Justinian. As soon as they reached the walls of the city, Justinian through a herald demanded immediate surrender of the capital and recognition of his imperial authority. In spite of being caught unawares, the emperor Tiberius declined to capitulate and attempted to organize resistance. On the fourth night of the siege Justinian with a small band crept into the city through the water pipes. As soon as they appeared on the streets the defenders were panic-stricken, and before long the population went over to Justinian's side (705).[238]

Having recovered his throne Justinian, true to his vow, disposed of his enemies with harsh cruelty. As to Tervel, he received exceptional honors. The restored emperor dressed the khan in imperial vestments and granted him the rank of Caesar. A throne was then

236. Theophanes, p. 373.
237. *Idem,* pp. 373-374.
238. Kulakovskii, III, 288-289.

placed near Justinian's throne for Tervel, and the people were ordered to make the same obeisances to the new Caesar as to the emperor himself. Tervel also received rich presents, in addition.[239]

The crowning of the Bulgarian khan as Caesar was an important precedent for the subsequent development of the monarchical idea both in Bulgaria and in Russia. In the system of Roman imperial power as set up by Diocletian (A.D. 284-305) the rank of Caesar was second to that of Augustus. The imperial authority, according to Diocletian, was to be represented forever by two Augusti and two Caesars.[240] Diocletian's system was shattered by subsequent events: the division of the empire into two portions—the Western and Eastern—and the downfall of the Western Empire (476). In the Eastern Roman, or Byzantine, Empire the emperor continued for a long time to enjoy the title of Augustus, which was used at ceremonial receptions and on other fit occasions, but two other titles were used even more generally, that of "autocrat" (αὐτοκράτωρ) which was meant to correspond to the Latin *imperator;* and that of *basileus* (βασιλεύς, "king").[241] As to the title of Caesar (Καίσαρ), it gradually lost its former prominence and assumed the connotation of the highest rank in Byzantine administration next to the emperor.[242] It appears that now, in ordering royal honors for Tervel, Justinian wanted to restore to the title of Caesar its former splendor. In any case the Bulgars, including Tervel himself, must have understood the title as a royal one.[243]

Attention should be paid in passing to the rather involved problem of the relation of the title "Caesar" to the Russian *tsar*. There were two different systems of transcription of "Caesar" in old Slavic literature. Under the influence of the Greek rendering of "Caesar" the Slavic word *kesar'* was formed, which was used by the East Slavs as well as by the Bulgars. On the other hand, among the West Slavs and in the Balkans the term Caesar was borrowed in Latin

239. Theophanes, pp. 374-375; Nicephorus Patriarcha, p. 42. Cf. Ostrogorsky, p. 93; Zlatarski, I, 1, pp. 166-167.

240. On the system of Diocletian see W. Ensslin, "The Reforms of Diocletian," *CAH,* XII, 383-388.

241. Bury, *Constitution,* pp. 19-21; Ostrogorsky, *Avtokrator,* pp. 97-121.

242. See Bury, *System,* p. 36; Ostrogorsky, pp. 64-65, 93; Stein, pp. 161-163; Zlatarski, I, 1, pp. 166-167.

243. I disagree here with S. Runciman, who in my opinion underestimates the implications of the event (Runciman, p. 30).

form, hence the Slavic *tsesar',* from the shortening of which it is supposed the Russian title *tsar'* was derived. Comparing the Slavic words with the Byzantine terminology, the words *tsesar* and *tsar* correspond to the Greek *basileus* ("king"), while the term *kesar* corresponds to the Greek "Caesar" (Καίσαρ). Thus, for example, in the New Testament: "We have no King but Caesar."[244] In the Greek original: οὐκ ἔχομεν βασιλέα εἰ μὴ Καίσαρα. In the medieval Balkan codices of the Church Slavonic version: *ne imamy tsesaria tokmo kesaria.* In Russian codices from at least the late Middle Ages: *ne imamy tsaria tokmo kesaria.*

It should be noted that the word *tsar* was used in Russia at least as early as the tenth century, since we find its derivative *tsarstvo* ("kingdom") in Igor's treaty with the Byzantines, A.D. 945.[245] It seems probable that the Russian title *tsar* originated independently of the Bulgarian *tsesar;* if so, its origin may perhaps be connected with the Iranian word *sar* ("head," "chief"). The use of the Iranian title by the Antic tribes may easily be admitted in view of the connection between the Antes and the As—and, as we know, the chief of the Caucasian As was known as *sar.*[246]

Altogether, it cannot be denied that the granting of the title Caesar to Tervel must have impressed the Bulgars very deeply and laid a foundation for the subsequent claims of the Bulgarian khans to the imperial title. Having paid his debt of gratitude to Tervel, Justinian had now to settle his relations with the Khazars. We have seen that he left his wife, the Khazar princess, behind him in Khazaria when starting on his daring adventure. In his absence she had given birth to a son, whom they called Tiberius. On regaining his throne Justinian immediately sent envoys to Khazaria to bring his consort and the infant heir apparent to Constantinople. As soon as they arrived, they were both crowned, and his son proclaimed co-emperor.[247] Some time later Justinian's father-in-law, the Khazar kagan, arrived in Constantinople as well. He was given a ceremonious reception similar to that which Tervel had received

244. St. John, 19. 15.

245. Hyp., col. 38; cf. Sreznevskii, III, col. 1434. On the correlation of the titles *tsesar* and *kesar* in medieval Bulgaria see S. Romanski, "Simeonovata titla tsesar," *BP,* I, 1 (1929), 125-128.

246. *Sar-i-os* (Σαρώσιος), Menander, frg. 4 (p. 4).

247. Kulakovskii, III, 290.

before him.[248] Whether the Khazar khan was likewise granted the title of Caesar we do not know.

The establishment of friendly relations with the northern neighbors of the empire seemed a good start for the further development of Justinian's foreign policy. He was now in an advantageous position for concentrating all the forces of the empire against the Arabs. However, he preferred to wreak vengeance on his enemies both in Italy and in the Taurida, and accordingly sent instead punitive expeditions to Ravenna as well as to Cherson.[249] By doing this he spread his forces thin over too large an area; the expeditions were costly in men and funds and met with desperate resistance of the population in both cases; besides, on its return cruise from the Crimea the Byzantine fleet was scattered by storm. The feeling of opposition to Justinian flared anew, and before long another general revolt broke out against his rule. The emperor, who was at this time in Asia Minor preparing a campaign against the Arabs, was compelled to call upon the Bulgar khan—the Caesar, Tervel—for assistance. Tervel immediately sent three thousand troops. However, when the Bulgars arrived in Asia Minor the whole country was already in a state of civil war, and the Bulgar commander preferred not to interfere, leaving Justinian to his doom.

Abandoned by almost everyone, Justinian was arrested and one of the army generals proclaimed emperor in his stead, after which both Justinian and his infant son were executed.[250] This was the end of Heraclius' dynasty. The Khan-Caesar Tervel deemed it proper to avenge the murder of his Augustus and in 712 invaded southern Thrace looting everything in his path. He reached the capital port, the Golden Horn, but did not dare to storm Constantinople itself and turned back, carrying prisoners and immense booty. Meanwhile the Arabs, taking advantage of the disorganization of the Byzantine Government, kept overrunning Asia Minor until by 716 they controlled most of the *themes* there. They were now in a position to threaten Constantinople itself. In view of this danger the Byzantine Government hastened to conclude a peace treaty with the Bulgars. According to its provisions the khan was to receive annually a tribute to the amount of 30 pounds of gold paid in sumptuous tissues and furs; licensed merchants of each side were

248. *Idem,* pp. 290-291.
249. *Idem,* pp. 293-301.
250. *Idem,* p. 302.

granted permission to import goods without paying customs duties; an exchange of prisoners was arranged. A new boundary line was established between the empire and the khanate, from the Bay of Burgas on the Black Sea to the Maritsa River, so drawn that the city of Adrianople remained in Greek possession.[251]

While by this treaty the Balkan frontier of the empire was made secure, Arab pressure continued and the situation became especially grave with the approach of the Arab fleet to the Dardanelles. Since the leaders of the Byzantine army and navy had no confidence in the then reigning emperor, they deposed him and in March, 717, put on the throne the general, Leo the Isaurian (Leo III as emperor), whom they considered, and who indeed proved to be, a man of great strategic abilities and a first-rank statesman. Leo's first move was to confirm the peace treaty with the Bulgars. Tervel was induced to send some auxiliary troops with the help of which the Arabs were prevented from completely surrounding Constantinople by land. As to the sea warfare, the Byzantine navy gained the upper hand with the help of the reliable Greek fire, and in 718 the Arabs were compelled to lift the siege of the Byzantine capital and to retreat both on land and sea.[252] While the war between the Byzantines and the Arabs was to last for several centuries to come, Arab forces were never again able to threaten Constantinople, and thus the year 717 proved an important landmark in Byzantine-Arab relations. It is interesting to note that while the Arabs were beaten off on the Byzantine front they continued their offensive in Spain with considerable success, and in 719 were able to cross the Pyrenees and invade southern France.[253]

During the whole period of his reign (717-41) Leo III[254] maintained friendly relations with the Bulgars in order to be able to concentrate all the forces of the empire on the struggle against the Arabs, in which he was quite successful, so that before long most of Asia Minor was regained. In his religious policy Leo opened the era of so-called iconoclasm, which met with stubborn opposition from the clergy and especially from the monks and also spoiled Constantinople's relations with Rome. Because of the firmness of Leo's

251. Theophanes, p. 497; Zlatarski, I, 1, pp. 178-183.

252. Bury, *1889*, pp. 401-405.

253. Halphen, pp. 143-144.

254. On Leo III and his reign see Bury, *1889*, pp. 401-449; Ostrogorsky, pp. 103-111

rule, however, the opposition was not able to stop the movement.

Since there were no wars with Bulgaria in Leo's time, there is little information on Bulgarian affairs in the Byzantine sources of this period. The Khan-Caesar Tervel, died in 718[255] and the name of his successor is unknown. The next khan, who ruled from 724 to 739, bore the name of Sevar.[256] The Bulgaro-Byzantine boundary line as defined by the treaty of 716 underwent no changes during Sevar's reign. How far the Bulgar possessions extended at this time to the northwest, up the Danube River, is not known; probably as far as the Iron Gate.

The Bulgars were rapidly abandoning their nomadic way of life and most of the boyars became owners of large land estates. It is possible that individual Anto-Slavic elders were accepted into the ranks of the landowning aristocracy, but the bulk of the Anto-Slavs in Bulgaria must have been peasants who worked for the boyars. Speaking generally, while the Bulgars had not yet merged with the Slavs, the tendency of the period was already toward such a fusion.

8. The As and the Rus in the Azov Area.

We have already pointed out[257] the difficulty of properly differentiating the Aso-Slavs (Antes) from the Aso-Iranians (Alans, Ossetians) in this age. Because of the fact that the ruling clans of the Antes were of Alanic origin, the connection between the Antes and the Ossetians must have been close, especially in the Azov and North Caucasian area.

Prior to the downfall of Great Bulgaria[258] the As were settled in three different regions, each group separated from the next by wedged-in Bulgar and Ugrian tribes. The three As groups are as follows: the western Antes in the region of the lower Danube; the eastern Antes in the upper Donets region; and the As (Ossetians) in the North Caucasian area. The migration of the Bulgars and the Ugrians in the middle and the second half of the seventh century affected considerably the fortunes of the As as well. The western Antes were conquered by the Danubian Bulgars. Part of the eastern Antes were subdued by the Ugrians (Magyars); another section of

255. Runciman, p. 33.
256. *Idem*, p. 35.
257. See Chap. IV, Secs. 6 and 8.
258. See Chap. V, Sec. 8.

them, profiting by the *Pax Khazarica,* were able to come down from the upper Donets to the lower Don and Sea of Azov regions. The North Caucasian As had to recognize the authority of the Khazars, but preserved their autonomy.[259] They must soon have established some kind of contact with the eastern Antes who now settled in the lower Don area. These Antes, or As, of the lower Don and Azov regions, together with the North Caucasian As, were included in the area controlled by the Khazar kagan. It is known that the As played an important role in the Khazar army and administration. Some of them became officers of the highest rank (*tarkhans*). One such As *tarkhan* was put in charge of a fort near the Khazar capital Itil.[260] Another, by the name of Yuri, was an influential official in the city of Sugdaea (Surozh) in the Crimea at the end of the eighth century.[261]

Some of the As clans, and among others those living in the Azov area, were known from at least the fourth century as Rukhs-As ("the light As"), alias Roxolani, alias Rocas (Rogas).[262] In the fifth century the Patriarch Proclus, commenting on the Hunno-Alanic invasion, quotes Ezekiel's prophecy about the people of Rhos (Ῥῶς).[263] In the compilation known as the *Church History* by Zechariah the Rhetor (555), among the tribes living north of the Caucasus one named Hros is mentioned.[264] According to A. P. Diakonov this is an exact Syriac transcription of the Greek Ῥῶς.[265] It is apparently the tribe which Proclus had in mind.

If we compare Zechariah's statement on the Hros with Procopius' evidence on the eastern group of the Antes[266] we see that both the Hros and the eastern Antes should be referred to the same area, north of the Sea of Azov. The obvious inference is that the Hros must be identified as part of the eastern Antes. Hros (Ῥῶς) is apparently the same name as Roc-As, or Rukhs-As, an Antic clan. It may be added in this connection that in some Oriental sources

259. See Sec. 2, above.
260. *Ibid.*
261. Vasilievskii, III, 93.
262. See Chap. III, Sec. 9.
263. See Chap. IV, Sec. 4.
264. Zacharias Rhetor, p. 253
265. A. P. Diakonov, "Izvestiia Psevdo-Zakharii o drevnikh Slavianakh," *VDI,* IV (1939), 86-87.
266. Procopius, VIII, 4, 9.

of the ninth and the tenth centuries the Don River is called the Russian, or the Slavic, River.[267] It is likewise in the Don area that the anonymous Ravenna geographer of the seventh century places the people of the Roxolani.[268] And he also mentions a town of Malorosa (Mal-i-Ros) in the Kuban delta.[269] All these names are but different variations and transcriptions of the same basic name, Rukhs-As.

From Ibn-Rusta we know that the Rukhs-As, or Rukhs clan, was considered the most prominent clan among the north Caucasian Alans.[270] Thus, the Ros (*Rus', Ros'*), whose name was to be in the course of time assumed by Norse newcomers, were originally an Irano-Slav tribe. The Rus mentioned in Balami's Persian translation of Tabari's *History*, in connection with the events of 643, must have been the same Rukhs-As. According to Balami, when the vanguard of the Arab army approached Derbend, its ruler made the following statement to the Arab commander: "I am caught between two enemies, the Khazars and the Rus. The latter are enemies of the whole world [i.e., of the whole North Caucasian area]. Since we alone know how to fight them, let us fight them instead of your exacting tribute from us." [271] There is nothing unacceptable in Balami's story. It seems quite possible that the Rukhs-As helped the Khazars in the latter's effort to control Derbend as one of the gates to Transcaucasia.[272]

Since the As and the Rus had settlements both in the lower Don region and at the Kuban delta, it may be suggested that they must have had boats to sail across the Sea of Azov or along its shores. It is significant that among words borrowed by the Magyars from the Slavs we find the term *ladik*[273] ("boat"; from the Slavic *lodia, lodka*).

Under the protection of the Khazars the Rus-As of the Azov area enjoyed peace and prosperity for about a century, except for having to help the master-nation to protect the Caucasian mountain passes against the Arabs. However, a time came when the

267. Minorsky, pp. 216-218.
268. Rav. An., IV, 3 (p. 45).
269. See Chap. IV, Sec. 6.
270. Minorsky, p. 445.
271. Harkavy, p. 74.
272. See Sec. 2, above, on the Khazaro-Arab wars in Transcaucasia.
273. Ballagi, *s.v.*

Khazars were no longer able to stop their enemies. In 737 the Arab general Marvan broke the line of Khazar defenses and raided not only the North Caucasian area but the region of the lower Don as well. Twenty thousand Slavs (that is, As, or Rus) were captured in the Don area and sent to Syria, where they were settled along the Byzantine frontier to protect the integrity of the Caliphate.[274]

274. Harkavy, pp. 38, 76.

CHAPTER VII.

THE NORSEMEN AND THE RUSSIAN KAGANATE, 737-839.

1. Preliminary Remarks.

IN the middle of the eighth century there began a period of turbulent expansion of Scandinavian peoples, known as the era of the Vikings.[1] The Vikings were intrepid mariners and pirates who explored both to the west and to the east in their search of adventure, booty, and glory. Within the frame of Russian history we may think of them as forerunners of the Kozaks. However, while the Kozak host was a democratic organization, the Viking movement was of an aristocratic nature, each band being led by some experienced leader who more often than not belonged to a royal clan.

The Viking expansion of the eighth, ninth, and tenth centuries was an elemental thing, a northern counterpart to the cases of sudden growth of power of some nomad peoples of the steppes. Figuratively, it may be characterized as a projection into the plan of human history of an early geological process, the expansion of the Scandinavian glacier to the south in the ice age. In old Russia the Norsemen were known as Varangians. Their penetration to the eastern Baltic littoral started long before the Viking era. As early as in the sixth and seventh centuries the Norsemen explored the course of the western Dvina River and before long from its upper parts reached the region of the middle Russian Mesopotamia—that is, of the upper Volga and Oka rivers. Probably not later than 737 they discovered the sources of the Donets River, defeated the Donets horde of the Magyars, and seized Verkhni Saltov. From there they went down the course of the Donets and the Don and eventually reached the Azov and North Caucasian regions. Thus, the Donets-Don riverway must have been controlled by the Norsemen long before the Volga and Dnieper ways. This may be explained by the fact that the

1. See T. D. Kendrick, *A History of the Vikings* (London, 1931).

Volga was barred by the Bulgars, and the Dnieper way offered no direct connection with the Orient and because of that did not at first attract their attention. Moreover, in its middle and lower parts the Dnieper offered an obstacle in the shape of the Magyars, and after the seizure of Verkhni Saltov by the Norsemen the remnants of the former Donets Magyar horde must have retreated to the Dnieper region and thus reinforced their kinsmen there.

It is the history of the seizure of the Donets-Don riverway by the Norsemen and their conquest of the Azov region that will constitute the main subject matter of the present chapter. In order to appreciate adequately the importance of these events we must examine them within the general frame of the history of the Pontic area as a whole. The Norse drive to the south affected the fortunes not only of the South Russian As, or Antes, but also of the Khazars, the Magyars, and the Byzantines, and as was always the case in years of trouble, Byzantine diplomacy was active in spreading intrigues among the Pontic peoples. An important factor in the political history of the period was also the Bulgaro-Antic state in the Balkan peninsula. While extending their control to the south, the Bulgar khans did not neglect the situation on the northern frontiers of their state, which eventually led to a clash with the Magyars in the area of the Bug and the lower Dnieper.

Ultimately all this intricate diplomatic game resulted in the barring of the Donets-Don riverway by the Khazars and the decline of the Swedish-Russian state in the Azov region. After losing the Donets-Don way the Norsemen had to find some other route to the south and thus became interested in the Dnieper. Their conquest of the middle Dnieper region will be dealt with, however, in the next chapter and not in the present one.

With the emergence of the Varangians on the Russian historical stage, Norse sources become important for our study. Unfortunately most of the extant written sources bear on a later period, but we must take into consideration that the authors of some of the sagas and chronicles drew extensively upon oral tradition, in which fragments of much older historical narratives were preserved. Heroic poems glorifying the deeds of valiant Norse knights were compiled by professional poets, the renowned scalds, and recited by them at the court of every Scandinavian ruler as early as the ninth and tenth centuries. Later it was Iceland that became the storehouse of ancient Norse poetry.[2]

The sagas form a branch of Norse folklore of their own. The saga is a narrative of heroic deeds couched in prose and not in verse. It was likewise in Iceland that the saga reached its full blossoming. In the Middle Ages (eleventh to thirteenth centuries) an urge for a scholarly treatment of history made itself felt in the Scandinavian countries. Latin being the language of medieval scholarship, the early Scandinavian chronicles were written in Latin. At the end of the twelfth century there appeared the *History of the Danes* by Saxo Grammaticus, likewise in Latin. Presently Latin was replaced by one of the native Norse tongues. In such cases the dependence of the chronicle on the sagas was even more marked. The most accomplished master of the saga was Snorri Sturluson (1178-1241). His *Heimskringla,* the history of the kings of Norway, is particularly important for the student of Russian history.

Snorri Sturluson belonged by birth to an aristocratic Icelandic clan and was brought up in the tradition of the sagas, for which he conceived a liking from childhood. He received a good education, mastered Latin and studied law, but his main ambition was still to become a scald, and he fully succeeded. In 1218, already well known for his sagas and poems, he went to Norway and was received there with honors, pledging his loyalty to King Haakon. The rest of Snorri's life was spent in constant trouble. When he returned to Iceland a feud broke out between himself and the Sturlungs. There began a protracted war between the two clans, both looking to Norway for support. In 1237 Snorri went to Norway for the second time for a short visit. He was killed by his enemies in 1241. Snorri's own life was thus spent in the spirit and tradition of the sagas, and his literary work was but a natural counterpart of his real life. The motives and feelings of the heroes he glorified in his books were quite close to his own; on the other hand, while describing the feuds and battles of old he may, in certain cases, have added to the old stories some features from his own experience.

Generally speaking, while some of the sagas are based upon old traditions, they were written down much later than the events they described and it is only in the versions of the thirteenth and four-

2. For a recent general survey of the subject see Halvdan Koht, *The Old Norse Sagas* (New York, 1931).

teenth centuries that we know them. We must also remember that the saga is not a chronicle and not a critical history of the past. Therefore, before using it as a source we must sift its contents carefully. Characteristic features of the past are well rendered in some of the sagas, but only a few of them can help us in approaching a specific event, much less in dating it.

In addition to the Norse folklore we have also some contemporary Runic inscriptions engraved on stone. Unfortunately such inscriptions are rather scant, and those which bear on Norsemen in Russia are comparatively late, eleventh to thirteenth century.[3]

As to the Byzantine and Oriental sources, most of those referred to in the two preceding chapters[4] may be used for the period covered in the present chapter. While Theophanes Confessor's chronicle dealt with events down to 813 only, in the reign of Constantine Porphyrogenitus, by order of that emperor, a continuation of Theophanes' chronicle was begun and later brought down to 961.

Of the Latin chronicles of the period the so-called *Bertinian Annals* are of special importance for us since they contain the note concerning the arrival of the Rus envoys at Ingelheim in 839.

Let us turn now to the treatment of the events of our period in the works of modern scholars. To our regret, Kulakovskii's *History of Byzantium* does not come down to the period we are discussing, since it ends with the accession to the throne of Leo III (717). Instead of Kulakovskii, reference may be made here to F. I. Uspenskii's *History of the Byzantine Empire.* Uspenskii was a prominent Byzantinologist but his *History* is, on the whole, less successful than some of his special studies. Volume II of Uspenskii's *History* was to cover the period from 717 to 1057; however, only part of it was published, dealing with events down to 867.

With the appearance of the Varangians we enter on a period which has been treated more or less fully in most of the courses and outlines of Russian history. It goes without saying that no general outline of Russian historiography can be given here.[5] We only can refer the reader—in both this chapter and the following one—to those outlines and monographs which have most direct importance for the study of the events dealt with in each of these two chapters.

3. On Norse Runic inscriptions see Sources, I, 1.

4. See Chap. V, Sec. 1; and Chap. VI, Sec. 1.

5. Reference may be made here to *An Outline of Modern Russian Historiography* by Anatole G. Mazour (Berkeley, California, 1939).

From this point of view, the first work to be mentioned here is the *Russian History* of V. N. Tatishchev (Volume I published in 1768), especially since it contains fragments from chronicles which have since been lost. For a similar reason, no student of Russian history can neglect N. M. Karamzin's (1766-1826) famous *History of the Russian State,* first published in 1818. Karamzin's work is indeed classic, and in the wide range of his interests and his familiarity with west European historiography Karamzin has few peers, if any, among Russian historians. It is symbolic that by his contemporaries Karamzin was called the Columbus of Russian history. This is of course exaggerated, since the Russian past was "discovered" before him by Tatishchev and Prince Shcherbatov; moreover, there was no need of discovering it, since the history of Russia has been continuously studied by generations of scholars, beginning with the compiler of the *Primary Chronicle.* It would be more to the point to call Karamzin the Russian Gibbon.

Of the subsequent outlines of the pre-Varangian and Varangian periods, those by K. N. Bestuzhev-Riumin and M. S. Hrushevskyi are of special value. As to monographs, P. P. Smirnov's *Volga River Way* (1927) and B. D. Grekov's *Kievan Russia* (1939) must be mentioned here in any case. Speaking of the "Varangian-Rus" problem,[6] there is now a comprehensive outline of the historiography of it by V. A. Moshin (1930). A. A. Kunik's and F. Kruse's studies form the foundation of the writing of the "Norse" party in Russian historiography; as to their opponents, the "anti-Norse" party, S. Gedeonov's work *The Varangians and the Rus* is most prominent.

2. *The Norsemen in North and Central Russia.*

Due to the roughness of the Scandinavian climate and topography, man could only secure his livelihood there by toiling much harder than the inhabitants of more fertile countries. In spite of the scarcity of population in old Scandinavia, it rose from time to time above the country's capacity for producing food, which, because of the primitive methods of husbandry, was rather small. In such cases there was no alternative to emigration of at least a part of the tribe, or tribes. Thus, as we already know,[7] around the beginning of the Christian era the Goths emigrated to the southern littoral of the Baltic Sea, whence they eventually moved to the Pontic steppes;

6. See Sec. 4, below.
7. See Chap. III, Sec. 6.

and so on. In the fifth and the sixth centuries the Norsemen were exploring extensively both the southern and the eastern shores of the Baltic Sea, and in the sixth century a group of them settled at the mouth of the western Dvina. In the seventh century the kings of southern Sweden had oversea possessions in Kurland. By the beginning of the eighth century Livonia and Estonia were part of the realm of Ivar, king of southern Sweden and Denmark.[8]

Scandinavia is rich in both iron and timber, and the Norsemen thus had plenty of the materials they needed for forging weapons and for shipbuilding. In earlier times only small boats were built, but in the ninth century larger vessels better fitted for distant cruises appeared. They became known as *koggi* (*koch* in North Russian dialect) and were built in Friesland.[9] The Varangian boat of the early type was an open rowboat, in which, however, sail could be set as well.[10] It was much higher at bow and stern than amidships, and the bow and the stern end staffs were set even higher. The boat of a prominent chieftain would be ornamented with carving, and its prow more often than not had the shape of a dragon's head. Olaf Trygvasson, according to the saga, had two such ships, known as the *Long Dragon* and the *Short Dragon*.[11] The former was provided with thirty-four benches for oarsmen. The dragon head on the bow was gilded as well as the end of the stern staff. From the Russian *bylinas* it is known that some Varangian boats built in Russia were painted red.[12]

Having consolidated their control over the Livonian littoral, the Varangians began to penetrate deeper into the country. Originally, one may suppose, only small bands of trappers and fur traders ventured into the woods. The course of the Western Dvina River offered the natural route inland, and it became the first path to facilitate the Varangian advance in Russia. The native population along the banks of the Western Dvina consisted of small tribes of Balts and Finns and was both scarce and lacking in unity, so that the Varan-

8. See B. Nerman, "Die Verbindungen Zwischen Skandinavien und dem Ostbaltikum in der jungeren Eisenzeit," *VHA, 40* (1929), 15.

9. Beliaev, p. 240.

10. On the Vikings' ships see Kendrick, pp. 23-27. A ship belonging "to the pagan Anglo-Saxon period" has been recently excavated near Woodbridge, Suffolk, England. On this magnificent find see C. W. Phillips, "The Excavation of the Sutton Hoo Ship-Burial," *AJ*, XX (1940), 149-202.

11. Monsen, 182.

12. Aristov, p. 100.

FINDS OF SCANDINAVIAN ANTIQUITIES IN RUSSIA

gians met no trouble and no opposition in at first trading with the natives and then subduing them.

Reaching the upper parts of the river the Varangians penetrated into the zone of Slavic colonization. It appears that the Slavic communities around the sources of the Western Dvina and the vicinity were, except for Novgorod, small and weak. It is characteristic that in their further drive inland the Varangians by-passed Novgorod and occupied it only much later. Due to the mutual proximity of the sources of the Western Dvina, Dnieper, and Volga,[13] once the Varangians reached the upper parts of the western Dvina, they were likely to explore the upper parts of both the Dnieper and the Volga as well. We may imagine that they reached the sources of these two rivers as early as the seventh century. With regard to the Dnieper, the Varangians could hardly go down it very far since the Lithuanian and Slavic tribes in the upper Dnieper region must have been strong and well organized. Their most important city in that area was at the site of Gnezdovo, near Smolensk.[14]

On the other hand, the Varangians met with no barrier on the upper Volga down to the region of the Cheremissians, a tribe under the authority of the Bulgars. This means that they could hardly navigate the river below the present city of Yaroslavl. Using the Kotorosl, a tributary of the Volga discharging into it near Yaroslavl, the Varangian boats could go up to Lake Nero, on the banks of which the town of Rostov is situated. From here there existed a portage to the river Nerl, a tributary of the Klyazma, which is in its turn a tributary of the Oka. In such a way the Varangians were able to penetrate to the Oka basin. It is significant that objects of Scandinavian origin such as oval fibulas and swords have been found in the mounds of the Rostov, Suzdal, and Murom regions. In the opinion of Count A. S. Uvarov, who together with P. S. Saveliev explored these mounds in the middle of the nineteenth century, they may be referred to the eighth and the ninth centuries.[15] A study of the finds in both the mounds and the sites of settlements shows that in many cases the Varangians lived in close proximity to the natives; the latter belonging to the Meria tribe, of Finnish extraction. Judging from what we know from literary sources of Varangian-Finnish relations of the ninth and the tenth centuries, we may assume that

13. Cf. Kerner, pp. 1-15 and map 2.

14. See Chap. VI, Sec. 4.

15. A. S. Uvarov, "Meriane i ikh byt." *TAS*, I, *2* (1871).

it was the Varangians who ruled over the Finns in the Rostov-Suzdal region, even in the eighth century.

If we assume that the Varangians must have conquered the Rostov region and reached the Oka River not later than A.D. 700, we may surmise that it could not be long before they started to explore the Oka River upstream. Now the upper parts of the Oka and its tributary the Zusha come close to the upper parts of the Don and the latter's tributary, the Sosna. And the upper parts of the Tim, a tributary to the Sosna, run near the upper parts of the Oskol.[16] Another connection between the Oskol and the upper Don is along the Khalan (tributary to the Oskol) and the Koroch (tributary to the Don). In view of this network of riverways, the Varangians could easily penetrate from the upper Oka River to the region of the upper Donets and Oskol rivers, that is, into the old area of As settlements. As we have mentioned before,[17] Verkhni Saltov must have been controlled by the Magyars from the end of the seventh century.

It must be noted in this connection that the Varangians might easily reach the upper parts of Oka not only from the east, going upstream, but also from the northwest, that is, from the upper Dnieper basin.[18] The Osma, a tributary of the Dnieper discharging into it near Dorogobuzh, comes close to the upper course of the Ugra, a tributary of the Oka which discharges into the latter at Kaluga. It is probable that there was a fort on the banks of the Ugra, garrisoned by Magyars.[19]

In view of all the above consideration it seems likely that around the 730's the Varangians came in touch with the Magyars in the area of the upper Oka and upper Donets rivers. The Magyars were presumably defeated and the Varangians seized the fortified town of Verkhni Saltov. As to the native population, the As, they must have joined the Varangians against the Magyars.

We admit that the argument is rather hypothetical, but there are nevertheless some points of support for these conclusions. There is, first of all, the archaeological evidence. A beautiful sword of Norse type has been found near Krasnianka in the district of Kupiansk;

16. Kerner, pp. 58-60, 108, 158. Generally speaking, Professor Kerner pays less attention to the rivers of the Don basin than to those of the Dnieper and the Volga basins.

17. See Chap. VI, Sec. 5.

18. Kerner, pp. 109-131.

19. See Chap. VI, Sec. 5.

that is, in the Oskol region.[20] On the other hand, a great number of "Oriental" things found in Sweden are strikingly similar to some of the items excavated at Verkhni Saltov.[21] From the archaeological argument we turn to the interpretation of certain statements in Constantine Porphyrogenitus' book *De Administrando Imperii.*

While discussing the origins and the history of the Magyars ("Turks") in Chapter 38 of his book, Constantine says that originally, when the Magyars lived in Lebedia "near Khazaria," they were "for some reason" known not as the "Turks"[22] but as Savartoiasphali (Σαβαρτοιασφάλοι).[22] Subsequently, speaking of the defeat of the Magyars by the Patzinaks, Constantine says that as a result of this defeat the Magyar horde split into two parts, one going east in the direction of Persia and the other west to Atelkuzu. The first group is "still known" under their old name of Savartoiasphali.[23] Both these statements are rather puzzling, and so far have not been satisfactorily explained. In general, Constantine's information on the contemporary situation and the immediate past is very precise, but for the more remote past he sometimes uses fragments of tradition which he does not himself understand, as indeed he does not conceal in this particular case ("for some reason," etc.). To begin with the name, Savartoiasphali. Markwart[24] rightly suggests that this name must be a combination of two names which should be read separately: Σαβάρτοι 'Ασφάλοι, Savarti Asphali. Markwart compares the first of these names, Savarti, with the name Sevordik which is quoted in some Armenian sources. *Sevordik* means in Armenian "Black Sons." In the Arabic sources this people is called Savardjia.[25] According to the Armenian chronicles the Sevordik migrated to Armenia from the north between 750 and 760 A.D.[26] If we accept Markwart's identification of Sevordik as Savarti, we have here a corroboration of Constantine Porphyrogenitus' statement about the migration of the Savartoiasphali toward the con-

20. Arne, p. 58.

21. *Idem,* pp. 93-95, 121-122.

22. It should be noted that Constantine Porphyrogenitus called the Magyars "Turks."

23. *De Adm.* 38, On the *Savartoiasphali* see Brun, II, 328; Grot, p. 217; Macartney, pp. 86, 174-176; Markwart, pp. 36-40; W. Pecz, *BZ, 7* (1898), 618-619; Roesler, p. 150; Zeuss, p. 749.

24. Markwart, p. 36.

25. *Idem,* pp. 36-39.

26. *Idem,* p. 37.

fines of Persia. There is, however, a discrepancy as to the date of the event. According to Constantine, the migration occurred after the clash of the Magyars with the Patzinaks; that is, in the middle of the ninth and not in the middle of the eighth century.

The evidence of the Armenian sources in this case should be given preference, and so we must make a correction to Constantine's narrative. The Caucasian drive of the Savarti was obviously the result not of the clash between the Magyars and the Patzinaks but of the former's clash with some other people. What people could this be? According to Constantine the clash occurred in the part of Lebedia which was "near Khazaria" and was the region occupied by the Magyars before their drive to the west. This region may be safely identified as that of the upper Donets and the Oskol; that is, the region in which Verkhni Saltov was situated and which, so far as we may judge from archaeological evidence, was eventually occupied by the Norsemen. We thus have sufficient ground for thinking that it is to the Norsemen and not to the Patzinaks that Constantine's information must be referred. May we not now take a step further and suggest that the Norsemen are meant in Constantine's work, under the name of Savarti? To be sure, Constantine applies this name to the Magyars, or to one branch of them. However, in view of the confusion of his statements in this case we may admit that he did not well understand what was said in his source in that regard. His source may have mentioned the name Savarti in connection with the Magyar defeat, and it may have been that the name referred originally not to the Magyars themselves (as Constantine suggests), but to their conquerors. It will not be amiss to recall in this connection that cases are numerous in the age we are studying of a people being renamed as a result of its conquest by another people. We know, for example, from Ammianus Marcellinus that some tribes conquered by the Alans (As) assumed the name of the latter.[27] Could not the case of the Savarti be similar? In other words, may we not suppose that the Magyars (or part of them) were called Savarti because they (or part of them) had been conquered by the Savarti?

If the Savarti are to be identified as the Norsemen (as we have suggested), the question arises of the origin of the name itself. I must confess that I have so far no definite answer to this question

27. See Chap. III, Sec. 3.

and am only able to submit three possible explanations; any one of which, if true, would be adequate.

(1) The name Savarti may be derived from the name *Svitjord* ("Sweden").[28] In this case, Savarti would mean just "Swedes."

(2) *Svartr* in old Norse, means "black."[29] We have mentioned that according to the Chinese tradition apparently accepted by most of the steppe peoples, black was the color of the north (cf. Black Bulgars, Black Ugrians, etc.).[30] Moreover, as we have already seen, in Armenian sources the Savarti were called *Sevordik,* or "Black Sons."[31]

(3) "Sverth" in Old Norse means "sword."[32] The sword was a typical Scandinavian weapon and it may be argued with some degree of probability that at the coming of the Varangians to the Donets region the natives would at once find out from the newcomers what the word for their chief weapon was in their own language, and would then call it accordingly.

So much for the Savarti. Let us now turn to the second half of the compound Savartoi-Asphali—the Asphali. Here we seem to be on firmer ground. As we know,[33] in the region of the upper Donets and Oskol a people known as Spali lived from at least Pliny's time, and we may safely assume that the name Asphali was nothing more than a variation of the name Spali. As we have mentioned,[34] there was a close connection between the Spali and the As (Antes). Therefore, in the Asphali of Constantine Porphyrogenitus we may see the Antes. The compound name Savartoi-Asphali might then be understood as the Swedes and the Antes.

3. *The Norsemen, the As, and the Rus in the Azov Region.*

By seizing Verkhni Saltov the Varangians opened for themselves the gates to the Donets-Don riverway down to the Sea of Azov.

28. See Rafn, I, 245.

29. *Svartr* or *svart,* see Cleasby, p. 607; Gordon, p. 361. Brun, II, p. 328, derived the name Savarti from the word *Swart* which he referred to the Crimean Goths. Zeuss (p. 749) also connected the name with the word "black," referring to the German *swart, schwarz;* he interpreted the name *Savartoiasphali* as "Black Ugrians." Cf. Roesler, p. 150.

30. See Chap. VI, Secs. 3 and 5.

31. Markwart, pp. 36-39.

32. *Sverth,* see Cleasby, p. 610; Gordon, p. 361; in East Norse, *swaerth,* Gordon, p. 361.

33. See Chap. III, Sec. 7.

34. *Ibid.*

They probably lost no time in exploring this way. In their southern drive the Varangians must have been greatly helped by the As, who had settlements both in the upper Donets region and on the lower Don, as well as in the North Caucasian area. We repeat that some of these As were Slavs organized by Iranians, while other As groups were purely Iranian. The As, or rather in this case, the Aso-Slavs, who lived in the upper Donets region and had been subdued by the Magyars, must have welcomed the arrival of the Varangians to Verkhni Saltov, supporting them against the Magyars. In this way the coöperation must have started between the Varangians and the As which was to become an important factor in the further Varangian drive to the south, because of the close connection between the upper Donets As and the Azov As.

We have furthermore to take into consideration that there were special reasons for the Azov As to welcome the coming of the Varangians at this moment. As we know, in 119 A.H. (A.D. 737/38) the Arabs raided the whole North Caucasian area including even the region of the lower Don, taking thousands of Aso-Slav prisoners.[35] The Khazars, overlords of the As, were not able to protect them, and the As must have been in search of some other suzerain. We may assume that when news came of the Varangians' appearance in the upper Donets region and their liberation of the Donets As from the Magyars, the Azov As and Rukhs-As (Rus)[36] must have been eager in their turn to beg the assistance of the Varangians against the Arabs (around A.D. 739). In such a case we may perhaps admit that this was the first instance of the "calling of the Varangians" for help by the Slavs, an event which tradition refers to a much later date—i.e. to A.D. 862.

In any case it seems probable that in, or soon after, the year 739 the Varangians reached the shores of the Sea of Azov, after which they must have at once started to explore the Caucasus. Having in mind our identification of the Savarti as Norsemen, and knowing from analysis of Constantine Porphyrogenitus and the Armenian sources that the Savarti invaded Armenia between 750 and 760, may we not see in this event the first Varangian drive to Transcaucasia?

To sum up the preceding argument, it seems highly probable that in the course of the eighth century a band of Norsemen—more

35. See Chap. VI, Sec. 8.
36. *Ibid.*

exactly, of Swedes—established their control over the lower Don and Azov area. It is significant that according to the Ynglinga-Saga, which was included in part in Snorri Sturluson's *Heimskringla* (thirteenth century), this area was known as Great Sweden (*Svitjort en mikla*).[37] The band of Swedes who controlled the native tribes of the As and Rukhs-As (*Rus*) was probably not numerous, and gradually the Swedes not only merged with their vassals but even accepted their name and themselves became known first as the As and then as the Rus.

It is well known that the Norse sagas are full of legends about the Asi (Aesir). By the time the sagas were written down the Asi were part of Scandinavian mythology and were included in the number of gods under the authority of Odin. We meet them as such in the Ynglinga-Saga, for example. However, remnants of an ancient historical foundation can be easily detected under the mythological façade.[38]

We read in the Ynglinga-Saga:[39] "The land in Asia to the east of the Tanakvisl [Tanais, i.e., Don River] was called Asaland or Asaheim and the chief town in the land was called Asagard [As-Grad, i.e., City of the As]."

It is clear from this passage that As-Grad could be reached by crossing the Don eastward; it must have been situated on the eastern or southeastern shore of the Sea of Azov, possibly on the Kuban delta, where there is a hill still called As-Dag (the Hill of the As).[40] If so, As-Grad was in or near the same locality as Malorosa and Tmutorokan. We may add that the name As-Grad which originated on the Sea of Azov appeared later on in the Baltic region. This

37. Rafn, I, 245.

38. It was Gibbon (II, 241) who first attempted to connect the story of Odin with South Russian historical background. While his suggestion has received little credit, his approach, in my opinion, has been fundamentally sound. We have of course to recall that already in the sixth century Jordanis noted that the Goths called their victorious leaders "not mere men, but demigods, that is Ansis" (Jordanis, Sec. 78). I do not enter here into the discussion of possible interrelation of the name *Ansis* with the name As; however, even if there was no connection between Jordanis' *Ansis* and the As, the close contacts between the Norsemen and the As in the eighth and ninth centuries might have easily resulted in a complete fusion of the legend and history. On the Aesir see Munch, pp. 1-10 and *passim*. It is significant that the feminine form derived from the Norse word *as* is *asynja* (Munch, pp. 287-288) which is strikingly similar to the old Russian *iasynia*, "an As [Ossetian] woman" (see, for example, *PSRL*, IX, 150).

39. Rafn, I, 246; cf. Monsen, p. 2.

40. "Asso-Dag," Goertz, I, 79.

second As-Grad, or Asagard, on the banks of the Western Dvina, is now known as Ascheraden.[41] The naming of this second As-Grad is not hard to explain. While the terminal of the old Varangian way from the Baltic to the Sea of Azov was at the mouth of the Don, its entry was at the mouth of the Western Dvina. It was a two-way passage, since not all the Norse warriors and merchants who went to the Orient stayed there permanently; many a Swedish adventurer, even if he now called himself an Asian or a Russian, would—after spending a number of years in the Orient and getting rich —eventually return home to the Baltic area, and would call old places by new names which recalled to him the fabulous land of his exploits and adventures.

It was under the influence of similar motives that As (feminine, Asa) became a popular personal name in Scandinavia. Several Norwegian princesses in the ninth and tenth centuries bore the name Asa.[42] And the syllable "As" was also used in forming such men's names as Asmund, Askold etc.[43]

As we know, the name Rus was closely connected with the name As.[44] The capital of the Norsemen in the Azov country, As-Grad, was probably close to the "Swamp City" of the Rus, Malorosa. The Kuban delta where As-Grad and Malorosa were situated was called the Rus Island by Arabic writers.[45] While the Azov Norsemen at first familiarized themselves with the name As, eventually they assumed the name of Rus, so that the state they founded in the Azov region subsequently became known as the Russian Kaganate.

4. The Varangian-Russian Problem.

While discussing in the preceding section the possible paths of expansion of the Norsemen in Russia, we have deliberately postponed until now a general treatment of the so-called "Varangian-Russian problem" which has played such an important role in Russian historiography, and on which there exists an immensely vast bibliography. We have done so purposely because we deemed it necessary first to assemble some data essential for the solution of

41. Taube, p. 385.
42. See Monsen, Index, *s.v.*
43. Taube, p. 385; M. Olsen derives such names from *ans* (Jordanis' *Ansis*) (Munch, p. 287).
44. See Chap. VI, Sec. 8.
45. See Sec. 5, below.

the question; also because our information on the Norsemen in Russia for the period of the eighth century is somewhat nebulous and scarce. It is only for the ninth century that more definite data on the Norsemen in South Russia are available. Now, as we are about to enter upon the ninth century, we cannot any longer postpone the discussion of the Varangian-Russian problem at large.

Let us then turn to an appraisal of the results of the tournament of the *Norsephiles* ("Normanists") and *Mysonorses* ("Anti-Normanists"), so famous in the annals of the Russian historiography. For a bibliography and comprehensive outline of the problem we refer the reader to V. A. Moshin's excellent studies.[46]

Generally speaking, there cannot be any doubt that in the ninth and tenth centuries, under the name of Russians (Rus, Ros), Norsemen are meant more often than not. To show this, it will be sufficient to mention the following three cases only:

(1) According to the *Bertinian Annals,* several "Russians" came along with the Byzantine envoys to Emperor Louis in 839; according to their own statement they were Swedes by origin.[47]

(2) In the treaty between Prince Oleg and the Byzantine Empire in 911, names of "Russian" envoys are listed; most of them are obviously Norse.[48]

(3) Constantine Porphyrogenitus quotes in his book *De Administrando Imperii* (written around 945) the names of the Dnieper cataracts both in Slavic and in "Russian." Most of the "Russian" names may be easily derived from the Norse.[49]

It is therefore incontestable that in the ninth and the tenth centuries the name "Rus" was applied to the Norsemen. If so, it may seem that the whole controversy between the Normanists and the Anti-Normanists is based on a misunderstanding on the part of the latter, and that their efforts have been, at best, quixotic. And yet such is not the case, since the value of the contributions of the Anti-Normanists to the study of ancient Russia cannot be denied. It was the Anti-Normanists who first called the attention of the students of Russian history to the evidence of the expansion of the Rus in the south long before the appearance of Riurik in Novgorod in A.D. 862, according to the traditional date. Thus the original, over-

46. Moshin, "Nachalo"; Moshin, "Vopros."

47. *MGH,* Scriptores, I, 434.

48. *Khristomatiia,* I, 1; cf. Cross, p. 151.

49. *De Adm.,* 9. For the interpretation of the names see Moshin, Nachalo, pp. 36-37; Thomsen, *Origin,* pp. 54-66.

simplified theory of the first Normanists, by which the whole history of the Norsemen in Russia was to start with Riurik and from Novgorod, was broken down. And yet the whole argument of the first Normanists was based on the premise that the very name of Rus spread from north to south and not otherwise. To prove this, it would be necessary to prove first that the tribe of Rus originated somewhere in Scandinavia and from there came to Novgorod. In such a case the name must have been mentioned in Scandinavian sources. And yet no tribe of Rus was known in Scandinavia and none was mentioned in the Norse sagas. In the latter, the name of Russia (*Rysaland*) refers to the organized Russian state of the eleventh and twelfth centuries, and even in that sense it is rarely used, the common name for Russia being that of *Gardariki,* "the realm of castles."

The only supporting hint the Normanists could find in Sweden for their thesis was the name Roslagen, a province in Sweden. This is, however, the name of a province and not of a tribe; moreover, it may be argued that the name was imported to Sweden by Norsemen returned from Russian campaigns, as was the case with the name As-Grad as applied to a town on the western Dvina.[50] Recognizing the failure of the Roslagen argument, A. A. Kunik, one of the leading Normanists and a conscientious and untiring explorer of the problem, shifted his attention to the Swedish term, *rodsen* ("rowers"), as the inhabitants of the shore section of Roslagen were known.[51] He suggested that this word, *rodsen* (Rodsi), or in Finnish pronunciation, *ruotsi,* gave birth to the name Rus. Some students of linguistics voiced their approval of the theory.[52] It was argued that according to the laws of linguistics such a transmutation, of *ruotsi* to *Rus,* would be possible. But if the philologist can be satisfied with this interpretation of the origin of the name Rus, the historian cannot. Is it indeed possible that Norsemen coming to Russia would accept as their own name a distorted appellation given them by the Finns on their way? Besides, the alleged name "Rodsi" is itself hypothetical.[53] Moreover, as has now been sufficiently shown, the first Norsemen penetrated to Russia not by the way of the Neva River but by the way of the Western Dvina, and the first natives

50. See Sec. 3, above.
51. Kunik, *Berufung,* I, 165-167.
52. Shakhmatov, *Sudby,* p. 50.
53. See A. Pogodin, "Les Rodsi: un peuple imaginaire," *RES, 17* (1937), 71-80.

they met were necessarily Lithuanians and not Finns. Finally, if the name Rus were derived from the alleged Finnish *ruotsi,* how are we to explain the fact that the name Rus (in the form of Ros, Ῥῶς) was known to the Byzantines long before the coming of the Varangians to Novgorod?[54]

We have already dealt in the preceding chapters with many a case of the early use of the name Rus, or Ros, in South Russia. It hardly can be denied that it existed there from at least the fourth century. To recapitulate our previous argument, the name was originally connected with one of the Alanic clans, that of the Light As (Rukhs-As). Not later than at the beginning of the ninth century the name must have been assumed by the Swedish warriors who established their control over the Don and Azov area. These Russianized Swedes became subsequently known as Rus both in Byzantium and in the Near and Middle East. As we shall see in due course,[55] upon the coming of Prince Riurik to Novgorod (around 856) an attempt was made to transplant, so to say, the name Rus from the south to the north, and to connect its origin with Riurik's clan. But this new theory was dictated by political considerations and cannot in any case cover the earlier Russian background.

5. The First Russian Kaganate.

The first host of Norsemen who appeared in the Azov area in the middle of the eighth century could hardly have been numerous. Moreover, part of them seem before long to have moved to Transcaucasia. However, when the road south was discovered, new bands of adventurers were probably not slow to follow the first pioneers. Rumors of the the rich countries of the Orient must have spread at once all over Scandinavia.

The exodus of the Varangians from Scandinavia and their rush to the Orient must have been also the result of domestic troubles in Scandinavian countries. King Ivar, whose possessions in Livonia and Estonia have already been mentioned,[56] succeeded in uniting southern Sweden and Denmark under his authority. His grandson Harald had to cope with an uprising in Sweden and was eventually defeated by the Swedes at Bravalla, eastern Gotland, around 770.[57]

54. See Chap. VI, Sec. 8.
55. See Chap. VIII, Sec. 3.
56. See Sec. 2, above.
57. Beliaev, p. 219

His kingdom disintegrated and many a follower of Harald was forced to emigrate. Some of them, it may be surmised, crossed the Baltic Sea to Livonia whence they could go farther east and south using the newly established road to the Azov area.

Being a seafaring nation, the Norsemen might be expected to build ships at the mouth of Don and to sail both the Azov and Black Seas. It should be mentioned that even before their coming, the As and the Rus traversed the Sea of Azov.[58] In this connection a passage in Theophanes Confessor's chronicle dealing with "Russian ships" in the Byzantine fleet commands special attention. While discussing Constantine V's campaign against the Bulgars in 773, Theophanes says that Constantine first sent against the Bulgars his main fleet of two hundred ships (*chelandia*) and then put to sea himself with his special flotilla of "Russian ships" (ῥούσια χελάνδια).[59] The Latin translator of Theophanes' chronicle, the Pope's librarian Anastasius who wrote at the end of the ninth century, rendered the Greek word ῥούσια not as "Russian" but as "red" (*rubea*).[60] We may recall that according to the Russian epic poems (*bylina*) red was the typical color for the early Russian battleships.[61] Thus it may well have been that "Russian ships" could be characterized as "red ships." [62] As to the possibility of the presence of Russian ships or sailors in the Byzantine fleet of 773, it must not be discarded without due examination.[63] From its agents in Cherson the Byzantine Government must have received news of the appearance of the Norsemen in the Azov region soon after their arrival there. We must take into account that for the later period—that of the tenth century—we have positive evidence of Russian sailors being in Byzantine service. According to the *Ceremonial Book* of Constantine Porphyrogenitus seven hundred Russians took part in the Crete expedition of 903; also seven Russian ships joined the Byzantine fleet in the Italian expedition of 935.[64] When speaking of Russian sailors in the imperial service, Constantine Porphyrogenitus does it in a matter-of-fact manner, so

58. See Chap. VI, Sec. 8.
59. Theophanes, p. 446.
60. *Idem,* II, 295.
61. Aristov, p. 100.
62. The "red ship" used by the emperor is mentioned by Constantine Porphyrogenitus (*De Adm.,* 51). He calls it, however, an *agrarium* (Ῥούσιον ἀγράριον), and not a *chelandium* (χελάνδιον) as in our case.
63. Cf. Moshin, *Vopros,* p. 131.
64. *De Cer.,* II, 44.

that apparently there was nothing new or unusual for him in such an arrangement. We may thus suppose that the practice started much earlier. There is nothing against a surmise that the first case of Russian naval coöperation with Byzantium took place in 773. On the other hand we must make it clear that, when all is said, this is still merely conjecture.

Chronologically the next possible case of Russian activity in the Black Sea seems to be contained in the story of the attack of the Russian Prince Bravlin on the town of Surozh (Sugdaea) in Crimea, appended to the Life of St. Stephen of Surozh.[65] This cannot, however, be dated with any precision. The Life of St. Stephen of Surozh is available in two versions of which the short one is in Greek and the expanded one in Russian. Both are known in later manuscript copies only, the Russian version being referred by V. G. Vasilievskii to the sixteenth century. However, both of them, according to Vasilievskii, have preserved the tradition of their early original.[66] The Russian Life of St. Stephen contains four appendices in which various miracles wrought by the saint both in life and after his death are described. It is in one of these appendices that the story of Prince Bravlin is told. According to the story the prince was stricken by palsy at the moment when he burst into St. Stephen's church after having stormed the city of Surozh. It is said that the miracle occurred "a few years" after the saint's death. St. Stephen died in 786. The definition "a few years after" is certainly not very precise. However, since Archbishop Philaret is mentioned in the story, and he was the immediate successor of St. Stephen, there is some reason to refer the episode to the end of the eighth century.[67] With regard to Prince Bravlin, N. T. Beliaev suggested that his name should be considered as an epithet connecting the prince with the battle of Bravalla (770) which we have mentioned in the beginning of this section.[68] In this case we are forced to recognize that the Prince Bravlin who attacked Surozh "a few years" after 786 had in 770 taken part in the battle of Bravalla and acquired fame by his exploits during this battle. All this is nothing more than a chain of conjectures, but it must be said that Beliaev's theory on the

65. Vasilievskii, III, 95-96.

66. *Idem,* pp. ccxx, cclviii. G. Da Costa-Louillet has recently voiced her doubts with regard to the authenticity of the source. She has, however, offered no new evidence on the matter (Da Costa, pp. 243-244).

67. Vasilievskii, p. 96.

68. Beliaev, p. 220.

name of Prince Bravlin is the only explanation so far given which has at least a degree of probability.[69]

On the ground of all that has been said we may venture a tentative conclusion that the Norsemen who penetrated into the Azov area about the middle of the eighth century and merged with the native As and Rus assumed considerable strength by the end of the century, so that they were even in a position to threaten the Crimea. We may suppose that by this time they had succeeded in building up not only a fighting force but an organized state as well. Their ruler must have eventually assumed the Khazar title of kagan. Says Ibn-Rusta: "The Rus have a ruler who is called *Khaqan-Rus*."[70] Ibn-Rusta wrote in the beginning of the tenth century but he is supposed to have used in this case a source of the middle of the ninth century, to which date his statement may be referred. Even more direct is the evidence of the *Bertinian Annals*, A.D. 839, which we have mentioned in the preceding section.[71] The Russians (Swedes) who came in that year to Ingelheim said that their ruler was known as kagan (*Chacanus*).

In view of the above information there can be no doubt that the Russian Kaganate existed as early as the first half of the ninth century; there is, however, no agreement among students of Russian history as to where to locate it. The orthodox Normanists have been inclined to consider Novgorod as its capital, which does not fit the geographic and political background of the period in any way.[72] In 1927 P. P. Smirnov's study on the Volga riverway was published, in which the whole problem was reconsidered from a new angle; since in Smirnov's opinion the kaganate was situated in the Russian "Mesopotamia"—the region between the upper Volga and Oka rivers.[73] While giving full credit to Smirnov's ingenuity and the large amount of source material used by him, we are not able to accept his final conclusions. Smirnov connects the very name Rus with the Volga River, which was mentioned as Ra in Ptolemy's work, and attempts to prove that the Russian Kaganate meant the Volga

69. *Ibid.*, and nn. 26-27; Vasilievskii, p. cclxxxiv.

70. Macartney, p. 213.

71. See Sec. 4, above.

72. Shakhmatov (*Sudby*, p. 56) considers Staraia Rusa (instead of Novgorod) the capital of the kaganate, which is no more acceptable. I admit, however, that the Swedish colony at Staraia Rusa was to a certain extent connected with the kaganate. See Chap. VIII, Sec. 3.

73. Smirnov, p. 130.

Kaganate.[74] His argument misses the point, however, since we know that the middle Volga region was controlled by the Bulgars and the lower Volga area by the Khazars. While the Russians eventually penetrated to the lower Volga, they came there via the Don River. Moreover, it is hardly possible to admit that both the commercial and the military activities of the Rus in the Near and Middle East could be directed from a faraway northern center. It is much more likely that the center of their state was in the south and not in the remote north. Finally, the very title of the Rus ruler—that of kagan—points to the neighborhood of the Khazars, from whom it was undoubtedly borrowed. By assuming this title the ruler of the Rus most likely wanted to emphasize his independence from the Khazars in contrast to the submission to the Khazar kagan of the Azov As and Rus prior to the coming of the Norsemen. This assumption of the kagan title would be natural and easy to explain in the background of the lower Don and Azov area, but entirely out of the picture when it comes to the upper Volga region.

However, while we insist on locating the center of the Russian Kaganate of the first half of the ninth century in the Azov area, we shall not deny the possibility of a close connection between the south and the north in this period, via the Donets-Don riverway. Verkhni Saltov on the upper Donets must have been an important station on this way. Commercially, the Russian Kaganate must have been based chiefly upon fur trade, and in this respect it fulfilled an economic function parallel to that of the Volga Bulgars. In order to secure the delivery of furs from the north the Russian kagan had to be in touch with some of the Slavic and Finnish tribes of the upper Volga region.

All told, we may assume that the Russian Kaganate of this period was a strong power of the same type as the Khazar and the Volga Bulgar states; that is, with the control of important routes of international trade as its main objective. From the Azov region as their base the Rus merchants of the ninth century traveled as far as Bagdad. Information as to their route may be found in the book of Ibn-Khurdadhbih, the postmaster general of the Caliphate.

"Tanais, the Slavonic River" (Don) was the first section of their route, according to Ibn-Khurdadhbih,[75] the lower Volga being the next section, and the Caspian Sea, the third. Ibn-Khurdadhbih wrote

74. *Idem,* pp. 7-9, 120-121.

75. Ibn-Khurdadhbih, p. 115 (of the French trans.); p. 154 (of the Arabic text).

about 847, but his information may be in this case referred to an earlier date. It is characteristic that he does not mention the Khazar fortress Sarkel on the Don, which was built in 833[76] and at which customs duties were paid by travelers of the Don riverway. According to Ibn-Khurdadhbih, the Rus merchants paid their customs duties at Khalmij on the Volga River,[77] an indication that the source he used refers to the situation as it was prior to the building of Sarkel.

It is obvious that Rus merchants used the portage between Don and Volga at the place where these two rivers come close together, on the parallel of Stalingrad (Tsaritsyn). The question is whether they descended the Don downstream to its bend in the direction of the Volga, or came upstream from the mouth of the Don. The French translator of Ibn-Khurdadhbih's work in the *Bibliotheca Geographorum Arabicorum* has the Russian merchants descend the Don (*descendent le Don*).[78] Such a translation is apparently based upon the preconceived idea that they must have arrived directly from the north, from Novgorod. Now in the Arabic original, it is simply said that the Russian merchants "go" (*sārū*)[79] the way of Don, and it seems almost certain that they used to come from the Sea of Azov up the stream and not downstream from the north. In Ibn-al-Faqih's revision of Ibn-Khurdadhbih's work (903) the town of Samakars is mentioned[80] as one of the stations used by the Russian merchants. This points to the Kuban delta as the base from which they started their trips, and thus gives us further evidence for locating the headquarters of the Russian Kaganate somewhere near Malorosa or Tmutorokan.

It is to the Kuban delta, the "Swamp of the Rus" (*Mal-i-Ros*), that the information of the Arabic and Persian sources on the Rus Island must be referred.

Says Ibn-Rusta: "The country of the Rus is an island in a lake (cf. Gardizi: "in a sea"); the island is a three-day journey through forests and swamps, and it is a damp morass, such that when a

76. See Sec. 10, below.
77. Ibn-Khurdadhbih, *loc. cit.*
78. *Idem*, p. 115 (of the French trans.).
79. Ibn-Khurdadhbih, p. 154 of the Arabic text.
80. Ibn-al-Faqih, p. 271 (of the Arabic text). De Goeje suggests the reading "Samkush" instead of "Samakars." The name may be referred either to Kerch (Sam-Kerch) or to some town in the Taman peninsula. Could not "Samakars" be considered a corruption of *Tamatarcha* (Tmutorokan)?

SEA OF AZOV
CRIMEA
Kerch
Enikale
Lighthouse
Pavlovskaia Battery
STRAIT
KERCH
Northern Spit or Chushka
Southern Spit or Tuzla
C.Tuzla
C.Panagia
C.Kishla
Columns under water
Coast Guard
Stony Tomb
Kuchugury
FONTAN PENINSULA
Fontan
Stony Battery
MT. KUKUOBA
Coast Guard
Battery
GULF OF TAMAN
TMUTOROKAN
Shimardan Bay
Artiukhov Farm
Semeniaki Farm
MT. SHUMUKOI
MT. KUSUOBA
Akhtanizovskaia
Sennaia St.
PHANAGORIA
MT. BLEVAKI
Peresypnoe Mouth
Peresypnaia St.
Kurchanskoe Mouth
KURCHANSKII LIMAN
Suvorovskii Redoubt
Adass
Mouth
MALOROSA
Temriuk
to Kurki
KANDAUR
AKHTANIZOVSKII LIMAN
C.Rakhmanovskii
C.Dubovyi Rynok
Titorovskaia
Temriuk
Perevoloka R.
Little Perevolochnaia Battery
MT. LYSAIA
Old Turkish Fort
Taman
Fort Phanagoria
MT. AS-DAG
BARROW VASIURINSKII
Gorodishche
BARROW BLIZNITSY
Gorodjshche
Stebleevskaia
MT. ZELENAIA
MT. KRUGLAIA
TSUKUR LIMAN
Kormussa
Gorodishche
Gorodishche
Bugaz
C.Kiziltash Burun
Shirochanskii St.
Bugaz Mouth
KUBANSKII LIMAN
Kuban R.
Djemiteiskaia Spit
KIZILTASHSKII LIMAN
BLACK SEA

man puts his foot on the ground it quakes owing to moisture."[81] According to Mirkhwand[82] certain islands were given to the Rus by the Khazar kagan; presumably the same Russian island as described by Ibn-Rusta and Gardizi is meant.

Gardizi puts the number of the Rus at one hundred thousand. According to both Ibn-Rusta and Gardizi "the Rus go out to raid the Slavs in boats and they take the Slavs prisoner and sell them to the Khazars and the Bulgars. They have no cultivated lands, and obtain grain from the Slavs."[83] The Slavs in question were probably the Aso-Slavs of the Don and Azov region. It is apparent that they paid their tribute to the Rus in grain, just as they had previously to the Magyars.

Speaking of the relations between the Rus and the Khazars, we may suppose that at the time of the first appearance of the Norsemen in the Azov region, around 739, the Khazars must have used them as allies against the Arabs. The migration of the Savarti, or Sevordik, to Transcaucasia[84] may have been undertaken at the advice of the Khazars. The Varangians who extended their control over the As in the Azov region may have first become vassals of the Khazar kagan,[85] as the As themselves had been before the coming of the Varangians. In such a case the As auxiliary brigade in the Khazar army must now have been replaced by the "Russian" one, and the chief of the Rus—the Rus *tarkhan*—must have assumed the position hitherto belonging in the Khazar system to the chief of the As —the *As-tarkhan*. It is possible that the *Ras-Tarkhan* mentioned in Tabari's book was in reality the *Rus-Tarkhan*.[86] It has been said[87] that the *As-Tarkhan* gradually assumed in Khazaria the position of a deputy kagan (*ansha* or *aysha*). It seems probable that now the *Rus-Tarkhan* may have achieved the same honor, and if so, this was the origin of the title of kagan among the Rus.

We may imagine that eventually altercations sprang up between the Khazars and the Rus, and the *Rus-Tarkhan,* or deputy kagan,

81. Macartney, p. 213.
82. B. D'Herbelot, *Bibliothèque Orientale* (Paris, 1697), *s.v.* Rous (pp. 722-723).
83. Macartney, p. 213.
84. See Sec. 3, above.
85. Cf. Mirkhwand's information that the kagan gave some island to the Rus (n. 82, above).
86. See Sec. 6, below.
87. See Chap. VI, Sec. 2.

proclaimed himself an independent ruler with the title of kagan. There is some reason to refer this event to A.D. 825.[88] In my opinion, it is to the struggle between the Khazars and the Rus that Chapters 10 and 11 in Constantine Porphyrogenitus' book *De Administrando Imperii* may be referred. To be sure, Constantine does not mention the Rus in these chapters, which deal with the Alans. But as we have suggested, the Alans, or As, were at that time under the authority of the Rus. Thus it may be argued—tentatively, of course—that "the ruler of Alania" whom Constantine mentions may have been the Russian kagan.

In Chapter 10 of his work Constantine speaks of the peoples who may be used against the Khazars in case of a war between these latter and the Byzantine Empire. "Note that the Uzes may wage war against the Khazars, since they live near by. Likewise, the ruler of Alania, since the nine *climata* ["districts"] of Khazaria are close to Alania, and the Alan may, if he chooses, devastate them and thus do much harm and damage to the Khazars, since it is from those nine *climata* that all means of livelihood and prosperity of Khazaria are derived." In the next, the 11th, chapter Constantine says that the ruler of Alania may also attack the Khazars when they are on their way either to Sarkel or to Cherson. Since Sarkel was built in 833, Chapter 11 must refer to the situation after that date, while Chapter 10 probably reflects conditions as they had been prior to 833. The mention of Sarkel is significant since, as we shall see,[89] it was built to prevent Russian attacks on Khazaria. Thus it seems quite probable that the Russians are meant in Chapter 11 as the possible foes of the Khazars, which consideration also adds support to our conjecture that the ruler of Alania should be identified as the Russian kagan.

At the time of Constantine's writing Kiev became a more important Russian center than Tmutorokan, and since Constantine paid much attention to the Kievan Rus in some other chapters of his work he may have chosen to omit the name Rus from Chapters 10 and 11, which deal with the Azov area, in order to prevent confusion. The name Alania was used in these chapters as a geographical term rather than an etnographical one; moreover, the original tribe of the Rus—as well as of the As—was Alanic or Alano-Slavic anyway.

88. See Sec. 6, below.
89. See Sec. 10, below.

6. *The Khazar State in the Second Half of the Eighth and the Beginning of the Ninth Century.*

The Arabic invasion of 737 administered such a severe blow to the Khazar state that it was only gradually able to put itself in order again. Baladhuri says that the supreme chief (*azim*) of the Khazars—that is, the kagan—was overcome with fear. He therefore accepted Marvan's offer of conversion to Islam as the preliminary condition of peace.[90] By converting to Islam the kagan placed himself under the authority of the caliph. In this respect the policy of the Arabs was similar to that of the Byzantines: any people accepting Greek Orthodoxy from the Patriarch of Constantinople was considered as being under the authority of the emperor as well. However, since the kagan's conversion to Islam was not the result of inner religious conviction but only desperate military and political necessity, the change was neither sincere nor lasting. In any case, the convert caliph's successors were not Moslems, and it was only a small part of the Khazar people who remained loyal to Islam.[91]

After his successful campaign of 737 Marvan spent several years in establishing his control over the Caucasian mountain tribes. In 742 he became caliph—the last of the Umayyad Dynasty. Following his death unrest sprang up in the Caliphate which resulted in the establishment of a new dynasty of Caliphs, that of the Abbassides, under whom Arab policy became less bellicose. During the period of trouble and the concomitant weakening of the central authority, an opposition movement started in some of the border provinces of the Caliphate, in Transcaucasia among others. There is some archaeological evidence to illustrate the troublesome situation in Transcaucasia at this period. A hoard of Arabic coins was recently found near Gandja.[92] Some may be dated 130 A.H. (A.D. 747/48) or earlier, while others belong to 144 A.H. (A.D. 762) or a later year, but there are no coins in this hoard for the years between 130 and 144 A.H., which may be explained by the owner's burying treasure during these many years because of the riotous situation in the country.

It is exactly to this decade of the 750's that the invasion of

90. Baladhuri, Hitti's trans., I, 325-326.
91. Vernadsky, *Conversion*, p. 80.
92. S. A. Pakhomov, "Gandjinskii Klad," Marr volume, pp. 737-744.

Transcaucasia by the Savarti (Sevordik) may be referred.[93] It is possible that the Savarti—that is, from our point of view the Varangians—undertook their campaign with the sponsorship of the Khazars, since the latter were interested in undermining Arab control over Transcaucasia. The Savarti destroyed the city of Shamkor, west of Gandja, and succeeded in seizing the whole Gandja region.[94] They were not able, however, to hold the rich city of Berda'a in spite of their attempt to do so. We may note that the city of Berda'a which attracted the attention of the Savarti was to become, later on, the objective of the Russian campaign in Transcaucasia in 943/44. It is possible that the Rus of the middle of the tenth century were partly guided in their drive to Berda'a by old tales and traditions, originating among the Rus of the middle of the eighth century, concerning the Savarti drive.

In 754 Caliph Al-Mansur became worried by the unceasing troubles in Transcaucasia and appointed as his lieutenant in Armenia Yazid ben Usaid as-Sulami, to restore Arab control in those parts. Yazid began a new campaign against the Khazars, directing his attack at the Alan Gate, that is, the fort of Daryal.[95] The Khazars were defeated and the kagan sued for peace, which was granted and secured by matrimonial ties, for Yazid married a Khazar princess who, according to the Armenian historian Levond, was the kagan's daughter.[96] In 764 the war between the Arabs and the Khazars broke out once more, this time with the advantage on the side of the Khazars, who captured the city of Tiflis and devastated Armenia.[97] It was on this occasion that the Khazar troops were commanded by Ras-Tarkhan. In some of the sources he is called a Khoresmian mercenary.[98] Markwart[99] suggests the reading As-Tarkhan. In our opinion, the reading Rus-Tarkhan would be more plausible, and if this is correct, he may have been the leader of the Rus brigade fighting for the Khazars. Following this episode there was peace between the Khazars and the Arabs for more than thirty years. In 182 A.H. (A.D. 798/99) the reigning kagan's daughter

93. See Sec. 3, above.
94. Mas'udi, II, 75.
95. Markwart, p. 37.
96. Brosset, I, 257, n. 1.
97. Brosset, *loc. cit.;* Grigoriev, p. 56.
98. Minorsky, p. 451.
99. Markwart, *Bericht,* p. 271.

was engaged to a Barmakide prince in Armenia. The fiancée arrived safely at Berda'a but there fell ill and died before the marriage could take place. The Khazars suspected poisoning, and the angry kagan sent his troops to Transcaucasia (799-800).[100]

The Khazar army again invaded Armenia, plundering the country and taking many prisoners. The Arabs had insufficient forces in Transcaucasia, since they were obliged at the time to send many troops to Sogdiana and Fergana to suppress opposition there. It was only in 822 that the Transcaucasian situation became more favorable to them, and Caliph Mamun was in a position to start an offensive against the Khazars.[101] There is little information in the sources about this war. Muqaddasi, who wrote in 375 A.H. (A.D. 985/86), comments as follows: "I have heard that Mamun attacked the Khazars from Gurjania and compelled their king to accept Islam."[102] If this statement is to be credited, we may think of another case of temporary conversion of the Khazars to Islam—around 825—but, like the first (737), it cannot have been lasting. It is probable that the Rus took advantage of the kagan's defeat, and we may even tentatively refer to this date (825) the emancipation of the Russian Kaganate from the Khazars.[103] We may note that Muqaddasi adds to his statement on the kagan's conversion the following line: "I have likewise heard that Roman warriors, known as Rus, conquered the Khazars and seized their land."[104] Since Muqaddasi wrote his book after Prince Sviatoslav's attack on the Khazars (969), it is possible to refer the above statement to Sviatoslav's campaign. In my opinion, however, Muqaddasi may have merged information concerning two different Khazaro-Russian wars, of which one took place around 825 and the other in 969.

Let us now turn to the relations between the Khazars and the Byzantine Empire. For the period of the second half of the eighth and the beginning of the ninth century our information is scant. It is in any case obvious that two opposing tendencies ruled the course of Khazaro-Byzantine relations. On one hand, because of common danger from the Arabs the two powers were inclined toward a *rapprochement*. On the other hand, their respective interests in the

100. *Idem*, pp. 5-6.
101. *Idem*, p. 476.
102. *Idem*, p. 3.
103. Cf. Sec. 5, above.
104. Harkavy, p. 282.

Taurida were antagonistic. We have mentioned in a previous section the possibility of Russian participation in Constantine V's naval campaign of 773.[105] At that time the Rus-Tarkhan must still have been under the authority of the Khazar kagan, and if there were Russians in the Byzantine navy they may have been sent there by the kagan's order.

Around 787, as we know from the Life of St. John of Gothia, the Khazars occupied the main city of the Crimean Goths, Doras, and a Khazar governor (*tudun*) was appointed there.[106] Presently an uprising took place at Doras against the Khazars. The latter, however, succeeded in crushing it; but apparently not for long, since in the 790's the city was already under the rule of a Gothic chief (*toparch*) responsible to the Byzantines.[107] It may be argued that the retreat of the Khazars from Doras was the result of coöperation between the Byzantines and the Rus. We have already mentioned [108] that according to Constantine Porphyrogenitus the ruler of Alania was in a position to help the empire to forestall Khazar attack on both Cherson and the *climata*. In our opinion this "ruler of Alania" may have been the Rus-Tarkhan. It seems even possible that prince Bravlin's Crimean campaign was started under the sponsorship of Byzantine diplomacy, with the object on the part of the Byzantines of shattering Khazar authority in the Crimea.

One result of the close relations between the Khazars and the Byzantines was the expansion of Christianity in Khazaria. Christianity, as earlier Judaism, penetrated to Khazaria from both Transcaucasia and the Taurida.[109] The Taurida was by the eighth century considerably Christianized. An interesting list of bishoprics of the eparchy of Gothia is preserved in a fourteenth-century manuscript, first edited by De Boor in 1894.[110] Until recently the list has been considered as of the middle of the eighth century; which date, however, cannot be accepted, and the list should be referred to the middle of the ninth century.[111] On the other hand, there cannot be

105. See Sec. 5, above.

106. Vasiliev, p. 91. See also V. P. Babenchikov, "Iz istorii Krymskoi Gotii," *GA*, *117* (1935), 147-152.

107. Vasiliev, p. 105.

108. See Sec. 5, above.

109. See Chap. VI, Sec. 2.

110. C. de Boor, "Nachträge zu den Notitiae Episcopatuum," *ZK*, XII (1891), 520-534

111. See Chap. VIII, Sec. 5.

any doubt that there were many well-organized Christian communities in the Crimea even in the eighth century.

The middle of the eighth century was a period of serious crisis in the religious life of the Byzantine Empire, due to the iconoclastic policies of the emperors of the Isaurian Dynasty.[112] Crimea, as well as the Caucasus, became a place of exile for many a Byzantine monk deported from Constantinople for his defense of the icons. Other monks migrated thither voluntarily because of their repugnance for the imperial decrees. A number of these newcomers settled in the caves in which the Crimean rocks abound, and turned some of them into chapels.[113] The influx of refugee monks contributed much to the intensity of religious spirit among the Crimean Christians. Incidentally, it also intensified the Hellenistic aspects of the Christian culture there.

In 787, in the reign of Empress Irene, the Seventh Ecumenical Council which had its sessions in Nicea voted to restore the veneration of icons.[114] While there was to be a later iconoclastic intermission, from 815 to 842,[115] the decisions of the Seventh Council were of paramount importance for both the Byzantine Church at large and the Crimean parishes as well. The cessation of fratricidal struggle within the Church resulted in a considerable consolidation of Christian communities in Crimea, and it also made possible the expansion of Christianity further east to Khazaria.

By the middle of the eighth century the traditional religion of the Khazars—which presented a mixture of the Altaic Shamanism and worship of the firmament (*tangri*) with the native Caucasian cults—was on the wane because of the missionary activities of Christians, Moslems, and Jews.[116] Representatives of each of these three great religions tried to convert the kagan to their respective faiths. Owing to considerations of a political nature the kagans proved reluctant to accept either Christianity or Islam, since conversion to Christianity would mean recognition of the supreme authority of the Byzantine emperor rather than merely that of the patriarch, while conversion to Islam would equally make the kagan a vassal of the caliph, at

112. On the iconoclastic movement see Bury, *1889*, pp. 428-438; Ostrogorsky, pp. 103-119.

113. Vasiliev, p. 89.

114. Bury, *1889*, pp. 497-498.

115. Bury, *Eastern*, pp. 56-76; Ostrogorsky, pp. 138-146.

116. Vernadsky, *Conversion*, pp. 78-79.

least nominally. On the other hand, Judaism was politically neutral, and conversion to this faith would not involve political commitments to any of his neighbors. And so Judaism eventually became the religion of the kagan and his court.

The precise date of the kagan's conversion is not known. According to the expanded version of the alleged letter of King Joseph, the kagan accepted Judaism around A.D. 620,[117] which is impossible in view of the whole historical background. Moreover, as we have mentioned,[118] Joseph's alleged letter is a rather dubious source. On the basis of a statement by Jehuda Halevy it has been suggested that the conversion took place not in 620 but a century later, about 740;[119] but this date is also hardly credible since from the Life of St. Abo it is known that the kagan was still a "pagan" in 782.[120] According to Mas'udi the Khazars accepted Judaism in the reign of the caliph Harun ar-Rashid (786-809).[121] However, we may recall that the kagan remained "pagan" even at the time of the mission of Constantine the Philosopher (St. Cyril, apostle of the Slavs), around 861.[122] Therefore the conversion to Judaism cannot have taken place until some time after that date.

7. Byzantium and the Bulgars, the Franks and the Avars, 739-805.

From the fortunes of the Don and Azov area we have now to turn once more to the Danube region and the Balkans, in order to take up the study of the Bulgaro-Antic state. With the death of Khan Sevar (739) the Dulo Dynasty came to an end, and trouble started immediately since the *boils* were not able to come to any agreement as to the election of a new khan. Each *boil* clan supported its own elder as candidate for the throne. Finally, Kormisosh of the Vokil (or Ukil) clan was elected khan.[123]

The position of the new khan was very difficult and it appears that in the beginning of his reign his authority was nominal only. The influential *boils* considered themselves not at all bound to submit to him, and were always ready openly to defy him. Generally

117. Kokovtsov, pp. 89-103.
118. See Sec. 1, above.
119. Kokovtsov, pp. 131-132.
120. St. Abo, pp. 23-28.
121. Mas'udi, II, 8.
122. See below, Chap. VIII, Sec. 5.
123. Runciman, p. 35.

speaking, there were two parties among the *boils* at the time. One advocated friendship with the Byzantine Empire and would not have objected to a complete Byzantinization of their country. The other party, which may be called that of the Old Guard, hated both the empire and Christianity and called for war. It is not clear to which of the two parties Kormisosh himself belonged. In any case he sustained peaceful relations with the empire during about fifteen years.

In 755 an event happened which closed the era of peace. Emperor Constantine V, son and successor to Leo III, an iconoclast like his father and like him an able military leader idolized by his troops, decided to fortify the Thracian border for any future eventuality.[124] He therefore had a chain of strong forts built in Thrace along the Bulgarian border, and settled there several thousands of Syrians and Armenians on whose loyalty he could depend. This move met with hostility on the part of the Bulgars, who saw in it a violation of the provisions of the treaty of 716. They demanded some kind of compensation, and when Constantine refused any a war started between the empire and the Bulgars which was to last, with intermissions, for several decades.[125]

The war began with an impetuous foray of the Bulgars, who succeeded in penetrating as far as the Long Wall. There, however, they were attacked and defeated by Constantine's imperial troops (756). Soon after the battle the khan, Kormisosh, died and was replaced by his son Vinek. The Slavs (or the Anto-Slavs) in Thrace and Macedonia profited by the clash between the Bulgars and the empire in an attempt to revolt against both. Constantine on his way back from the Bulgarian campaign succeeded in suppressing the insurrection (758), but when he returned to Constantinople leaving only a small force on the frontier the Slavs rose up again and this time called the Bulgars to their assistance. The Byzantine troops were now defeated (759), but dissension among the Bulgar chieftains prevented the Bulgars and Slavs from getting the full benefit of their victory. In 761 Khan Vinek was assassinated with all his kin and the leader of the revolt, one Telets from the Ugain clan, was elected the new khan.[126]

Preparing himself and his army for a new war against the empire,

124. Bury, *1889*, p. 470.
125. *Idem*, pp. 471 ff.
126. Runciman, p. 37.

Telets decided to use the Slavs to reinforce his regular army and demanded from them a levy in mass. The Slavs of southern Thrace and Macedonia, being weary of constant warfare, proved reluctant to comply with the order, to avoid which they decided to emigrate to more quiet regions. While during the past few years they had wavered between the empire and the Bulgars, they now reckoned that subjection to the latter would be heavier to bear, and consequently petitioned the emperor, Constantine, pledging their loyalty and asking for permission to move to some peaceful district of Asia Minor. Constantine graciously agreed, whereupon several Slav tribes, numbering over two hundred thousand, moved to Bithynia to lands allotted them along the Artan River (762).[127] Simultaneously other Slavic tribes—those of central and northern Thrace—accepted the demands of the Bulgar khan and mustered an auxiliary corps twenty thousand strong. With his army thus reinforced Telets invaded southern Thrace, seized some of the Byzantine forts, and began building new ones of his own.[128]

Realizing the seriousness of the situation, Constantine shipped part of his cavalry by sea to the mouth of the Danube in order to create a diversion in the Bulgars' rear while he personally led his main army to the city of Anchial, where a bloody encounter took place resulting in a defeat of the Bulgars (763).[129] The imperial army itself, however, suffered such losses, that Constantine was not able to pursue the enemy and chose to return to his capital instead, where he celebrated his triumph by circus games. The khan, Telets, paid for his failure with his life, being murdered by the hostile *boils* in the same way he himself had killed his predecessor two years before.[130] Riots then started in Bulgaria, one candidate for the throne superseding another in rapid succession, and some asking for Byzantine support. The power of the Bulgars was seriously undermined, and in 768 they sued for peace.[131]

Constantine accepted, since in his opinion they were so much weakened that they ceased to constitute any threat to the empire.

127. Nicephorus Patriarcha, pp. 68-69; Theophanes, p. 432.

128. Runciman, p. 38.

129. The date 763, is according to A. Lombard, *Constantin V* (Paris, 1902), p. 48; Ostrogorsky, p. 114, follows Lombard. Zlatarski, I, 1, p. 213, dates the battle 762, in which he is seconded by Runciman, p. 38.

130. Runciman, p. 39.

131. Bury, *1889*, pp. 472-473; Runciman, pp. 39-40.

He miscalculated, however, since after a year or two of peace they recovered from the effects of their defeat and under a new khan, the energetic Telerig, were again ready for any adventure. Therefore Constantine reopened military operations, and in May 773 a fleet of two thousand boats was mustered and sent to the mouth of Danube. It was in this fleet that the "Russian" or "Red" squadron mentioned above[132] was included. Simultaneously the imperial army set forth overland. Caught between two fires the Bulgars once more sued for peace. The emperor agreed to discontinue his military activities and to receive the Bulgar envoy at Constantinople, whither one of the leading *boils* was accordingly sent. While the negotiations were dragging along without achieving quick result, the khan Telerig prepared an expedition against a Slav tribe settled in Berzetia (or Verzitia) in Thessaly.[133] His plan was to compel this tribe to move into the confines of the Bulgar Khanate. Consequently a Bulgar brigade twelve thousand strong was dispatched to Thessaly. Telerig's scheme became known to the emperor Constantine in advance through spies. The emperor immediately concentrated an army eighty thousand strong on the outskirts of Constantinople, pretending to the Bulgar envoy that it was intended for a campaign against the Arabs. He then secretly led the army by forced marches to a mountain pass on the route of the Bulgarian expedition, where he attacked the unsuspecting Bulgars, who fled panic-stricken.[134]

Following this event the Bulgars accepted a peace treaty by which each side pledged to abstain from any act of aggression toward the other. Actually, however, both sides immediately began to prepare themselves for a continuation of the struggle. Telerig somehow succeeded in obtaining a list of Byzantine secret agents in Bulgaria, and ordered all of them slain, after which the emperor Constantine moved his army against the Bulgars.[135] It was only his unexpected death from ague in the beginning of the campaign (775), that saved Bulgaria from Byzantine invasion. The Bulgars, however, did not profit by this mercy, since another spell of internal turmoil now fell upon them and in 777 Khan Telerig was compelled to flee to Con-

132. See Sec. 5, above.
133. Theophanes, p. 447.
134. Runciman, p. 41.
135. *Idem,* p. 42.

stantinople, where he was promptly baptized and married to a Greek girl.[136] He never after had occasion to return to his native country.

A decade of peace between Byzantium and Bulgaria followed, after which new clashes ensued, with intermittent fortune for either side. In 797 the empress Irene came to the throne after having her son Constantine VI arrested and blinded.[137] In spite of this cruel deed she proved to be of placid disposition in her international policies and succeeded in restoring peace in Thrace. Feeling secure from any further threat from Byzantium, the Bulgars could now divert their attention to the middle Danubian problem. While the Avar horde centering in Pannonia had been by this time considerably weakened, it was still able to hold its ground until the end of the eighth century, when it had to face the Frankish menace. In 791 Charlemagne after inflicting a series of defeats on the Avars penetrated as far east as Raab. In 796 his son Pipin routed the Avars on the banks of the Tisa River, seizing the khan's headquarters and immense booty. In order to protect the Frankish kingdom from any future Avar raid a new border province was organized by the Franks, known as *Ostmark* (Austria).[138]

The assumption of the imperial title by Charlemagne (800) was an event of paramount significance for the further development of international politics in Europe, and it also had important repercussions in the Near East. Theoretically Charlemagne restored the Roman Empire; actually, it was a new political body—the Holy Empire of the German Nation—which now came to being.[139] It could be expected that the new empire would not be held valid by the Byzantine Government, since according to the Byzantine doctrine the Roman Empire had never died but continued to live in Constantinople, the "new Rome." However, Empress Irene who now represented the new Rome was not in a position to stop Charlemagne and chose to compromise.[140] The activities of Charlemagne, conqueror both of the once dread Avars and of a number of west Slavic tribes, deeply impressed the southern Slavs as well,

136. *Idem,* p. 43.

137. Bury, *1889,* p. 488.

138. Halphen, p. 241.

139. The standard, though now somewhat antiquated, work is J. Bryce, *The Holy Roman Empire* (rev. ed., New York and London, 1904). See also K. Heldmann, *Das Kaisertum Karls des Grossen* (Weimar, 1928).

140. Bury, *1889,* p. 490; Ostrogorsky, pp. 126-128.

and it is supposed that the Slavic word for king (*kral', korol'*) is nothing more than a transliteration of Charlemagne's name (Karl).[141]

As to the Franko-Avar War, the Bulgars did not fail to take advantage of the weakening of the Avars. As we have seen,[142] after the dismemberment of Great Bulgaria one of the Bulgarian hordes migrated to Pannonia and submitted itself to the Avar kagan. Now these Pannonian Bulgars revolted against their masters and got in touch with their Balkan kin. In 803 the Avars were attacked from two sides: Charlemagne fell upon them from the west and the Bulgarian khan, Krum, from the east. The war ended with the complete destruction of the Avar Kaganate, its possessions being divided between the Franks and the Bulgars.[143] The latter occupied both banks of the Danube up to the mouth of the Tisa. Above the Tisa the left bank was held by the Franks, while the Slavic tribes on the right bank as far as the mouth of the Drava recognized the authority of Khan Krum, who succeeded in clearing his new possessions of the remnants of the Avar horde by 805.

8. Byzantium and the Bulgars during the Reign of Khan Krum.

The downfall of the Avar Kaganate made a powerful impression on the whole Slavic world. The tradition about it was alive even in the eleventh century, and the compiler of the Russian *Primary Chronicle* inserted the following note into his manuscript: "The Obry [i.e., Avars] were large in stature and proud in spirit, and God destroyed them, and they all perished, and not one of them survived. And there is to this day a proverb in Russia, which runs: They perished like the Obry." [144]

It is but natural that through his victory over the Avars Khan Krum[145] was now considered by the Balkan Slavs the successor of the once dreaded Avar kagan, and the Bulgars became to a certain extent political heirs of the Avars. According to the Byzantine lexicographer Suidas, of the tenth century, following their victory

141. Shakhmatov, *Sudby,* p. 26.
142. See Chap. V, Sec. 8
143. Howorth, pp. 801-805; Runciman, p. 50.
144. Adapted from Cross, p. 141.
145. On Krum see Runciman, pp. 51-70; Zlatarski, I, 1, pp. 247-292.

over the Avars the Bulgar grandees began to wear clothes of Avar style. Suidas likewise informs us that Krum asked advice of his Avar prisoners with regard to legislation.[146] Krum's possessions now extended far to the north. The course of the river Tisa marked the boundary between the Frankish and the Bulgar states. From the upper parts of Tisa the Bulgar boundary line turned east, and on the eastern side of the Carpathian Mountains reached the upper section of the Pruth River. It then followed the course of the Pruth downstream, south to Leovo, whence it turned east again, crossing Bessarabia to the Dniester River. This overland line across Bessarabia was fortified by a fosse and earthen rampart.[147] Continuing along the course of the lower Dniester the boundary then touched the Black Sea shore at the mouth of the Dniester. It is to be noted that the areas of Moldavia and southern Bessarabia, included in the Bulgarian state, had been for centuries settled—at least in part—by the Antes. A strong Bulgarian garrison was probably stationed in southern Bessarabia to watch over the movements of the Magyars and the Slavs in the Dnieper area.

The consolidation of Bulgarian rule over the newly acquired territories north of the Danube and the strengthening of the northern frontier must have required several years. Simultaneously Khan Krum paid much attention both to the reorganization of his army and to administrative reforms aimed at weakening the Bulgar aristocracy, the *boils*. With such an object in mind he decided to increase the role of his Slavic subjects, and some of the Slavic elders (*zhupan*) appeared at his court to be entrusted with various commissions. One of them, Dragomir, was Krum's envoy to Constantinople in 812. Slavic was widely spoken at Krum's headquarters, and it is said that at court banquets he used to drink the health of his guests in Slavic.[148] It is hard to obtain a definite idea of Krum's legislation from Suidas' statements, but his plan appears to have consisted in limiting the sway of the aristocracy over the common people. Thus according to Suidas[149] the rich were ordered by Krum to help the poor, under threat of confiscation of their possessions. Those who harbored "thieves" faced the same threat

146. Suidas, *s.v.* Βούλγαροι (I, 483-484).
147. Feher, pp. 8-23; Zlatarski, I, 1, pp. 248-249.
148. Zlatarski, I, 1, pp. 262, 290.
149. Suidas, as in n. 146, above.

under another of his laws, which may have been intended not against petty thieves but against political offenders, and which in such a case we may interpret as an attempt to stop the custom of private warfare between the grandees.[150] As to the army, it was now reinforced by the incorporation into it of Slavic detachments as regular units; with Bulgar officers, however, to command them.

The Byzantine War started in 807 and proceeded with intermittent success, but on the whole with marked advantage to the Bulgars. In 809 the strong Byzantine fortress of Sardica (modern Sofia) surrendered. Among the prisoners the most valuable proved to be an Arab engineer, who agreed to enter Krum's service and take charge of machinery necessary for besieging fortresses.[151] In order to avenge the loss of Sardica, Emperor Nicephorus laid siege to the Bulgarian capital Pliska, which was taken and destroyed, and most of its inhabitants slain (811). After this, however, the Byzantine army was surrounded by the Bulgars in a mountain gorge and completely routed. Nicephorus himself perished in battle, and Krum ordered a goblet made from the emperor's skull.[152] The goblet was plated with silver, and the victorious khan used it for toasts at state banquets.

Next year the Bulgars set forth to Constantinople and succeeded in seizing some of the forts in the outer line of fortifications protecting the Byzantine capital. Not expecting to take the city by either siege or storm, Krum offered peace based on the provisions of the treaty of 716, which seemed quite reasonable, but in spite of his moderation the new emperor Michael I declined the offer. Krum then decided to occupy the important fortress of Mesembria on the gulf of Burgas, which could serve him as a base for future operations. Taking the fortress with the help of siege machinery, the Bulgars seized large booty, among which was a supply of the secret stuff for the "Greek fire" and thirty-six flame throwers.[153] In 813 Krum again approached Constantinople. By this time another change had occurred on the Byzantine throne, and sly Leo the Armenian was occupying it. He professed his readiness to conclude

150. Zlatarski, I, 1, pp. 285-287.

151. Runciman, pp. 54-55. On Krum's poliorcetic machines see Zlatarski, I, 1, pp. 415-420.

152. Runciman, p. 57.

153. *Idem*, p. 61.

peace, but demanded a personal interview with Krum, intending to seize the latter treacherously during the meeting. The plot did not work, however, and the infuriated khan retaliated by laying waste the suburbs of the capital.[154] Krum then turned his attention to the city of Odrin (Adrianople) which had already been surrounded by the Bulgars but was still holding. When the khan ordered the siege machines to be brought close to the walls, the inhabitants of the city surrendered, the more so since there was no food left in the city. The city was destroyed and the remaining population, about ten thousand families, moved north to Bessarabia. Among those deported were Archbishop Manuel and several Byzantine officials with their families, including the parents of the future emperor Basil I. Since Adrianople belonged to the Macedonian *theme* (military district), the section of Bessarabia to which the inhabitants of Adrianople were moved also became known as Macedonia.[155] The settlers were given arms and organized as frontier guards to protect the boundary against any Magyar raid. Slavs were settled in the Adrianople district instead.

Under the Bulgarian pressure the Byzantine Government decided to ask the Frankish emperor Louis I for assistance. Envoys were sent to him, accordingly, to negotiate a military alliance of the Western and Eastern Empires against the Bulgars.[156] Before the Byzantine envoys reached their destination, news of Krum's death was received in Constantinople. The dreaded khan had died of stroke, on April 13, 814.[157]

9. *Bulgar Policies under Khan Omortag, 814-831.*

Krum's successor was his young son Omortag. Taking advantage of his youth and inexperience the *boils* seized the reins of government. Their most prominent leader was Chok (Τζόκος).[158] The *boils* represented the conservative Bulgar party, opposed to Chris-

154. *Idem,* pp. 63-64.

155. *Idem,* p. 65. Recently, H. Grégoire (*Habitat,* pp. 270-274) has suggested that it was these Macedonian settlers on the Danube who were mentioned by some Oriental writers under the name of *Vnndr*. Grégoire's theory is very ingenious but the problem of *Vnndr* requires further investigation.

156. *Idem,* pp. 67-68.

157. *Idem,* p. 68.

158. On Chok see Bury, *Eastern,* p. 359; Grégoire, *Sources,* p. 767; Runciman, p. 71; Zlatarski, I, 1, pp. 293-294.

tianity and apparently also to Slavdom. Christians were subjected to persecution and many of them slain, among others Manuel, the former archbishop of Adrianople. The ruling *boils* were, however, wise enough to restore friendly relations with the Byzantine Empire, and in the winter of 816 a peace treaty was concluded for the term of thirty years, subject to renewal every ten years.[159] By the provisions of the treaty the fortress of Sardica was returned to the empire.

The attention of the Bulgar Government now turned to the north. According to an inscription dated between 818 and 820,[160] a Bulgar *kopan* (a title which probably corresponded to the Slavic *zhupan*) named Okors, of the clan of Chakagar, was drowned in the Dnieper during a campaign. We may thus assume that the Bulgars undertook at that time a campaign, or perhaps several campaigns, against the Magyars and the Dnieper Slavs. The name of the clan to which the drowned Bulgar chieftain belonged, Chakagar (which is the plural form), may be compared to the name Chok. It is to be noted in this connection that a similar name was known to old Kievan tradition recorded in the Russian *Primary Chronicle*.[161] According to the Kievan legend, the name of one of the three brothers who founded Kiev was Shchok (the other two were Kiy and Khoriv).[162] This name is obviously very close to such Bulgarian names as Chok and Chakagar. The question naturally arises, could not one of the Bulgarian chieftains (perhaps Chok himself, or one of his clan) have penetrated as far as Kiev during a Bulgar campaign of this period?

In the beginning of Omortag's reign a new palace was built in the old khan's capital, Pliska,[163] to replace that destroyed by the Greeks in 811. Omortag later decided to move his headquarters farther to the south, closer to the Balkan mountain passes, so as to be in a better position to watch events in southern Thrace. Accordingly, a new palace was built on the bank of the Tutsa River, a

159. Runciman, pp. 72-73. Doelger, I, 48, refers the treaty to 814.

160. Aboba-Pliska, p. 190. Beshevliev, No. 1 (p. 43) and pp. 65-69; Runciman, p. 81; Zlatarski, I, 1, p. 294.

161. Cross, p. 145.

162. See below, Chap. VIII, Sec. 4.

163. The site of Omortag's castle has been excavated by the Russian Archaeological Institute in Constantinople under the direction of F. I. Uspenskii and K. Shkorpil. See *Aboba;* also, Feher, pp. 41-52

tributary to the Dotsin River which discharges into the Black Sea south of Varna. The building was completed by 821, the new capital receiving the Slavic name of Preslav.[164]

Omortag maintained friendly relations with the empire and was able to give valuable assistance at the time of the revolt of Thomas "the Slav" (821-823).[165] Thomas' rebellion was the upshot of the palace revolution which took place in Constantinople in 820, when Emperor Leo V was murdered by the captain of his guard, who then proclaimed himself emperor under the name of Michael II. While most of the leading officials and army generals recognized the usurper, Thomas refused to do so. He commanded one of the Byzantine army corps in Asia Minor which consisted mostly of Slavs, descendants of the Slavs who had settled in Bithynia in the eighth century.[166] It is possible that Thomas himself was of Slavic origin. His rebellion was supported by some other army corps stationed in Asia Minor, as well as by Georgians and Armenians. He likewise succeeded in taking advantage of the opposition of a part of the clergy and the population at large to the iconoclastic policy of the Constantinople government, and proclaimed a restoration of the veneration of icons as his major objective. Another aspect of Thomas' uprising was that of social revolution. He was supported by peasants, most of whom by that time had become serfs.

Since he controlled part of the Byzantine fleet, Thomas was able to besiege Constantinople from both sea and land. As soon as he crossed the Bosporus, crowds of Macedonian and Thracian Slavs rushed to his banners. It was at this juncture that the emperor Michael II asked Khan Omortag for assistance.[167] The latter was probably himself worried enough by the spread of the revolutionary spirit among his Slavic subjects, and was consequently ready to oblige the emperor by sending a Bulgar army to help him. While the Bulgars took care of Thomas' overland troops, the flotilla was destroyed by what navy remained at the emperor's disposal, and thus the abortive revolution came to a close. Thomas himself was taken prisoner and executed.[168]

164. Feher, pp. 52-58; Runciman, pp. 77-78.

165. On the uprising of Thomas "the Slav" see Bury, *Eastern*, pp. 84-110; E. Lipshits, "Vosstanie Fomy Slavianina," *VDI*, I (1939), 352-365; Ostrogorsky, pp. 142-143; Vasiliev, Arabes, I, 22-49. Vasiliev considers Thomas an Armenian.

166. See Sec. 7, above; also Chap. VI, Sec. 6.

167. Bury, *Eastern*, pp. 100-102.

168. *Idem*, p. 106.

By this time the attention of the Bulgars had shifted to the northwest, where serious complications with the Franks were threatening. As we have seen,[169] following the downfall of the Avar Khanate, the Slavic tribes of the Srem region, between the Sava and the Danube, recognized the authority of the Bulgar khan. The Croats, however, whose abodes were west of Srem, submitted themselves to the Franks. Apparently neither of those two Slavic groups were satisfied with their respective suzerains, since in 818 the Srem tribes asked Emperor Louis to receive them under his authority, while in 819 the Croat prince Ludevit revolted against him.[170] The Srem leaders then decided to join Ludevit, and it looked as if a new Croat-Srem-Slav state had come into being, but after a few years the Franks succeeded in suppressing Ludevit's rebellion and both Croatia and Srem were occupied by the Franks (822).[171]

At this point the Bulgars, who considered Srem within their sphere of influence, voiced their protest. Negotiations between Omortag and Louis dragged on for several years, but the Franks were not willing to make any concessions and in 827 a war started between them.[172] Bulgarian troops were sent in boats up the Danube and the Drava. The Slavs drove away the Frankish administration officials, who were now replaced by Bulgarian agents. The Franks came back next year only to be expelled once more, after which they agreed to negotiate for peace. In 832 the Bulgar envoys were received by Louis, and a peace treaty was concluded the exact provisions of which are not known.[173] In any case the Srem region remained under Bulgar control, and it was from that time that the old fortress Singidun at the confluence of the Sava and the Danube became known by the Slavic name of Belgrad (Beograd).

10. The Political Crisis in the North Pontic Area, 831-839.

We have now to turn our attention back to the Russian Kaganate. Unfortunately, information for this period is extremely scarce. The Arabic geographers paid little attention to the history of the kaganate, and by the time Constantine Porphyrogenitus wrote his book the political center of the Rus had shifted from the Azov region to Kiev.

169. See Sec. 6, above.
170. Dvornik, *Slaves,* p. 47.
171. *Idem,* pp. 48-49.
172. *Idem,* p. 50.
173. Runciman, p. 83.

We may suppose that after the seizure of the city of Doras in Crimea by the Khazars, around 787, the Byzantine Government attempted to use the Russians against the Khazars.[174] As was repeatedly the case, a barbaric nation, drawn by Byzantine diplomacy into the vortex of international politics with the object of assisting the empire, later at the first opportunity turned against the empire's possessions. It appears that this is precisely what happened in Crimea after 787. The Russians helped to expel the Khazars from Doras, and seized Surozh (Sugdaea), which made them a menace to all the Byzantine possessions in Crimea.[175] For a number of years the Byzantine Government was not in a position to retaliate, since until 815 the empire was engaged in a disastrous war with the Danubian Bulgars, and then the uprising of Thomas the Slav endangered its very existence, after which there was also a war against the Arabs.

It was only in the reign of Emperor Theophilus (829-42) that the Byzantine Government was able to pay greater attention to the Russian problem, and even then the initiative was taken by the Khazars, to whom the growing strength of the Rus meant a great deal of trouble. Around 833 the Khazar kagan dispatched envoys to Emperor Theophilus asking him to send competent engineers for building a fortress on the Don River, because of the danger from enemies.[176] Unfortunately, neither the author of the continuation of Theophanes' chronicle nor Constantine Porphyrogenitus, both of whom record this episode, explain what enemies are meant. Some modern students of the problem have suggested their identification as the Patzinaks, others have been ready to see the Magyars in them.[177] However, the Patzinak inroads reached their climax much later, and the Magyars were still at the time of the Khazar embassy the kagan's vassals. Therefore we must agree with such scholars as J. B. Bury[178] and A. A. Vasiliev,[179] who identify the Khazars' enemies as the Russians (*Rus*). However, I cannot accept these scholars' explanation that the Russians in question were the Novgorod Varangians. It seems much more plausible that the

174. See Sec. 6, above.

175. On the Russian attack on Sugdaea (Surozh) see Sec. 5, above. That the Russians may have helped the Goths to expel the Khazars from Doras is my surmise only.

176. *De Adm.*, 42; Theophanes Continuatus, pp. 122-124.

177. Vasiliev, p. 109.

178. Bury, *Eastern*, p. 418.

179. Vasiliev, p. 111.

Russians against whom the Khazars wanted a fortress built were the Azov Rus. It was to bar their way from the Sea of Azov to the Volga that the fortress was needed; also possibly, as a secondary object, to sever their lines of communication with their kin in North Russia, who did not as yet, however, control the city of Novgorod.

Emperor Theophilus agreed to assist the Khazars and sent them an impressive expedition headed by the *spatharo-candidate* Petronas Kamateros.[180] Petronas' flotilla set forth for Cherson (Korsun) where it was joined by another squadron sent from Paphlagonia. In Cherson the materials were reloaded into smaller boats, in which the troops and the engineers were then shipped through Kerch Strait and across the Sea of Azov to the mouth of the Don, and up the Don to the site selected for the fortress, at the mouth of Tsymla River near the modern town of Tsymlianskaya. The fortress was built on the left bank of the Don.[181] The central castle was of white stone, while the outer wall was of brick with boulders used as foundation. Brick had been made on the spot in kilns built by Byzantine technicians.

The fortress became known as Sarkel, which means in Ugric "White House."[182] The Russian chroniclers call it the "White Tower" (*Belaia Vezha*).[183] It is probable that smaller forts were built along the Don both above and below.

Having executed his mission, Petronas presented to his government a general report in which he stressed the desirability of strengthening the imperial power in Crimea by appointing a military governor (*strategos*). The project was approved by Emperor Theophilus, and Petronas himself was appointed to the post with the title of "Military Governor of the Climates," as the mountain districts of Crimea inhabited by the Goths were known.[184] The city of Cherson which had been autonomous since the times of Justinian II[185] was now subject to the new governor.

We may suppose that before long the Russians must have felt

180. *Idem,* 115.

181. M. I. Artamonov, "Srednevekovye poseleniia na nizhnem Donu," *GA, 131* (1935); *Idem,* "Sarkel," *SA,* VI (1940), 130-165. Of the older literature on Sarkel see Kh. I. Popov, "Gde nakhodilas Khazarskaia krepost Sarkel?," *TAS,* IX, *1* (1895).

182. In Greek, *Ἄσπρον Ὀσπίτιον.*

183. Cross, p. 171.

184. Vasiliev, p. 108.

185. See Chap. VI, Sec. 6.

painfully the new pressure imposed on them by both the building of Sarkel and the consolidation of imperial military power in the Crimea, and probably because of this they decided to send envoys to Constantinople for negotiations. The Russian embassy arrived in the imperial city some time in 838.[186] Nothing is known of the course of the negotiations, but it is obvious that they ended in an impasse, since the envoys were not allowed to return home but were, under a suitable pretext, sent west instead. It may be assumed that the emperor was not willing to make any concessions to the Russians, since it was not in his interest to quarrel with the Khazars.

The pretext by which the envoys were prevented from proceeding homeward was that a dangerous situation had developed along their return route, due to the attacks of some barbaric tribes. Probably the appearance of the Magyars in the lower Danube area was meant in this case. This was all connected with the Bulgarian troubles. In 836 the second decade since the conclusion of the peace treaty between Byzantium and the Bulgars came to an end, and according to the provisions of the original treaty (concluded in 816) it had to be renewed every ten years.[187] It appears that the treaty was not renewed in 836 and that the Bulgar khan Malamir, Omortag's successor, seized Sardica and started a campaign against Salonika. The sequence of events and their chronology is not quite clear, however, because of some confusion in the sources.[188] In any case it has been sufficiently established that relations between the Byzantine Government and the Bulgars at the end of the 830's were strained, and that the former started secret parleys with the Macedonians who had been deported by Khan Krum from Adrianople to Bessarabia.[189] They were now eager to return to their old abodes. In order to ship them back, Emperor Theophilus sent a flotilla of boats to the mouth of the Danube. Since the main Bulgar army was at the time engaged in the Salonika campaign, the Bulgars had insufficient forces to prevent the Macedonian exiles from reaching the boats sent to their rescue, and in consequence invited a Magyar horde from beyond the Dniester River to attack the exiles. However, the latter were well organized and beat the Magyars off.[190]

186. Bury, *Eastern,* p. 418.

187. See Sec. 9, above.

188. On the Danubian crisis of 836-839 see Bury, *Eastern,* pp. 370-373; Grot, pp. 225-233; Runciman, pp. 85-88; Zlatarski, pp. 337-341.

189. See Sec. 8, above.

190. Grot, p. 227.

After this the "Macedonians" boarded the boats and were brought safely to Constantinople, in the outskirts of which lands were allotted them for settlement.

It is probably these troublesome events which served the Byzantine Government as a pretext for not allowing the Russian envoys to proceed homeward. They were obliged instead to join the Byzantine embassy which was at that juncture being sent to Emperor Louis I at Ingelheim. The arrival of this embassy has been recorded in the *Bertinian Annals* under the date of January 17, 839,[191] and a resumé of the contents of the letter sent by Theophilus to Louis was likewise inserted which, so far as it concerns the Russian envoys, reads as follows:

> He [Theophilus] also sent along with them [the Byzantine envoys] certain men who stated that their tribe is known as Rus and that their ruler is known as the kagan [*Chacanus*]; he [Theophilus] asked that the emperor [Louis] allow them to return home across his possessions since the roads by which they had come to Constantinople were cut by wild and cruel tribes, and he did not want them to face danger in case of returning by the same route.

According to the chronicler these men (the Russian envoys) proved to be Swedes by birth (*eos gente esse Suenorum*). Considering them suspicious the Frankish emperor ordered them arrested for more complete investigation. We may suppose that this move was the result of secret advice from Constantinople.

191. *Ann. Bert. s.a.* 839; cf. Kruse, pp. 132-133.

CHAPTER VIII.

THE BACKGROUND OF KIEVAN RUSSIA, 839-878.

1. The Russian Tribes in the Ninth Century.

THE *Book of Annals* (*Povest' Vremennykh Let*) compiled in the twelfth century on the basis of the *Primary Chronicle* of the eleventh century opens with a general ethnographic and geographic introduction, after which entries arranged by years follow. In the introductory part the compiler of the *Book* deals in a general way with the aboriginal Slavic tribes including the Russian. However, no comprehensive survey of these tribes is offered; several lists of tribes are quoted separately of which none is identical with any other. It seems probable therefore that the compiler of the *Book* had at his disposal a number of sources which he did not succeed in digesting, also that he may have arranged certain tribes in groups because of the particular historical background they had in common.

Let us examine from this point of view the two lists of Russian tribes on folio 4 and folio 6 of the Hypatian manuscript respectively.[1] The first list contains the following names: the Polianians, Drevlianians, Dregovichians, Polochanians, Slovenians (of Novgorod) and Severians (*Severo*). To this list the Krivichians should be added, of whom the Polochanians formed only a branch. Smolensk was the chief town of the Krivichians. Generally speaking, tribes of western and northern Russia are comprised in this list. The second list is as follows: the Polianians, Drevlianians, Severians, Radimichians, Viatichians, Khorvatians, Dulebians, Ulichians, and Tivertsi. We may note that the tribes mentioned here are those of central and southwestern Russia, or of Ukraine.

By comparing these two lists we may see that three tribes: The Polianians, the Drevlianians, and the Severians, are included in both of them. All three were living either in the Kiev area or close to it. We may suppose therefore that both lists were compiled by chroniclers who in each case started their survey of tribes from

1. Hyp., cols. 5-6 and 10. On the ethnography of the *Book of Annals* see Barsov, pp. 7-13; A. Pogodin, "Die Bericht der russischen Chronik ueber die Gruendung des russischen Staates," *ZOG, 5* (1931), 194-214.

Kiev. If we now consider not the tribes common to the two lists but those mentioned in one of the lists only, we may speak of two groups of Russian tribes: the northwestern, and the southern. While these lists were recorded in the eleventh century, there is no doubt that most of the tribes mentioned in them existed much earlier. We have seen[2] that Procopius, historian of the sixth century, gives the names of only two major Slav groups, the Sclaveni and the Antes. However, each of them must have comprised a number of smaller divisions, and Procopius himself speaks on one occasion of the "innumerable tribes of the Antes." [3] Jordanis, who knows both the Sclaveni and the Antes (as well as the Venethi in the north), likewise states that the names of the Slavic tribes vary in different clans and localities.[4] Unfortunately neither he nor Procopius took the trouble to give even a tentative list of these smaller tribes and clans.

If we turn to the Byzantine sources of the eighth and ninth centuries, we shall find information concerning the Balkan Slavs only. We have already met some of these tribes in dealing with the southern expansion of the Danubian Bulgars.[5] We have now to examine their names more closely. According to the chronicle of Theophanes Confessor, when the Bulgars started their drive into Thrace at the end of the seventh century,[6] they first conquered the Severians (Σέβερεις) and the Seven Clans (ἑπτα γενεαί).[7] The name "Severians" is of course identical with the name of one of the Russian tribes quoted above. As to the Seven Clans, in my opinion they may be identified with one of the two other Russian tribes, the Radimichians and Viatichians. It is significant that the Russian Radimichians and Viatichians lived in close proximity to the Russian Severians, just as did the Balkan Severians and the Seven Clans. Furthermore, turning to the archaeological evidence, among the antiquities of the Radimichians and the Viatichians characteristic seven-petaled pendants have been found. Each petal of the Viatichian pendant is shaped like an oblong shield, while the Radimichian has a triangular shape.[8] In my opinion this pendant may be considered as the tribe emblem, and the number of petals

2. See Chap. III, Sec. 7.
3. Procopius, VIII, 4, 9.
4. Jordanis, Sec. 34.
5. See Chap. VI, Sec. 6.
6. *Ibid.*
7. Theophanes, p. 359; cf. Niederle, II, 415-416.
8. Gotie, pp. 212-215.

shows that the tribe was composed of seven clans, just as the Balkan Seven Clans. It must also be noted that while most of the names of the Russian tribes are repeated in the Balkans, the name of neither Radimichians nor Viatichians is ever mentioned, which makes it even more likely that these two tribes, or at least one of them, was represented in the Balkans by the Seven Clans. It should be noted that seven was a sacred number with the Iranians and the old Iranian name of the city of Theodosia in Crimea, for example, was Abdarda, which means "Seven Sides."[9]

South of the Balkan Severians and the Seven Clans, in the Rodop Mountains, the tribe of the Dregovichians had their abodes. One of the members of the Church Council at Constantinople in 879 was Bishop Peter of the Dregovichians (ὁ Δρουγοβιτίας).[10] The Polianians and the Smolianians (Σμολαίνοι or Σμολεάνοι) are mentioned among the Macedonian tribes of the tenth century.[11] The tribes of Polianians, Krivichians, and Drevlianians are known to have settled in the Peloponnesus.[12]

The coincidence of tribal names between the Balkan Slavs and the Russian Slavs cannot be accidental. It is obvious that the Balkan and Russian tribes in question are but different branches of the same original tribes. Some of them must have belonged to the Sclaveni group, others to the Antes. In Procopius' time both the Sclaveni and the Antes occupied vast regions north of the lower Danube. Later on, part of them moved south to Thrace and Macedonia. As a result of subsequent events, especially of the Avar invasion, the Anto-Slavic bloc on the lower Danube was split, part of each tribe or group of tribes going south to be subsequently subdued by either Byzantium or the Bulgars, and the others going north to become eventually members of the Kievan Rus federation.

We have now to determine, however tentatively, which of the Slavic tribes belonged to the Sclavenian group and which to the Antic. To start with the Balkan tribes, in my opinion both the Severians and the Seven Clans belonged to the Antic group. Their geographic location in the northeastern section of Thrace is an evidence in itself, since it is known that in the sixth and seventh

9. Miller, *Sledy*, p. 240.
10. Dvornik, *Slaves*, pp. 235-236; Niederle, II, 424.
11. Dvornik, *Slaves*, pp. 13 and 237; Niederle, II, 428.
12. Dvornik, *Slaves*, pp. 15-16; Niederle, II, 370.

centuries the Antes occupied the eastern portion of the lower Danube area, and the Sclaveni the western. Moreover, the very name of the Severians points to the Azov-North Caucasus connections of this particular tribe, being obviously another form of the name Sabeiri, or Saviri, that of a Bulgaro-Hunnic people of the North Caucasian area.[13] If the Balkan Severians were Antes, so must the Russian have been, and if the Seven Clans are to be identified as the Radimichians or Viatichians, this means that the Russian tribes bearing these names belonged likewise to the Antic group. The Polianians—both in the Balkans and in Russia—must be considered an Antic tribe as well. Incidentally, their very name may have been a translation of the name Antes, which originally meant the "Steppe People,"[14] as did also the name Polianians.[15] On the other hand, such tribes as the Drevlianians, the Dregovichians, the Krivichians, and the Smolianians, were most likely Sclaveni and not Antes, since in Russia these tribes formed the northwestern group, the northern spearhead of which had even preserved the actual name of the Sclaveni (the *Slovene* of Novgorod). It is characteristic that the list of northwestern tribes in the Russian *Book of Annals* (the first of the two discussed at the beginning of this section) is followed by the remark, "and thus the Slovenian nation spread about" (*i tako razydesia slovensk yazyk*).[16]

With these preliminary observations let us now turn to a survey of the expansion and the way of life of the Russian tribes of the eighth and ninth centuries. Unfortunately, on this occasion as on many others the evidence of the written sources is very scant. More can be obtained from archaeological data, but here again not enough has so far been done for our period, and most of the systematically studied Slavic kurgans and *gorodishcha* belong to a later time, that of the tenth through the thirteenth centuries.[17]

For the sake of convenience we shall examine here the background of the Russian tribes, grouping them by geographical provinces as

13. See Chap. IV, Sec. 7.
14. See Chap. III, Sec. 2.
15. From *pole*, "field"; in Old Russian, "steppe."
16. Hyp., col. 6.
17. For general information on the expansion of the Russian tribes see Barsov, pp. 67-205; Gotie, pp. 204-209; Hrushevskyi, I, 143-211; Niederle, IV, 127-213; Shakhmatov. *Sudby*, pp. 28-39; Spitsyn, *Rasselenie;* P. N. Tretiakov, "Rasselenie drevnerusskikh plemen po arkheologicheskim dannym," *SA*, IV (1937), 33-51. For general orientation in the study of the archaeological materials see Niederle, IV, 240-277, and Niederle, *Rukovet.*

follows: (a) the southwestern area; (b) the southeastern area; (c) the west; (d) the Pripet marshes area; and (e) the north.

(*a*) *The Southwestern Area.*

We include in this area the right-bank Ukraine (without Volynia and Galicia) and Bessarabia; that is, the territory from the Pruth River in the west to the lower Dnieper (below Kiev) in the east. This is the home of the western group of Antes in the sixth century. By the end of the eighth century the Magyars had penetrated to the lower Bug region. Even thereafter, single Antic settlements may have held their ground, but generally speaking the boundary between the Magyar-controlled territory and that of the Antes followed the line from Tiraspol on the lower Dniester to the mouth of the Ros on the Dnieper. The Magyars lived, in the ninth century, east of this line and the Slavs west of it.

In the ninth and the tenth centuries, within the southwestern area with which we are now dealing the following Russian tribes were settled: the Polianians, the Ulichians, and the Tivertsi. The Polianians occupied by this time most of Kiev province, the Tivertsi southern Bessarabia, and the Ulichians northern Bessarabia and the southern section of Podolia province.

The name, Tivertsi,[18] may be derived from the name of the fortress Tura (Tvra, Turris) in which Emperor Justinian I settled one of the Antic tribes, apparently the forefathers of the Tivertsi.[19] The name Tura is of course somehow connected with the ancient name of the Dniester River, Tyras (Τύρας), mentioned by Herodotus. The Greek letter υ (upsilon) was apparently used to render a sound alien to the Greek language. The original name is derived from an Iranian root (*tur* or *tvr*).[20] Therefore the Tivertsi (or Turtsi) were the Dniester River tribe.

As to the Ulichians,[21] in the various chronicles their name is read differently (*Ulichi, Uluchi, Uglichi, Ulutichi, Liutichi, Luchane*). Some scholars have accepted the form *Uglichi* which they derive from the Russian word *ugol* ("corner"), and suggest accordingly that the home of the *Uglichi* was in the southern section of

18. On the Tivertsi see Barsov, pp. 97-99; Hrushevskyi, I, 179-180; Niederle, IV, 161-162.

19. See Chap. IV, Sec. 10.

20. Sobolevskii, I, 4-5, 277.

21. Barsov, pp. 96-100; Hrushevskyi, I, 176-179; Niederle, IV, 157-161.

Bessarabia, known as "the Corner" (*Ugol*, Ὄγγλος) between the Pruth and the lower Danube.[22] At first sight the explanation seems plausible, but there are several considerations against it. First of all, in the so-called *Nikon Chronicle* Peresechen, city of the Ulichians, is mentioned.[23] This city must have been located not in the southern part of Bessarabia but in its central part, north of Kishinev.[24] Moreover, the *Nikon Chronicle* also says that the Ulichians originally lived in the lower Dnieper region and moved west of the Dniester only later on.[25] The *Nikon Chronicle* is a late compilation, however (sixteenth century). But there is one more reason not to place the Ulichians in the Bessarabian "Corner": that corner was from the sixth century occupied by the Tivertsi.[26] It thus appears that the form *Uglichi*, has insufficient support, and the form *Uluchi* or *Ulichi* should be preferred. The name *Uluchi* may be derived from the Russian *luka* ("bend").[27] We may remember in this connection the bend of the Black Sea shore between the mouths of the Dnieper and the Dniester. It is precisely here that Jordanis places the Antes generally. *"Antes vero . . . qua Ponticum mare curvatur, a Danastro extenduntur ad Danaprum."*[28] The Uluchian Antes were, in the second half of the sixth century, subject to the inroads of the Kutriguri and the Avars and were probably pushed inland and cut off from access to the sea for some time, but later, in the seventh and the eighth centuries they must have appeared on the Pontic littoral once more. By the end of the eighth century the lower Bug area was occupied by the Magyars, who were obliged to move west a century later in their turn to make room for the Patzinaks pressing on from the east.

The Polianians (*Poliane*),[29] at the time of the compilation of the *Primary Chronicle* inhabited the Kiev region. In the seventh and the eighth centuries however, their abodes must have been in the south. Since the lower Bug area was then occupied by the Uluchians, we may locate the Polianians in the Ingul region. It is probable that

22. See Chap. III, Sec. 3; cf. Barsov, pp. 96-97
23. *PSRL*, IX, 26.
24. N. I. Nadezhdin, "O polozhenii goroda Peresechna," *OO*, *1* (1844), 235.
25. *PSRL*, IX, 26.
26. See n. 19, above.
27. Brun, I, 1?,-182; Niederle, IV, 158.
28. Jordanis, Sec. 35.
29. Barsov, pp. 128-129; Hrushevskyi, I, 167-169; Niederle IV, 178-182; Parkhomenko, pp. 57-59.

they controlled likewise the mouth of the Dnieper. Even as late as in the tenth and eleventh centuries, Oleshie at the mouth of the Dnieper served as a station for Kievan (i.e., Polianian) merchants on their way to Constantinople.[30] On the coming of the Magyars—at the end of the eighth century—the Polianians were compelled to withdraw northward to the Kiev region, which seems to have been occupied by the Drevlianians until that time. The tribal name of the Polianians (like that of the Drevlianians) may have been given them, or assumed by them, as a reference to the nature of the country in which they originally lived. As we have already mentioned, the name, Polianians, means "Steppe People." We may recall in this connection some of the other Slavic tribal names similarly derived: *Iezerity* ("the Lake People"), *Pomorane* ("the Seashore People"), *Doliane* ("the Valley People").[31] On the other hand, the names Polianian and Drevlianian may also refer to the previous political connections of each of these two tribes respectively. We know[32] that one of the Gothic tribes was called the Greutungi, which corresponds exactly to the Slavic name of the Polianians; the name of another Gothic tribe, the Tervingi, has the same connotation as that of the Drevlianians. We may suppose that at the time of Gothic supremacy, in the third and the fourth centuries, the forefathers of the Polianians were subject to the Greutungi, and those of the Drevlianians to the Tervingi.

Let us now turn to the archaeological evidence. The antiquities of both the Ulichians and the Tivertsi have been insufficiently studied. The region of their original settlement was later flooded by various nomadic tribes, mostly of Turkish extraction, so that few traces of these two Antic tribes can have remained and even fewer have actually been found. The author of the *Primary Chronicle* says that in his time (eleventh century) some cities of the Ulichians and Tiverians still existed (*sut' grady ikh i do sego dnia*).[33] Some of the kurgans, faced with stone, which have been excavated in the southern part of Podolia province are tentatively considered Ulichian. Vases with ashes and burned bones have been found in these kurgans, but little else.[34]

30. Hrushevskyi, I, 254.
31. Dvornik, *Slaves*, p. 15.
32. See Chap. III, Sec. 9.
33. Cross, p. 141.
34. Gotie, p. 225.

More material has been found in various sites (*gorodishcha*) of Kiev province,[35] to the northern part of which the Polianians moved only later on, but which, in the south, may have had Polianian settlements even in the earlier period. Some of these sites, such as Paster and Motronino in Cherkassy district, have existed from remote antiquity, and the finds there illustrate primarily the early cultural stage, that of the funeral urns.[36] In the Paster *gorodishche* some ornaments have been excavated—pendants, stylized effigies of horses, etc.—which are to be referred to the period of the fifth and sixth centuries, but to which other objects of later periods, even of the eleventh century, bear a resemblance.[37] In some other sites of Kiev province, in particular Kniazha Gora at the mouth of the Ros River, the earlier (fifth and sixth centuries) and the later (tenth and eleventh centuries) stages of cultural development are equally better represented than the intermediary period of the eighth and ninth centuries. However, since there is similarity in style and inventory between the earlier and the later findings, some idea may be obtained of the intermediary period as well. Among items found in these *gorodishcha* iron tools and accessories may be noted here, such as knives, axes, nails, sickles, locks, and hoops.[38] It is obvious that the iron industries of the Polianians were on a high level.[39] It may be added that they were renowned for their skill in the forging of weapons, especially of swords. The *Primary Chronicle* contains a characteristic story of the Polianians' answer to the Khazars when the latter were about to impose a tribute on them. The Polianians offered to pay in swords.[40] Generally speaking, we may suppose that the cultural level of the Polianians was comparatively high even in the eighth and the ninth centuries, although the accumulation of wealth, jewelry, and art objects cannot at that time have reached such proportions as later, in the eleventh and twelfth centuries.

35. *Idem,* pp. 7-8, 236-237.
36. See Chap. II, Sec. 1.
37. Rybakov, p. 336.
38. Gotie, p. 93.
39. Cf. G. Vernadsky, "Iron mining and iron industries in Mediaeval Russia," *Études dediées à la mémoire d'André Andréadès* (Athens, 1939), pp. 363-364.
40. Cross, p. 143.

(*b*) *The Southeastern Area.*

We are dealing here with the territory to the south of the river Ugra and its continuation, the Oka River. On the west the territory is bounded, roughly speaking, by the course of the Dnieper River downstream from Mogilev; on the east, by the course of the Don River; on the south, by the Black Sea. We also include in this area the Azov region and the Kuban delta.

At the time of the compilation of the *Primary Chronicle* in the eleventh century, the whole southeastern portion of the territory in question was controlled by the Cumans, and only in the Kuban delta the "island" of Tmutorokan remained in Russian hands. The situation was different in the earlier period, and we have already seen[41] sufficient evidence for the assumption that in the eighth century there were Russian (Aso-Slav) settlements in the lower Don and Azov areas. Russians may also have penetrated into the Crimea.[42]

The *Primary Chronicle* contains the names of three southeastern Russian tribes, to wit: the Severians (*Severo* or *Severiane*); the Radimichians (*Radimichi*); and the Viatichians (*Viatichi*). In the eleventh century the Severians[43] were settled in the basins of the following eastern tributaries of the middle Dnieper: Psiol, Sula, and Desna, with the latter's tributary, the Seim; this corresponds to the area of Chernigov, Kursk, and the northwestern part of Poltava provinces. The Radimichians[44] inhabited the basin of the Sozh River, that is, the left bank portion of Mogilev province. The Viatichians[45] controlled the southern part of the Oka basin and the upper Don region, covering the territory of Orel, Kaluga, Tula, and Riazan provinces. We may be sure that in the earlier period all three of these tribes extended much farther to the southeast, being pushed north only as the result of Patzinak and Cuman inroads. It may be suggested that in the first half of the ninth century the Severians occupied the whole Donets basin, and the Radimichians the Desna basin. When the Severians were driven northwest from the Donets

41. See Chap. VI, Section 8.
42. See Chap. IV, Sec. 8.
43. Niederle, IV, 182-186.
44. *Idem,* pp. 189-191; P. Rykov, "Iugovostochnye granitsy Radimichei," Sar. Univ., X, *3,* 39-53.
45. M. Hrushevskyi, "Do pytannia pro rozselenne Viatichei," *NTS, 118* (inaccessible to me); Niederle, IV, 191-197.

basin by the Patzinaks, they in their turn pushed the Radimichians north from the Desna to the Sozh region. As to the Viatichians, we may suppose that their original settlements were in the Don area at least as far south as Boguchar.[46] We have no information as to the name of the Aso-Slavic tribe that was settled, in the eighth and the ninth centuries, in the lower Don and Azov region, but it may be argued with great plausibility that its name was Rus or Ros, since in this region the Russian Kaganate was founded early in the ninth century.[47]

Let us now turn to the archaeological data. The antiquities of the Severians, the Radimichians, and the Viatichians, within the confines of their respective territories of the eleventh century, have been fairly thoroughly studied. On the other hand, Slavic antiquities in the Donets and Don area have not been systematically explored, and for the lower Don and the Azov areas even the possibility of the existence of things Slavic has been denied by some scholars. In any case, no group of burial furniture of that area has been defined as Slavic, and on this ground the archaeologist Yu. V. Gotie has expressed his belief that there were no Slav settlements in the lower Don and Azov area in the pre-Kievan period.[48] Exception must be taken to such an assertion. The *argumentum a silentio* has much less weight in archaeological speculation than positive evidence, especially with regard to regions which have not yet been systematically explored. We may agree that no traces of a specific culture have as yet been found in such-and-such a region, but this does not necessarily mean that no such traces will be found in the future. The evidence may be right there, but so long as it remains buried we are not aware of it. Little was suspected of the riches gathered by Antic chieftains of the sixth and seventh centuries before the discovery of the Pereshchepino and Sudzha treasure hoards, and both were found rather recently, the first in 1911 and the second in 1927.[49] Moreover, even objects known for some time are not always at once

46. Niederle, IV, 193; Shakhmatov, *Poseleniia.*

47. See Chap. VI, Sec. 8.

48. Gotie, 228. Equally skeptical are I. I. Liapushkin, "Slaviano-russkie poseleniia IX-X vv. na Donu i Tamani," *IIM, 6* (1940) 89-92, and A. N. Nasonov, "Tmutorokan," *IZ,* VI (1940), 80. See, however, V. Mavrodin, "Po povodu odnoi teorii o mestopolozhenii Tmutorokani," *PIDO,* No. 9-10 (1936), which I know only from Nasonov's reference; also, V. Mavrodin, "Slaviano-russkoe naselenie nizhnego Dona i Severnogo Kavkaza v X-XIV vekakh," *PIG, 11* (1939), reviewed by I. Liapushkin, *VDI, I* (1940), 150-153.

49. See Chap. IV, Sec. 8.

adequately identified; for example, some antiquities of Verkhni Saltov were referred to the Magyar "cultural sphere" by Arendt and Fettich only as late as 1934-37.[50] We know also of regions in which the existence of Slavic settlements is well documented by written sources, but so far not by archaeological findings. Thus there is no doubt of the existence of the tribes of the Ulichians and the Tivertsi but we have little if any archaeological evidence to support that of the literary sources. Furthermore, there is no doubt that in the eleventh century Tmutorokan was a Russian city, but except for the famous stone with Prince Gleb's inscription[51] there is no monumental evidence whatever to illustrate the flourishing of Russian culture there.[52] In view of these considerations we can hardly reject the evidence of Arabic sources as to the Slavic population of the lower Don area in the eighth century.[53]

We turn now to the Severians.[54] According to materials found in the Severian kurgans of the tenth and eleventh centuries, the prevailing funeral rite was by cremation. However, kurgans with inhumated remains are also known. Some of the Severian kurgans are poor in grave furniture. A few earrings inlaid with silver or glass, buckles, and beads have been found in them. Another group is much richer. The inventory of a typical kurgan of the other type contains temple rings made of wire spirally bent; copper and iron torques; pendants for necklaces, spheric and crescent-shaped; bracelets; rings; nimbus-shaped decorative plates for headdresses. In some of the Severian kurgans as well as in the *gorodishcha,* weapons have been found. In the Gochevo Kurgan, Kursk province, a sword of the Polianian type was excavated.[55] In view of the differ-

50. See Chap. VI, Sec. 5.

51. Orlov, pp. 1-2; A. Spitsyn, "Tmutorakanskii Kamen," *ORSA, 9* (1915), 103-132.

52. For older reports on the progress of the archaeological research on the Taman peninsula see Goertz, II; Minns, pp. 21-24, 566; for recent exploration see A. S. Bashkirov, "Arkheologicheskoe obsledovanie Tamanskogo poluostrova letom 1927 goda," *IAI,* III (1928), 71-86; D. Eding, "Ekspeditsionnaia rabota moskovskikh arkheologov v 1937 godu," *VDI,* I (1938), pp. 141-142; V. Blavatskii, "Raskopki v Fanagorii v 1940 godu," *VDI,* I (1941), pp. 220-222. The scarcity of monuments may be partly explained by the change in the sea level, as a result of which portions of old sites have been covered by water. See Goertz, I, 48, and *VDI,* I (1938), p. 141.

53. Harkavy, pp. 38, 76.

54. Barsov, pp. 147-152; Hrushevskyi, I., 170-174. For archaelogical evidence see N. Makarenko, "Otchet ob arkheologicheskikh izsledovaniiakh v Poltavskoi gubernii," *AK, 22* (1907), 38-90; D. Samokvasov, *Mogily russkoi zemli* (Moscow, 1908), pp. 188-220; *idem.,* "Severianskie kurgany," TAS, III, *1*.

55. Rybakov, p. 337.

entiation of the two types of Severian graves it has been suggested that the two groups represent burials of men of different social status: the grandees and the common people.[56] It is also possible that the difference is not that of economic but of tribal groups.

An examination of the antiquities of the Radimichians and the Viatichians[57] leads to the conclusion that in spite of some difference in details these two groups had much in common. We have already mentioned (at the beginning of this section) that a seven-petaled pendant is characteristic of both Radimichian and Viatichian antiquities, although the shape of the petal is different for the two tribes. We repeat that either or both of these tribes may be connected with the Seven Clans tribe (ἑπτὰ γενεαί) of Thrace. The pendant was apparently the tribal emblem, symbolizing the union of seven clans in each case, but the two tribes as a whole must have been closely affiliated also. According to a story in the *Book of Annals* the tribes were the descendants of two brothers, Radim and Viatok (or Viatko).[58] We read that these two brothers were Poles (*Liakh*), or rather, lived among the Poles (*v Liasekh*). Commenting on this statement and taking into consideration the possibility of an eastward migration of certain West Slavic tribes following the downfall of the Avar Kaganate, the late A. A. Shakhmatov built up an hypothesis of Polish origin for the Radimichians and Viatichians.[59] Such an hypothesis cannot be supported, and is even definitely contradicted, by archaeological evidence available.[60] We must thus reject Shakhmatov's surmise. It is quite probable that the legend of the Polish origin of the Radimichians and the Viatichians was launched at the time of the seizure of Kiev by King Boleslaw I of Poland (1018).[61] It is also possible that the text of the legend as it reads in the *Book of Annals* may be faulty. According to this text, "there were two brothers among the Poles" (*biasta dva brata v Liasekh*). May we not conjecture that in the original text "among the As" (*v Iasekh*) was read instead of "among the Poles" (*v Liasekh*)?

56. Gotie, pp. 226-227.

57. Artsikhovskii, *Kurgany;* P. M. Eremenko and A. A. Spitsyn, "Radimichskie kurgany," *RAO 8* (1895); B. A. Rybakov, "Radzimichy," *BAN,* III (1932); inaccessible to me, see Grekov, p. 28.

58. Hyp., col. 10; cf. Cross, p. 141.

59. Shakhmatov, *Sudby,* pp. 37-39.

60. Gotie, pp. 218-219.

61. Vernadsky, *PDH,* p. 50.

There is in any case much more reason to derive both the Radimichians and the Viatichians from the As than from the Poles. In Viatichian and Radimichian kurgans of the tenth and the eleventh centuries, inhumation prevailed over cremation as a funeral rite. Cremation is very rare with the Radimichians and even rarer with the other tribe.[62] Presumably inhumation was the old habit for both. Now, we know this was the prevailing custom with the Alans (As) as well.[63] Moreover, the very names of the two mythical brothers, Radim and Viatok, may be derived from the Ossetian. For Radim we may quote the Ossetian word *rad* ("order," "line"), and for Viatok, the Ossetian *faetaeg* ("leader").[64]

The Viatichian kurgans[65] are usually not high—from 0.7 to 1.4 meters. The skeletons are found placed with head oriented toward the west or northwest. Apparently the idea was to orient the head toward sunset, and the variation was according to seasons. The inventory of grave goods is fairly uniform in most of the kurgans. The following are typical items: seven-petaled temple pendants, beads, torques, bracelets, and plate rings and crosses of the *ajour* technique. The crosses may have been mere ornaments and their discovery is not necessarily to be taken as evidence of Christianity.[66] In the Radimichian kurgans[67] the body was deposited on a special bed made of cinder and earth 0.5 meter above the ground level. A spheric tumulus was then built over the burial bed. The corpse was always laid with the head oriented to the west. For the inventory of the grave furniture the seven-petaled temple pendants, plate necklaces, and pendants for necklaces, may be considered typical.

62. Gotie, pp. 212-215.

63. *Idem,* pp. 54-62.

64. Miller, *Slovar,* pp. 934, 1407. There is also a possibility of deriving the name *Radimichi* from Ossetian *radomun* (*radaemun*), "to tame," "to subdue" (Miller, *Slovar,* pp. 934-935). Niederle accepts the Russian chronicler's theory that the names of the Radimichians and the Viatichians should be derived from the personal names Radim and Viatko; the latter, according to Niederle is a contraction from Viacheslav (Niederle, IV, 190, 194). Shakhmatov suggested the derivation of *Viatichi* from *Venti,* which he compared with the name of Tacitus' Veneti (Venedi) and that of the Keltic tribe of Venetes. See A. Shakhmatov, "Zu den aeltesten slavisch-keltischen Beziehungen," *ASP, 33* (1912), 61. Cf. also his "Poseleniia," p. 728. Later on Shakhmatov introduced an intermediary Polish form, "Wetic" (*Sudby,* p. 38). Cf. Artsikhovskii, *Kurgany,* p. 152, and Niederle, IV, 194-196.

65. Artsikhovskii, *Kurgany;* Gotie, p. 212.

66. Gotie, p. 212.

67. *Idem,* p. 214.

(*c*) *The Western Area.*

In this subsection we have to deal with western Volynia and Galicia. Western Volynia in the eighth and ninth centuries was the home of the Dulebians, and Galicia, situated on the northeastern slopes of the Carpathian Mountains, the home of the Khorvatians (*khorvaty,* Croats).[68] The Yugoslav scholar L. Hauptmann has recently offered a plausible conjecture that the Khorvatians were a Slavic tribe controlled by an Alanic clan.[69] In other words (from our point of view) the Khorvatians may be considered one of the As, or Antic, tribes. The country in which they settled was known as White Khorvatia, and both geographically and ethnographically it formed a juncture of the Russian, Polish and Czech tribes. According to Hauptmann it was from Galicia that the Khorvatians (Croats) crossed the Carpathian Mountains southward and penetrated, first into the basin of the upper Elbe (Laba) and then into the region of the middle Danube, until they finally settled to the south of that river. Part of the tribe, however, remained in Galicia and at the end of the ninth century recognized the authority of the Moravian prince, Sviatopolk.[70] At the end of the tenth century the prince of Kiev, Vladimir, made claims on Galicia in his turn.[71]

As to the Dulebians,[72] their history was closely interlocked with that of the Khorvatians. We have seen that in the second half of the sixth century the Avars conquered the Dulebians and compelled part of them to migrate to Moravia. The main bulk of the tribe remained, however, in Volynia, moving a little northward down the western Bug. It was probably after this that they became known as the Bugians (*buzhane*). The name Dulebians is older. In the list of Slavic tribes in the *Book of Annals,* quoted at the beginning of the section, a note is inserted to define the location of the Dulebians: the country of the Dulebians is that "where now the Volynians (*Volyniane*) are." According to Barsov this note may have been inserted in the *Book of Annals* by a later copyist, most likely by the compiler of the fourteenth-century digest of chronicles.[73] Barsov's suggestion is quite acceptable. If so, the name Volynians came into

68. Barsov, p. 95; Hrushevskii, I, 184-187; Niederle, IV, 154-156.
69. Hauptmann, *Kroaten,* pp. 343 ff.; Vinski, pp. 20-21.
70. See Secs. 6 and 8, below.
71. Vernadsky, *PDH,* p. 46.
72. Barsov, pp. 100-102; Hrushevskyi, I, 180-184; Niederle, IV, 172-175.
73. Barsov, p. 101.

use in a comparatively late period. This is apparently at variance with the mention of an allegedly similar name, *Valinana,* or *Velinana,* in Mas'udi's chapter on the Slavs (tenth century).[74] The identification of the name mentioned by Mas'udi as *Volyniane* (Volynians) seems hardly possible, however. According to Mas'udi, the tribe he described was the most powerful and ancient among the Slavic tribes. Now, from no other sources do we know of an old Slavic tribe bearing the name of *Volyniane.* Markwart suggests therefore that the Antes are meant in Mas'udi's book. The name of the leader of the tribe is quoted by Mas'udi as Majak. Markwart attempts to identify him as Mezamer (Bezmer), the Antic prince of the sixth century killed by the Avars.[75] In my opinion the name Majak may rather be considered a distortion of the name Boz (alias Bus), that of the ruler of the Antes at the time of the Alano-Gothic war of the end of the fourth century.[76] In any case, Mas'udi's *Velinana* can hardly have any connection with the Russian *Volyniane.* It must be added that the reading *Valinana* (or *Velinana*) in Mas'udi's text is doubtful. In the Leiden manuscript the name is written without diacritical marks;[77] it may be read in several different ways, to suit any commentator's imagination: *Veliamana, Veliamata, Velinamia,* etc. In the manuscript of Al-Bakri's work—and Al-Bakri used Mas'udi's original book—the name is spelt *Velinbaba.*[78]

Archaeological evidence is likewise against the supposition that the Volynians, or rather their predecessors the Dulebians, were a strong tribe in a position to dominate over other Slavic tribes. The inventory of the Volynian kurgans is very poor. In some of the kurgans no grave goods whatever have been found. In cases where there have been grave furnishings, they have been plain pots, wooden buckets, primitive ornaments.[79] The Volynian kurgans are low. Funeral by inhumation was apparently the prevailing custom, although cases of cremation are also known.

74. Mas'udi, III, 65.
75. Markwart, p. 147.
76. Taking into consideration the possibility of the interchange of *m* and *b* not only in Turkish, but also, under certain conditions in Ossetian (for the latter see Miller, *Sprache,* p. 34). Cf. Chap. V, Sec. 3.
77. Charmoy, p. 311, n. *bbb.*
78. Kunik, *Al-Bekri,* p. 33.
79. Gotie, p. 241. For details see V. Antonovich, "Raskopki kurganov v zapadnoi Volyni," *TAS,* XI, *1;* E. N. Melnik, "Raskopki v zemle luchan," *TAS,* XI, *1* (1902).

(*d*) *The Pripet Forest Region.*

North of the Pripet River the Dregovichians (*Dregovichi*) had their abodes; south of it, the Drevlianians (*Drevliane*). In the tenth century the Drevlianians[80] kept to the forest and swamp area between the courses of the rivers Irsha and Teterev in the south, and the Pripet in the north. It may be argued however that in older times, prior to the retreat of the Polianians from the lower Dnieper to the Kiev area as a result of Magyar pressure, the Drevlianians had expanded much farther to the south than the region occupied by them in the tenth century. They may have then controlled the Kiev area, at least the region around Kiev itself; in other words, they may have extended to the northern fringe of the steppe zone. While the name of the Drevlianians means "Forest People," it may, as has been mentioned above,[81] refer to political conditions rather than natural environment; it may point, that is, to their previous subjugation by the Tervingi Goths. In any case, burials similar to the Drevlianian have been excavated near Kiev.[82] It is likewise possible that before the end of the eighth century part of the Drevlianians were established east of the Dnieper, from which area they were later pushed westward across the river by the Radimichians and the Severians. All this, however, is a matter of conjecture; only the antiquities of the area occupied by the Drevlianians in the tenth century may safely be considered Drevlianian.

Over seven thousand Drevlianian mounds have been excavated.[83] They are referred to the period from the ninth to the thirteenth century. Inhumation is the prevailing type of burial. The inventory of objects is poor. Plain pots, wooden buckets, glass beads, earrings of bronze or of poor silver, have been found. Among other items excavated, flints, small iron knives, sickles, remnants of woolen cloth and leather shoes, may be mentioned here. On the whole, the Drevlianian material culture was in the ninth and tenth centuries on a lower level than that of the Polianians. Was the situation similar in the seventh and eighth centuries, or was the Drevlianian wealth

80. Barsov, pp. 127-128; Niederle, IV, 177-178.
81. See beginning of this section.
82. Parkhomenko, p. 45.
83. Gotie, pp. 240-241; Niederle, IV, 257. See also V. Antonovich, "Raskopki v strane Drevlian," *MAR, 11* (1813).

reduced after they were pushed north from the Kiev area? It is hard to say.

In his chapter on the Slavs Mas'udi mentions a powerful kingdom of ad-Dir, with big cities and a strong army.[84] It has been suggested by some scholars that the name ad-Dir should be interpreted as a personal one, and the king ad-Dir identified as the Norseman Dir who, according to the *Primary Chronicle,* together with Askold established himself in Kiev around 860.[85] The theory seems hardly acceptable; moreover, in my opinion, the name ad-Dir should be interpreted as a tribal rather than a personal name. If so, it is possible that Mas'udi meant the Drevlianians in this case. The Drevlianians are described in the *Book of Annals* as proud and warlike people, in spite of the fact that by the time of the compilation of the chronicle they were confined to a backwood swamp area. If it could be proved that they controlled Kiev in the seventh and eighth centuries, Mas'udi's comment would fit them well.

As to the Dregovichians,[86] they likewise disposed of their dead by inhumation. The inventory of their grave goods is unimpressive. Among other things, filigree beads and temple pendants with overlapping ends were found, which according to Gotie[87] are closer to the style of the Krivichian ornaments than to that of the Radimichians; this in spite of the fact that the latter lived just across the Dnieper from the Dregovichians.

(*e*) *The North.*

There were two major tribes in the northern and northwestern area, the Krivichians (*Krivichi*)[88] and the Slovenians (*Slovene*).[89] The Krivichians settled around the headwaters of the Dnieper, western Dvina, and Volga, thus commanding an important junction of river ways. The Slovenians in their drive north from the middle Dnieper[90] must have reached the banks of Lake Ilmen not later than the sixth century, and the city of Novgorod probably existed as early as in the seventh century.

84. Mas'udi, III, 64.
85. Hrushevskyi, I, 364. On Dir see Sec. 4, below.
86. Barsov, pp. 124-128; Niederle, IV, 186-189; V. V. Zavitnevich, "Formy pogrebalnykh obriadov v kurganakh Minskoi gubernii," *TAX*, IX, *2* (1897).
87. Gotie, p. 217.
88. Barsov, pp. 174-180; Niederle, IV, 197-199.
89. Barsov, pp. 191-192; Niederle, IV, 202-203.
90. See Chap. III, Sec. 7.

Judging from the archaeological evidence, the Krivichians had much in common with the Slovenians. For both, the cremation of their dead was typical. It is only in the eleventh century, under the influence of Christian rites, that burial by inhumation spread among the Krivichians.

The Slovenian kurgans[91] are usually high, from 10 meters up. The people of the Novgorod and Pskov provinces used to call the kurgan of such type *sopka* (plural, *sopki*).[92] The oldest *sopki* are referred to the seventh century, and in one of them a Sassanian coin dated A.D. 617 was found.[93] Most of the *sopki*, however, are of the eighth and ninth centuries. The inventory of the objects is mostly poor. Pottery and burned bones, human as well as animal, have been excavated.

In the Smolensk region—the area of Krivichian expansion—most of the mounds are of lesser height and size than the Slovenian kurgans. The most important concentration of the Krivichian kurgans is at Gnezdovo.[94] Most of the Gnezdovo mounds may be dated in the tenth century, but a number belong to an earlier period. The furniture of the Gnezdovo mounds is much richer than that of the Slovenian *sopki*. Even in the early kurgans ample ornaments were found, such as iron and copper torques, copper fibulas, crescent- and cross-shaped pendants, metal figurines of birds, etc.

As we have seen, the migration of several South Russian tribes such as the Uluchians, Polianians, Severians, Radimichians, and Viatichians was in a general direction from south to north; it was a retreat caused by pressure from the Magyars and other nomadic peoples. The migration of northern tribes beginning in the seventh century was, on the contrary, not a retreat but a forward expansion in the general direction from west to east, from Smolensk and Novgorod areas to the "Russian Mesopotamia" (*Mezhdurech'e*) between the upper Volga and Oka rivers.[95] The Krivichian pioneers reached the upper Volga via the course of the Vazuza River.[96]

91. Gotie, pp. 206-207; Niederle, IV, 267-268. For details see N. Brandenburg, "Kurgany yuzhnogo Priladozh'ia," *MAR, 18* (1895); V. N. Glazov, "Gdovskie kurgany," *MAR, 29* (1903); L. K. Ivanovskii, "Kurgany Peterburgskoi gubernii," *MAR, 20* (1896).

92. *Sopka,* in local dialects, means a volcano, also any hill of conic shape.

93. Gotie, p. 207.

94. See Chap. VII, Sec. 4.

95. Gotie, pp. 207-208; Niederle, pp. 202-203; Tretiakov, pp. 69-97. Tretiakov's study has become available to me too late to make full use of it.

96. Kerner, pp. 109-113.

The Slovenians went up the Msta River, from the headwaters of which they used the portage to the upper Mologa and from there reached the Sit and the Kashinka.[97] Early burials of Slovenian type have been found near Bezhetsk and on the banks of the Sit River.[98]

The two streams of colonization—the Slovenian and Krivichian—merged in the Rostov-Suzdal region. In the ninth and tenth centuries there were already numerous Slavic settlements in that area which had been originally inhabited by Finno-Ugrian tribes. The first Slavic pioneers must have appeared there in the eighth if not in the seventh century. Unfortunately we obtain no clear picture from the results of archaeological research. Over seven thousand kurgans were excavated in that area by Count A. S. Uvarov and P. S. Saveliev in the middle of the nineteenth century,[99] but the work was done hastily and without registering the exact location of each item found. Therefore it is now impossible to classify the strata or to differentiate the Finnish from the Slavic deposits. It is in any case clear that most of the kurgans reveal a mixed Finno-Slavic culture. Such items as thin temple pendants, fibulas and neck bands resemble closely similar things found in Gnezdovo graves.[100] That at least part of the kurgans of the Rostov-Suzdal area belonged not to the Finns but to settlers of other race is evidenced by numerous cases of burial by cremation, which was not characteristic of the Finns. On the other hand, both the northern Slavs (the Krivichians and the Slovenians) and the Norsemen practiced cremation. The archeologist I. A. Tikhomirov suggested on this ground that non-Finnish items of the Rostov-Suzdal kurgans must be considered Teutonic.[101] Recently P. P. Smirnov has seconded his opinion.[102] We have seen[103] that the Norsemen might have penetrated to the Rostov-Suzdal area as early as at the end of the seventh or the beginning of the eighth century. However, they probably followed in the wake of the Slavic colonization which cleared the path for them. Therefore, while some

97. *Idem*, pp. 115-116.
98. Gotie, p. 222.
99. *TAS, I, 2.*
100. Niederle, IV, 248-266; cf. A. A. Spitsyn, "Vladimirskie kurgany," *AK, 15* (1905).
101. I. A. Tikhomirov, "Kto nasypal Yaroslavskie kurgany?" *Trudy* of the Second Tver Region Archaeological Congress" (Tver, 1906) (inaccessible to me, see Smirnov, p. 145).
102. Smirnov, p. 145.
103. See Chap. VII, Sec. 2.

of the non-Finnish items of the Rostov-Suzdal kurgans may be considered Norse, the bulk of them are probably Slavic.

We may now venture to offer some general observations upon the way of life and civilization of the early Russian tribes.

With regard to their economic life: the Russian tribes of the eighth and ninth centuries were thoroughly familiar with agriculture, which was in most cases the foundation of their economic activities.[104] In the steppes, horse and cattle breeding constituted another prominent branch of economic life, while in the northern forests hunting and apiculture must have assumed considerable importance. The Russian tribes were, as to their material culture, in the Iron Age. Many household articles and agricultural tools—as, for example, sickles—were made of iron. Iron weapons—such as swords—were forged. Bronze and silver were used for ornaments. The finding of spindles indicates a familiarity with weaving, while pieces of woolen cloth point to the development of the process of fulling.

The practice of two different types of burial—by inhumation and by cremation—reflects the existence of two different trends of religious belief. Cremation of the dead was an old habit with at least some of the Slavic tribes, which should be connected with the worship of Perun, God of Thunder and Lightning. We have seen that in the eighth and the ninth centuries the rite of cremation dominated among the Krivichians and the Slovenians. As to the Polianians and the Severians, the evidence we have for cremation refers to the tenth century and we cannot be sure that the practice was the same in the earlier period.

In the burial rites of all other Russian tribes—the Radimichians, the Viatichians, the Dulebians, the Drevlianians, and the Dregovichians—the custom of inhumation seems to have prevailed. The same probably applies to the Khorvatians. We must recall in this connection that inhumation was typical for the North Caucasian cultural sphere, particularly for the Alans. Since the Antes were, in our opinion, closely connected with the Alans, the spread of this form of funeral among such Antic tribes as the Radimichians, the Viatichians, the Severians, and the Dulebians may be ascribed to

104. Until recently, students of medieval Russia have emphasized the development of foreign trade as the characteristic feature of Russian economics of the early Kievan period. Kliuchevskii was the standard-bearer of this theory. The tendency now is to pay most attention to the agricultural background. See especially Grekov, pp. 21-33. The problem will be discussed in Volume II.

the Alanic origin of the ruling clans of these tribes. As to the Drevlianians and the Dregovichians, they may have accepted the ritual from the Dulebians, their neighbors.

The difference in funeral ritual among the Russian tribes is undoubtedly evidence of a duality of their religious beliefs. It is apparent that the religion of the Antic tribes must have been influenced by Iranian creeds and mythology. We have already mentioned the veneration of the mythical bird-dog Senmurv in the Scythian and Sassanian periods.[105] Veneration must have been still rendered to Senmurv in the Khazar and early Varangian period, and a ceramic plate found in Gnezdovo[106] and referred to the eighth or ninth century is characteristic in this respect. In the *Book of Annals* Senmurv is mentioned under the name of Simargl,[107] which is close to "Simurg," as the Persian poet Firdausi calls the mystic bird in his *Shah-Nama*.[108]

After the political unification of the Russian tribes under the authority of the Kievan princes, religious beliefs of various tribes were syncretized, and in the second half of the tenth century, prior to Vladimir's conversion to Christianity, the Kievan pantheon included both the Slavonic Perun and the Iranian Simurg.[109]

With regard to the social stratification of the Russian tribes of the eighth and ninth centuries, the archaeological evidence points to a cleavage between the wealthy upper classes and the common people, in any case among the Polianians, Severians, and Krivichians. Grandees and merchants of such large cities as Kiev or Smolensk accumulated considerable wealth.[110] The finding of numerous hoards of Oriental coins located in various provinces points to the wide range of foreign commerce. Leaving aside the treasure hoards of a later date and taking into account only those containing Oriental coins of the eighth and ninth centuries, most of these have been found in the land of the Severians, the Radimichians, and the Viatichians; while not a few such hoards were located in the country of the Krivichians and the Slovenians, as well as in the Rostov-

105. See Chap. III, Sec. 8.

106. Trever, *Senmurv*, p. 324.

107. Hyp., col. 67; Laur., col. 79.

108. Firdausi, Warner's trans., I, 241, 246, 253, 276, 302; III, 158, 313, 330; V, 132-133.

109. On the pagan cults in Kiev prior to Vladimir's conversion see Mansikka, *Religion*, and Niederle, *Zivot*, II, 1, pp. 116-128.

110. Gotie, pp. 235-239.

Suzdal area, likewise colonized by both these two tribes. As to the Kiev area, little has been found for the period prior to the tenth century, and only one hoard has so far been excavated in the lower Don area.[111]

In conclusion, let us refer to the anthropological evidence. A considerable number of skeletons and skulls found in various barrows and funeral sites all over Russia have been examined by students of anthropology, but the data arrived at are not exhaustive or conclusive. According to Yu. D. Talko-Gryntsevich (Hryncewicz)[112] no general type of the East Slav may be established, and there is not only difference between different tribes as to anthropological type, but in some cases there are different groups within the same tribe.

With regard to stature, the Novgorodian *Slovene,* the Polianians, and part of the Severians were taller than men of other tribes. The Drevlianians and the Radimichians were of medium height (above 165 centimeters); the Krivichians were the smallest (around 157 centimeters). With regard to the structure of the cranium (cephalic index), the Polianians were subbrachycephalic; the Severians, the western Krivichians, the Drevlianians, and the Novgorodians, subdolichocephalic; the eastern Krivichians, dolichocephalic. As to width of forehead, the Severians, the Polianians, the Drevlianians, and the Krivichians had rather broad foreheads, but the Novgorodians only medium. The Polianian had a broad occiput (back part of the head), and this also applies to the Severian, Drevlianian, and Krivichian; the Novgorodian had a medium occiput. The Drevlianians and Krivichians had large faces, while those of the Novgorodians, Severians, and Polianians were rather small.

Taking into consideration these marks as well as a number of others, and their combination, Talko-Gryntsevich has suggested the following classification of the old Russian tribes:

(1) The Novgorodians
(2) The Polianians and the Severians
(3) The Drevlianians and the Krivichians

The classification is incomplete, since not all the Russian tribes are included in it. Still, it may help the historian, and if valid

111. For the geographical distribution of the findings of Oriental coins in Russia see Liubomirov and Markov.

112. Yu. D. Talko-Gryntsevich, "Opyt fizicheskoi kharakteristiki drevnikh vostochnykh Slavian," *Stat'i po Slavianovedeniiu,* III (1910), 109-111, 123-124. Cf. Parkhomenko, p. 24.

reveals a difference in anthropological type between the Antic tribes (Group 2) and the Slovenian tribes (Group 3).

It should be noted, however, that the validity of Talko-Gryntsevich's classification was questioned by Jan Czekanowski, who emphasized even more than Talko-Gryntsevich the mixture of anthropological types in the territory of western Eurasia which makes the establishment of any definite geographic boundaries between anthropological groups very difficult. As to Czekanowski's own classification, it may be mentioned that he refers the Polianians to what he calls the "Eastern" or "pre-Slavic" anthropological type and the Severians (or rather part of them) to the "Mediterranean" type.[113]

2. *The Extension of Khazar and Magyar Control over the South Russian Tribes.*

The compiler of the *Book of Annals,* who used some old unwritten traditions, had a vague idea that the South Russian tribes had in some remote time belonged to a great state, or federation, within which each tribe was able to preserve its own customs. This federation "was called Great Scythia by the Greeks; [each tribe] kept their own customs, and the laws (*zakony*) and traditions of their fathers, and each [had] their own character."[114] In this tradition of Great Scythia reminiscences of the Sarmatian and Hunnic epoch may be seen, but it seems more natural to refer the Great Scythia of the *Book of Annals* to the Khazaro-Magyar period, when incidentally the Khazars themselves used the Slavic word *zakon* for "law."

At the end of the seventh century the As and Rus tribes of the lower Don area submitted themselves to the Khazars, while the As tribes in the upper Donets region were conquered by the Magyars. The latter, however, considered themselves the supreme local authority for the Khazars. According to our conjecture[115] in the 730's the Swedes appeared in the upper Donets region and clashed with the Magyars. These latter now moved west to the lower Dnieper and Bug area and partly conquered, partly pushed north the Polianians and the Ulichians.[116] The Donets-Don riverway was now controlled by Swedes, who eventually merged with the As and the

113. Jan Czekanowski, "Anthropologische Beiträge zum Problem der Slawisch-Finnischen Beziehungen," *SMYA, 35,* 4 (1925).

114. Hyp., col. 10.

115. See Chap. VII, Sec. 3.

116. See Sec. 1, above.

Rus and assumed the latter's name. The new united Rus must at first have recognized the authority of the Khazars but eventually, around 825, broke with them and founded their own kaganate. Around 833 the Khazars retaliated by building the fortress of Sarkel, the object of which was to cut off the Russians from the Don riverway.[117]

The erection of Sarkel proved to be only a first move in the Khazar effort to encircle the Russian Kaganate. In order to make their control over the lower Don area secure, and to prevent any new Varangian bands from coming out of the north to the assistance of the Russians, the Khazars had to control the upper Don and upper Donets region as well. Such a policy was dictated by economic considerations likewise. It was from the north through the upper Donets way that the Azov Russians received furs. It is noteworthy that as soon as the Khazars conquered Russian tribes in the Oka region they imposed tribute in fur.

Work on the building of Sarkel began around 833. We may imagine that by 840 the Khazars must have conquered both the Severians and the Viatichians, and later on the Radimichians as well. As to Khazar control of the Polianians, the evidence is contradictory. Under A.M. 6367 (A.D. 859) the chronicler records that Polianians paid tribute in fur to the Khazars.[118] However, according to another story,[119] when the Khazars demanded tribute from the Polianians, the latter offered to pay in swords. The chronicler comments that the Khazar elders were suspicious of the offer and warned their "prince" (i.e., kagan) in the following words: "Evil is this tribute, Prince. We have won it with a one-edged weapon, called a saber, but the weapon of these men is sharp on both edges and is called a sword. These men shall impose tribute upon us and upon other lands. All this has come to pass."[120] The story as it reads in the *Book of Annals* is obviously the fruit of poetic elaboration. In the original version only the plain fact that the Polianians once offered to pay tribute to the Khazars in swords must have been recorded. Subsequently, the tribute was apparently discontinued, which called for the chronicler's comment and explanation.

We may assume that while Khazar troops reached Kiev they

117. See Chap. VII, Sec. 10.
118. Cross, p. 144.
119. Hyp., cols. 12-13.
120. Cross, p. 143.

hardly stayed there long. In view of other information available we must suppose that the actual control of Kiev was taken over by the Magyars. Since the Magyars themselves were Khazar vassals, there is no contradiction in the sources when some of them mention the Khazars and others the Magyars as rulers of Kiev. The *Book of Annals* speaks only of Khazars in this connection.[121] The Magyar version is given in the chronicle of King Bela's notary.[122] This was written in the thirteenth century, but its compiler used an older Magyar chronicle, the so-called *Gesta Hungarorum,* which was written in the beginning of the twelfth century—that is, simultaneously with the Russian *Book of Annals.*[123] According to Bela's notary the Magyar duke (*voevoda*) Olom (alias Almus) defeated the Kievans, who were then compelled to recognize his authority.[124] It must be noted in this connection that the *Book of Annals* mentions Olom's palace (*Olmin dvor*), which was situated on a hill near Kiev.[125] The hill was known as the Ugrian (i.e., Magyar) settlement (*Ugorskoe*).[126]

The *voevoda* Olom (Ἀλμούτζης, cf. Almus) is likewise mentioned in Constantine Porphyrogenitus' book *De Administrando Imperii.*[127] Macartney thinks that Olom's son was born around 840.[128] If so, Olom's birth may be dated some time before 820, in any case not later than that year. He was probably in his prime at the time the Khazars appeared at Kiev, around 840. We may suppose that an agreement was reached between the Khazars and the Magyars, by which Kiev was left in Olom's charge.

An analysis of the legend recorded in the *Book of Annals* as to the founding of the city of Kiev shows that the Kiev people had even in the eleventh century some vague recollection of Khazar-Magyar background. According to the legend, there were once upon a time three brothers, Kiy, Shchok, and Khoriv, and their sister, Lybed. Each of the brothers settled on a near-by hill, and this was the beginning of the city, which was named Kiev from the name of the elder brother, Kiy.[129]

121. *Idem,* p. 145.
122. *An. Bel.,* p. 11.
123. Vernadsky, *Lebedia,* p. 199.
124. *An. Bel.,* p. 11.
125. Hyp., col. 18.
126. *Ibid.*
127. *De Adm.,* 38.
128. Macartney, p. 109.
129. Cross, pp. 140, 145.

The name Kiy may be derived from the Turkish word *kiy* ("bank of a river").[130] Since the ruling clan of the Khazar state was of Turkish extraction, we may connect the naming of Kiev with the coming of the Khazars. Khazar troops must have reached the city from the east, and have been impressed by the steep hills (*kiy*) across the Dnieper. Hence, possibly, the name of the city.

The name of the third brother, Khoriv, seems to be of Biblical origin. Khoriv is the Russian transcription for Horeb. The name should be connected with the hill Khorivitsa, apparently the site of a settlement of Khazar Jews in Kiev.[131]

As to the second brother, Shchok, he may be tentatively identified as Chok, the Bulgar *boil* who led a campaign in the Dnieper region in the beginning of the ninth century.[132] It should be noted, however, that a similar name, Shok (Saac), is mentioned in old Magyar chronicles.[133]

The name of the sister of the mythical brothers, Lybed, points clearly to the Magyar background, since it must be connected with the name of the Magyar *voevoda* Lebedias (*Lebed*).[134] It is significant that Princess Lebed became a popular personage in Russian *bylinas* and folk tales.[135]

3. Riurik and the Varangian-Russian Principality of Novgorod.

By the middle of the ninth century Ukraine—both the left-bank and the right-bank Ukraine—was controlled by the Khazars and the Magyars. At the same time the Varangians were strengthening their grip on North Russia. Thus the whole area between the Baltic Sea and the Black Sea was divided into two spheres of influence: the Khazaro-Magyar in the south and the Varangian in the north. This situation is adequately described in the *Book of Annals* under the year A.M. 6367 (A.D. 859), in the following words: "The Varangians from beyond the sea imposed tribute on the Chud, the Slovenians, the Merians, the Ves, and the Krivichians, while the Khazars imposed tribute on the Polianians, and the Severians, and the Viatichians."[136]

130. Gordlevskii, *Slovar*, p. 594.
131. Vernadsky, *Lebedia*, p. 202.
132. See Chap. VII, Sec. 9.
133. *An. Bel.*, p. 8.
134. See Chap. VI, Sec. 5.
135. Vernadsky, *Lebedia*, p. 203.
136. Cross, p. 144.

Commenting on the date of this statement we must say that in the original version of the *Primary Chronicle* no dates were indicated for the early period; such dates as we find in this part of the *Book of Annals* were supplied by the compiler of the *Book* as an afterthought, and therefore do not always fit the narrative.[137] In any case we may assume that by the middle of the ninth century the Slovenians recognized the authority of the Varangians. Little is known of the activities of the latter in North Russia prior to the coming of Riurik. Generally speaking, Varangian policies in the north are to be connected with the plight of the Russian Kaganate in the south.

The news of the Khazar pressure on the Russian Kaganate must have been brought to North Russia first of all by the Russian envoys who were prevented by the Byzantine Government from returning to the kaganate in 839 and were sent to Germany instead; whence, we may imagine, being eventually released by Emperor Louis, they went to Sweden and then possibly to Staraia Rusa.[138] In addition, news of the establishment of Khazar control over the Viatichians and the Severians and of the cutting, in this way, of the Donets riverway must have reached Novgorod from the merchants now prevented from going south.

We have to take into account that in the first half of the ninth century—after the establishment of the Russian Kaganate in the Azov area and prior to the Khazar offensive—relations between the Russian north and the Russian south must have been lively and extensive. The upper Dvina and Lake Ilmen region played the role of an important commercial station on the road between Scandinavia and the Orient, and vice versa. Finds of weapons and fibulas of the Norse type together with Oriental coins in Livonian graves[139]—among other sites, in Asheraden[140]—are characteristic enough. Some of the Swedish warriors and merchants who went in search of adventure to the Azov area, after getting rich there or getting weary would return north and settle in North Russia, whence they were still able to participate in the profits of Oriental trade. Of the new bands of adventurers who headed east from Scandinavia some would likewise stop in North Russia; thus by the middle of the ninth cen-

137. On the chronology of the *Book of Annals* see Cross, pp. 109-115.
138. See Chap. VII, Sec. 10.
139. Arne, p. 20; Markov, pp. 16-23.
140. On Ascheraden-Asgard see Chap. VII, Sec. 2.

tury a community of Swedish merchants, through their commercial activities connected in one way or another with the Russian Kaganate, came into being in the Lake Ilmen area. The center of this northern agency of the Russian Kaganate was probably in Staraia Rusa, and both Shakhmatov and Platonov even suggest that this latter city must be identified as the "Russian island" of the Arabic writers,[141] which suggestion is unacceptable from our point of view.

The break in relations with the south resulting from the Khazar offensive must have painfully affected the economic life of the Novgorod area. We may recall that even in later times, in the Kievan period, the Novgorod population depended on the Oka region for grain supplies. And the Ilmen "Russia company" of Swedish merchants and their agents must have sustained serious losses because of the severance of their ties with the Russian Kaganate. New bands of Varangians who kept coming from Scandinavia and stopped in North Russia on their way to the Azov region, now—being prevented from going south—began to loot the native population of North Russia. There is mention of one such episode in the Life of St. Anscarius, according to which some Danes sailed in 852 across the Baltic Sea and seized a city in the land of the Slavs (*in finibus Slavorum*). This city should be identified as Novgorod.[142] Receiving a large ransom, the Danes went home. It is possible that the same episode has also been recorded in the Russian *Book of Annals* under A.D. 862.[143] "And they [the Slovenians] chased the Varangians away and did not give them [permanent] tribute, and set out to govern themselves."[144] According to the so-called Joakim's chronicle, the text of which has been lost but which V. N. Tatishchev was able to use in excerpts, the name of the Slovenian prince who ousted the Varangians was Gostomysl.[145] Judging from Tatishchev's résumé of Joakim's story about Gostomysl, it is in the nature of a legend.

While the Danes were repulsed, the situation in the Novgorod area did not improve so long as the road south was not cleared. Therefore the crisis continued "and there was no justice in the administration, and clan rose against clan, and a civil war started."[146] In order to ease the situation and to open the way south a campaign

141. S. F. Platonov, "Rusa," *DD*, I (1920), 1-5; Shakhmatov, *Sudby*, p. 56.
142. Rimbert, *Vita Anskarii*, p. 43.
143. On the unreliability of the date 862 see Kliuchevskii, I, 101.
144. Hyp., col. 15.
145. Tatishchev, I, 33.
146. Hyp., col. 15.

against the Khazars was necessary, but for such an undertaking troops were needed which apparently were not then available in the Ilmen area. This must have been the main cause of the "calling of the Varangians."[147]

Let us now analyze that famous story as recorded in the *Book of Annals*. It runs differently in the Hypatian and in the Laurentian versions. According to the Hypatian version, "The Rus, the Chud, the Slovenians, the Krivichians, and the Ves, said [to the Varangians]: 'our land is great and abundant but there is no order in it: come to rule and reign over us.'" (*rkosha Rus', Chud', Slovene, Krivichi i Vsia: zemlia nasha velika i obilna, a nariada v nei net: da poidete kniazhit' i volodet' nami*).[148] It is obvious that under the name Rus the members of the Swedish colony at Staraia Rusa are meant here, chiefly merchants transacting business with the Russian Kaganate in the Azov area. Their object in "calling the Varangians" must have been primarily that of reopening the way to the south with the help of new bands of Norsemen.

Subsequently the meaning of the original story was forgotten and in a later variant, preserved in the Laurentian version, the Rus are no longer mentioned among the Ilmen tribes who call the Norsemen to their assistance, but on the contrary, according to some codices of the Laurentian version it is the Rus whom those tribes call to rule over them: "The Chud, the Slovenians, the Krivichians, and the Ves said to the Rus, etc." (*resha Rusi Chud', Slovene, Krivichi i Ves', etc.*).[149]

In connection with this story the *Book of Annals* contains, both in the Hypatian and in the Laurentian version, a list of the Norse ("Varangian") tribes, including the Rus as one of them: "And they went beyond the sea to the Varangian Rus: that tribe of the Varangians was called Rus, as each of the other Varangian tribes has its own name, to wit: the Swedes, the Norwegians, the Angles, and the the Gotlanders." (*sitse bo zvakhut' ty variagi Rus', iako se druzii zovutsia Svei, druzii zhe Urmane, Angliane, inei i Gote, tako i si.*)[150]

147. For the history of the text and the literary background of the legend of the "Calling of the Varangians" see A. A. Shakhmatov, "Skazanie o prizvanii Variagov," *ANORI, 9,* 4 (1904), 284-365. Cf. Smirnov, pp. 151-152; Stender-Petersen, pp. 42-76.

148. Hyp., col. 15.

149. Laur., col. 19. The reading *Rusi* ("to the Rus") appears in the Radzivill and the Moscow Ecclesiastical Academy codices. The Laurentian and the Trinity Laura (Troitsa) codices have *Rus'* as in the Hypatian version.

150. Hyp., col. 15.

This statement must be considered a later interpolation, which we may refer to the time of the compilation of the *Book of Annals*—that is, to the beginning of the twelfth century. It is extremely interesting as an attempt to derive the name Rus not from the south but from the north, so that the compiler of the *Book of Annals* may be called the fountainhead of the "Normanizing School."

No Norse tribe called "Rus" is known. But it is sufficiently clear from the story of the *Book of Annals* just what tribe is meant under that name. Let us indeed examine the list of the Varangian peoples as given above. Besides the Rus, the following peoples are mentioned: the Swedes (*Svei*), the Norwegians (*Urmane*), the Angles (*Angliane*),[151] and the Gotlander (*Gote*). We notice that there is no mention of the Danes. Consequently, the Rus of the *Book of Annals* must be identified as the Danes, which is another reason for distinguishing between the Old Rus of the south and the New Rus of the north; since, as we know, the Rus of the Russian Kaganate were Swedes.[152]

The leader of the Rus, who according to the *Book of Annals* accepted the invitation to come to rule over the Ilmen tribes, was called Riurik. And he may be considered indeed one of the Danish feudal lords, to be identified with Roric of Jutland of western annals. The identification of Riurik of Novgorod as Roric of Jutland was first suggested by Friedrich Kruse in 1836,[153] but not then widely accepted. In 1929 N. T. Beliaev approached the problem once more and with the use of some new materials and certain new arguments fully confirmed Kruse's theory.[154] The identification is certainly valid.

We are thus in a position to make a brief sketch of Riurik's life.[155] His father, of the clan of Skioldung, had been ousted from Jutland and had pledged allegiance to Charlemagne, from whom around 782 he received Friesland as his fief. Riurik was born about the year 800. His childhood passed in turbulent surroundings since his father, and after the latter's death his elder brother, were constantly at war with the usurping rulers of Jutland. In 826 or thereabouts, Riurik's elder brother Harald, who had succeeded in

151. Since the *Book of Annals* was compiled after the Norman conquest, the word *Angliane* should perhaps be translated "the English" rather than "the Angles."

152. See Chap. VII, Secs. 3 and 5.

153. F. Kruse, "O proiskhozhdenii Riurika," *ZMNP*, *9* (1836), 43-73.

154. Beliaev, pp. 237-239.

155. *Idem*, pp. 225-270.

seizing part of Jutland but was later expelled from it, placed himself under the protection of Emperor Louis the Pious and was baptized at Ingelheim, near Mainz.[156] As Harald came thither with all his family we may surmise that Riurik was baptized as well. If so, he can hardly have taken his conversion seriously, for he later returned to paganism.

After Harald's conversion the emperor granted him as his fief the district of Rustringen in Friesland. Riurik received his share in it and after his brother's death became lord of the whole fief. Even before Harald's death the two brothers had to fight stubbornly to protect their lands from attack on the part of the king of Denmark, and after the death of Emperor Louis Riurik's position became quite precarious. According to the Treaty of Verdun (843) Friesland was included in Lothaire's portion of the empire and it appears that Riurik lost his fief. During the next few years Riurik led the life of an adventurer, taking part in several raids both on the continent and on England. In the annals of those years he became known as *fel Christianitatis*, "the gall of Christendom."[157] In 845 his boats sailed up the Elbe River, and in the same year he raided northern France. In 850 Riurik launched a fleet of three hundred fifty boats with which he looted the coastal districts of England.[158] In the next years he turned his attention to the mouth of the Rhine and to Friesland. Lothaire was compelled to compromise, and returned Friesland to Riurik on condition that he would defend the shores of the empire from the attacks of other vikings.[159] Since Riurik was now prevented from looting the shores of the North Sea he must have thenceforth shifted his attention to the Baltic, being probably well informed of the Danes' raid on Novgorod of 852.

Riurik's interest in the Baltic area must have received a new impetus when he was forced by Lothaire to give up Friesland once more, and was granted in its place another fief in Jutland (854).[160] Becoming master of southern Jutland, Riurik acquired direct access to the Baltic Sea, and was thus in an even better position than before to take active part in Baltic affairs. The compiler of the *Book of Annals* refers Riurik's arrival in Novgorod to the same year in which the Danes were compelled to leave the city ("862,"

156. Kruse, pp. 88-103.
157. Beliaev, p. 230.
158. Kruse, pp. 164-167, 190.
159. Beliaev, p. 232; Kruse, pp. 190-191.
160. Kruse, p. 233.

that is, 852). Actually two or more years may have passed between these two events, and in any case Riurik's expedition to the Novgorod area cannot have been undertaken before his establishment in Jutland; that is, not before 854. Most probably it took place in 855 or even in 856.

The *Book of Annals* states that Riurik came to Russia with two brothers, Sineus and Truvor. No such names are recorded in western chronicles. According to N. T. Beliaev, Sineus and Truvor must be interpreted not as personal names but as epithets for Riurik himself. In Norse, Signjotr means "victorious" and Thruwar, "trustworthy." [161] In medieval storytelling the legend of three brothers founding a city or a state was a popular motif, and since there was such a story about Kiev the chronicler would not hesitate to apply it to the Novgorod area as well.

We have now to return to the analysis of the name Rus, the origin of which is in the *Book of Annals* connected with the advent of Riurik. We have seen that by the Rus the compiler of the *Book of Annals* meant the Danes. As the lord of Jutland, Riurik certainly might have been considered a Dane and there must have been many Danes in his retinue. But no portion of Jutland proper is known as Rus. However, since Riurik was for some time the ruler of Friesland, an attempt has been made by N. T. Beliaev to interpret the name Rus as the Finnish mutilation of the name Fries.[162] The hypothesis is hardly plausible, but Beliaev mentions—albeit casually—another possibility: the derivation of the name Rus from that of Rustringen, which was Riurik's original fief; the name "Rustringen" being abridged to "Rus." [163] The name Rus in its original meaning of the southern Rus, those of the Russian Kaganate, was sufficiently familiar in Novgorod by the time of Riurik's arrival, and it may now have been used instead of the lengthy Rustringen. We have seen that in the *Book of Annals* (Hypatian version) there is a patent contradiction concerning the Rus. It is the Rus who lead the other tribes in extending their invitation to the Varangians, and on the other hand it is the Varangian tribe of Rus who answer the call. The puzzle may be solved if we admit the existence of two Rus: the old Swedish Rus of the Russian Kaganate and the new Friesian Rus of Riurik.

161. Beliaev, pp. 244-245.
162. *Idem,* pp. 246-247.
163. *Idem,* p. 251.

4. The Rus in the Dnieper and Pontic Area.

According to the *Book of Annals,* Riurik upon his coming to Russia settled himself in Ladoga, while Sineus took charge of Beloozero, and Truvor, Izborsk.[164] We have seen that Riurik's alleged brothers Sineus and Truvor probably never existed,[165] but it is quite likely that he placed some of his relatives or followers in other cities in the capacity of his lieutenants or vassals. Having spent most of his life in the west, Riurik must have been well acquainted with the nascent feudal system and might be prepared to apply its principles to his new possessions in Russia. From this angle the statement of Joakim's chronicle concerning the organization of North Russia under Riurik, known to us in Tatishchev's résumé, deserves attention. According to Tatishchev[166] "Riurik set up in all of the cities princes of either Varangian or Slavic descent, and he himself was known as the Grand Duke (*kniaz velikii*), which is equal to the Greek terms of *archicrator* or *basileus,* and those princes were his vassals." The Greek terms do not, of course, belong to the picture, since Riurik's notions of suzerainty must have been patterned according to the standards of the Western Empire with which he was quite familiar.

Tatishchev's statement may be compared with that of the *Book of Annals.* According to the latter Riurik's brothers Sineus and Truvor, died two years after their coming to Russia. After their death Riurik moved from Ladoga to Novgorod and built a castle there. "And there he stayed as the prince and assigned other cities to his barons (*muzhi*), instructing them to build castles; to one of them he gave Polotsk; to another, Rostov; and to still another, Beloozero; and so in all those cities the Varangian newcomers rule." [167]

Busy with the organization of his new realm, Riurik was not apparently thinking of any campaign to the south. And yet it was almost certainly in the hope of promoting such a campaign that the old Rus colony of Staraia Rusa called Riurik to Novgorod. They must now have decided to attempt to break their way to the south without Riurik's help. From this point of view we may approach the

164. Hyp., col. 15.
165. See Sec. 3, above.
166. Tatishchev, I, 34.
167. Hyp., col. 15.

chronicler's story of Askold's expedition to Kiev. The beginning of the story reads as follows: "And he [Riurik] had two men [Askold and Dir], not of his own kin, but barons [boyars, *boiarina*], and they asked his permission to go to Constantinople with their kin, and they went, accordingly, down the Dnieper River."[168] It is obvious that the initiative in this matter belonged not to Riurik but to the two barons themselves. The words "not of his kin" (*ne plemeni iego*) may perhaps be interpreted in the sense "not of his tribe," that is, not of his Friesian retinue. They started "with their kin" (*s rodom svoim*), that is with the members of the Old Rus (Swedish) colony.

As to the chronicler's assertion that Askold's goal was Constantinople, it sounds like the chronicler's own comment rather than a mere recording of a fact. It is hardly conceivable that at that time any Novgorod man would think of a campaign against Constantinople.[169] Askold's idea must have been indeed that of breaking south, but chiefly, we may think, in order to restore connections with the Russian Kaganate in the Azov area. Since the traditional Donets-Don riverway was barred by the Khazars, a new route had to be established. Krivichian merchants must by this time have explored the Dnieper Riverway from Smolensk down to Kiev, and it was probably through them that Askold came by the idea of going to Kiev, whence he might hope to find some way farther south.

To continue the chronicler's story:

> and they [Askold and Dir] went down the Dnieper River and saw a town on the hill and asked: "whose town is it?" And they [the town people] said: "there were three brothers, Kiy, Shchok, and Khoriv who founded this city and perished, and we now live in it and pay tribute to the Khazars." Askold and Dir stayed in the town and assembled many Varangians and began ruling over the Polianian land.[170]

The story is legendary but must have preserved some sound historical features as well. As to the Khazar tribute, we have already seen[171] that the tribute may have been collected for the Khazars by the Magyar *voevoda* Olom. It was probably in the name

168. *Idem*, col. 16.
169. I cannot therefore accept the opinion of N. T. Beliaev, who suggests that Askold was commissioned by Riurik to raid Constantinople (Beliaev, p. 241).
170. Hyp., col. 16.
171. See Sec. 2, above.

of Olom that Askold and Dir ruled in Kiev. When Oleg later seized Kiev[172] and he said to Askold and Dir: "you are not princes, nor of princely clan," his words may be interpreted in the sense that Askold and Dir were not considered independent rulers, but rather someone else's lieutenants. If so, whose? After they were killed by Oleg's order, their bodies were carried to Olom's palace on the Ugrian Hill.[173] Why? Apparently because they ruled in Olom's name from his palace, which served as the governor's mansion.

Under A.M. 6374 (A.D. 866) the *Book of Annals* records that Askold and Dir undertook a campaign against Constantinople.[174] From the Byzantine sources we know that the first Russian attack on Constantinople took place in 860 and not in 866.[175] Therefore we must admit a chronological error of six years in this passage of the *Book of Annals*. With regard to the campaign, we cannot think that Askold and Dir had a large enough army to undertake it by themselves. The Magyars, even if we suppose that they agreed to let the Rus go through the lower Dnieper region, had no boats and were not familiar with sea warfare, so that they were not in a position to give material help. Only from the Russian Kaganate in the Tmutorokan area can assistance have been expected. The campaign must have been, then, a joint undertaking of the Russian kagan and of Askold and Dir. Probably the Tmutorokan kagan took the initiative in this matter. In any case the establishment of a connection with the Tmutorokan Kaganate was, as we have suggested above,[176] Askold's original aim, and he must have sent messengers to Tmutorokan soon after his coming to Kiev. It was possible to get from Kiev to the shores of the Sea of Azov by boat, using the steppe rivers and the portages.[177] One of these riverways was up the Orel River (a tributary of the Dnieper) and from its headwaters by portage to the tributaries of the Donets, then down the Donets and the Don. This way, however, was barred by the Khazars. It is more conceivable therefore that another way was used: up the Samara (a tributary of the Dnieper farther to the south) and its tributary the Volchya, and by portage to the Kalmius and thus to the Sea of Azov.

There is little information concerning conditions in the Russian

172. See Sec. 8, below.
173. Hyp., col. 18.
174. Cross, p. 145.
175. Ostrogorsky, p. 159.
176. See above, at the beginning of this section.
177. Brun, I, 174-209.

Kaganate in these years. As we have seen,[178] the envoys of the kagan who came to Constantinople in 838 were not allowed to return but were sent to Germany. We do not know whether they finally succeeded in getting back to Tmutorokan over the roundabout way—from Ingelheim to Novgorod and so on. In any case the detention of the envoys by the Byzantine emperor meant a severance of diplomatic relations between the Russian Kaganate and Byzantium, and it is possible that this was the cause of the Russian raid on Amastris in or around the year 840[179]—if we admit that such a raid actually took place.[180] There is no evidence of any further Russian naval activities in the Black Sea between 840 and 860. While the alleged raid of 840 was directed against Asia Minor, now in 860 the Rus decided to strike at Constantinople itself.

The campaign of 860[181] seems to have been carefully prepared and well timed. The empire was at the time in the midst of a hard war against the Arabs. In 859 the latter administered a severe defeat to the Byzantine troops and the emperor himself barely escaped capture. From the early spring of 860 the empire was busy organizing its forces for a new campaign against the Arabs and at the beginning of June the emperor and his assistant, the *curopalates* Bardas, led the Byzantine army to Asia Minor. Precisely such an opportunity was what the Russians awaited for their attack on Constantinople.

It is not know what route the Russians chose to bring their fleet from the Cimmerian Bosporus (Kerch Strait) to the Thracian Bosporus (Bosporus Strait). It seems certain that the Byzantines were caught unawares, having no intelligence of the advance of the Russians until Russian boats appeared at the Strait of Bosporus. On the other hand it seems equally certain that the Byzantine navy must have kept watch over both the Crimean coast line and the shore of Asia Minor to prevent any Russian activities, especially after the Russian raid on Amastris in 840. We may think therefore that the

178. See Chap. VII, Sec. 10.

179. On the Russian raid on Amastris see Vasilievskii, III, i-cxli.

180. G. da Costa-Louillet has recently attempted to undermine the validity of the Life of St. George of Amastris as a source for the study of the Russian raid on that city. She suggests that the passage on the raid in the Life is a later interpolation and refers it to Igor's campaign of 941 (Da Costa, pp. 246-248). Such an interpretation is not new and Vasilievskii has already weighed and criticized it (Vasilievskii, III, cxxxvi-cxxxviii). A. A. Vasiliev connects the Amastris episode with the Russian campaign of 860 (Vasiliev, *Arabes,* I, 243).

181. Bury, *Eastern,* pp. 419-422; Ostrogorsky, p. 159; Vasiliev, *Arabes,* I, 240-247.

Russians appeared from a quarter in which the Byzantines never expected them. They may have used the roundabout way through the Sea of Azov and northern Tauria to the mouth of the Dnieper;[182] that is, crossing first the Sea of Azov to its northern shore, then going up the river Berda and down the river Konskaya, a tributary of the Dnieper. Quite possibly it was in the lagoon formed by the Konskaya's approach to the Dnieper, below the present town of Zaporozhie, that the expeditionary force of the Russian Kaganate joined the unit of Askold and Dir coming from Kiev. The joint flotilla of Russian boats must then have sailed down the Konskaya and lower Dnieper to the Black Sea and crossed it directly south to the Bosporus.

On June 18, 860, the combined Russian fleet consisting of two hundred boats appeared before the walls of Constantinople.[183] Both the authorities and the population were in complete confusion. Had the Russians immediately stormed the city they would probably have taken it, meeting with no resistance on the part of the inhabitants. But instead they began to loot the rich palaces and monasteries outside the walls. Meanwhile Patriarch Photius rallied the population and formed hastily an improvised militia to defend the city. A messenger was sent to the emperor's headquarters in Asia Minor with a report of the critical situation in the capital.[184]

In order to raise the spirit of the people Photius organized a religious procession to the embankment of the Golden Horn, the inner harbor of Constantinople. A sacred relic known as the Blessed Virgin's vestment was dipped into the water, after which, according to the tradition, a storm came up by which the Russian boats were dispersed. Photius himself, however, says in one of his homilies that the Russians began to retreat even before the storm.[185] They lingered for some time in the near-by waters where they were eventually attacked by the Byzantine fleet sent by the emperor, who also hastened back to his capital with the land army. The Russians apparently suffered heavy losses and only some of the boats made their escape.

182. See n. 177, above.
183. For the date see Ostrogorsky, p. 159.
184. Vasiliev, *Arabes,* I, 244.
185. Photius, *Homily II,* p. 222.

5. *The Khazaria Mission of Constantine the Philosopher and the First Conversion of the Rus.*

After the retreat of the Russian fleet from Constantinople the Byzantine authorities must have immediately considered measures which could prevent any future onslaught. One of the methods of Byzantine diplomacy in dealing with the "Northern Barbarians" was to sponsor their conversion to Christianity. We have seen that in the sixth century the "Hunnic" prince Grod was invited to Constantinople to be baptized there[186] and in the seventh century the young Bulgarian khan Kurt was converted.[187] It was only natural that following the Russian raid of 860 the Byzantine authorities—both secular and church—should recur to the idea of mitigating the fierce spirit of the Rus by preaching Christianity to them.

At the time of the Russian raid the patriarchal throne was as we have seen[188] occupied by Photius, a man of high intellect and profound education, one of the greatest spiritual leaders in the entire history of the Byzantine world.[189] As head of the Byzantine Church, Photius played an important role in state affairs as well. Emperor Michael was little over twenty in 860; he was, moreover a pithless youth, lacking in firmness.[190] His chief assistant, the *curopalates* Bardas, was a great friend of Photius and always valued his advice. Photius' enlightened object was to sponsor the advancement of philosophy as the foundation of the Church, and also to spread the Byzantine spiritual civilization beyond the borders of the empire. Therefore the period of his first tenure of the patriarchal office (858-867) witnessed a revival of the missionary activities of the Byzantine Church. The attempt to convert the Rus to Christianity was only one of several such moves of Photius' policy.

As we know, the Rus were as harmful to the Khazars as they

186. See Chap. IV, Sec. 10.
187. See Chap. V, Sec. 6.
188. See Sec. 4, above.
189. On Photius see F. Dvornik, "Études sur Photius," *Byz. 11* (1936), 1-19; Dvornik, *Slaves,* pp. 119-146; J. Hergenröther, *Photius,* 3 vols. (Ratisbonn, 1869); T. M. Rosseikin, *Pervoe Patriarshestvo Fotiia* (Sergiev Posad, 1915), inaccessible to me.
190. H. Grégoire's recent studies (*Byz., 4,* 437-468; *5,* 327-246; *8,* 515-550) have shown that Michael III was a better ruler than had been formerly supposed, and that his reign had great significance in Byzantine history. It is, however, not Michael personally but his advisers, chiefly Bardas and Photius, who must be given chief credit for the success of his policies. Cf. Ostrogorsky, p. 155.

were to the Byzantines, and some coördination between Byzantine and Khazar policies toward the Rus seemed essential. While Christianity was striking root in Khazaria,[191] it was not firmly established there and the kagan himself was a pagan. Still, Photius might entertain the hope of converting both the Khazars and the Rus by one stroke. According to the Life of Constantine the Philosopher, it was from the Khazars that the initiative for his mission actually came, but in any case Photius must have been quite eager to take advantage of the coming of Khazar envoys to Constantinople, with the request that preachers be sent to them (probably late in 860).

The statement made by the Khazar envoys upon their arrival at Constantinople is recorded in the Life of Constantine as follows: "We have known God the Lord of everything [Tangri, the Altaic God of Heaven] from time immemorial . . . and now the Jews are urging us to accept their religion and customs, and the Arabs, on their part, draw us to their faith, promising us peace and many gifts."[192] In these words the religious situation in Khazaria is pretty accurately described. We have already mentioned[193] that both Judaism and Islam, as well as Christianity, had been spreading in Khazaria for some time, and the Arabs considered the kagan's conversion to Islam a prerequisite for peace. It is apparent that by the time of the Khazar embassy to Constantinople the kagan was about to decide which of the three foreign faiths of Khazaria he would accept to replace his primitive Shamanism.

Photius appointed the ablest of his pupils, Constantine, known as the Philosopher, to head the mission. Constantine was to become known under the name of Cyril, which was given him together with the highest monastic rank (*skhima*) just before his death, as one of the two Apostles of the Slavs, the other being his brother Methodius.[194] There is no doubt that Constantine was a man of powerful intellectual ability, a great dialectician and an even greater linguist. According to his biographer he was considered in Constantinople the only eligible candidate for the Khazaria mission: "no other would be able to undertake it."[195] Aside from Con-

191. See Chap. VI, Sec. 2.

192. Life, chap. 8.

193. See Chap. VI, Sec. 2.

194. There is an extensive literature on *SS.* Cyril and Methodius and their life work, for the bibliography of which see Ilyinskii. The most important recent work is Dvornik, *Légendes*.

195. Life, chap. 8.

stantine's general philosophical and theological background, probably his linguistic abilities and familiarity with dialectics mattered most in determining his choice. Several years before, he had been sent as a missionary to Syria, where he must have obtained not only some knowledge of Moslem dialectics but probably also some idea of the elements of both the Arabic and the Hebrew languages, which was to be of great help in his discussions with the Jews and the Moslems in Khazaria.[196] On his way to Khazaria Constantine stopped in Cherson in Crimea to complete his Hebraic studies. Incidentally, through a Samaritan he met in the Crimea he also obtained some reading knowledge of the Samaritan tongue.[197]

No less important was Constantine's familiarity with Slavic. Both he and his brother Methodius, who was to accompany him to Khazaria, were born in Salonika where their father occupied a position of some importance in the army administration.[198] Slavic was spoken in the family, as probably in many Macedonian families, together with the Greek. Knowledge of Slavic was imperative for the head and members of the Khazaria mission, for that language was widely spoken at the time both in Crimea and in Khazaria proper, especially by some of the As and Rus tribes. We may add to prevent any misunderstanding that some other clans—especially in the North Caucasian area—spoke pure Iranian (Ossetian), and in some border districts a mixture of Slavic and Ossetian may have been used. Even after the coming of the Swedes and the establishment of their rule over the As and the Rus, the linguistic situation cannot have been radically changed. The Swedish ruling group was not numerous, and far from imposing their language on the peoples they ruled, they themselves were probably rapidly Slavified, as was to be later the case with the Kievan rulers.

However this may be, knowledge of Slavic proved very useful to Constantine even during his stay at Cherson.

And he found there a copy of the Gospel and the Psalms written in Russian characters (*ros'sky pismeny pisano;* variant: *rous'sky*) and he found

196. Life, chap. 6; cf. Dvornik, *Légendes,* pp. 85-111.

197. Life, chap. 8; Dvornik, *Légendes,* p. 185. A. Vaillant suggests that the mention of the Samaritan in Constantine's Life should be understood metaphorically: "Le Samaritain que Constantin a trouvé à Cherson, c'est le bon Samaritain, ou la Samaritaine, de l'Evangile" (*RES, 15,* 76). However, not only the Samaritan but Samaritan books are mentioned in the Life, so Vaillant's comment misses the point.

198. He was a *drungarius.* See Dvornik, *Légendes,* pp. 2-19.

a man speaking that language and spoke to him and understood the meaning of what he said, and, adjusting it to his own dialect, he analyzed the characters, both for the vowels and the consonants, and praying to God, started quickly to read and speak [Russian].[199]

Since Constantine himself has been generally acclaimed as the inventor of the Slavic alphabet, and since there is no definite evidence of the previous existence of any developed Slavic script,[200] the above famous passage in the Life of Constantine has mystified several generations of scholars. A number of theories have been suggested to identify the "Russian characters" in question.[201] Until recently the "Gothic" theory was generally considered the most plausible.[202] According to this, the manuscript Constantine found in Cherson was in Gothic (of the Crimean Goths). In 1935 an entirely different hypothesis was suggested by A. Vaillant,[203] namely, that the text of the above passage of the Life of Constantine should be considered faulty, and instead of "Russian characters" (*rous'sky*), "Syriac characters" (*sour'sky*) is meant. In our opinion neither the Gothic nor the Syriac theory is valid. The Crimean Goths were well known even in Constantinople, and so much the more so in Cherson; Constantine could not possibly mistake them for the Russians. As to the Syriac hypothesis, it is more plausible than the Gothic in view of Constantine's general educational and cultural background,[204] but at the same time we are faced with the fact that in none of the codices of Constantine's Life is *sour'sky* read in this passage, while some manuscripts have not *rous'sky,* but *ros'sky* or *rousky,* so that the possibility of deriving *roussky* from *sour'sky* in this passage is scant. Furthermore, from the contents of the story it is plain that the main difficulty for Constantine was in analyzing the characters, and not in understanding the language, which he mastered easily, comparing it with his own (*svoei besede prikladaia*)—that is, obviously comparing the Russian with the Macedonian Slavic dialect. Altogether, it seems

199. Life, chap. 8.

200. On the problem of the existence of a Runic script among the Slavs see V. Jagić, "Vopros o runakh u Slavian," *ESF,* III, 1-36.

201. See Dvornik, *Legendes,* pp. 185-188; Ilyinskii, pp. 66-67.

202. See Vasiliev, p. 113.

203. A. Vaillant, "Les lettres russes de la Vie de Constantin," *RES, 15* (1935), 75-77.

204. Dr. R. Jakobson informed me, in private conversation, that he is in favor of the Syriac hypothesis.

the simplest explanation to accept the reading as it stands, and to agree that the manuscript was actually in Russian; that is, in the language of the southern Rus (As, Antes), or more specifically that of the Crimean As or Rus.

In his subsequent polemics with the Roman clergy, when Constantine had to defend the right of the Slavs to have their church books and to conduct the liturgy in their own language, he compiled a list of the peoples who use their own language in church literature and the church service. The list contains the names of the following peoples:[205] the Armenians, the Persians, the Abasgians, the Iberians, the Sugdeans, the Goths, the Avars, the Turks, the Khazars, the Arabs, the Egyptians, and the Syrians. While there is no specific mention of the Russians, attention should be called to the name "Sugdeans." These are certainly to be identified as the inhabitants of the city and district of Sugdaea, in eastern Crimea. And in this part of the Crimea the As constituted the bulk of the population. Thus under the name of Sugdeans Constantine must have meant the As—and the Rus, since the Rus were but a clan of the As.

While the problem of the language of the manuscript Constantine studied in Cherson is, in our opinion, easy to solve, the nature of the characters in which it was written constitutes a much more involved problem, and in this matter we offer no more than a surmise. It is known that Christianity penetrated to the peoples of the North Caucasian area chiefly from the south, from Georgia and Armenia. Both Armenian and Georgian missionaries visited Khazaria from time to time. Thus in the year 681/82 an Albanian bishop, Israel, preached among North Caucasian "Huns."[206] It is probable that among his converts were Ossetians (As) as well. At the end of the eighth century a Georgian monk, St. Abo, traveled in Crimea and Khazaria.[207] It seems quite plausible that Christian communities formed in the North Caucasian area in the course of the seventh and eighth centuries, including the Ossetian (As) communities, must have used Armenian or Georgian characters for writing down liturgical texts or prayers. From the North Caucasian As, the Crimean (Sugdean) As may have borrowed the former's alphabet, which probably consisted of Armenian or Georgian characters (or a mixture of both) adapted to the As language. And it was probably with

205. Life, chap. 16.
206. See above, Chap. VI, Sec. 2.
207. See above, Chap. VII, Sec. 6.

a Russian manuscript, written in such an adapted Armenian or Georgian alphabet, that Constantine had to deal in Cherson.[208]

We may think that Constantine stayed in Crimea during the winter of 861 and in the spring of that year set forth to the kagan's headquarters in Khazaria. The route chosen by the missionary commands attention.[209] He went first of all to northern Tauria, where he was attacked by the Magyars; who, however, did not turn him back, so he proceeded to one of the harbors on the northern shore of the Sea of Azov, where he boarded a ship and sailed along the "Khazarian Way." The question may be asked why did not Constantine board a ship right in Cherson, or at any rate in Kerch, which would have saved him the trouble of the overland route through northern Tauria, exposed as it was to Magyar raid. There must have been some good reason for the detour. Apparently the sea route through Kerch strait was barred by someone so that Constantine could not use it. But who could bar navigation through Kerch strait? Hardly anybody but the Russians, whose headquarters were across the strait in Tmutorokan, but who apparently at that time controlled Kerch as well. It follows that the Russians were not yet willing to accept the Byzantine missionaries. Be this as it may, Constantine had to use a different route, the one which in his Life is called the Khazarian Way. This is undoubtedly the old road of the Rus merchants through Khazaria as described by Ibn-Khurdadhbih;[210] that is, up the Don River to Sarkel, then by portage to the Volga and down the Volga to the city of Itil.

At the time of Constantine's mission the kagan's headquarters were not at Itil, however, but at Samandar, which was located either on the site of the present town of Kizliar, or on the site of Tarku.[211] In any case, Constantine had to travel from Itil southward along the western shore of the Caspian Sea, down to the mouth of the Terek River. After his arrival at the kagan's headquarters Constantine was to confront his opponents, the Hebrew and the Moslem missionaries. In the Life, his dispute with the Jew is described in some length while little is said of his polemics against the Moslems. In Methodius' Life[212] no dispute with the Moslems is mentioned. We

208. See n. 234, below.
209. *Life,* chaps. 8 and 9; cf. Vernadsky, *Eparchy,* pp. 70-71.
210. See Chap. VII, Sec. 5.
211. See Chap. VI, Sec. 2.
212. Life of Methodius, chap. 4.

may recall that the book of the Arabic author, Al-Bakri, contains a story about the religious disputes in Khazaria between the Christians and the Jews, in which apparently Constantine's mission is meant.[213] According to Al-Bakri, the Jew was victorious against his Christian opponent, and as to the Moslem missionary, he was not able to take part in the debates, having been poisoned by the Jews. According to the Life of Constantine it was he who defeated all the arguments of the Jew, and not vice versa; but any other approach can hardly be expected in such a literary document as the life of a saint.

In any case, even from the Life it is clear that the kagan was not converted by Constantine's arguments. However, he allowed his courtiers and his people to be baptized if they chose. Around two hundred of them were actually baptized. Moreover, the kagan wrote a polite letter to the emperor, which read in part as follows: "You have sent us, Sire, a worthy man who by his words and deeds showed us that the Christian faith is holy; and we have understood that it is the true faith and we let those who like it be baptized and hope that we ourselves will be ready to do the same [in due time]. And we are friends and associates of your majesty and are ready to serve you when you require our service." [214] Thus, while reserving his freedom as to religion, the kagan announced friendship and alliance between himself and the emperor. We may say therefore that from the political angle Constantine's mission was fully successful, but only partially so from the point of view of the Church. While new impetus was given to the expansion of Christianity in Khazaria, it did not become the official religion and the kagan himself remained aloof. It should be added that within three or four years after Constantine's journey to Khazaria the kagan was converted to Judaism (around 865).[215]

In seeing Constantine off the kagan offered him rich presents, but Constantine declined to accept them, asking the kagan instead to do him the favor of freeing the Byzantine prisoners without ransom, which he agreed to do.[216] Since there had been no war between Byzantium and the Khazars prior to Constantine's mission, the question naturally arises what Byzantine prisoners were in Khazaria and how they got there. The only possible explanation is that these

213. Macartney, pp. 201-202; cf. Vernadsky, *Conversion,* p. 84.

214. Life, chap. 11.

215. Vernadsky, *Conversion,* p. 85.

216. Life, chap. 11.

were Greeks taken prisoners by the Russians during their raid on Constantinople, then brought to Tmutorokan and sold to the Khazars.

For his return Constantine chose the overland route across the North Caucasian area. He first went to the Caspian Gates; that is, the Daryal Gorge. From there he directed his journey to the eastern shore of the Sea of Azov across arid steppes, where both he and his companions suffered much from thirst and exhaustion.[217] We may wonder why he did not chose the much more convenient route down the Kuban River to Tmutorokan. And once more the answer is, apparently, that the Tmutorokan Russians would not let him pass through their territory. Moreover, he had with him the freed Greek prisoners whom they would have been eager to seize.

After crossing the Sea of Azov Constantine came back to the Crimea and it was during this second Crimean sojourn that he converted the people of Phullae to Christianity.[218] The city of Phullae was situated northeast of the Crimean mountain range, near the modern town of Karasubazar. According to Constantine's Life the Phullaeans worshiped a sacred oak, which Constantine cut down. This story is similar to that of the conversion of the "Huns" in northern Caucasus by the Albanian bishop, Israel, in 681/82.[219] The Huns, like the Phullaeans, worshiped a sacred oak; and Israel, like Constantine, felled it. According to Markwart the worship of trees was widely spread among the Kasogians (Circassians) and the Abasgians, from whom the Alans (As) borrowed it.[220] We may mention in this connection that Constantine Porphyrogenitus, writing in the middle of the tenth century, relates that the Russians (who by that time controlled Kiev) used to sacrifice cocks before a huge oak in the Island of St. Gregory, to be identified as the Khortitsa island on the Dnieper.[221] The Kievan rulers were of Norse descent, but in their army were many Polianians and these were one of the Antic, or As, tribes. By the time of the conversion of the Phullaeans (around 861), part of both the Caucasian and the Crimean As and Rus were already Christian, and the Sugdean Rus even had church books in their own language and script—the "Russian characters"

217. *Idem,* chap. 12.
218. *Ibid.*
219. Brosset, III, 484.
220. Markwart, p. 15.
221. *De Adm.,* 9.

—but further inland, as in Phullae until the arrival of Constantine, the As and the Rus were still pagan.

While he succeeded in the promotion of Christianity in the Crimea and the North Caucasian area, Constantine failed to convert the Tmutorokan Russians, who apparently refused flatly to admit him. However, the example of the Crimean and North Caucasian As and Rus must have gradually impressed the Tmutorokan Rus as well, and in 867 Patriarch Photius was able to announce with exultation that the people of Rhos, once known for their ferocity, now accepted a bishop and performed Christian custom with great zeal.[222] Unfortunately Photius does not state in his epistle where the see of the Rhos bishop was located, but we may safely suppose that it was in Tmutorokan itself, since the see of Tmutorokan is mentioned in the list of bishoprics of the Eparchy of Gothia, which in my opinion must have been compiled by Constantine upon his return from Khazaria.[223] We must therefore consider the bishopric of Tmutorokan the original nucleus of the Russian Church.[224]

6. The Pannonia Mission of Constantine and Methodius and the Commencement of the Slavic Letters.[225]

A year after Constantine's return from Khazaria, he and his brother Methodius assumed a new mission, the results of which proved even more far-reaching for the whole course of development of Slavic culture. This time they were called to the west instead of to the east. The initiative for the new mission came from Prince Rostislav of Moravia. In 862 his envoys came to Constantinople and requested the emperor to send preachers to Moravia to urge the cause of Christianity there. By this time part of the Moravian people including Prince Rostislav himself were already converted to Christianity, chiefly through German missionaries. The latter, however, were not familiar with the Slavic tongue, which was a serious handicap to their preaching. Moreover, the church books they brought with them and the church services they conducted were in Latin, and so incomprehensible to the natives.

In order to grasp fully the significance of Rostislav's decision to

222. Photius, "Epistola 13," Sec. 35 (*PG, 102,* cols. 736-737); Cf. *Les Regestes des Actes du Patriarcat de Constantinople,* I, 2, No. 481 (Istanbul, 1936), pp. 88-89.

223. Vernadsky, *Eparchy,* pp. 70-75.

224. See Vernadsky, *Status,* pp. 300 ff.

225. See Dvornik, *Legendes,* pp. 212-230; Dvornik, *Slaves,* pp. 147-183; Ilyinskii, pp. 71-84.

apply to Constantine for missionaries, we must consider the involved political and ecclesiastical background of the area of the middle Danube, known as Pannonia in the wider sense of the name. Ecclesiastically the area was within the jurisdiction of Rome, but more specifically the bishop of Salzburg claimed authority over the region. With regard to international politics, in the first quarter of the ninth century, as we have seen,[226] the area of the middle Danube was the object of dispute between the Franks and the Bulgars. Moravia remained within the Frankish sphere of influence and in 840 King Louis the German installed Prince Rostislav there as his vassal. Rostislav was at first loyal to Louis, but later attempted to emancipate himself and his country from the German domination.[227] Although he had had himself baptized Rostislav resented the haughty ways of the German bishops. In 855 Louis sent troops to Moravia, but these were defeated by the Moravian prince. Later, Louis offered to Khan Boris of Bulgaria, at that time still a pagan, an alliance against Moravia.[228] It was to forestall the danger of being attacked by the Bulgars in addition to the Germans that Rostislav decided to ask the Byzantine emperor for assistance, both diplomatic and ecclesiastical.

It was natural enough for the Patriarch Photius to entrust the new mission to the two Salonikan brothers, in view both of their knowledge of Slavic and the experience in missionary activities they had acquired in Khazaria; where, it must be remarked, the leading role belonged to Constantine, while Methodius showed no particular initiative. Constantine was leader of the Pannonia mission as well but this time Methodius was also very active, and after Constantine's death in 869 Methodius alone continued the work, proving himself a worthy successor of his great brother.

While discussing the plan of the missionary work in Moravia, Constantine from the outset insisted on the use of the Slavic language for the Moravian Church. His idea was approved by both Photius and the emperor, Michael. It must be noted that the Byzantine Church authorities proved ready on several occasions to recognize the use of native languages in the church, in contrast to the usually uncompromising attitude of Rome. Once the decision to use the Slavic language for church services in Moravia was taken, the

226. See Chap. VII, Sec. 9.

227. On Rostislav see Grot, pp. 97-119; Uspenskii, *Monarkhii,* pp. 40-52.

228. Bury, p. 383; Zlatarski, pp. 14-15.

immediate problem was that of having at least the basic church books translated into Slavic and written in Slavic; and there was no established Slavic alphabet at the time. We may assume that in many cases the Slavs used the Greek alphabet, which however was not quite suited to the Slavic language; as we have seen above,[229] the Crimean As and Rus used some kind of alphabet of their own. Now before launching the Pannonia mission, Constantine had either to agree to the use of the Greek alphabet for Slavonic letters or to approve the "Russian characters" he had studied in Crimea, or else to invent an entirely new Slavic alphabet. According to the Life, Constantine chose the latter course and compiled an alphabet of his own: "And the Philosopher, according to his custom, first started praying together with his assistants; and before long, God responded to the prayer of his servitors, and the divine idea came upon Constantine, and he compiled the characters." [230]

The Slavic alphabet used in the church books and, in a revised form, in the secular literature of the Russians, the Ukrainians, the Bulgars, and the Serbs, is still known as Cyrillic, according to Constantine's monastic name. However, most scholars now doubt that this was the alphabet invented by Constantine (Cyril), and refer the invention of the Cyrillic script to a Bulgarian pupil of Constantine's brother Methodius, at the end of the ninth century.[231] As to Constantine, he is now generally considered the inventor of the so-called Glagolitic alphabet. The problem is hard to solve, since not only no autograph of Constantine has been preserved, but no Slavic manuscript whatever of his time has been found. The earliest specimens of both Glagolitic and Cyrillic script so far known are referred to the reign of Tsar Simeon of Bulgaria (892-927).[232]

The Cyrillic alphabet is based on Greek uncials with the use of some additional characters to denote sounds not covered by the Greek letters. As to the Glagolitic alphabet, its origin is still a mystery. At one time it was generally agreed that it was derived from the Greek cursive, but confidence in this theory has been

229. See Sec. 5, above.

230. Life, chap. 14.

231. Dvornik, *Slaves,* p. 318; G. Ilyinskii, "Gde, kogda, kem i s kakoiu tseliu glagolitsa byla zamenena kirillitsei?," *BS, 3* (1931) 87.

232. On the problem of the origins and the interrelation of the Cyrillic and Glagolitic script see V. Jagić, "Glagolicheskoe pismo," *ESF,* III, 51-230; Karskii, *Paleografiia,* pp. 158-223; V. N. Shchepkin, *Uchebnik Russkoi paleografii* (Moscow, 1918), pp. 11-20; Vajs, pp. 13-21.

considerably shaken.[233] The derivation of the Glagolitic from one or another of the Oriental alphabets, such as the Coptic, the Hebrew, the Samaritan, the Armenian, or the Georgian, has also been suggested by various scholars.[234] Not being a special student of linguistics, nor of paleography, I can hardly claim to be a competent judge of the issues of the Glagolitic controversy. However, since students in these special fields have not so far come to any definitive conclusion I have no alternative to forming some kind of opinion of my own. A certain similarity between the Armenian and Georgian alphabets on the one hand and the Glagolitic alphabet on the other cannot be denied. Since according to my conjecture the "Russian characters" Constantine found in Crimea must have been similarly derived from the Armenian or Georgian (or both), I am ready to second, with certain reservations and to a certain extent, N. K. Nikolskii's theory that the "Russian characters" mentioned in Constantine's Life were the Glagolitic characters.[235] It is significant in this connection that from the inscription on the Reims copy of the Gospel, which is of the fourteenth century, we may conclude that the Glagolitic was known as the "Russian" script.[236]

If so, the obvious conclusion is that Constantine did not invent the Glagolitic alphabet, consequently the alphabet *he* invented must have been the Cyrillic. How then explain the use of the Glagolitic as a second of the two early Slavic alphabets? It may be argued that while inventing the Cyrillic for general use, Constantine kept using the Glagolitic as a kind of cryptic script for confidential messages, initiating into its use only the most trustworthy of his disciples.[237]

233. A. Rahlfs, "Zur Frage nach der Herkunft des Glagolitischen Alphabets," *ZVS, 45* (1913) 285-287. See, however, Vajs, p. 39.

234. On the similarity of the Glagolithic alphabet to the Georgian, see R. Abicht, *Ist die Aehnlichkeit des glagolitischen mit dem grusinischen Alphabet Zufall?* (Leipzig, 1895), inaccessible to me; on Armenian parallels see M. Gaster, *Ilchester lectures on Greeko-Slavonic Literature* (London, 1887), pp. 209-229. The importance of the Caucasian background for the study of the problem was emphasized by V. F. Miller, "K voprosu o slavianskoi azbuke," *ZMNP, 232* (1884), 1-35. He suggested the derivation of the Glagolitic script from the Avestian, which is not convincing. In 1927 V. Pozhidaev offered another hypothesis in connection with the Caucasian background. According to him the Glagolitic should be derived from the Caucasian clan emblems (*tamga*), see M. Grunskyi, "Nova teoriia pro pokhozhdennia Glagolitsy," *UAN, 19* (1928), 266-277. The theory seems hardly plausible.

235. Nikolskii, *Pismena.*

236. *Idem,* pp. 36-37.

237. For the use of the Glagolitic as cryptic script in some of the Cyrillic manuscripts see Karskii, pp. 249-250.

Later, after Constantine's death, secrecy may have lifted and the Glagolitic may have been used together with the Cyrillic or, in some regions, even preferred to it.

While inclined myself to interpret the interrelation of the two scripts in the way just explained, I am also ready in principle to admit the possibility of an alternate approach to the problem. It may be argued that Constantine did not accept the "Russian characters" as he found them, but revised and adapted them more closely to the needs of the Slavic language. Such revision and adaptation may have been called his invention. In such a case, Constantine may still be considered the inventor of the Glagolitic alphabet, which would refer the invention of the Cyrillic to Methodius' disciples.

In the year 863 Constantine and Methodius appeared in Moravia at the court of Prince Rostislav. The history of their activities there is outside the scope of our present work and we must limit ourselves here to some general remarks only. The specific difficulty of the missionary brothers' position was that they had to be on good terms with Byzantium and Rome simultaneously. As a matter of fact there was as yet no schism between the Western and the Eastern Church. Even the denunciation of the Pope's policies by Photius which was to come in 867,[238] did not break the community of churches, the less so since later on Photius himself resumed relations with Rome. The final break was to come two centuries later, under the patriarch Michael Cerularius (1054). The delicacy of Constantine's and Methodius' position resulted from the fact that they were sent as missionaries by the Patriarch of Constantinople into an area which traditionally belonged to the jurisdiction of the Pope of Rome. Had the brothers coming to Moravia insisted on its ecclesiastical submission to Constantinople (as Photius may have instructed them) they would have committed a breach of canonical discipline. But they did nothing of the sort, being imbued by a truly Christian spirit and not by considerations of church policies. Their object was to organize a Slavic Church in Moravia and not to extend the boundaries of the Byzantine Patriarchate. The opposition they met at the onset was not from Rome but from the German clergy.[239] Since these latter were canonically subordinated to the Pope, it was to the Pope that Constantine and Methodius addressed

238. See Sec. 7, below.

239. See P. J. Alexander, "The Papacy, the Bavarian Clergy, and the Slavonic Apostles," *SR, 20* (1941), 206-293.

themselves for a confirmation of their authority in Pannonia. Theoretically, the Pope had the power to organize a new eparchy in Pannonia despite any protest of the Bishop of Salzburg. Actually the Germans put as many obstacles in the brothers' way as they could. Both the German and the Italian clergy opposed vigorously the use of the Slavic language in church services.

In 868 Constantine and Methodius went to Rome in order to defend the rights of the Slavic language, a mission in which they completely succeeded, and Pope Hadrian solemnly deposited copies of Slavic liturgical books on the altars of several churches in Rome.[240] By this time Constantine's health was completely shattered by his intense labors and he died in Rome after receiving the highest monastic rank (*skhima*)[241] under the name of Cyril (869). Methodius was ready to go on with the work alone, and in 870 Pope Hadrian II ordained him Bishop of Pannonia, to have his see at Sirmium (Mitrovica).[242] It seemed that the cause of the Slavic Church was now secured, but just at this moment a palace revolution occurred in Moravia. The Germans skillfully took advantage of the disagreement between Prince Rostislav and his nephew Sviatopolk. With the help of the Germans Sviatopolk arrested his uncle and seized the Moravian throne for himself. Before long the Germans betrayed him and invaded Moravia. It was only in 874 that Sviatopolk succeeded in ousting them and restoring his authority.[243]

While opposing the Germans politically, Sviatopolk proved ready to compromise with them in church matters. He recognized Methodius as archbishop but at the same time sought the advice of a German priest, Wiching. Wiching opposed the Slavic liturgy and in various ways intrigued against Methodius, reporting the latter to the Pope.[244] Methodius went to Rome once more, but although he succeeded in exculpating himself the Pope, in order not to irritate the German prelates, gradually began to curtail the use of Slavic in the Moravian Church. Following Methodius' death (885) the use of the Slavic for the liturgy was barred in Moravia. Methodius' disciples were expelled from the country and had to take refuge in Bulgaria.[245]

240. Life, chap. 17; cf. Dvornik, *Slaves*, p. 199.

241. *Skhima* is a transcription of the Slavic term corresponding to the Greek σχῆμα.

242. Dvornik, *Slaves*, p. 207.

243. On Sviatopolk see Grot, pp. 121-124; Uspenskii, ***Monarkhii***, pp. 63-94.

244. Dvornik, *Slaves*, pp. 262-270.

245. See Sec. 7, below.

While the main results of the Pannonia mission were thus forfeited, the historic work of Constantine and Methodius was not in vain since they laid a solid foundation for building up Slavic letters and Slavic civilization at large, for which they certainly deserve their name as Apostles of the Slavs. In the midst of their hard administrative and missionary work in Pannonia, and in spite of all obstacles, they found time for literary activities, of which the Slavic translation of the Gospels, the Psalms, and some church service books,[246] were the most important fruits. The Slavic language of Constantine's and Methodius' works, which had as its linguistic base the Macedonian dialect,[247] became the language of all Slavic churches—that is, of the Orthodox Slavs—and is therefore known now as Church Slavonic. It was the language of most of the Slavic literati during the Middle Ages and early modern period, and it was also to become the foundation from which the Russian literary language developed. Thus, while the blossoming of Slavic letters in Moravia was of short duration, it lasted long enough to carry the torch first to Bulgaria and Serbia, and then to Russia.

7. *The Conversion of the Danubian Bulgars.*[248]

As we have seen,[249] the diplomatic move of the Moravian prince Rostislav which resulted in sending Christian missionaries from Constantinople to Pannonia was meant to ward off the danger to Moravia of a Franko-Bulgar *rapprochement*. Little is known of the course of negotiations between King Louis the German and Khan Boris of Bulgaria in 862 and 863, but it may be surmised that questions of ecclesiastical policy were among those discussed.[250] While the majority of both the Bulgars and the Slavs subject to them were still pagan, Christianity had started to spread in Bulgaria, chiefly through Greeks; both those who became subject to the khan and the Greek merchants coming to and from Bulgaria. And more generally speaking, as the empire's closest neighbor Bulgaria was

246. It appears that at first only the set of selections from the New Testament for religious service was translated, see Dvornik, *Slaves,* p. 166. Gradually, further translations were made, cf. Ilyinskii, pp. 115-136.

247. N. Durnovo, "Mysli i predpolozheniia o proiskhozhdenii staroslavianskogo yazyka," *BS, 1* (1929), 48-85 and *3* (1931) pp. 68-78; Ilyinskii, pp. 136-164.

248. See Bury, *Eastern,* pp. 381-392; Dvornik, *Slaves,* pp. 184-195; Runciman, pp. 99-130; Zlatarski, I, 2, pp. 21-201.

249. See Sec. 6, above.

250. Bury, *Eastern,* p. 383.

naturally open to Byzantine cultural influences. Khan Boris had thus the same dilemma before him as later on Prince Vladimir of Kiev was to face: whether to oppose Christianity or to promote it in the state interest.[251] A conversion to Christianity offered many advantages, such as enhancing the ruler's prestige, both nationally and internationally, and placing a staff of educated men at his service. On the other hand, Boris could not fail to recognize certain dangers in receiving Christianity from Byzantium. Recognition of the authority of the Patriarch of Constantinople over the would-be Bulgarian Church might lead to the necessity of recognizing the authority of the Byzantine emperor over the Bulgarian state. It seems quite probable that Boris would therefore prefer to receive Christianity not from Byzantium but from Rome, or more particularly from the German prelates under Roman jurisdiction. If this reasoning is correct, church matters must have played a certain role in the parleys between the Franks and the Bulgars.

It is known that in 863 Louis advised Rome of Boris' intention to accept the true faith.[252] An important though delicate point was the problem of the future organization of the Bulgarian Church. Boris must have insisted on a certain autonomy for the Bulgarian Church, in any case of organizing it as a diocese. Later, the Russian princes of Kiev were to make precisely the same demands.[253] While the negotiations between the Franks and the Bulgars dragged along, Byzantine troops entered Bulgaria and Emperor Michael III demanded that Boris break his Frankish alliance. Receiving no help from Germany, Boris was compelled not only to accept the Byzantine ultimatum but even to express his desire to become a Christian. He was baptized, together with some of his courtiers, in 864.[254] The emperor himself was Boris' godfather and consequently Boris accepted the emperor's name, Michael, as his Christian name.

However, the pagan party was still strong among the *boils,* and before long a plot was formed against the khan. The conspirators surrounded the palace, but Boris did not lose courage and with the small retinue of loyal guards made a sortie and dispersed the plotters. The ringleaders were arrested and immediately executed

251. Priselkov, pp. 21-35; Vernadsky, *Status,* pp. 294-302.

252. Dvornik, *Slaves,* p. 186.

253. Priselkov, pp. 10-11, 35-36; Vernadsky, *Status,* p. 298.

254. A. Vaillant and M. Lascaris, "La date de la conversion des Bulgares," *RES, 13* (1933), 5-15.

together with their children in order to prevent any possibility of revenge.[255] The execution of the leaders of the pagan party, most of whom were Bulgars and not Slavs, increased the weight of Slavs at the khan's court. While Boris connected himself with the Christian party without reservations, he was not ready to submit unconditionally to Byzantine leadership. On the contrary, he was soon disappointed in Byzantine coöperation.

We must realize that Patriarch Photius' policy towards the Bulgarian and Moravian churches was entirely different. In sending his missionaries to Pannonia, Photius was ready to have the Pannonian Church organized as an autonomous diocese, and recommended the use of Slavic for the liturgy.[256] Nothing of the sort was meant for Bulgaria. Following Boris' conversion, Greek and Armenian priests were sent thither; no bishop was appointed for Bulgaria and Photius appears to have planned to keep the Bulgarian Church under the direct rule of the patriarchal throne at Constantinople. It is not difficult to understand the causes of difference in Photius' respective attitude toward Moravia and Bulgaria. Moravia was outside the boundaries not only of the Byzantine Empire but of the Constantinople Patriarchate as well. Photius had nothing to lose by the establishment of a national church in Moravia. All the troubles were for the Pope. The territory of Bulgaria, on the contrary, had been from of old within the imperial boundaries, and from the ecclesiastical point of view Thrace was always considered part of the Constantinople Patriarchate and not under Rome.[257] In any case, considerations of imperial centralism and Greek nationalism prevailed in Photius' treatment of Bulgaria.

The Byzantine policy in this matter proved to be very shortsighted. When Boris accepted Christianity he must from the very beginning have insisted on having a bishop in charge of the Bulgarian Church, to make it potentially autonomous. Now that from his point of view the Byzantine authorities had cheated him, he sent envoys to Rome asking the Pope, Nicholas, to dispatch a bishop and priests to Bulgaria (August, 866).[258] Boris also addressed himself to King Louis the German, asking his help in the matter through his influence with the Pope. The Pope did not need any prompting,

255. Runciman, pp. 105-106.
256. See Sec. 6, above.
257. N. Suvorov, *Uchebnik tserkovnogo prava* (Moscow, 1912), pp. 31-32.
258. Dvornik, *Slaves*, p. 191

however, since he was only too eager to seize the opportunity of spreading his control over the Balkan peninsula. He immediately sent to Boris two legates for the organization of the Bulgarian Church under the authority of Rome. By making this move the Pope trespassed upon the prerogatives of the Constantinople Patriarchate, and Photius' irritation may be easily imagined. A violent conflict between the Pope and the Patriarch now developed and Photius solemnly denounced Nicholas' action, pointing likewise to what he considered theological errors of the Roman Church, the most important of them being the Filioque clause in the Latin Creed (867).[259]

The danger of a complete break between the Eastern and the Western Church was averted by a palace revolution in Constantinople. Emperor Michael III was assassinated by Basil the Macedonian, who seized the throne himself (September 23, 867). Simultaneously Photius was deposed and Ignatius elected patriarch instead.[260] While Ignatius wanted a compromise with Rome on theological differences, he proved no less ready than Photius to insist on Byzantine prerogative with regard to the Bulgarian Church. We must take into consideration that the khan, Boris, was by this time himself disappointed in the Pope's attitude. Of the two legates sent to Bulgaria one—Formozo, Bishop of Port—succeeded in winning Boris' confidence. Formozo showed great consideration of the needs of the Bulgarian Church and intended to organize it as a separate unit. This was apparently contrary to the Pope's secret plans, and Formozo's enemies in Rome voiced their suspicions that he was thinking more of his own interests than of those of the Roman see. For this reason, when Boris asked the Pope to appoint Formozo as the first Bishop of Bulgaria he not only refused but even called Formozo back to Rome.

Boris was deeply offended and addressed himself once more to Constantinople for guidance in church affairs. The matter was referred to the Eighth Ecumenical Council which met in Constantinople in 869-70. The council (subsequently repudiated by the Orthodox) anathematized Photius, but on the other hand, in spite of the protest of the Pope's legates, reaffirmed the authority of the Patriarch of Constantinople over Bulgaria.[261] The controversy did

259. Bury, *Eastern*, pp. 200-203.
260. *Idem*, pp. 203-204.
261. Runciman, pp. 113-114.

not end here, however, since the Pope was not willing to revoke his claims.

The struggle between Byzantium and Rome affected painfully the development of the young Bulgarian Church, the more so since neither Pope nor Patriarch was ready to recognize the validity of the Slavic language in the church service. It was only after the coming of Methodius' disciples—Clement, Nahum, and others—from Moravia to Bulgaria (886) that a Slavification of the Bulgarian Church became possible. Slavonic schools were established for the training of Bulgarian priests and Slavonic copies of the most important church books were prepared. Finally the Bulgarian national assembly of 893, which proclaimed Boris' son Simeon ruler (*archont*) of Bulgaria, simultaneously recognized the Slavic language as the official language of the Church.[262] Clement was appointed Bishop of Velich. The period of the reign of Tsar Simeon (893-927) was one of rapid rise and flowering for Slavic letters in Bulgaria.[263]

8. Kiev in the 870's and its Capture by Oleg.

We have now to turn back to Kiev. As we have seen,[264] in 860 Askold and Dir joined forces with the Azov-area Russians for an attack on Constantinople. It is known that after the campaign of 860 at least some of the Russians were converted to Christianity, and were put under the authority of a bishop whose see was, presumably, at Tmutorokan.[265] In connection with these developments, we would naturally very much like to know the attitude towards Christianity of those Russians who were controlled by Askold and Dir, and whether Askold and Dir themselves were ready to promote Christianity in Kiev. Unfortunately there is no information available in our sources.[266]

On the other hand, it seems quite probable that in the 860's and 870's some Christian missionaries may have reached Kiev not only from the south but from the west as well, namely from Moravia. We

262. *Idem,* pp. 134-135; Zlatarski, pp. 253-277.

263. On letters and art in the age of Simeon see Runciman, pp. 138-143; Zlatarski, pp. 282-284.

264. See Sec. 4, above.

265. See Sec. 5, above.

266. For a survey of the problem of the spread of Christianity in Russia prior to Vladimir's conversion see N. Polonskaia, "K voprosu o khristianstve na Rusi do Vladimira." *ZMNP, 71* (1917), 33-80.

have seen,[267] that by the labor of the saints Cyril and Methodius, Christianity was firmly established in Moravia with Slavic as the first, though only temporary, language of the Moravian Church. For a number of years Moravia thus became an important center of Slavic culture and education. Although Prince Sviatopolk (870-894) was not a champion of the Slavic Church,[268] he helped the expansion of the Church indirectly by extending the boundaries of his state. To his realm we may refer the mention by Al-Bakri and some other Oriental writers of a mighty Slavic kingdom, the capital of which was called al-Firaq (Prague). According to Gardizi the name of the Slavic ruler was Svet-Malik.[269] This king controlled among other lands the province of Jervab, that is, of the Khorvatians (Croats).

There cannot be any doubt that the Khorvatians of Galicia are meant here.[270] The city of Jervab mentioned by Al-Bakri is probably Krakow. These Khorvatians were of the same stock as the southern Croats (the Balkan ones), but because of their geographic location they became closely connected with the East Slavs and subsequently joined the federation of the Russian tribes ruled by Kievan princes. Even at that remote period there must have been commercial relations between Kiev and Galicia,[271] and with the merchants, as was often the case elsewhere, Christian missionaries may have come. We may safely surmise that some of St. Cyril's and St. Methodius' disciples went preaching to Galicia, and from there some of them may have tried to communicate with Kiev.[272] It is to this "Moravian period" that the origin of the idea of the unity of three Slavic tribes—the Czechs, the Poles, and the Russians[273]—may be referred; later the legend of the three brothers, Czech, Liakh (Pole), and Rus was launched to express the idea of the unity of these three Slavic peoples even more clearly.[274]

267. See Sec. 6, above.

268. *Ibid.*

269. Macartney, p. 211, *Malik* means "king" in Arabic.

270. See Sec. 1, above.

271. Cf. A. V. Florovskii, *Chekhi i Vostochnye Slaviane* (Prague, 1935), pp. 158-182.

272. It appears that the compiler of the Russian *Primary Chronicle* used some Moravian literary materials. See Nikolskii, *Povest*, pp. 45-84. Exception has been taken to some of Nikolskii's conclusions by V. M. Istrin, "Moravskaia istoriia Slavian," *BS*, *3* (1931), 308-331, and *4* (1932), pp. 36-55, but even Istrin admits that copies of Moravian manuscripts were in circulation in Kievan Russia in the eleventh "and possibly even in the tenth century" (p. 54).

273. Hyp., col. 19.

274. Nikolskii, *Povest*, pp. 78-83.

In speaking of the expansion of Kievan commerce in the 870's we may now emphasize the growing importance of the upper Dnieper way. The story of the capture of Kiev by Oleg (878) as told by the chronicler of the eleventh century[275] is characteristic. According to this tale, Oleg pretended to be a merchant and it was with the help of this artifice that he succeeded in seizing the city. The obvious implication of the story is that by this time there was nothing unusual in the arrival of merchant boats at Kiev from Smolensk.

Because of the dearth of evidence we are unable to give any precise data on the cultural and economic development of Kiev in the 870's. However, taking into consideration that the city must have maintained fairly close relations—commercial and other—with Smolensk on the north, Galicia in the west, and the Azov area on the southeast, we may assume that, born of these various influences, important cultural changes were taking place in Kiev. Politically, as has been already mentioned,[276] Kiev seems to have been controlled by the Magyars at this time.

At the end of 870's the seemingly peaceful development of Kievan life was broken by the arrival of a new band of Varangians who reached the city from Novgorod. In order to understand the background of this event we have now to turn our attention to Novgorod. We have seen that the Jutland prince Riurik appeared in Ladoga around 856[277] and that some time later he took hold of Novgorod.[278] Several years must have elapsed while Riurik put in order his new possessions in the Novgorod area. He continued, however, to watch the development of events in the west, and in 867 made a vain attempt to regain Friesland with the help of the Danes.[279] The death in 869 of Lothaire, king of Lotharingia, who had in 854 received Friesland as a fief from his father the emperor Lothaire,[280] called for a general redivision of all the holdings in the Frankish Empire, and Riurik decided that the moment was propitious for presenting his claims as well. He went, accordingly, to Nimwegen for an interview with Charles the Bald (a brother to Emperor Lothaire) and promised to support him for due consideration. In 873 Riurik received Friesland back, and thereafter his name receives no fur-

275. Cross, p. 146.
276. See Sec. 4, above.
277. See Sec. 3, above.
278. See Sec. 4, above.
279. Kruse, p. 328.
280. See Sec. 3, above.

ther mention in the Frankish annals.[281] In the Russian *Book of Annals* Riurik's death is recorded under the year 879.[282] If we admit here the same chronological error as in the story of the Russian attack on Constantinople—that is, an error of six years—we may refer Riurik's death to the year 873. But, as we shall presently see, the chronicler's computation was gradually being corrected, and the error in this case may have been four or three years instead of six. In any case, Riurik must have died not long after regaining his old fief.[283]

According to the tradition of the *Book of Annals* Riurik left in Novgorod an infant son, Igor, in whose name his kinsman Oleg ruled at first.[284] The name Igor occurs in the Skioldung clan. The ancestor of the Skioldungs—Riurik's great-great-great-grandfather—was called Ivar, which may be considered another form of the name Ingvar, or Igor.[285] According to the chronicles, Riurik's son was the same Igor who became Prince of Kiev after Oleg's death and who reigned, according to the tradition, from 912 to 945.[286] The identity of the two Igors is hardly acceptable, however. In that case Igor of Kiev would have had to be over 70 at the time of his death (born not later than 873, died 945). Meanwhile there is no indication in the chronicles that Prince Igor was that old. In 941-44 he personally led a campaign, full of hardships, against the Byzantine Empire.[287] In 945 he also personally directed a raid on the Drevlianians, during which he was killed.[288] In addition, his son Sviatoslav was born in 942.[289] In view of these considerations we may suggest that between Riurik of Novgorod and Igor of Kiev there was at least one intermediary generation, possibly two.[290]

As to Oleg, in the so-called Joakim's chronicle he is called "Urmanin," that is a Norwegian.[291] He may be identified as the Odd of

281. Beliaev, p. 269.
282. Cross, p. 146.
283. According to Kendrick, p. 206, n. 1, Roric of Jutland [i.e., Riurik of Novgorod] died in 876.
284. Cross, pp. 146-147.
285. Beliaev, p. 243.
286. Cross, pp. 157-164.
287. *Idem*, pp. 157-159.
288. *Idem*, p. 164.
289. *Idem*, p. 158.
290. Cf. Hrushevskyi, I, 391.
291. Tatishchev, I, 35.

the Norse sagas.[292] It is possible that the name under which he is mentioned in Russian chronicles is but a derivation from the name of his native country. "Oleg" is a Russian transcription of "Helgi," which may mean a native of Halogaland (Helgaland) in Norway.[293] In Oleg we have thus a representative of the third stream of the Scandinavian flood in North Russia, the first two being the Swedish (Askold and Dir), and the Danish (Riurik). We assume that Oleg must have come to Novgorod not alone but as the leader of a strong retinue, consisting of course chiefly of Norwegians, which may explain the fact that he became ruler after Riurik's death, or even earlier, after Riurik's final departure to the west. Sailing westward, Riurik must have taken with him at least part of his Danish retinue, and what Danes remained in Novgorod had probably to compromise with the Norwegians and to pledge their allegiance to Oleg. We have already seen[294] that the break of communication with the Azov area which occurred around 840 must have painfully affected the welfare of the north. While Askold and Dir succeeded in reaching Kiev, they in turn lost their connection with Novgorod. On the other hand, Riurik, even after he became the ruler of Novgorod, being still intent on regaining his western possessions was little interested in any expansion to the south.

It is thus to Oleg that credit must be given for uniting the north and the south of Russia. The beginning of his campaign to the south is described in the chronicle in the following words: "Oleg set forth, taking with him many warriors from among the Varangians, the Chud, the Slavs, the Merians, the Ves, and the Krivichians."[295] It is plain that Oleg was by this time the recognized leader of all the northern tribes. It is also characteristic that Russians (*Rus'*) are not mentioned among his supporters, and for obvious reasons. The old *Rus'* (of Swedish extraction and Azovian background) must have left Novgorod for Kiev much earlier with Askold and Dir, while the new Frisian *Rus'*, or rather what was left of them after

292. Beliaev, p. 257.

293. *Idem*, p. 256. As R. Jakobson has suggested to me, the name *Helgi* means in Norse "the Holy" (cf. Cleasby, p. 255); the Russian *Veshchii Oleg* ("Oleg the Wise") would be *Helgi Helgi* in Norse, so that the Russian epithet *Veshchii* ("the Wise") is apparently only a trans. of the Norse name into Russian. A. Liashchenko's study on Oleg, quoted by Beliaev, p. 257, is inaccessible to me.

294. See Sec. 3, above.

295. Hyp., col. 17; cf. Cross, p. 146.

Riurik's departure for Friesland, were now merged with Oleg's Varangians.

Oleg's campaign is dated in the *Primary Chronicle* A.M. 6390 (A.D. 882).[296] As before, we must expect a chronological error, although not to the extent of six years as in the episode of the Russian attack on Constantinople. We must take into consideration that the chronicler's date for Oleg's treaty with the Greeks is correct (911). It is apparent that in the course of his narrative the chronicler was gradually adjusting his computation. Therefore we may suppose that the error in dating Oleg's first campaign was less than in the dating of Askold's raid on Constantinople—perhaps not six but, let us say, between four and two years. In this case, Oleg's campaign to Kiev may be referred to between A.D. 878 and 880 (tentatively, 878).

Oleg advanced cautiously, trying to secure his control over the most important points along the Dnieper riverway, in each of which he left some of his soldiers as garrison. "And he took the city (Smolensk), and set up a garrison there. Thence he went on and captured Liubech, and set up a garrison there. He then came to the hills of Kiev."[297] According to the *Primary Chronicle,* Oleg captured Kiev by ruse. He concealed his troops near the bank of the river and then sent messengers to Askold and Dir to announce the arrival of a trade caravan.[298] It is quite possible that Oleg's messengers were some Smolensk merchants who had come to Kiev even earlier, so that their appearance was not suspicious to the Kievan rulers. The device worked: both Askold and Dir went to the boats without sufficient protection and were slain on the spot by Oleg's warriors. As we have already mentioned,[299] their bodies were then carried to Olom's palace. With their assassination the Magyar rule in Kiev came to a close. "And Oleg set himself up as prince in Kiev."[300]

296. Cross, p. 146.
297. Hyp., col. 17.
298. *Ibid.; PSRL,* IX, 15.
299. See Sec. 4, above.
300. Cross, p. 146.

9. *Concluding Remarks.*

The seizure of Kiev by Oleg opens a new period in Russian history, that of the so-called Kievan state or Kievan Russia (*Rus'*). In contrast with the previous South Russian state-like formations of the Antic and the Khazar periods, based upon the Don and Azov area, it is the Dnieper riverway—"from the Varangians to the Greeks" (*iz Variag v Greki*)—which now becomes the geographic pivot of the Russian state. For Oleg, however, Kiev was only the first, be it the most important, station on his drive south. The southern Dnieper area remained for a number of years in the hands of the Magyars, and it was not until about thirty years after his conquest of Kiev that Oleg was able to start his first campaign to Constantinople. Nevertheless, Kiev was his base for any further expansion southward and that is why we consider the date of his coming to Kiev an important landmark, with which we may conveniently conclude this volume.

In this last chapter of our outline of the history of ancient Russia we have dealt with variegated events which took place during some twoscore years between the Russian embassy to Constantinople in 838-39 and the conquest of Kiev by Oleg, around 878. At first glance it may seem that there is little organic connection between the events discussed, save mere chronological sequence. Such an impression—if the reader happens to have it—must be partly the result of the width of the geographical background we have taken into account. We have had to shift our attention constantly from north to south, from east to west, watching closely important political developments not only in the Baltic region but also on the southeastern shore of the North Sea; traveling now to the Caucasus and now to the middle Danube. In addition to outlining the political and military events we have also reviewed ecclesiastical policies and trends of cultural progress, since this is a significant period—the age of the formation of the medieval Slavic civilization at large. It is in this age that the cultural foundation for so-called Kievan Russia was laid. True, Christianity became the official religion of the Kievan *Rus'* only at the end of the tenth century. But the flourishing of Christianity in Russia in the eleventh century can never be properly understood unless we realize that part of the Russian tribes—the southeastern and the western ones—had been influenced by the

Christian idea since at least the 860's. The appearance of such accomplished spiritual leaders as for example the metropolitan Hilarion, in the eleventh century, is an evidence that Christianity must have struck root in Russian society at a much earlier period. Without some knowledge of that early background the maturity of Russian Christian culture in the eleventh century would seem an unexplained miracle. It was indeed in the ninth century and in regions as far apart as the Azov area, Moravia, and Bulgaria that the spadework was done for the growth of Christianity in Russia.

The foundations of the economic regime of Kievan Russia were likewise laid long before the tenth century. Agriculture made considerable progress all over Russia in the course of the eighth and ninth centuries. As to commerce, Tmutorokan was still in the ninth century a more important center than Kiev, and it kept its position even in the early part of the Kievan period. Both in the tenth and in the first half of the eleventh century, when the Dnieper riverway had already been firmly established, Russian princes tried to keep intact their connections with Tmutorokan and watched closely the events of the Azov area.

From the political as from the strategic point of view, Tmutorokan as late as in the tenth century was almost as important as Kiev. Vladimir's Crimean campaign of 989[301] was partly motivated by his desire to secure his hold over Tmutorokan, the old capital of the first Russian Kaganate. And it is characteristic that following his Crimean campaign Vladimir himself assumed the title of kagan, which his son Yaroslav also held after him.[302] The rulers of Kiev thus became political successors of the *Rus'* kagans of Tmutorokan. The use of the title of kagan by the first Kievan princes shows clearly the wide range of their political interests as well as their dreams of empire. The new inroads of the Turkish nomads, first of the Patzinaks and then of the Cumans, severed Kiev from the Azov region and thus made the realization of the imperial plan impossible. The position of the city—would-be capital of an empire—was thus undermined. In due time, the loss of Kiev's connection with the Azov and North Caucasian areas proved to be one of the major, although not immediate, causes of the subsequent decline and final downfall of the Kievan Kaganate.

301. Vernadsky, *Status*, pp. 297-302.

302. Both Vladimir and Yaroslav were referred to as kagans by the Metropolitan Hilarion. See Vernadsky, *Status*, p. 301; also, *RIB*, *36* (1920), 103.

ABBREVIATIONS

AA *American Anthropologist.*

Abaev V. I. Abaev, "Alanica," *ANOO* (1935), pp. 881-894.

Aboba F. I. Uspenskii, K. V. Shkorpil and others, "Materialy dlia Bolgarskikh drevnostei: Aboba-Pliska," with an album of plates, *RAIC, 10* (1905).

AH *Archaeologia Hungarica.*

AIK *Annales de l' Institut Kondakov.*

AIM Académie des Inscriptions, *Mémoires présentés par divers savants.*

AJ *The Antiquaries Journal.*

AJA *American Journal of Archaeology.*

AK Arkheologicheskaia Komissiia, *Izvestiia.*

AN Akademiia Nauk, *Izvestiia.*

An. Bel. "Anonymi Belae regis notarii de Gestis Hungarorum liber." See Sources, II, 1.

ANIR Akademiia Nauk, *Izvestiia po Russkomu Yazyku i Slovesnosti.*

ANM Akademiia Nauk, *Mémoires.*

ANOO Akademiia Nauk, *Izvestiia,* Otdelenie Obshchestvennykh Nauk.

ANORI Akademiia Nauk, Otdelenie Russkogo Yazyka i Slovesnosti, *Izvestiia.*

ANORS Akademiia Nauk, Otdelenie Russkogo Yazyka i Slovesnosti, *Sbornik.*

ANSR Akademiia Nauk, *Sbornik po Russkomu Yazyku i Slovesnosti.*

ANZ Akademiia Nauk, *Zapiski.*

ANZI Akademiia Nauk, *Zapiski po istoriko-filologicheskomu otdeleniiu.*

Aristov N. Aristov, *Promyshlennost drevnei Rusi* (St. Petersburg, 1866).

Arne T. J. Arne, *La Suède et l'Orient* (Upsala, 1914).

Artamonov M. I. Artamonov, *Ocherki drevneishei istorii Khazar* (Leningrad, 1936).

Artsikhovskii, *Kurgany* A. V. Artsikhovskii, *Kurgany Viatichei* (Moscow, 1930).

ASP *Archiv für slavische Philologie.*

AUA Aarhus Universitet, *Aarskrift.*

AWB Preussische Akademie der Wissenschaften, Berlin, *Sitzungsberichte* (Phil.-Hist. Klasse).

AWV Akademie der Wissenschaften, Vienna, *Denkschriften* (Phil.-Hist. Klasse).

Ballagi M. Ballagi, *Wörterbuch der Ungarischen und Deutschen Sprache,* Vol. I (Pest, 1872).

BAN Akademiia Nauk BSSR., Institut Istorii, *Pratsy sektsii arkheologii.*

Barsov N. P. Barsov, *Ocherki Russkoi istoricheskoi geografii* (2d ed. Warsaw, 1885).

Bartold W. Barthold, *Turkestan Down to the Mongolian Invasion* (London, 1928).

Beliaev N. T. Beliaev, "Rorik Iutlandskii i Riurik nachalnoi letopisi," *SK, 3* (1929), 215-270.

Berneker E. Berneker, *Slavisches Etymologisches Wörterbuch* (Heidelberg, Vol. I, 1908-13; Vol. II, Fasc. 1, *s.a.*).

Beshevliev V. Beshevliev, "Prvobolgarski nadpisi." See Sources, I, 1.

BGA *Bibliotheca Geographorum Arabicorum*, ed. M. J. de Goje (Leyden).

BNJ *Byzantinisch-Neugriechische Jahrbücher.*

Bogaevskii P. M. Bogaevskii, "Ocherki religioznykh predstavlenii Votiakov," *EO* (1890): I, No. 2, 116-163; II, No. 2, 77-109; III, No. 4, 42-70.

Book of Annals *Povest Vremennykh Let.* See Sources, II, 3.

BP *Bolgarski Pregled.*

Braun F. Braun, "Razyskaniia v oblasti Goto-Slavianskikh otnoshenii," *ANORS, 64,* No. 12 (1899).

Bromberg J. Bromberg, "Toponymical and Historical Miscellanies," *Byz. 12* (1937), 151-180, and 449-475; *13* (1938), 9-71.

Brosset M. Brosset, *Histoire de la Géorgie,* Vol. I (St. Petersburg, 1849); Vol. III, *Additions et Eclaircissements* (1851); Vol. IV, *Introduction et Tables des Matières* (1858).

Browne E. G. Browne, *A History of Persian Literature under Tatar Dominion* (Cambridge, 1920).

Brueckner A. Brueckner, *Dzieje Kultury Polskiej,* I (Krakow, 1930).

Brueckner, *Litwa* A. Brueckner, *Starozytna Litwa* (Warsaw, 1909).

Brun F. K. Brun [Bruun], "Chernomor'e," I-II (*NU, 28* and *30,* 1879-80).

BS *Byzantinoslavica.*

Bury J. B. Bury, *History of the Later Roman Empire,* Vols. I-II (London, 1923).

Bury, *Constitution* J. B. Bury, *The Constitution of the Later Roman Empire* (Cambridge, 1910).

Bury, *Eastern* J. B. Bury, *A History of the Eastern Roman Empire* (London, 1912).

Bury, *System* J. B. Bury, "The Imperial Administrative System in the Ninth Century," British Academy, Supplemental Papers, I (London, 1911).

Bury, *1889* J. B. Bury, *A History of the Later Roman Empire,* Vol. II (London, 1889).

Byz. *Byzantion.*

BZ *Byzantinische Zeitschrift.*

CAH *Cambridge Ancient History.*

CGU Corpus der Griechischen Urkunden des Mittelalters und der neueren Zeit.

Charanis P. Charanis, *Church and State in the Later Roman Empire* (Madison, Wisconsin, 1939).

Charmoy F. Charmoy, Relation de Masoudy. See Sources, II, 2, A.

Charpentier Jarl Charpentier, "Die ethnographische Stellung der Tocharer," *ZDMG, 71* (1917), 347-388.

Cleasby *An Icelandic-English Dictionary,* based on the ms. collections of the late Richard Cleasby, enlarged and completed by Gudbrand Vigfusson (Oxford, 1874).

Cross S. H. Cross, *The Russian Primary Chronicle* (Cambridge, Mass., Harvard University Press, 1930).

Da Costa G. Da Costa-Louillet, "Y eut-il des invasions Russes dans l'Empire Byzantin avant 860?," *Byz. 15* (1941), 231-248.

DD *Dela i Dni.*

De Adm. Constantine Porphyrogenitus, *De Administrando Imperii, PG, 113.*

De cer. Constantine Porphyrogenitus, *De Ceremoniis Aulae Byzantinae, PG, 112.*

Deguignes Deguignes, *Histoire Générale des Huns,* Vol. I, in two parts (Paris, 1756).

Doelger, Regesten F. Doelger, Regesten der Kaiserurkunden des Ostroemischen Reiches, *CGU,* Ser. I, Pt. 1 (Munich, 1941).

Dopsch A. Dopsch, *Grundlagen der Europäischen Kulturentwicklung,* I-II (2d ed. Vienna, 1923-24).

There is a somewhat abridged English ed., under the title, *The Economic and Social Foundations of European Civilization* (New York and London, 1937). The German ed. is cited, unless otherwise stated.

Dovnar-Zapolskii *Russkaia istoriia pod redaktsiei M. V. Dovnar-Zapolskogo,* Vol. I (Moscow, 1910).

Dvornik, *Légendes* F. Dvornik, *Les Légendes de Constantin et de Methode vues de Byzance* (Prague, 1933).

Dvornik, *Slaves* F. Dvornik, *Les Slaves, Byzance et Rome au IX Siècle* (Paris, 1926).

Ebert M. Ebert, *Suedrussland im Altertum* (Bonn and Leipzig, 1921).

Eck A. Eck, *Le Moyen Age Russe* (Paris, 1933).

Efimenko P. P. Efimenko, *"Dorodovoe obschestvo," GA, 79* (1934).

EI *Encyclopaedia of Islam.*

EO *Etnograficheskoe Obozrenie.*

ES Brockhaus-Efron, *Entsiklopedicheskii Slovar.*

ESA *Eurasia Septentrionalis Antiqua.*

ESF *Entsiklopediia Slavianskoi Filologii.*

Exc. Ins. *Excerpta de Insidiis,* see Constantine Porphyrogenitus, *Excerpta Historica,* III. See Sources, II, 1.

Fehér G. Fehér, "Les monuments de la culture Protobulgare," *AH, 7* (1931).

Fettich N. Fettich, "Die Metallkunst der landnehmenden Ungarn," *AH, 21* (1937).

FFC *FF Communications ed. for the Folklore Fellows* (Helsinki).

FUF *Finnisch-Ugrische Forschungen.*

GA Gosudarstvennaia Akademiia Istorii Materialnoi Kultury, *Izvestiia.*

GAM Gosudarstvennaia Akademiia Istorii Materialnoi Kultury, *Memoirs.*

Gedeonov S. Gedeonov, *Variagi i Rus,* I-II (St. Petersburg, 1876).

Gibbon *The History of the Decline and Fall of the Roman Empire* by Edward Gibbon, ed. by J. B. Bury (London, 1898-1900). 7 vols.

Goertz K. K. Gerts, *Sobranie Sochinenii,* I-II (St. Petersburg, 1898).

Gordlevskii, *Slovar* *Turetsko-Russkii Slovar,* sostavil D. A. Magazanik pod redaktsiei V. A. Gordlevskogo.

Gordon E. V. Gordon, *An Introduction to Old Norse* (Oxford, 1927).

Gorodtsov V. A. Gorodtsov, "Dako-Sarmatskie elementy v Russkom narodnom iskusstve," *IMT*, I (1926).

Gotie Yu. V. Gotie, *Zheleznyi Vek v Vostochnoi Evrope* (Moscow-Leningrad, 1930).

Gotie, *Ocherki* Yu. V. Gotie, *Ocherki po istorii materialnoi kultury Vostochnoi Evropy*, I (Moscow, 1925).

Grégoire, *Habitat* H. Grégoire, "L'Habitat primitif des Magyars," *Byz.* *13* (1938), 267-278.

Grégoire, *Sources* H. Grégoire, "Les sources épigrafiques de l'histoire Bulgare," *Byz.*, *9* (1934), 745-786.

Grekov B. D. Grekov, *Kievskaia Rus* (3d ed. Moscow-Leningrad, 1939).

Grigoriev V. V. Grigor'ev, *Rossiia i Aziia* (St. Petersburg, 1876).

Groot, *Hunnen* J. J. M. de Groot, *Chinesische Urkunden*. See Sources, II, 2, C.

Grot K. Ya. Grot, *Moraviia i Madiary* (St. Petersburg, 1881).

Grousset R. Grousset, *L'Empire des Steppes* (Paris, 1939).

Haloun G. Haloun, "Zur Ue-tsi Frage," *ZDMG*, *91* (1937), 243-318.

Halphen L. Halphen, *Les Barbares des grandes invasions aux conquêtes Turques du XI-e siècle* (Paris, 1926).

Harkavy A. Harkavy [Garkavi], *Skazaniia musulmanskikh pisatelei o Slavianakh i Russkikh* (St. Petersburg, 1870).

Hauptmann, *Kroaten* L. Hauptmann, "Kroaten, Goten und Sarmaten," *Germanoslavica*, Vol. III (1935).

Herrmann A. Herrmann, "Tocharoi," *PW*, Ser. 2, *12* (1937).

HGM *Historici Graeci Minores*, ed. L. Dindorf, Vols. I-II (Leipzig, 1870-71).

Howorth H. H. Howorth, "The Avars," *JRAS*, *21* (1889), 721-810.

Hrushevskyi M. S. Hrushevskyi [Grushevskii], *Istoriia Ukrainy-Rusi*, Vol. I (Lvov, 2d ed. 1904); Vol. VII (Kiev-Lvov, 1909).

Hyp. Hypatian version of the *Book of Annals*. See Sources, II, 3.

IAI Institut Arkheologii i Iskusstvoznaniia (Moscow, RANION), Otdelenie Arkheologii.

IBG Irkutsk, Biologo-Geograficheskii Institut, *Izvestiia*.

Ibn-Fadhlan Fadhlan, Ibn, Krachkovskii's ed. See Sources, II, 2, A.

IF *Indogermanische Forschungen*.

IIM Akademiia Nauk, Institut Istorii Materialnoi Kultury, *Kratkie Soobshcheniia*.

Ilyinskii G. A. Il'inskii, *Opyt sistematicheskoi Kirillo-Mefodievskoi bibliografii* (Sofia, 1934).

IMO Istoricheskii Muzei, *Otchet*.

IMT Istoricheskii Muzei, *Trudy*.

IPE V. V. Latyshev, *Inscriptiones Antiquae*. See Sources, I, 1.

Istrin, *Khronika* George Hamartolus, *Khronika*. See Sources, II, 3.

IUT Irkutsk, Universitet, *Trudy professorov i prepodavatelei*.

IZ *Istoricheskie Zapiski*.

JAIG *Journal of the Anthropological Institute of Great Britain and Ireland*.

JAOS *Journal of the American Oriental Society*.

JKGS *Jahrbücher für Kultur und Geschichte der Slaven*.

JHS *The Journal of Hellenic Studies*.

Jordanis Jordanis, *Getica*. See Sources, *II*, 1.

JRAS *The Journal of the Royal Asiatic Society.*

Kalaidovich K. Kalaidovich, *Ioann Eksarkh Bolgarskii* (Moscow, 1824).

Karskii, *Paleografiia* E. F. Karskii, *Slavianskaia Kirillovskaia Paleografiia* (Leningrad, 1928).

KCA *Körösi Czoma Archiwum.*

Kendrick T. D. Kendrick, *A History of the Vikings* (London, 1930).

Kerner R. J. Kerner, *The Urge to the Sea: the Course of Russian History* (Berkeley and Los Angeles, 1942).

Khristomatiia M. F. Vladimirskii-Budanov, *Khristomatiia po istorii Russkogo prava,* Vol. I (6th ed. St. Petersburg and Kiev, 1908).

Khudiakov M. G. Khudiakov, "Votskie rodovye deleniia," *KUO, 30,* 3, pp. 339-356, and *31,* 1, pp. 1-18 (1920).

Kletnova E. Kletnova, "Velikii Gnezdovskii Mogilnik," *Niederlův Sbornik* (Prague, 1925), pp. 309-322.

Kliuchevskii V. O. Kliuchevskii, *Kurs Russkoi Istorii,* Vol. I (Petrograd, 1918).

Kniga *Kniga Bolshomu Chertezhu* (2 ed. St. Petersburg, 1858).

Kokovtsov P. K. Kokovtsov, *Evreisko-Khazarskaia perepiska v X veke* (Leningrad, 1932).

Kondakov, *Drevnosti* Count I. I. Tolstoy and N. P. Kondakov, *Russkie Drevnosti* (St. Petersburg, 1889-99), 6 vols.

Kondakov, *Ocherki* N. P. Kondakov, *Ocherki i Zametki po istorii srednevekovogo iskusstva i kultury* (Prague, 1929).

Kruse F. Kruse, *Chronicòn Nortmannorum* (Hamburg and Gotha, 1851).

Kulakovskii Yu. Kulakovskii, *Istoriia Vizantii,* Vols. I-III (Kiev, 1910-15).

Kulakovskii, *Alany* Yu. Kulakovskii, *Alany po svedeniiam klassicheskikh i vizantiiskikh pisatelei* (Kiev, 1899).

Kulakovskii, *Tavrida* Yu. Kulakovskii, Proshloe Tavridy (2d ed. Kiev, 1914).

Kunik, Al-Bekri A. Kunik and Baron V. Rosen, "Izvestiia Al-Bekri i drugikh avtorov o Rusi i Slavianakh," *ANZ, 32,* Suppl. No. 2 (1878).

Kunik, *Berufung* Ernst [i.e., Arist] Kunik, *Die Berufung der schwedischen Rodsen durch die Finnen und Slaven* (St. Petersburg, 1844).

KUO Kazan, Universitet, Obshchestvo Arkheologii, Istorii i Etnografii, *Izvestiia.*

Latyshev V. V. Latyshev, *Scythica et Caucasica,* Vols. I-II (St. Petersburg, 1890-1904).

Levchenko M. V. Levchenko, "Vizantia i Slaviane v VI-VII vekakh," *VDI, 4* (1938), 23-48.

Liddell-Scott *Greek-English Lexicon,* by H. G. Liddell and R. Scott (new ed. in 2 vols., Oxford, 1925-40).

Life The Pannonian Life of Constantine the Philosopher (St. Cyril). See Sources, II, 3.

Liubomirov P. G. Liubomirov, "Torgovye sviazi Rusi s Vostokom v VIII-IX vekakh," Sar. Univ., I, *3* (1923), 5-38.

Longnon, *Géographie* A. Longnon, *Géographie de la Gaule au VIe siècle* (Paris, 1878).

Longnon, *Noms* A. Longnon, *Les Noms de lieu de la France* (Paris, 1920-29).

Lot F. Lot, *Les Invasions Germaniques* (Paris, 1935).

LUA *Lunds Universitets Arsskrift.*

Macartney C. A. Macartney, *The Magyars in the Ninth Century* (Cambridge, Cambridge University Press, 1930).

McGovern W. M. McGovern, *The Early Empires of Central Asia* (Chapel Hill, N.C., 1939).

MAE Akademiia Nauk, Muzei Antropologii i Etnografii, *Sbornik.*

Mansikka, *Religion* V. J. Mansikka, "Die Religion der Ostslaven," *FFC, 43* (1922).

MAR Arkheologicheskaia Komissiia, *Materialy po arkheologii Rossii.*

Markov A. Markov, *Topografiia kladov vostochnykh monet* (St. Petersburg, 1910).

Markwart J. Marquart, *Osteuropäische und ostasiatische Streifzüge* (Leipzig, 1903).

Markwart, *Bericht* J. Markwart, "Ein arabischer Bericht uber die arktischen (uralischen) Länder," *UJ, 4* (1924), 262-334.

Markwart, *Chronologie* J. Marquart, *Die Chronologie der alttürkischen Inschriften* (Leipzig, 1903).

Marr N. Ya. Marr, *Izbrannye raboty,* Vols. I-V (Leningrad, 1933-35).

Marr, *Sostav* N. Ya. Marr, *Plemennoi sostav naseleniia Kavkaza* (Petrograd, 1920).

Marr Volume *Akademiia Nauk Akademiku Marru* (Moscow-Leningrad, 1935).

ME Russkii Muzei, *Materialy po etnografii.*

Melioranskii, I P. M. Melioranskii, "Turetskie elementy v yazyke Slova o Polku Igoreve," *ANORI, 7,* 2 (1903), pp. 273-302.

Melioranskii, II P. M. Melioranskii, "Vtoraia statia o turetskikh elementakh v yazyke Slova o Polku Igoreve," *ANORI, 10,* 2 (1905), pp. 66-92.

Melioranskii, III P. M. Melioranskii, "Zaimstvovannye vostochnye slova v russkoi pismennosti domongolskogo vremeni," *ANORI, 10,* 4 (1905), pp. 109-134.

Menghin O. Menghin, *Weltgeschichte der Steinzeit* (Vienna, 1931).

MGH Monumenta Germaniae Historica.

MIAS Akademiia Nauk, Institut Istorii Materialnoi Kultury, *Materialy i Issledovaniia po arkheologii S.S.S.R.*

Miklosich, I F. Miklosich, "Die Fremdwörter in den Slavischen Sprachen," *AWV, 15* (1867).

Miklosich, II F. Miklosich, "Die Slavischen Elemente im Magyarischen," *AWV, 21* (1872).

Miklosich, III-IV F. Miklosich, "Die Türkischen Elemente in den südost- und osteuropäischen Sprachen," *AWV, 34-35* (1884-85).

Miller V. F. Miller, "Osetinskie Etiudy," Part III, *MU, 8* (1887).

Miller, *Sledy* V. F. Miller, "Epigraficheskie sledy iranstva na yuge Rossii," *ZMNP, 247* (1886), 232-283.

Miller, *Slovar* V. F. Miller, *Osetinsko-Russko-Nemetskii Slovar* (Leningrad, 1927-34), 3 vols.

Miller, *Sprache* V. F. Miller, "Die Sprache der Osseten," *Grundriss der Iranischen Philologie,* I, Suppl. (Strasbourg, 1903).

Minns E. H. Minns, *Scythians and Greeks* (Cambridge, 1913).

Minorsky V. Minorsky, *Hudud al-Alam* (London, 1937).

Mommsen Th. Mommsen, "Index Locorum" to Jordanis' *Romana et Getica.* See Sources, II, 1.

Monsen *Heimskringla, by Snorre Sturlason,* ed. by E. Monsen (New York, D. Appleton & Co., 1932).

Moravcsik J. Moravcsik, "Zur Geschichte der Onoguren," *UJ, 10* (1930), 53-90.

Moshin, *Nachalo* V. A. Moshin, "Nachalo Rusi," *BS, 3* (1931), 38-58, 285-307.

Moshin, *Vopros* V. A. Moshin, "Variago-Russkii Vopros," *Slavia, 10* (1931), 109-136, 343-379, 501-587.

MP Akademiia Nauk, Muzei Paleografii, *Trudy.*

MSE *Malaia Sovetskaia Entsiklopediia.*

MU Moscow, Universitet, *Uchenyia Zapiski,* Otdel istorikofilologicheskii.

Muellenhoff K. Muellenhoff, *Deutsche Altertumskunde,* Vol. II (2d ed. Berlin, 1906).

Munch P. A. Munch, *Norse Mythology,* revised by M. Olsen (New York, 1926).

Niederle L. Niederle, *Slovanské Starožitnosti,* Vol. I (2d ed. 1925-26); Vol. II (1906-10); Vol. III (2d ed. 1927); Vol. IV (1924) (Prague).

Niederle, *Rukovet* L. Niederle, *Rukovet' Slovanské Archeologie* (Prague, 1931).

Niederle, *Zivot* L. Niederle, *Život starých Slovanů* (Series 2 of the Slovanské Starožitnosti), Vol. I (1911-13); Vol. II, 1 (1924); Vol. II, 2 (1934); Vol. III (Prague, 1921-25).

Nikolskii, *Pismena* N. K. Nikolskii, "K voprosu o russkikh pismenakh," *ANIR,* I, 1-37.

Nikolskii, *Povest* N. K. Nikolskii, "Povest Vremennykh Let," *ANSR,* II, 1-106.

NTS Naukove Tovarystvo imeni Shevchenka, *Zapiski.*

NU Odessa, Novorossiiskii Universitet, *Zapiski.*

NUIF Odessa, Novorossiiskii Univeritet, Istoriko-Filologicheskoe Obshchestvo, *Letopisi.*

NYPL New York Public Library, *Bulletin.*

OO Odessa, Obshchestvo Istorii i Drevnostei, *Zapiski.*

Orlov A. S. Orlov, *Bibliografiia Russkikh nadpisei XI-XV vekov* (Moscow-Leningrad, 1936).

ORSA Russkoe Arkheologicheskoe Obshchestvo, Otdelenie Russkoi i Slavianskoi arkheologii, *Zapiski.*

Ostrogorsky G. Ostrogorsky, *Geschichte des Byzantinischen Staates* (Munich, 1940).

Ostrogorsky, Avtokrator G. Ostrogorsky, "Avtokrator i Samodrzhats," *SKA, 164* (1935).

PA *Przeglad Archeologiczny.*

Parkhomenko V. A. Parkhomenko, *U istokov Russkoi Gosudarstvennosti* (Leningrad, 1924).

PG J. P. Migne, *Patrologiae Cursus Completus.* Series Graeca.

PIDO *Problemy istorii dokapitalisticheskikh obshchestv.*

PIG Pedagogicheskii Institut imeni Gertsena, Leningrad, *Uchenye Zapiski.*

PL J. P. Migne, *Patrologiae Cursus Completus,* Series Latina.

Priselkov M. D. Priselkov, *Ocherki po tserkovno-politicheskoi istorii Kievskoi Rusi* (St. Petersburg, 1913).

Procopius Procopius, *History of the Wars.* See Sources, II, 1.

PSRL *Polnoe Sobranie Russkikh Letopisei.*

PW Pauly-Wissowa-Kroll, *Realencyclopaedie der Klassischen Altertumswissenschaft.*

Radlov V. V. Radlov, "Sibirskie Drevnosti," *MAR, 3,5,15,27.*

Rafn C. C. Rafn, *Antiquités Russes.* See Sources, II, 4.

RAIC Russkii Arkheologicheskii Institut, Constantinople, *Izvestiia.*

RAO Russkoe Arkheologicheskoe Obshchestvo, *Zapiski.*

Rav.An. Ravennas Anonymus. See Sources, II, 1.

RES *Revue des Études Slaves.*

RGA J. Hoops, *Reallexikon der Germanischen Altertumskunde.*

RH *Revue Historique.*

RHD *Revue historique de droit français et étranger.*

RIB *Russkaia Istoricheskaia Biblioteka.*

RK *Recueil Kondakov* (Prague, 1926).

RL M. Ebert, *Reallexikon der Vorgeschichte.*

Roesler R. Roesler, *Romänische Studien* (Leipzig, 1871).

Rostovtzeff M. Rostovtzeff, *Iranians and Greeks* (Oxford, 1922).

Rostovtzeff, *Animal Style* M. Rostovtzeff, *The Animal Style in South Russia and China* (Princeton, 1929).

Rostovtzeff, *Centre* M. Rostovtzeff, *Le Centre de l'Asie, la Russie, la Chine et le style animal* (Prague, 1929).

Rostovtzeff, *Hellenistic World* M. Rostovtzeff, *The Social and Economic History of the Hellenistic World* (Oxford, 1941).

Rostovtzeff, *Roman Empire* M. Rostovtzeff, *The Social and Economic History of the Roman Empire* (Oxford, 1926).

Rostovtzeff, *Sarmatae* M. Rostovtzeff, "The Sarmatae and the Parthians," *CAH, XI, chap. iii.*

Rostovtzeff, *Skythien* M. Rostowcew, *Skythien und der Bosporus* (Berlin, 1931).

Rostovtzeff, *Zhivopis* M. Rostovtzeff, *Antichmaia dekorativnaia zhivopis na yuge Rossii,* Vol. I (St. Petersburg, 1914); Album of Plates (1913).

Runciman S. Runciman, *A History of the First Bulgarian Empire* (London, 1930).

Rybakov B. A. Rybakov, "Anty i Kievskaia Rus," *VDI, 1* (1939), 319-337.

SA *Sovetskaia Arkheologiia.*

Safarik P. J. Schafarik [Šafarík], *Slawische Alterthuemer,* Vols. I-II (Leipzig, 1843-44).

Sar. Univ. Saratov, Universitet, *Uchenye Zapiski.*

Semenov, *Slovar* P. P. Semenov, *Geograficheskо-Statisticheskii Slovar Rossiiskoi Imperii* (St. Petersburg, 1865-85), 5 vols.

Setälä T. Ya., and S., "Finskii yazyk," *ES, 71,* pp. 23-26.

SF *Südostdeutsche Forschungen.*

SFO Société Finno-Ougrienne, *Mémoires.*

Shakhmatov, *Poseleniia* A. A. Shakhmatov, "Yuzhnye poseleniia Viatichei," *AN* (1907), pp. 715-729.

Shakhmatov, *Sudby* A. A. Shakhmatov, *Drevneishie sudby Russkogo plemeni* (Petrograd, 1919).

SK *Seminarium Kondakovianum* (Prague).

SKA Srpska Kraljevska Akademija, *Glasnik.*

Slovo *Slovo o polku Igoreve.* See Sources, II, 3.

Smirnov P. P. Smirnov, *Volz'kyi shliakh i starodavni Rusy* (Kiev, 1928).

Smirnov, *Populations* I. N. Smirnov, *Les populations Finnoises des bassins de la Volga et de la Kama,* Vol. I (Paris, 1898).

Smirnov, Tmutorokan V. D. Smirnov, "Chto takoe Tmutorokan?," *VV, 23* (1923), 15-73.

SMK *Sbornik Materialov dlia opisaniia mestnostei i plemen Kavkaza* (Tiflis).

SMYA *Suomen Muinaismuistoyhdistyksen Aikakauskirja* (Helsinki).

Sobolevskii, I A. I. Sobolevskii, "Russko-Skifskie Etiudy," *ANORI, 26* (1923), 1-44; *27* (1924), 252-332.

Sobolevskii, II A. I. Sobolevskii, "Slaviano-Skifskie Etiudy," *ANIR,* I (1928), 376-390.

SOF Societas Orientalis Fennica, *Studia Orientalia* (Helsinki).

Spitsyn, *Drevnosti Kamy* A. A. Spitsyn, "Drevnosti basseinov rek Oki i Kamy," *MAR, 25* (1901).

Spitsyn, *Rasselenie* A. A. Spitsyn, "Rasselenie drevne-russkikh plemen po arkheologicheskim dannym," *ZMNP, 324* (1899), 301-340.

SR *Slavonic and East European Review.*

Sreznevskii I. Sreznevskii, *Materialy dlia slovaria drevnerusskogo yazyka,* I-III (St. Petersburg, 1893-1912).

Stein E. Stein, *Studien zur Geschichte des Byzantinischen Reiches* (Stuttgart, 1919).

Stender-Petersen A. Stender-Petersen, "Die Varaegersaga als Quelle der Altrussischen Chronik," *AUA, 6* (1934).

STO *Sbornik Trudov Orkhonskoi Ekspeditsii.*

Stritter I. Stritter, *Izvestiia Vizantiiskikh istorikov,* I-IV (St. Petersburg, 1770-75).

SU Sofia, Universitet, *Godishnik.*

SZM Sarajevo, Zemaljski Muzej, *Glasnik.*

Tallgren, *Col. Zaus.* A. M. Tallgren, *Collection Zaoussailov,* I-II (Helsinki, 1916-18).

Tallgren, *Kupfer* A. M. Tallgren, "Die Kupfer—und Bronzezeit in Nord—und Ostrussland," *SMYA, 25,* 1 (1911).

Tallgren, *Orient* A. M. Tallgren, "L'Orient et l'Occident dans l'âge du fer finno-ougrien jusqu'au IX-e siècle de notre ère," *SMYA, 35,* 3 (1924).

Tallgren, *Pontide* A. M. Tallgren, "La Pontide préscythique," *ESA 2* (1926).

Tallgren, *Provinces* A. M. Tallgren, "Les provinces culturelles Finnoises de l'âge récent de fer dans la Russie du nord," *ESA, 3* (1928), 3-24.

Tarn W. W. Tarn, *The Greeks in Bactria and India* (Cambridge, 1938).

Tarn, *Alexander* W. W. Tarn, "Alexander and the Conquest of the Far East," *CAH, 7,* Chap. xiii.

TAS *Trudy Arkheologicheskikh S'ezdov.* (In quotation, the first number refers to the number of each of the archeological congresses in their sequence, and the second number to the volume.)

Taube Baron M. Taube, "Russische und litauische Fürsten an der Düna," *JKGS, 11* (1935), 367-502.

Teploukhov S. A. Teploukhov, "Opyt klassifikatsii metallicheskikh kultur Minusinskogo kraia," *ME,* IV, 1 (1927).

Thomsen, *Origin* V. Thomsen, *The Relations between Ancient Russia and Scandinavia and the Origin of the Russian State* (Oxford and London, 1877).

Tillemont L. S. le Nain de Tillemont, *Histoire des Empereurs,* vol. VI (1739).

TO Tavricheskoe Obshchestvo Istorii, Arkheologii i Etnografii (Simferopol), *Izvestiia.*

Toll N. P. Toll, *Skify i Gunny* (Prague, 1928).

Tolstov S. Tolstov, "Drevnosti Verkhnego Khorezma," *VDI, 1* (1941) 155-184.

TP *T'oung Pao.*

Tretiakov P. N. Tretiakov, "K istorii plemen Verkhnego Povolzhia v pervom tysiacheletii n.e.," *MIAS, 5* (1941).

Trever, *Pamiatniki* K. V. Trever, *Pamiatniki Greko-Baktriiskogo Iskusstva* (Moscow-Leningrad, 1940).

Trever, *Senmurv* K. V. Trever, "Sobaka-Ptitsa: Senmurv i Paskudj," *GA, 100* (1933), 293-328.

UAN Vseukrainska Akademiia Nauk, Istorychno-Filologichnyi Viddil, *Zapiski.*

UJ *Ungarische Jahrbücher.*

Uspenskii F. I. Uspenskii, *Istoriia Vizantiiskoi Imperii,* Vols. I-II (St. Petersburg-Leningrad, 1914-27).

Uspenskii, *Monarkhii* F. I. Uspenskii, *Pervye Slavianskie Monarkhii na severopzapade* (St. Petersburg, 1872).

Vajs J. Vajs, *Rukovet' Hlaholské Paleografie* (Prague, 1932).

Vasiliev A. A. Vasiliev, *The Goths in the Crimea* (Cambridge, Mass., 1936).

Vasiliev, *Arabes* A. A. Vasiliev, *Byzance et les Arabes,* Vol. I (Bruxelles, 1935).

Vasiliev, *Slaviane* A. A. Vasiliev, "Slaviane v Gretsii," *VV, 5* (1898), 404-438, 626-670.

Vasilievskii V. G. Vasilievskii, *Trudy,* I-IV (St. Petersburg-Leningrad, 1908-30).

Vasmer, *Beitraege* M. Vasmer, "Beitraege zur historischen Voelkerkunde Osteuropas," I-III, *AWB 24* (1932); *18* (1934); *19* (1935). (Part IV is said to have appeared in 1941.)

Vasmer, *Iranier* M. Vasmer, *Untersuchungen über die ältesten Wohnsitze der Slaven,* I: "Die Iranier in Südrussland" (Leipzig, 1923).

VDI *Vestnik Drevnei Istorii.*

Vernadsky, *Conversion* G. Vernadsky, "The Date of the Conversion of the Khazars to Judaism," *Byz., 15* (1941), 76-86.

Vernadsky, *Eparchy* G. Vernadsky, "The Eparchy of Gothia," *Byz., 15* (1941), 67-76.

Vernadsky, *Goten* G. Vernadsky, "Goten und Anten in Südrussland," *SF, 3* (1938), 265-279.

Vernadsky, *Lebedia* G. Vernadsky, "Lebedia: Studies on the Magyar Background of Kievan Russia," *Byz., 14* (1939), 179-203.

Vernadsky, *Origins* G. Vernadsky, "On the Origins of the Antae," *JAOS, 59* (1939), 56-66.
Vernadsky, *PHD* G. Vernadsky, *Political and Diplomatic History of Russia* (Boston, 1936).
Vernadsky, *Spali* G. Vernadsky, "The Spali of Jordanis and the Spori of Procopius," *Byz., 13* (1938), 263-266.
Vernadsky, *Zvenya* G. Vernadsky, *Zven'ia Russkoi Kultury,* Vol. I (Bruxelles, 1938).
VHA *K. Vitterhets Historie och Antikvitets Akademiens Handlinger.*
Vinski Z. Vinski, *Uz problematiku starog Irana i Kavkaza* (Zagreb, 1940).
VOZ Russkoe Arkheologicheskoe Obshchestvo, Vostochnoe Otdelenie, *Zapiski.*
VV *Vizantiiskii Vremennik.*
Wanstrat L. Wanstrat, *Beitraege zur Charakteristik des Russischen Wortschatzes* (Leipzig, 1933).
Westberg F. F. Westberg, "K analizu vostochnykh istochnikov o Vostochnoi Evrope," *ZMNP, 13* (1908), 364-412; *14* (1908), 1-52.
WNZ *Wiener Numismatische Zeitschrift.*
WPZ *Wiener Prähistorische Zeitschrift.*
Zakharov A. Zakharov and V. V. Arendt, "Studia Levedica," *AH, 16* (1935).
ZDMG *Zeitschrift der Deutschen Morgenlandischen Gesellschaft.*
Zeuss K. Zeuss, *Die Deutschen und die Nachbarstaemme* (Munich, 1837; reimpression, Heidelberg, 1925).
ZK *Zeitschrift für Kirchengeschichte.*
Zlatarski V. Zlatarski, *Istoriia na Bolgarskata Drzhava,* Vol. I 1-2 (Sofia, 1918-27).
ZMNP *Zhurnal Ministerstva Narodnogo Prosveshcheniia.*
ZOG *Zeitschrift für Osteuropäische Geschichte.*
ZSP *Zeitschrift für Slavische Philologie.*
ZVS *Zeitschrift für vergleichende Sprachvorschung.*

SOURCES

*I. Monumental Sources**

1. Epigraphic

Arne, pp. 7-14 ("Témoignage des pierres runiques").
Beshevliev, V., "Prvobolgarski Nadpisi," *SU, 31,* I (1934).
Braun, F., "Shvedskaia runicheskaia nadpis naidennaia na ostrove Berezani," *AK, 23* (1907).
Friesen, O. von., "Runenschrift," *RGA,* IV, 5-54.
Gordon, pp. 160-172 ("Runic inscriptions").
Grégoire, H., "Les sources épigraphiques de l'histoire Bulgare," *Byz., 9* (1934), 745-786.
Latyshev, V. V., *Inscriptiones Antiquae Orae Septentrionalis Ponti Euxini,* Vols. I-II, IV (St. Petersburg, 1885-1901).
—— *Sbornik grecheskikh nadpisei khristianskikh vremen iz Yuzhnoi Rossii* (St. Petersburg, 1896).
Orlov, A. S., *Bibliografiia Russkikh nadpisei XI-XV vekov* (Moscow-Leningrad, 1936).
Radlov, V. V., *Die alttürkischen Inschriften der Mongolei.* New Series (St. Petersburg, 1897).
Thomsen, V., "Alttürkische Inschriften aus der Mongolei," *ZDMG, 78* (1934), 121-175.
Uspenskii, F. I., "Nadpisi Starobolgarskie," *RAIC, 10* (1905), 173-212.

2. Numismatic and Sigillographic

Fraehn, C. M., "Drei Muenzen der Wolga-Bulgaren," *ANM,* Ser. 6, *1* (1832), 171-204.
Likhachov, N. P., "Materialy dlia istorii Vizantiiskoi i Russkoi sfragistiki," *MP,* I (1928).
Markov, A., *Topografiia kladov vostochnykh monet* (St. Petersburg, 1910).
Saveliev, P. S., *Mukhammedanskaia numizmatika* (St. Petersburg, 1846).
Schlumberger, G., *Sigillographie de l'Empire Byzantin* (Paris, 1884).
Vasmer, R., "Ueber die Muenzen der Wolga-Bulgaren," *WNZ, 57* (1924), 63-84.

* For the archaeological evidence see chap. I, Sec. 2, as well as works on archaeology referred to in the notes throughout.

II. Literary Sources

1. Greek and Latin

Agathias, *Historiae,* ed. Dindorf, *HGM,* II.

Ammianus Marcellinus, *Res Gestae,* J. C. Rolfe, ed. and trans., 3 vols. "Loeb Classical Library" (Harvard University Press).

Annales Bertiniani, see Prudentius.

"Anonymi Belae regis notarii de Gestis Hungarorum liber," *Rerum Hungaricarum Monumenta Arpadiana,"* ed. S. Endlicher (St. Gallen, 1849; reimpression, Leipzig, 1931).

Anskarius, see Rimbert.

Apollinaris Sidonius, C. Sollius, *Carmina,* ed. P. Mohr (Leipzig, 1895).

Chronica Gallica, ed. Mommsen, *MGH, Auctores Antiquissimi,* Vol. *9* (1892).

Chronicon Paschale, ed. Dindorf (Bonn 1832). 2 vols.

Codex Justinianus, see Corpus Juris Civilis.

Constantine Porphyrogenitus, *De Administrando Imperii, PG, 113.*

—— *De Ceremoniis Aulae Byzantinae, PG, 112.*

—— *De Thematibus, PG, 113.*

—— *Excerpta Historica,* ed. Boissevain, De Boor, Buettner-Wobst, Vols. I-IV (Berlin, 1906).

Cornelius Tacitus, see Tacitus.

Corpus Juris Civilis: I, Institutiones, Digesta, ed. P. Krueger (1920); II. Codex Justinianus, ed. P. Krueger (1914); III. Novellae, ed. R. Schoell and G. Kroll (1912).

Dexippus, *Fragmenta,* ed. Dindorf, *HGM,* I.

Dio Cassius, *Historia Romana,* ed. Dindorf. (Leipzig, 1863-65). 5 vols.

Drepanius, Latinius Pacatus, "Panegyricus Theodosio Augusto dictus," *Panegyrici Latini,* ed. A. Baehrens (Leipzig, 1874).

Ennodius, *Opera,* ed. Hartel (1882).

Eunapius, *Fragmenta,* ed. Dindorf, *HGM,* I.

Fredegar, *Chronicarum quae dicuntur Fredegarii Scholastici libri* IV, ed. B. Krusch, *MGH, Scriptores Rerum Merovingicarum,* II (1888).

Georgius Monachus, *Chronicon,* ed. De Boor, Vol. I (Leipzig, 1904).

Gregory of Tours, *Historia Francorum,* ed. W. Arendt and B. Krusch, *MGH Scriptores Rerum Merovingicarum,* I (1884).

Herodotus, *Historiae,* ed. H. Stein (Berlin, 1884). Also in "Loeb Classical Library," ed. A. D. Godley.

Isidore of Seville, *Etymologiae, PL, 82.*

Iustinus, M. Iunianus, see Trogus.

John Chrysostom, "Epistolae," *PG, 52.*

John Malalas, see Malalas.

John of Antioch, *Excerpta de Insidiis,* Constantine Porphyrogenitus, *Excerpta Historica,* III.

Jordanis (Jordanes), *Romana et Getica,* ed. Th. Mommsen, *MGH, Auctores Antiquissimi,* Vol. 5 (Berlin, 1882).

English trans. of the "Getica," by C. C. Mierow, *The Gothic History of Jordanes* (Princeton, Princeton University Press, 1915

MALALAS, JOHN, *Chronographia,* ed. Dindorf (Bonn, 1831).

MARCELLINUS, COMES, *Chronicon,* ed. Mommsen, *MGH, Auctores Antiquissimi,* Vol. XI (1894).

MAURICIUS, STRATEGICON, ed. J. Scheffer, *Arriani Tactica et Mauricii Ars Militaris* (Upsala, 1664).

Excerpts reprinted in Niederle, *Zivot,* I, 27-32. Russian trans. by S. A. Zhebelev and S. P. Kondratiev, *VDI* (1941), pp. 253-257.

MELA, see Pomponius Mela.

MENANDER PROTECTOR, *Fragmenta,* ed. Dindorf, *HGM,* II.

NICEPHORUS KALLISTUS XANTHOPULUS, *Church History, PG, 147.*

NICEPHORUS PATRIARCHA, *Opuscula Historica,* ed. De Boor (Leipzig, 1880).

Notitia Dignitatuum, ed. Seeck (1876).

Novellae, see Corpus Juris Civilis.

OLYMPIODORUS, *Fragmenta,* ed. Dindorf, *HGM,* I.

PACATUS, see Drepanius.

PHILOSTORGIUS, *Historia Ecclesiastica, PG, 65.*

PHOTIUS, "Epistolae," *PG, 102.*

—— *In Rossorum Incursionem Homiliae,* I-II, ed. A. Nauck, *Lexicon Vindobonense* (St. Petersburg, 1867), pp. 201-232.

PLINY, *Naturalis Historia,* ed. Jahn (Leipzig, 1870).

PLUTARCHUS, *Libellus de Fluviis,* ed. R. Hercher (Leipzig, 1851).

POMPEIUS TROGUS, see Trogus.

POMPONIUS MELA, *Chorographia,* ed. Frick (Berlin, 1880).

PRISCUS, *Fragmenta,* ed. Dindorf, *HGM,* I.

PROCOPIUS, *The Anecdota or Secret History,* H. B. Dewing, ed. and trans. "Loeb Classical Library."

—— *Buildings,* H. B. Dewing, ed. and trans. "Loeb Classical Library."

—— *History of the Wars,* H. B. Dewing, ed. and trans. 5 vols. "Loeb Classical Library."

PRUDENTIUS, *Annales,* ed. Pertz, *MGH, Scriptores,* I (1826), 429-454.

PTOLEMY, *Geographia,* ed. Noble (Leipzig, 1843).

RAVENNAS ANONYMUS, *Cosmographia,* ed. J. Schnetz, *Itineraria Romana,* II (Leipzig, 1940).

RIMBERT, *Vita Anskarii,* ed. G. Waitz (Hannover, 1884).

ST. GEORGE OF AMASTRIS, Life of, Vasilievskii, III, 1-71.

ST. JOHN OF GOTHIA, Life of, *Acta Sanctorum,* Junii Tomus VII, 167-71. Russian trans., Vasilievskii, II, 396-400.

ST. STEPHEN OF SUGDAEA (Surozh), Life of, Vasilievskii, III, 72-76.

SALVIANUS, *De Gubernatione Dei,* ed. Pauly (Vienna, 1883).

SAXO GRAMMATICUS, *Gesta Danorum,* ed. J. Olrik and H. Raeder (Copenhagen, 1931). 2 vols.

Scriptores Rerum Langobardorum, MGH (1878).

SIDONIUS, see Apollinaris Sidonius.

SIMOCATTA, see Theophylactus Simocatta.

SOCRATES, *Historia Ecclesiastica, PG, 67.*

STEPHANUS OF BYZANTIUM, *Ethnicorum quae supersunt,* ed. A. Meinecke (Berlin, 1849).

STRABO, *Geographica,* ed. H. L. Jones. "Loeb Classical Library."

SUIDA, *Lexicon,* ed. A. Adler (Leipzig, 1928-38). 5 vols.

TACITUS, CORNELIUS, *Germania,* ed. M. Hutton. "Loeb Classical Library."

—— *Historiae,* ed. C. Moore, "Loeb Classical Library."

THEOPHANES CONFESSOR, *Chronographia,* ed. De Boor (Leipzig, 1883-85). 2 vols.

THEOPHANES CONTINUATUS, ed. Bekker (Bonn, 1838).

THEOPHYLACTUS SIMOCATTA, *Historiae,* ed. De Boor (Leipzig, 1887).

TROGUS, *M. Iuniani Iustini Epitoma Historiarum Philippicarum Pompei Trogi,* ed. O. Seel (Leipzig, 1935).

ZOSIMUS, *Historia nova,* ed. Mendelssohn (Bonn, 1887).

2. *Oriental*

A. Arabic and Persian*

AL-BAKRI, see Bakri.

ATHIR, IBN AL-, *Chronicon quod perfectissum inscribtur,* ed. Tornberg. Excerpts in Marquart, see his Index of Authorities quoted, p. 554.

AUFI, *Jami al-Hikayat,* ed. Bartold, *VOZ, 9* (1896), 262-267.

BAKRI, *Kitab al-Masalik wa'l-Mamalik,* ed. A. Kunik and Baron V. Rosen, *ANZ, 32,* Suppl. No. 2 (1878), with Russian trans. Excerpts in English trans., Macartney, pp. 189-190, 192-208.

BALADHURI, *Liber Expugnationibus Regionum,* ed. De Goje (1866). English trans. by K. Hitti and F. C. Murgotten, *The Origins of the Islamic State* (New York, 1916-24). 2 vols.

BAL'AMI, see Tabari.

BALKHI, ABU ZAID, author of the work revised and ed. by Istakhri (see Istakhri). Excerpts in Russian trans., Harkavy, pp. 273-277.

EDRISI, see Idrisi.

FADHLAN, IBN, *Kitab* (report of his mission to the Volga Bulgars) known in two versions, as follows:

A. Yaqut's version (extensive excerpts). *Jaquts geographisches Woerterbuch,* ed. F. Wuestenfeld (6 vols., Leipzig, 1866-1873), I, 112-113, 468-469, 723-727; II, 438-440, 484-485, 834-840; IV, 944.

Yaqut's excerpts from Ibn-Fadhlan have been published separately with commentary and German trans., by C. M. Fraehn, in the following studies of the latter: (1) "De Chazaris," *ANM, 8* (1822); (2) "De Baschkiris," *ibid.;* (3) *Ibn-Foszlans und anderer Araber Berichte ueber die Russen* (St. Petersburg, 1823); (4) "Die aeltesten arabischen Nachrichten ueber die Wolga Bulgaren," *ANM,* Ser. 6, *1* (1832).

B. Original version (incomplete), in Codex No. 2 (III, 17, 2) of the Ali ibn-Riza Library at Meshed, Iran. *Puteshestvie Ibn-Fadhlana na Volgu,* ed.

* Diacritical marks in the transliteration of the Arabic and Persian names and titles are omitted.

by I. Yu. Krachkovskii (Moscow-Leningrad, 1939). Phototypical reproduction of the text, Russian trans., and commentary.

FAQIH, IBN-AL-, *Compendium Libri Kitab al-Boldan,* ed. De Goje, *BGA, 5* (1885).

FIRDAUSI, *Shah-nama,* done into English by A. G. Warner and E. Warner (London, 1905-25). 9 vols.

GARDIZI, *Zayn al-Akhbar,* ed. Bartold, *ANZI,* vol. I, No. 4 (1897), 80-103; Russian trans., pp. 103-126. Excerpts in English trans., Macartney, pp. 189-200, 203-215.

HAUQAL, IBN, *Viae et Regna, BGA, 2* (1873). Excerpts in Russian trans., (1) by Harkavy, pp. 218-222; (2) by N. A. Karaulov, *SMK, 38* (1908) 81-118.

Hudud al-Alam, ed. Bartold (Leningrad, 1930). Phototypical reproduction of the manuscript.

—— trans. and explained by V. Minorsky (London, 1937).

IBN AL-ATHIR, see Athir.

IBN-FADHLAN, see Fadhlan.

IBN-AL-FAQIH, see Faqih.

IBN-HAUQAL, see Hauqal.

IBN-KHURDADHBIH, see Khurdadhbih.

IBN-RUSTA, see Rusta.

IDRISI, *"Geographie d' Edrisi," traduite de l'arabe par A. Jaubert* (Paris, 1836-40). 2 vols.

—— *La Finlande et les autres pays baltiques orientaux (Geographie, VII, 4), édition critique par O. J. Tallgren-Tullio et A. M. Tallgren, SOF, 3* (1930).

—— O. J. Tullio (Tallgren), *Du nouveau sur Idrisi, SOF, 6,* 3 (1936).

ISTAKHRI, *Viae regnorum, BGA, 1* (1870). Excerpts in Russian trans., Harkavy, pp. 191-193.

KHURDADHBIH, IBN, *Kitab al-Masalik wa'l-Mamalik, BGA, 6* (1889), with French trans. Excerpts in Russian trans., Harkavy, pp. 48-49.

MARVAZI, *Taba'i al-haywan,* ed. V. Minorsky, forthcoming in the "Forlong Fund Publications." See "A List of Works" (1901-40) by V. Minorsky No. 110 (Cambridge, *s.a.* [1942]), p. 22.

MAS'UDI, *Muruj al-dhahab*

(a) Maçoudi, *Les Prairies d'or, texte et traduction par C. Barbier de Meynard et Pavet de Courteille* (Paris, 1861-77). 9 vols.

(b) M. Charmoy, *"Relation de Mas'oudy et d'autres Musulmans sur les anciens Slaves," ANM,* Ser. 6, *2* (1834) 297-408.

MAQDISI, see Muqaddasi.

MIRKHWAND, *Rawdatu's-Safa.* On editions of the text see Browne, pp. 431-432. Excerpts in French trans., B. D'Herbelot, *Bibliothèque Orientale* (Paris, 1697), *s.v.* "Rous," p. 722.

MUQADDASI, *Descriptio Imperii Moslemici,* ed. De Goje, *BGA, 3* (1877). Excerpts in Russian trans., Harkavy, pp. 281-283.

RUSTA, IBN, *Kitab al-Alak an-Nafisa,* ed. de Goje, *BGA, 7* (1892). An earlier edition, with Russian trans., by D. Khvolson (Chwolson), *Izvestiia o Khazarakh, Burtasakh, Bolgarakh, Madiarakh, Slavianakh i Russkikh Ibn-Dasta* (St. Petersburg, 1869). Russian trans. only, ZMNP, *140* (1868) 657-771. Excerpts in English trans., Macartney, pp. 191-215.

TABARI, *Annales,* ed. De Goje (Leyden, 1879-1901). German translation of a portion, by Th. Nöldeke, *Geschichte der Perser and Araber zur Zeit der Sassaniden* (Leyden, 1879).

Persian version, by Bal'ami: *Chronique de Tabari traduite sur la version persane* par H. Zotenberg (Paris, 1867-74). 4 vols.

B. DORN, "Tabary's Nachrichten ueber die Chasaren," *ANM,* Ser. 6, *6* (1844), 445-601; Russian trans., *ZMNP, 18* (1844). Excerpts in Russian trans., Harkavy, pp. 74-76.

YA'QUBI, *Kitab al-Boldan,* ed. De Goje, *BGA, 7* (1892). Excerpts in Russian trans., Harkavy, p. 63.

—— *Historiae,* ed. Houtsma (Leyden, 1883). 2 vols. Excerpts in French trans., Vasiliev, Arabes, I, 270-277.

YAQUT, *Geographic Dictionary,* ed. Wuestenfeld, *Jaquts geographisches Woerterbuch* (Leipzig, 1866-1873). 6 vols. See Fadhlan.

B. Armenian and Georgian

BROSSET, vols. I and III.

DJANASHVILI, M. "Izvestiia gruzinskikh letopisei i istorikov," *SMK, 22* (1897), 1-196; *26* (1899).

LEVOND [GHEVOND], *History of the Caliphs.* Russian trans. (by K. Patkanov), *Istoriia Khalifov* (St. Petersburg, 1862).

MOSES OF KHOREN, *History of Armenia.* Russian trans. by N. O. Emin, *Istoriia Armenii* (Moscow, 1893).

MOSES KALANKATVACI (KAGANKATVATSI), *History of the Albanians* (Agvanians) Russian trans. by K. Patkanov, *Istoriia Agvan* (St. Petersburg, 1861). Excerpts in Russian trans. by I. I. Shopen [Chopin], *Novyie Zametki* (St. Petersburg, 1866), pp. 417-501.

ST. ABO, Life of, Latin trans. by P. Peeters, "Les Khazars dans la passion de St. Abo of Tiflis," *Analecta Bollandiana, 52* (1934), 23-28.

C. Chinese

Annals of the Former Han (*Ch'ien Han Shu*). English trans. of chap. 96, by A. Wylie, "Notes on the Western Regions," *JAIG, 10* (1881) 20-48.

Annals of the Later Han (*Heou Han Shu*). French trans. of chap. 118, by Chavannes, "Les pays d'Occident d'après le Heou Han Chou," *TP, 8* (1907), 153-221.

BICHURIN, IAKINF, *Sobranie Svedenii o narodakh obitavshikh v srednei Azii* (St. Petersburg, 1851).

DE GROOT, J. J. M., *Chinesische Urkunden zur Geschichte Asiens,* Vols. I-II (Berlin und Leipzig, 1921-26).

Historical Records (*Shi-ki*). English trans. of chap. 123, by F. Hirth, "The Story of Chang K'ien," *JAOS, 37* (1917) 93-116.

D. Hebrew

P. K. Kokovtsov, *Evreisko-Khazarskaia perepiska v X veke* (Leningrad, 1932).

E. Syriac

Ab-ul-Faraj, Gregory, Chronology, ed. P. J. Bruns and G. G. Kirsch, with Latin trans. (Leipzig, 1788).

—— ed. E. A. W. Budge, with English trans. (London, 1932).

Bar Hebraeus, see Ab-ul-Faraj.

John of Ephesus, *Ecclesiastical History*. German trans. by I. M. Schoenfelder, *Die Kirchengeschichte des Johannes von Ephesus* (Munich, 1862).

Michael Syrus, ed. Chabot, *Chronique de Michel le Syrien,* Vol. II (Paris, 1902), with French trans.

Pigulevskaia, N. *Siriiskie Istochniki po istorii S.S.S.R.* (Moscow-Leningrad, 1941).

Zacharias Rhetor. German trans. by K. Ahrens and G. Krueger, *Die sogenannte Kirchengeschichte des Zacharias Rhetor* (Leipzig, 1899).

3. Slavic

Book of Annals ("Povest Vremennykh Let"): (a) Hypatian version, *PSRL,* Vol. II, Fasciculus 1 (3 ed. Petrograd, 1923); (b) Laurentian version, *PSRL,* Vol. I, Fasciculus 1 (2d ed. Leningrad, 1926).

Constantine the Philosopher, see St. Cyril.

Georgius Monachus, Slavic version, ed. V. M. Istrin, *Khronika Georgiia Amartola* (Leningrad, 1920-30). 3 vols.

John Malalas, Slavic version, ed. V. M. Istrin: Book I, *ANZI,* Ser. 8, *1,* No. 3 (1897); Book II, *NUIF, 10* (1902); Books IV-V, *NUIF, 13* (1905); Books VI-IX, *ANORS, 89,* No. 3 (1911) and No. 7 (1912); Book X, *NUIF, 17* (1913); Books XI-XIV, *ANORS, 90,* No. 2 (1913); Books XV-XVIII, *ANORS, 91,* No. 2 (1914).

English trans. of Books VIII to XVIII. *Chronicle of John Malalas,* M. Spinka and G. Downey, ed. and trans. (Chicago, 1940).

Nikon Chronicle ("Nikonovskaia Letopis"), *PSRL,* Vol. IX (1862).

St. Cyril (Constantine), Life of, the so-called Pannonian version.

Lavrov, P. A., "Materialy po istorii vozniknoveniia drevneishei Slavianskoi pismennosti," *Trudy Slavianskoi Komissii* (Akademiia Nauk), I (Leningrad, 1930), 1-66. Pastrnek, F. *Dějiny slovanských apoštolů Cyrilla a Methoda* (Prague, 1902), pp. 154-215. French trans., Dvornik, *Legendes,* pp. 349-380.

St. Methodius, Life of, the so-called Pannonian version: Lavrov (as above), pp. 67-78. Pastrnek (as above). French trans., Dvornik, *Legendes,* pp. 381-393.

St. Stephen of Surozh (*Sugdaea*), *Life of,* ed. V. G. Vasilievskii, III, 77-98.

Slovo o Polku Igoreve ("The Lay of Igor's Campaign") (Moscow, 1800; reimpression, Moscow, 1920).

4. Anglo-Saxon and Norse

Antiquités Russes d'après les monuments historiques des Islandais, ed. C. C. Rafn, Vols. I-II (Copenhague, 1850).

Beowulf, ed. W. J. Sedgefield (3d ed. Manchester, 1935).

Snorri Sturluson, *Heimskringla,* ed. by E. Monsen, trans. with the assistance of A. H. Smith (New York, 1932).

CHRONOLOGY

An asterisk (*) *shows that the date is tentative.*

B.C.	
*3000	Beginnings of the neolithic culture in Russia
*2500	Anau II culture
	Tripolie culture
*2100	The Maikop Kurgan
*2000	Anau III culture
	Afanasieva culture
	Kelteminar culture
	Fatianovo neolithic culture
*1800	End of the Tripolie culture
*1500	Fatianovo bronze culture
	Andronovo culture
	Tazabagiab culture
*1200	Borodino hoard
*1100	Seima culture
*1000	Koban culture
	Karasuk culture
	Cimmerians in South Russia
*900	Later Volosovo culture
	Earliest iron tools in central Russia and Ukraine
*900–500	Minusinsk culture, first stage
*700–200	Scythians in South Russia
*700	Beginnings of the Greek colonization of the northern shores of the Black Sea
*647–646	The city of the Boristhenites (Olbia) founded
*600–200	Ananyino culture
*512	Darius' campaign against the Scythians
*500–300	Minusinsk culture, second stage
*500	Panticapaeum (Kerch) founded
434/3	Treaty of friendship between the Bosporan kingdom and Athens
*400	Chersonese (Cherson) founded
335	Alexander the Great's Danubian campaign
330	Olbia besieged by Zopyrion
329–328	Alexander the Great's campaign in Turkestan
291	Lysimachus defeated by the Getae
*284	Kelts in western Ukraine and Bessarabia
*250	Beginnings of the Bactrian kingdom
*248	Foundation of the Parthian kingdom

A.D. 9	The dynasty of the Former Han in China
*200 B.C.– A.D. 180	The preponderance of the Sarmatians in South Russia
177	The Huns invade Kan-Su
165	Defeat of the Yue-chi by the Huns
	Migration of the Yue-chi to Jungaria
	The Osuns in Jungaria conquered by the Yue-chi
	The Yue-chi in the Semirechie area
140	The Huns invade the Semirechie area
	Migration of the Yue-chi to Ferghana and Soghdiana
*128	The people of An-tsai (Antes) in Kazakhstan mentioned in Chinese chronicles
108	The Roxolani defeated by Mithradates' troops in Crimea
	Mithradates becomes king of Bosporus
106	Cherson incorporated into the kingdom of Bosporus
62	Suicide of Mithradates
*50	Sack of Olbia by the Getae
24	Cherson receives a "Charter of Freedom" from Rome
A.D.	
25–220	The dynasty of the Later Han in China
49–62	Cotys, king of Bosporus
98	The Venedi (western Slavs) mentioned by Tacitus
101–102	Emperor Trajan's first Dacian campaign
105–106	Emperor Trajan's second Dacian campaign
*125	The An-ts'ai identified as Alans in Chinese chronicles
*165–180	Migration of the Goths to Ukraine
174	The Vandals admitted to Dacia by Marcus Aurelius
226–640	The Sassanian dynasty in Iran
251	Emperor Dacius defeated by the Goths in the Balkans
256	The Borani raid the Caucasian shore of the Black Sea
257	The Borani and the Ostrogoths sack Trapezunt
258	The Visigoths raid the Bosporus and Dardanelles
262–264	The Visigoths raid the littoral of Thrace and Bithynia
267	The Ostrogoths and the Heruls raid Athens and Corinth
268	The Visigoths raid Salonika
	Dacia evacuated by the Romans
*350–370	King Ermenrich of the Ostrogoths
*360	The Alans conquered by the Huns
*362	The Bosporan kingdom conquered by Ermenrich
*365	Ermenrich's campaign against the Slavs
	Migration of the Slovenians (*Slovene*) from the middle Dnieper area to the North (eventually to the Lake Ilmen area)
*370	The Ostrogoths defeated by the Huns
*373–376	The Alano-Gothic war
*374	The Antes defeated and their king Boz crucified by the Ostrogoths
*375	The Battle of Erak: defeat of the Ostrogoths by the Alans
*376	The Alans in Dacia
	The Visigoths invade Thrace

378	The battle of Adrianople between the Romans and the Goths. Death of Emperor Valens
	The Huns cross Kerch Strait
379–395	Emperor Theodosius I
*380	Scattered Alanic bands appear in the middle Danubian area
406	The Alans and the Vandals invade Gaul
409	The Alans and the Vandals invade Spain
410	The sack of Rome by the Visigoths
418	The Alans defeated by the Visigoths in Spain
	Remnants of the West Alanic horde merge with the Vandals
420	The Huns establish themselves in the middle Danubian area
427	The Vandals and the Alans occupy Carthage in North Africa (Tunisia)
434–453	Attila, khan of the Huns
434	Peace treaty between the Byzantine Empire and the Huns
448	Byzantine embassy to Khan Attila, recorded by Priscus
451	Attila's invasion of Gaul; the "Battle of Nations"
452	Attila's Italian campaign
453	Death of Attila
454	The dismemberment of the Hunnic Empire
468–469	The Danubian war between the Byzantines and the Huns
491–518	Emperor Anastasius I
493	"Scythians" (probably, Slavs) raid Thrace
514–516	The Revolt of Vitalian
517	The Slavs raid Macedonia and Illyricum
527–565	Emperor Justinian I
534	Chilbudius, Byzantine general, killed in a battle with the Slavs on the Danube
*543	Pseudo-Chilbudius (Khilbud), an Antic pretender to Chilbudius' office
*544	The Antes garrison Tyras
*550	Three Slavic peoples, the Venethi, the Sclaveni, and the Antes mentioned by Jordanis
*555	The people of Hros in the Don area mentioned in a Syriac chronicle
558–559	The Bulgar khan Zabergan's invasion of Thrace
559	The Avars in the North Caucasian area
561	Antic envoy Mezamer killed by the Avars
562	The Avars in Dobrudja
563	The arrival of the first Turkish envoy in Constantinople
568	The Avars in Pannonia
	The Byzantine-Turkish alliance
576	The Turks at the both sides of Kerch Strait
	Headquarters of the Turkish commander (*t'ma tarkhan*) established in the Taman peninsula (hence, the name of the city of Tmutorokan)
582–602	The reign of Emperor Mauricius
584–642	Khan Kurt of Great Bulgaria

592–597 Byzantine campaigns against the Slavs
588 Breaking of the Turkish Empire into the Eastern part (Mongolia) and the Western part (Turkestan)
*600 The Norsemen at the mouth of the Western Dvina in the East Baltic region
610–641 The reign of Emperor Heraclius
618–907 The Tang dynasty in China
622 The flight of Mohammed from Mecca (Hegira) which opens the Islamic era
*625 The formation of the Khazar state
626 The Avar raid on Constantinople
Defeat of the Avars
The Byzantino-Khazar alliance
632 The beginning of the Arab expansion
*643 Dismemberment of Great Bulgaria
*650 Migration of the Bulgar horde under Asparukh from the Azov region to the Lower Danube area
The beginnings of the state of the Volga Bulgars
The migration of the Ugrians (Magyars) from the North Caucasian Area to the Don and Donets area
The expansion of the Norsemen (Swedes) in the western Dvina area
The expansion of the Slavs in the upper Volga and Oka region
The city of Malorosa, in the Taman area, mentioned in Ravennas Anonymus' *Cosmographia*
651–652 The Arabs raid the North Caucasian area
658 Emperor Constans' expedition against the Macedonian Slavs
661–749 The Umayyad dynasty of the Caliphs
673 The defeat of the Arab fleet before Constantinople with the help of the "Greek fire"
679 The Bulgar invasion of Thrace
681–682 The arrival of a Christian mission from Armenia to the North Caucasian area
683 The Khazars raid Armenia
685–695 First reign of Justinian II
686 Thirty thousand Macedonian Slavs moved to Bithynia
692 Part of the Bithynian Slavs go over from the Byzantine to the Arab side: Seven thousand of them settle in Syria
696–704 Justinian II in exile in Khazaria
*700 The Norsemen (Swedes) in the upper Volga and Oka region
The Magyars consolidate their control of the upper Donets and Oskol region
701 Death of Asparukh, the first khan of the Danubian Bulgars
705–711 Second reign of Justinian II
705 Justinian II takes back Constantinople with the help of the Bulgars
The Bulgar khan Tervel proclaimed Caesar
711 Deposition and execution of Justinian II
712 Arab conquest of Khoresmia in Turkestan

714-717	War between the Arabs and the Khazars in the Caucasus
716	Peace treaty between the Byzantines and the Bulgars
717–741	Reign of the emperor Leo III
717–718	Defeat of the Arabs by Leo III
726–732	War between the Arabs and the Khazars in the Caucasus
*735	The Swedes defeat the Magyars in the upper Donets—Oskol region and seize Verkhni Saltov
	The Magyars move from the Donets to the Dnieper region
737–738	The Arabs under Marvan invade the Don area: Twenty thousand Slavs moved to Syria
739	Fall of the western Turkish Empire in Turkestan
741–775	Reign of the emperor Constantine V
749–1258	The Abbasid dynasty of the Caliphs
*750	The Swedes establish their control over the As and Rus tribes in the Azov area, as vassals of the Khazar kagan, assuming eventually the name of the Rus.
	The City of the As (As-Grad), mentioned in the Norse sagas, is founded, presumably in the Azov region
750–760	The people of Sevordik (Savarti, Swedes?) in Transcaucasia
756–759	War between Byzantium and the Bulgars
762	Two hundred thousand Slavs from Thrace and Macedonia moved to Bithynia
763	The battle of Anchial between the Byzantines and the Bulgars
764	Khazar troops commanded by Ras [Rus?]—Tarkhan capture Tiflis and devastate Armenia
*770	The Battle of Bravalla in Sweden, some of the survivors of which presumably migrate to Russia
773	Constantine V's campaign against the Bulgars
	Russian (or "red") ships join the Byzantine fleet
*782	St. Abo of Tiflis visits the Crimea and Khazaria
*787	The city of Doras (Dory) in Crimea occupied by the Khazars
*790	Uprising in Doras and retreat of the Khazars
•	Russian attack on Sugdaea (Surozh)
797–802	Empress Irene
800	Charlemagne crowned emperor of the Holy Roman Empire
*800	Riurik (Roric), of the clan of Skjoldungs, born
803–805	The Avar Kaganate destroyed by the combined efforts of the Franks and the Bulgars
805–814	Khan Krum of Bulgaria
807–816	War between the Byzantines and the Bulgars
813	Adrianople surrenders to the Bulgars
	Ten thousand Greek families moved from Adrianople to Bessarabia
814–831	Khan Omortag of Bulgaria
814–816	Rule of Chok and other *boils* in Bulgaria
816	Bulgaro-Byzantine peace treaty
821–823	Uprising of Thomas the Slav in the Byzantine Empire
*825	Emancipation of the Russians from the authority of the Khazars.

	Establishment of the Russian Kaganate, presumably at Tmutorokan
826	Riurik baptized at Ingelheim, Franconia, together with his elder brother. They are granted Rustringen in Friesland as fief by Emperor Louis
827–832	War between the Bulgars and the Franks
833	Khazar envoys request Byzantine assistance to build a fortress on the Don River, presumably against the Russians
*835	Sarkel on the Don built for the Khazars by Byzantine engineers
	The Khazars open a campaign against the Russian tribes in the middle Dnieper and Oka region
836–839	Troubles between the Bulgars and the Byzantines
838	Russian envoys in Constantinople
*838	Adrianople Greeks settled in Bessarabia revolt against the Bulgars and beat off a Magyar attack
839	Russian envoys prevented from returning home and sent from Constantinople to Ingelheim, Franconia
*840	Russian attack on Amastris
	Kiev occupied by the Khazars and the Magyars. The Magyar chieftain Almus (Olom) made governor (*voevoda*) of Kiev
842–867	Reign of the emperor Michael III
843	Treaty of Verdun. Riurik deprived of his fief
845–850	Riurik's raids on Saxony, France, and England
846–870	Prince Rostislav of Moravia
850	Rustringen returned to Riurik by Emperor Lothaire
*852	The Danes raid Novgorod
852–889	Khan Boris of Bulgaria
854	Riurik forced to give up Rustringen but given southern Jutland instead
*856	Riurik arrives in Russia and establishes himself at Ladoga
*858	Riurik moves to Novgorod
	Askold and Dir explore the Dnieper riverway and reach Kiev where they establish their rule, presumably as Olom's lieutenants
858–867	Photius Patriarch of Constantinople
860	Russian raid on Constantinople
*860–861	Mission of Constantine the Philosopher (St. Cyril) to Khazaria
*860	"Russian characters" studied by Constantine in Cherson
862	Constantine and Methodius sent to Moravia as missionaries
*862	The invention of the Slavic alphabet
864	Conversion of the khan Boris of Bulgaria to Christianity
*865	Conversion of the Khazars to Judaism
	Conversion of the (Tmutorokan) Russians to Christianity
866	Boris of Bulgaria breaks with the Byzantine Patriarch and sends envoys to Rome
867	The establishment of the first Russian bishopric, presumably at Tmutorokan
	The break between Patriarch Photius and Pope Nicholas
867–886	Reign of the emperor Basil I

867–878	Ignatius Patriarch of Constantinople
869	Death of St. Cyril (Constantine the Philosopher)
869–870	The Eighth Oecumenical Council (not recognized as such by the Orthodox) confirms the authority of the Patriarch of Constantinople over Bulgaria
870	Riurik's meeting with King Charles the Bald at Nimwegen
870–894	Prince Sviatopolk of Moravia
*873	Death of Riurik
*878	The seizure of Kiev by Oleg
885	Death of St. Methodius
886	Methodius' pupils expelled from Moravia and given refuge in Bulgaria
893	Bulgarian National Assembly recognizes Slavic as the language of the church

GENERAL INDEX

INDEX OF AUTHORS CITED

HIEBERT LIBRARY
3 6877 00042 9885